27

The Achievement of Ted Hughes

EDITED BY **KEITH SAGAR**

The Achievement of Ted Hughes

THE UNIVERSITY OF GEORGIA PRESS
Athens

Published in 1983 in the United States of America by
the University of Georgia Press, Athens, Georgia 30602.
Typeset in Great Britain and printed in Hong Kong

Library of Congress Cataloging in Publication Data

Main entry under title:

The Achievement of Ted Hughes.

  Includes bibliographical references and index.
  1. Hughes, Ted, 1930-   -Criticism and interpre-
tation-Congresses.   I. Sagar, Keith.
PR6058.U37Z52   1983   821'.914   82-13522
ISBN 0-8203-0650-9

The editor, contributors and publisher are grateful to the following for
permission to use copyright material: Faber & Faber Ltd. for extensive
quotation from the works of Ted Hughes published by them – *The Hawk in the
Rain* ©1957; *Lupercal* ©1960; *Meet My Folks!* ©1961; *The Earth-Owl and
Other Moon People* ©1963; *Nessie the Mannerless Monster* ©1964; *Wodwo*
©1967; *Poetry in the Making* ©1967; *Seneca's Oedipus* ©1969; *Crow* ©1970;
A Choice of Shakespeare's Verse ©1971; *Season Songs* ©1976; *Gaudete*
©1977; *Cave Birds* ©1978; *Remains of Elmet* ©1979; *Moortown* ©1979;
Selected Poems 1957-1981 ©1982; .Harper & Row Publishers, Inc. for
extensive quotation from the works of Ted Hughes published by them in the
U.S.A. – *The Hawk in the Rain* ©1957; *Lupercal* ©1960; *Wodwo*·©1967;
Crow ©1970; *Gaudete* ©1977; *Moortown* ©1979; *New Selected Poems*
©1982; Olwyn Hughes for all previously unpublished or uncollected material
by Ted Hughes.
  Seamus Heaney's chapter is part of a lecture given at the University of
California at Berkeley in May 1976, first published as 'Now and in England' in
Critical Inquiry 1977, and collected as 'Englands of the Mind' in *Preoccupa-
tions*, Faber and Faber 1980. Keith Sagar's chapter on 'Hughes and his
Landscape' was first published in *Poetry Wales* 1980. Jarold Ramsay's chapter
was first published in the *Massachusetts Review* in 1978.

CONTENTS

PART I

Background
and Context

Hughes and his landscape

A list of the best twenty living British poets would include a disproportionate number of Welsh, Scottish and Irish poets. The usual explanation for this would be the different and higher role of the poet in the Celtic cultures, the bardic tradition and so on. I should like here to suggest another possible reason, the deeper influence of landscape upon Celtic poets. The Celtic writer is more likely to live in a landscape, as opposed to a town, and that landscape is likely to be more dramatic, insistent and wild than most English landscapes which are gentler and more amenable to human purposes and perspectives.

I do not mean that the landscape is available to the Celtic poet simply as subject matter (though it is no coincidence that, for example, two of R. S. Thomas' best poems should be 'Welsh Landscape' and 'The Welsh Hill Country'), but that it can provide him also with a fund of vital images, and with a paradigm for his understanding of life itself and his own inner being.

I want to go even further than this. Poetry is religious or it is nothing. Its claim to be taken seriously – more seriously than any other form of art or language – is its ability to keep open and operative the connections between the depths of the human psyche and the hidden sources of everything in the non-human world. The poet is a medium for transmitting an occult charge from the non-human world into the psyche and thence into consciousness. The Celtic poet knows this in his blood. Most English poets have drifted into a rational humanism and arrogantly expect us to value their measured musings. Their verse is altogether lacking in what Lorca called *duende*, the spirit of life itself in its constant war with death, the spirit of the earth with its 'dark sounds':

These 'dark sounds' are the mystery, the roots thrusting into the fertile loam known to all of us, ignored by all of us, but from which we get what is real in art. . . . The *duende* is a power and not a behaviour, it is a struggle and not a concept. . . . It is not a matter of ability, but of real live form; of blood; of ancient culture; of creative action . . .

The appearance of the *duende* always presupposes a radical change of all forms based on old structures. It gives a sensation of freshness wholly unknown, having the quality of a newly created rose, of miracle, and produces in the end an almost religious enthusiasm . . .

The *duende* does not appear if it sees no possibility of death . . . The *duende* likes a straight fight with the creator on the edge of the well . . . The *duende* wounds, and in the healing of this wound which never closes is the prodigious, the original in the work of man. The magical quality of a poem consists in its being always possessed by the *duende*, so that whoever beholds it is baptised with dark water. Because with *duende* it is easier to love and to understand, and also one is *certain* to be loved and understood; and this struggle for expression and for the communication of expression reaches at times, in poetry, the character of a fight to the death.

(Lorca, 'Theory and Function of the *Duende*')

One of the primary manifestations of *duende* is in the spirit of place. Much of what we call civilisation has been characterised by efforts to kill or mutilate that. The surest way to kill it within the psyche is to learn to ignore it, or to sentimentalise or prettify it. It is emphatically not the loving mother of post-Wordsworthian English Nature poetry.

The Celtic writer takes for granted that the landscape shaped him, and probably assumes that this is not so true of his English counterpart, since the landscape of England is relatively bland. If, like Philip Larkin, you were born in Coventry, that might be true: 'Nothing, like something, happens anywhere.' But there are parts of England with every bit as much character as anywhere over the borders – for example, that stretch of the Pennine moors and valleys between Lancashire and Yorkshire which has Haworth at its northern edge and the Calder Valley running through the middle of it, from Todmorden to Halifax. It was once part of the ancient kingdom of Elmet, 'the last British Celtic kingdom to fall to the Angles' according to Ted Hughes, who was born there, and who celebrates its Celtic and more recent past in *Remains of Elmet*:

For centuries it was considered a more or less uninhabitable wilderness, a notorious refuge for criminals, a hide-out for refugees. Then in the early 1800s it became the cradle for the Industrial Revolution in textiles, and the upper Calder became 'the hardest-worked river in England'.

Throughout my lifetime, since 1930, I have watched the mills of the region and their attendant chapels die. Within the last fifteen years the end has come. They are now virtually dead, and the population of the valleys and the hillsides, so rooted for so long, is changing rapidly.

The poet is engaged in finding metaphors for his own nature, his only touchstone for human nature. His earliest metaphors are drawn from his immediate childhood world, his inheritance. These metaphors in turn give him a way of looking at the further and future world and a way of thinking about himself when he becomes self-conscious. Thus they shape his nature and bring it closer to the permanent realities. In a radio interview in 1961, Hughes said that the move to Mexborough when he was eight 'really sealed off my first seven years so that now my first seven years seems almost half my life. I've remembered almost everything because it was sealed off in that particular way and became a sort of brain – another subsidiary brain for me'. The geography of his childhood world became his map of heaven and hell; the distinctive interplay of the elements in that place gave him his sense of the creating and destroying powers of the world; the local animals became his theriomorphic archetypes. This landscape was imprinted on his soul, and, in a sense, all his poems are about it. When the poems are overtly, literally, about it, the magical change from description to metaphor to myth is enacted before our eyes, as in *Remains of Elmet*.

From these poems, and from many earlier texts, we can trace the evolution of the most penetrating, authentic and all-embracing poetic vision of our time.

Hughes was born in Mytholmroyd in 1930 in an end terrace house backing on to the canal. Beyond the canal was the main trunk road connecting the Yorkshire woollen towns and the Lancashire cotton towns, with its constant rumble of heavy lorries. Beyond that the railway. Then, rising almost sheer from the valley and seeming to fill half the sky, Scout Rock:

This was the *memento mundi* over my birth: my spiritual midwife at the time and my godfather ever since – or one of my godfathers. From my first day, it watched. If it couldn't see me direct, a towering gloom over my pram, it watched me through a species of periscope: that is, by infiltrating the very light of my room with its particular shadow.   ('The Rock')

It seemed to seal off everything to the South. Since to the North the land rose almost as steeply from immediately in front of the house up to the high bleak moors, 'the narrow valley, with its flooring of cricket pitch, meadows, bowling greens, streets, railways and mills, seemed damp, dark and dissatisfied' and felt like a trap.

The other spiritual midwives were scarcely more benign. In 'My Fairy Godmother' Hughes imagines himself at birth surrounded by the Wicked Powers. One of them says: 'The earth for him will have such magnet strength / It will drag all things from his hold, and his own body at length'. Another said: 'A misty rock is all this boy shall be / He shall meet nothing but ships in distress and the wild, empty sea'. Another: 'He shall be a ghost, and haunt the places of earth, / And all the stars shall mark his death as little as his birth'. His Fairy Godmother redeems his life by providing him with a ladder out of the trap, a magic ever-changing ladder which stands for life's perpetual capacity for transforming and renewing itself.

Crag Jack, one of Hughes' alter egos (in fact his grandfather), is more specific about the identity of those Wicked Powers:

The churches, lord, all the dark churches
Stooped over my cradle once:
I came clear, but my god's down
Under the weight of all that stone.   ('Crag Jack's Apostasy')

Mount Zion chapel literally stooped over his cradle:

Above the kitchen window, that uplifted mass
Was a deadfall —
Darkening the sun of every day
Right to the eleventh hour.

Later he was dragged there every Sunday in an atmosphere of terror:

The convicting holy eyes, the convulsed Moses mouthings.

Men in their prison-yard, at attention,
Exercising their cowed, shaven souls.
Lips stretching saliva, eyes fixed like the eyes
Of cockerels hung by the legs
As the bottomless cry
Beats itself numb again against Wesley's foundation stone.   ('Mount Zion')

The purpose of the chapel seemed to be simply to eradicate the joy of life, even if that meant eradicating life itself. Once the place was thrown into a state of battle-fury by a cricket singing from a crack in the wall:

Long after I'd been smothered in bed
I heard them
Riving at the religious stonework
with screwdrivers and chisels.

Now the cracks are widening and the only singing heard in many of the chapels is the singing of crickets.

What the boys preferred to do with their Sundays was to dig, Sunday after Sunday, with iron levers, even while the bells summoned them elsewhere, for the Ancient Briton supposed, according to local folk-lore, to lie under a half-ton rock:

We needed that waft from the cave
The dawn dew-chilling of emergence,
The hunting grounds untouched all around us.
('The Ancient Briton Lay Under His Rock')

That rock could not be shifted, nor what it hid, the buried life of England, the repressed needs of the human psyche, eradicated.

In the short story 'Sunday', the boy has to endure a stifling, scrubbed Sunday morning, the church-going slopes spotless and harmless, forbidden grass in the Memorial Gardens, even the pavements 'untouchably proper'. The men wear 'tight blue pin-stripe suits' and the boy his 'detestable blue blazer'. Sitting in chapel, the situation of greatest constraint he knows, he lets his imagination be taken over by the image of a wolf which 'urged itself with all its strength through a land empty of everything but trees and snow'. This wolf, the ghost of the last wolf killed in Britain, appears again and again in Hughes:

These feet, deprived,
Disdaining all that are caged, or storied, or pictured,
Through and throughout the true world search
For their vanished head, for the world

Vanished with the head, the teeth, the quick eyes —.   ('February')

The wolf is that in the boy which refuses to be constrained, tamed, disciplined, like those Vikings ('the snow's stupefied anvils') who spent themselves in 'beforehand revenge' For the gruelling relapse and prolongueur of their blood / Into the iron arteries of Calvin' ('The Warriors of the North')

The boy lives for the afternoon, when his father has promised to take him to Top Wharf Pub to see for the first time Billy Red kill rats in his teeth like a terrier. The Cretans sacrificed a living bull to Dionysos by tearing it with their teeth. Billy Red degrades this archaic religious act, communion with the god by eating the god, to a Sunday afternoon secular entertainment for a bored denatured public for a free pint. But the boy is not yet denatured. The thought of that savagery, that unthinkable closeness of the human and the animal, reduces everything else in his consciousness to unreality. The story is autobiographical. There really was a Billy Red.

Animals were of tremendous importance to Hughes from the beginning, living representatives of another world, 'the true world'. 'the world under the world'. Even the canal

Bred wild leopards – among bleached depth fungus.
Loach. Torpid, ginger-bearded, secretive
Prehistory of the canal's masonry,
With little cupid mouths.

Five inches huge!   ('The Canal's Drowning Black')

They were easily netted, and, after a night in a two-pound jam-jar

On a windowsill
Blackened with acid rain fall-out
From Manchester's rotten lung

were lobbed back, stiff, 'into their Paradise and mine'. Once, under the main road canal bridge, there was even a leaping trout:

A seed
Of the wild god now flowering for me
Such a tigerish, dark, breathing lily
Between the tyres, under the tortured axles.   ('The Long Tunnel Ceiling')

'The wild gentle god of everywhereness' was obviously responsible for these free lords, and for the demons like the weasels smoked out of a bank 'Furious with ill-contained lightning', demons 'Crackling with redundant energy'.

Yet the only relationship which seemed possible between town boys and the surrounding wildlife was to catch and kill. Hughes had an older brother:

His one interest in life was creeping about on the hillsides with a rifle. He took me along as a retriever and I had to scramble into all kinds of places collecting magpies and owls and rabbits and weasels and rats and curlews that he shot. He could not shoot enough for me.   ('Capturing Animals')

Later Hughes tried to keep wild animals as pets:

An animal I never succeeded in keeping alive is the fox. I was always frustrated: twice by a farmer, who killed cubs I had caught before I could get to them, and once by a poultry keeper who freed my cub while his dog waited.
                                                    ('Capturing Animals')

The lesson was being driven home that animals were, by nature, victims. It was the natural order of things that any creature outside the ordered world of men should be killed. And if a human being chose to step outside that ordered world, he became fair game. The lesson was reinforced by a story his brother told him 'of the tramp sleeping up there in the bracken, who stirred at an unlucky moment and was shot dead for a fox by an alert farmer and sent rolling down the slope'.

After the move to Mexborough when he was eight, Hughes was one day crawling silently up the side of a hollow scooped out by the Dearne to see what might be in the next hollow. As he reached the top and peered over, he found himself face-to-face with a fox, about nine inches away. They looked into each other's eyes, and it seemed that his own being was for a moment which was also an eternity supplanted by that of the fox. Then the fox was gone. But it remained in his unconscious as a symbol of unquenchable life whether in the natural world or in the human psyche.

In his second year at Cambridge Hughes went through a sort of crisis which caused a complete block in his ability to write essays. One night very late, very tired, he went to bed, leaving the essay he had been struggling with on his desk. Then he dreamed that he was still sitting at the desk when the door opened and a creature came in with the head and body of a fox, but erect, man-sized, and with human hands. He had escaped from a fire; there was a strong smell of burning hair and the skin was charred, cracked and bleeding, especially the hands. He came across the room, put his hand on the essay, and said 'Stop this. You are destroying us.' His hand left a blood-print on the page. Hughes connected the fox's command with his own doubts about the effect of the Cambridge brand of critical analysis on the creative spirit (he had written no more poems since leaving school), and decided to change from English to Archaeology and Anthropology.

The life which we have already killed off and got under, which now marauds destructively in the underworld of the unconscious is the wolf. The life now making its last stand in remote fastness is adder and otter. The life we keep trying to kill, but which somehow survives, is stoat (see 'Strawberry Hill') and fox. The landscape itself is a huge animal which seems to let itself be tamed. The network of walls is 'harness on the long moors'. But now those Pennine hills are breaking loose again, slowly shaking the mills, chapels and houses to pieces as in a great sieve.

The 'great adventure' was the attempt to bring the hills and moors with their resources of grass, water and stone, into the human economy. For a time it seemed to have succeeded. The hills were plotted and parcelled with mile after mile of stone walls raised with lifetimes of patient labour, and 'Spines that wore into a bowed / Enslavement' ('Walls'). Hill-stone seemed to be content

To be cut, to be carted
And fixed in its new place.
It let itself be conscripted
Into mills. And it stayed in position
Defending this slavery against all.   ('Hill-Stone Was Content')

Men got to the summit and

for some giddy moments
A television
Blinked from the wolf's lookout.   ('When Men Got to the Summit')

But now all that remains of the great enterprise is a hulk, 'every rib
shattered'. The spent walls are nothing but a 'harvest of long
cemeteries'. The stones of the mills are returning to the earth.

It is, of course, sad to see a thriving community in decay; and most of
Hughes' childhood in that valley was happy. But he feels little
nostalgia. It was a 'happy hell'. The lives of the farm workers 'went
into the enclosures / Like manure' ('Walls'). The lives of the factory
hands were sacrificed to the looms. But what really broke the spirit of
the community was the first world war.

First, Mills
          and steep wet cobbles
Then cenotaphs.

First, football pitches, crown greens
Then the bottomless wound of the railway station
That bled this valley to death.

All the young men of the valley were recruited into the Lancashire
Fusiliers and shipped to the Dardanelles. Seventeen, including Hughes'
father, came back. His father, saved by his pocket-book, would talk
endlessly to the boy about his 'four-year mastication by gunfire and
mud':

            While I, small and four,
Lay on the carpet as his luckless double,
His memory's buried, immovable anchor,
Among jawbones and blown-off boots, tree-stumps, shell-cases and craters,
Under rain that goes on drumming its rods and thickening
Its kingdom, which the sun has abandoned, and where nobody
Can ever again move from shelter.   ('Out')

These images superimposed in perfect register upon those impressed
on him by the surrounding landscape:

The throb of the mills and the crying of lambs
Like shouting in Flanders

Muffled away
In white curls
And memorial knuckles

Under hikers' heels.   ('The Sheep Went On Being Dead')

The whole valley was like a trench —

Over this trench
A sky like an empty helmet
With a hole in it.

And now — two minutes silence
In the childhood of earth.   ('First, Mills')

Even the beauty spots seemed haunted by the ghosts of the young men
who went there on Sunday jaunts before the war:

And the beech-tree solemnities
Muffle much cordite.
* * *
And the air-stir releases
The love-murmurs of a generation of slaves
Whose bones melted in Asia Minor.   ('Hardcastle Crags')

In a radio interview Hughes said that the First World War was more
part of his imagination than the second because 'It was right there from
the beginning, so it was going on in us for eight years before the Second
World War came along . . . The First World War was our sort of
fairy-story world – certainly was mine'.

So it seemed to the young Hughes that there was a mourning quality
in the spirit of the place, the *duende*. And the role of men in that place
was to provide the deaths and disasters and wastage for it to be in
mourning for:

Everything in West Yorkshire is slightly unpleasant. Nothing ever quite
escapes into happiness. The people are not detached enough from the stone, as
if they were only half-born from the earth, and the graves are too near the
surface. A disaster seems to hang around in the air there for a long time. I can
never escape the impression that the whole region is in mourning for the first
world war.   ('The Rock')

To confront the *duende* in its purity, it was necessary to go up onto the
moors. There you could listen to the 'dark sounds' of the spirit of the
moors: 'The peculiar sad desolate spirit that cries in telegraph wires on
moor roads, in the dry and so similar voices of grouse and sheep, and
the moist voices of curlews.' You could almost see the spirit because of

the strange eerie quality of the light (a quality wonderfully captured in
Fay Godwin's photographs) 'at once both gloomily purplish and
incredibly clear, unnaturally clear, as if objects there had less
protection than elsewhere, were more exposed to the radioactive
dangers of space, more startled by their own existence.'

What distinguishes the moors from the valley is the fact that, in
spite of the mourning, the accumulated deaths, 'the mood of moorland
is exultant'. Many of the finest poems in *Remains of Elmet* celebrate
the exhilaration which is the recognition that out of these uncompromising materials, this graveyard, this vacancy of scruffy hills and
stagnant pools and bone-chilling winds, the place is continually
renewing ife and making miracles. This was expressed finely in many
early poems:

Buttoned from the blowing mist
Walk the ridges of ruined stone.
What humbles these hills has raised
The arrogance of blood and bone,
And thrown the hawk upon the wind,
And lit the fox in the dripping ground.   ('Crow Hill')

Yet even this seems rhetorical against the transparent purity of his
latest testimony:

And now this whole scene, like a mother.
Lifts a cry
Right to the source of it all.

A solitary cry.

She has made a curlew.   ('Long Screams')

And this is why Hughes cannot regret that the moors are breaking
loose again from the harness of men:

The Trance of Light

The upturned face of this land
The mad singing in the hills
The prophetic mouth of the rain

That fell asleep

Under migraine of headscarves and clatter
Of clog-irons and looms
And gutter-water and clog-irons
And clog-irons and biblical texts
Stretches awake, out of Revelations
And returns to itself.

Chapels, chimneys, vanish in the brightening

And the hills walk out on the hills
The rain talks to its gods
The light, opening younger, fresher wings
Holds this land up again like an offering

Heavy with the dream of a people.

After his marvellous evocation of the spirit of the moors, Hughes ended that early essay 'The Rock' with these words: 'From there the return home was a descent into the pit, and after each visit I must have returned less and less of myself to the valley. This was where the division of body and soul, for me, began.' It was a great advantage to Hughes to have been born not in a town, where he might have allowed himself to be shut up in the little box of the exclusively human:

The country, to townies,
Is hardly more than nice,
A window-box, pretty
When the afternoon's empty;
When a visitor waits,
The window shuts.   (Kingsley Amis, 'Here Is Where')

nor in the country, where he might have become just another 'nature' poet, but on the very frontier where the two were engaged in a 'fight to the death'. He suffered in childhood the crisis of our civilisation in a very pure form. The experience forced him into a fiercely dualistic attitude to life which released the amazing energies of his first three books, *The Hawk in the Rain*, *Lupercal* and *Wodwo*. The subsequent books have been a gradual healing of that split. From that deep early dualism Hughes has moved painfully but surely towards 'a proper knowledge of the sacred wholeness of Nature, and a proper alignment of our behaviour within her laws.'

Most great writers want to save the world. Fiction and drama are partly modes of discourse and tend to get pulled towards other, non-imaginative forms of discourse such as politics, ethics or religion. The poet must recognise that he is not in the business of initiating a revolution or peddling propaganda or of merely ruminating in verse about political, ethical or religious matters. His business is to effect subtle changes, poem by poem, book by book, in the consciousness of his most responsive readers, towards a more whole and balanced sense of themselves and of their dependence on and obligation towards all that is not themselves. To do this, he need not be in possession of The Truth. What we require from him is not answers but metaphors — sparks which fly from the imagination of the poet to fire the imagination of the reader.

The great poet will have to do rather more than this. He will have to save himself, cure himself, in the role of Everyman. That is, to take himself to pieces and reconsistute himself in accordance with the inescapable facts. This process has to be lived through, not just imagined. But the imagining, the poetry, is part of the process, not just a record of it. The right metaphors are simply those which work, which actually do carry out the operation, or the required stage of it.

It is not only the chimneys and chapels of the Calder Valley which must collapse before there can be any new building. The image of stone returning to the earth is one of many images in Hughes for the restoration to Nature of its own, the healing and rededication of the holy elements before man can approach them again with clean hands, with respect and humility, and for purposes, one hopes, rather more natural, sane and worthily human than the enslavement of body and spirit which has characterised Protestantism and capitalism in England.

2 SEAMUS HEANEY

Hughes and England

One of the most precise and suggestive of T. S. Eliot's critical formulations was his notion of what he called 'the auditory imagination', 'the feeling for syllable and rhythm, penetrating far below the conscious levels of thought and feeling, invigorating every word; sinking to the most primitive and forgotten, returning to the origin and bringing something back', fusing 'the most ancient and the most civilised mentality'. I presume Eliot was thinking here about the cultural depth-charges latent in certain words and rhythms, that binding secret between words in poetry that delights not just the ear but the whole backward and abysm of mind and body; thinking of the energies beating in and between words that the poet brings into half-deliberate play; thinking of the relationship between the word as pure vocable, as articulate noise, and the word as etymological occurrence, as symptom of human history, memory and attachments.

It is in the context of this auditory imagination that I wish to discuss the language of Ted Hughes, Geoffrey Hill and Philip Larkin. All of them return to an origin and bring something back, all three live off the hump of the English poetic achievement, all three, here and now, in England, imply a continuity with another England, there and then. All three are hoarders and shorers of what they take to be the real England. All three treat England as a region — or rather treat their region as England — in different and complementary ways. I believe they are aflicted with a sense of history that was once the peculiar afflication of the poets of other nations who were not themselves natives of England but who spoke the English language. The poets of the mother culture, I feel, are now possessed of that defensive love of their territory which was once shared only by those poets whom we might call colonial — Yeats, MacDiarmid, Carlos Williams. They are aware of their English-ness as deposits in the descending storeys of the literary and historical past. Their very terrain is becoming consciously precious. A desire to preserve indigenous traditions, to keep open the imagination's supply lines to the past, to receive from the stations of Anglo-Saxon confirmations of ancestry, to perceive in the rituals of show Saturdays and race-meetings and seaside outings, of church-going and marriages at Whitsun, and in the necessities that crave expression after the ritual of church-going has passed away, to perceive in these a continuity of communal ways, and a confirmation of an identity which is threatened — all this is signified by their language.

When we examine that language, we find that their three separate voices are guaranteed by three separate foundations which, when combined, represent almost the total resources of the English language itself. Hughes relies on the northern deposits, the pagan Anglo-Saxon and Norse elements, and he draws energy also from a related constellation of primitive myths and world views. The life of his language is a persistence of the stark outline and vitality of Anglo-Saxon that became the Middle English alliterative tradition and then went underground to sustain the folk poetry, the ballads, and the ebullience of Shakespeare and the Elizabethans. Hill is also sustained by the Anglo-Saxon base, but his proper guarantor is that language as modified and amplified by the vocabularies and values of the Mediterranean, by the early medieval Latin influence; his is to a certain extent a scholastic imagination founded on an England that we might describe as Anglo-Romanesque, touched by the polysyllabic light of Christianity but possessed by darker energies which might be acknowledged as barbaric. Larkin then completes the picture, because his proper hinterland is the English language Frenchified and turned humanist by the Norman conquest and the Renaissance, made nimble, melodious and plangent by Chaucer and Spenser, and besomed clean of its inkhornisms and its irrational magics by the eighteenth century.

And their Englands of the mind might be correspondingly characte-rised. Hughes' is a primeval landscape where stones cry out and horizons endure, where the elements inhabit the mind with a religious force, where the pebble dreams 'it is the foetus of God', 'where the staring angels go through', 'where all the stars bow down', where, with appropriately pre-Socratic force, water lies 'at the bottom of all things / utterly worn out utterly clear'. It is England as King Lear's heath which now becomes a Yorkshire moor where sheep and foxes and hawks persuade 'unaccommodated man' that he is a poor bare forked thing, kinned not in a chain but on a plane of being with the animals themselves. There monoliths and lintels. The air is menaced by God's voice in the wind, by demonic protean crow-shapes; and the poet is a wanderer among the ruins, cut off by catastrophe from consolation and philosphy. Hill's England, on the other hand, is more hospitable to the human presence. The monoliths make way for the keeps and chantries if also for the beheading block. The heath's loneliness is kept at bay by the natural magic of the grove and the intellectual force of the scholar's cell. The poet is not a wanderer but a clerk or perhaps an illuminator or one of a guild of masters: he is in possession of a history rather than a mythology; he has a learned rather than an oral tradition. There are wars, but there are also dynasties, ideas of inheritance and order, possibilities for the 'true governaunce of England'. His elegies are not laments for the irrevocable dispersal of the *comitatus* and the ring-river in the hall, but solemn requiems for Plantagenet kings whose murderous wars are set in a great pattern, to be understood only when 'the sea / Across daubed rocks evacuates its dead'. And Larkin's England similarly reflects features from the period that his language is hived off. His trees and flowers and grasses are neither animistic, nor hallowed by half-remembered druidic lore; they are emblems of mutabilitie. Behind them lies the sensibility of troubador and courtier. 'Cut grass lies frail; / Brief is the breath / Mown stalks exhale'; his landscape is dominated neither by the untamed heath nor the totemistic architectures of spire and battlement but by the civic prospects, by roofs and gardens and prospects where urban and pastoral visions interact as 'postal districts packed like squares of wheat'. The poet is no longer a bardic remnant nor an initiate in curious learning nor a jealous master of the secrets of a craft; he is a humane and civilised member of the customs service or the civil service or, indeed, the library service. The moon is no longer his white goddess but his poetic property, to be image rather than icon: 'high and preposterous and separate', she watches over unfenced existence, over fulfilment's desolate attic, over an England of department stores, canals and floatings of industrial froth, explosions in mines, effigies in churches, secretaries in offices; and she hauls tides of life where only one ship is worth celebration, not a Golden Hind or a Victory, but 'black-/Sailed unfamiliar, towing at her back / A huge and birdless silence'.

Hughes' sensibility is pagan in the original sense: he is a haunter of the *pagus*, a heath-dweller, a heathen; he moves by instinct in the thickets beyond the *urbs*; he is neither urban nor urbane. His poetry is as redolent of the lair as it is of the library. The very titles of his books are casts made into the outback of our animal recognitions. *Lupercal*, a word infested with wolfish stinks yet returning to an origin in Shakespeare's *Julius Caesar*: 'You all did see that on the Lupercal / I thrice presented him a kingly crown.' Yet the word passes back through Shakespeare into the Lupercal, a cave below the western corner of the Palatine Hill in Rome; and the Lupercal was also the festival held on 15 February when, after the sacrifice of goats and a dog, youths dressed only in girdles made from the skins of these victims ran about the bounds of the Palatine city, striking those whom they met, especially women, with strips of goatskin. It was a fertility rite, and it was also a ritual beating of the bounds of the city, and in a way Hughes' language is just this also. Its sensuous fetch, its redolence of blood and gland and grass and water, recalled English poetry in the fifties from a too suburban aversion of the attention from the elemental; and the poems beat the bounds of a hidden England in streams and trees, on moors and in byres. Hughes appeared like Poor Tom on the heath, a civilised man tasting and testing the primitive facts; he appeared as *Wodwo*, a nosing wild man of the woods. The volume *Wodwo* appeared in 1967 and carried as its epigraph a quotation from *Gawain and the Green Knight*, and that deliberate affiliation is instructive. Like the art of Gawain, Hughes' art is one of clear outline and inner richness. His diction is consonantal, and it snicks through the air like an efficient blade, marking and carving out fast definite shapes; but within those shapes, mysteries and rituals are hinted at. They are circles within which he conjures up presences.

Hughes' vigour has much to do with this matter of consonants that take the measure of his vowels like calipers, or stud the line like rivets. 'Everything is inheriting everything', as he says in one of his poems, and what he has inherited through Shakespeare and John Webster and Hopkins and Lawrence is something of that primary life of stress which is the quick of the English poetic matter. His consonants are the Norsemen, the Normans, the Roundheads in the world of his vocables, hacking and hedging and hammering down the abundance and luxury and possible lasciviousness of the vowels. 'I imagine this midnight moment's forest' — the first line of the well-known 'The Thought Fox' — is hushed, but it is a hush achieved by the quelling, battening-down action of the m's and d's and t's: I iMagine this MiDnighT MoMenT's foresT. Hughes' aspiration in these early poems is to command all the elements, to bring them within the jurisdiction of his authoritarian voice. And in 'The Thought Fox' the thing at the beginning of the poem which lives beyond his jurisdiction is characteristically fluid and vowelling and sibilant: 'Something else is alive' whispers of a presence not yet accounted for, a presence that is granted its full vowel music as its epiphany — 'Something more near / Though deeper within darkness / Is entering the loneliness.' It is granted this dilation of its mystery before it is conjured into the possession of the poet-warden, the vowel-keeper; and its final emergence in the fully sounded i's and e's of 'an eye, / A widening deepening greenness,' is gradually mastered by the braking action of 'brilliantly, concentratedly', and by the shooting of the monosyllabic consonantal bolts in the last stanza:

Till, with a sudden sharp hot stink of fox
It enters the dark hole of the head.
The window is starless still; the clock ticks,
The page is printed.

Next a poem whose subject might be expected to woo the tender pious vowels from a poet rather than the disciplining consonants. About a 'Fern': 'Here is the fern's frond, unfurling a gesture'. The first line is an Anglo-Saxon line, four stresses, three of them picked out by alliteration; and although the frosty grip of those f's thaws out, the fern is still subsumed into images of control and discipline and regal authority:

And, among them, the fern
Dances gravely, like the plume
Of a warrior returning, under the low hills,

Into his own kingdom.

But of course we recognise that Hughes' 'Thistles' are vegetation more kindred to his spirit than the pliant fern. And when he turns his attention to them, they become reincarnations of the Norsemen in a poem entitled 'The Warriors of the North':

Bringing their frozen swords, their salt-bleached eyes, their salt-bleached hair,
The snow's stupefied anvils in rows,
Bringing their envy,
The slow ships feelered Southward, snails over the steep sheen of the water-
globe.

and he imagines them resurrected in all their arctic mail 'into the iron arteries of Calvin', and into 'Thistles'. The thistles are emblems of the Hughes voice as I see it, born of an original vigour, fighting back over the same ground; and it is not insignificant that in this poem Hughes himself imagines the thistles as images of a fundamental speech, uttering itself in gutturals from behind the sloped arms of consonants:

Every one a revengeful burst
Of resurrection, a grasped fistful
Of splintered weapons and Icelandic frost thrust up

From the underground stain of a decayed Viking.
They are like pale hair and the gutturals of dialect.
Every one manages a plume of blood.

Then they grow grey, like men.
Mown down, it is a feud. Their sons appear,
Stiff with weapons, fighting back over the same ground.

The gutturals of dialect, which Hughes here connects with the Nordic
stratum of English speech, he pronounces in another place to be the
germinal secret of his own voice. In an interview published in the
London Magazine in January 1971 he said:

I grew up in West Yorkshire. They have a very distinctive dialect there.
Whatever other speech you grow into, presumably your dialect stays alive in a
sort of inner freedom . . . it's your childhood self there inside the dialect and
that is possibly your real self or the core of it . . . Without it, I doubt if I would
ever have written verse. And in the case of the West Yorkshire dialect, of
course, it connects you directly and in your most intimate self to Middle
English poetry.

In other words he finds that the original grain of his speech is a chip off
the old block and that his work need not be a new planting but a new
bud on an old bough. What other poet would have the boldness to
entitle a collection *Wodwo*. Yet *Gawain and the Green Knight*, with
its beautiful alliterating and illuminated form, its interlacing and
trellising of natural life and mythic life, is probably closer in spirit to
Hughes' poetry than Hughes' poetry is to that of his English
contemporaries. Everything inherits everything — and Hughes is the
rightful heir to this alliterative tradition, and to the cleaving simplicity
of the Border ballad, which he elevates to the status of touchstone later
in that same interview. He says that he started writing again in 1955:

The poems that set me off were odd pieces by Shapiro, Lowell, Merwin, Wilbur
and Crowe Ransom. Crowe Ransom was the one who gave me a model I felt I
could use. He helped me get my words into focus . . . But this whole business of
influences is mysterious . . . And after all the campaigns to make it new you're
stuck with the fact that some of the Scots Border ballads still cut a deeper
groove than anything written in the last forty years. Influences just seem to
make it more and more unlikely that a poet will write what he alone could
write.

What Hughes alone could write depended for its release on the
discovery of a way to undam the energies of the dialect, to get a
stomping ground for that inner freedom, to get that childhood self a
disguise to roam at large in. Freedom and naturalness and homeliness
are positives in Hughes' critical vocabulary, and they are linked with
both the authenticity of individual poets and the genius of the
language itself. Speaking of Keith Douglas in 1964, Hughes could have

been speaking of himself; of the way his language and his imagination alerted themselves when the hunt for the poem in the adult world became synonymous with the hunt for the animal in the world of childhood, the world of dialect:

The impression is of a sudden mobilising of the poet's will, a clearing of his vision, as if from sitting considering possibilities and impossibilities he stood up to act. Pictures of things no longer interest him much: he wants their substance, their nature and their consequences in life. At once, and quite suddenly, his mind is whole . . . He is a renovator of language. It is not that he uses words in jolting combinations, or with titanic extravagance, or curious precision. His triumph is in the way he renews the simplicity of ordinary talk . . . The music that goes along with this . . . is the natural path of such confident, candid thinking . . . A utility general purpose style that combines a colloquial prose readiness with poetic breadth, a ritual intensity of music with clear direct feeling, and yet in the end is nothing but casual speech.

This combination of ritual intensity, prose readiness, direct feeling and casual speech can be discovered likewise in the best poems of *Lupercal*, because in *Hawk in the Rain* and indeed in much of *Wodwo* and *Crow*, we are often in the presence of that titanic extravagance Hughes mentions, speech not so much mobilising and standing up to act as flexing and straining until it verges on the grotesque. But in poems like 'Pike', 'Hawk Roosting', 'The Bull Moses' and 'An Otter' we get this confident, speedy, hammer-and-tongs proficiency. And in this poem from *Wodwo*, called 'Pibroch', a poem uniquely Hughesian in its very title, fetching energy and ancestry from what is beyond the Pale and beneath the surface, we have the elements of the Scottish piper's *ceol mor*, the high style, implicit in words like 'dead', 'heaven', 'universe', 'aeon', 'angels', and in phrases like 'the foetus of God', 'the stars bow down' — a phrase which cunningly makes its cast and raises Blake in the pool of the ear. We have elements of this high style, ritual intensity, whatever you want to call it; and we have also the 'prose readiness', the 'casual speech' of 'bored', 'hangs on', 'lets up', 'tryout', and the workaday cadences of 'Over the stone rushes the wind', and 'her mind's gone completely'. The landscape of the poem is one that the Anglo-Saxon wanderer or seafarer would be completely at home in:

The sea cries with its meaningless voice
Treating alike its dead and its living,
Probably bored with the appearance of heaven
After so many millions of nights without sleep,
Without purpose, without self-deception.

Stone likewise. A pebble is imprisoned
Like nothing in the Universe.
Created for black sleep. Or growing
Conscious of the sun's red spot occasionally,
Then dreaming it is the foetus of God.

Over the stone rushes the wind
Able to mingle with nothing,
Like the hearing of the blind stone itself.
Or turns, as if the stone's mind came feeling
A fantasy of directions.

Drinking the sea and eating the rock
A tree struggles to make leaves —
An old woman fallen from space
Unprepared for these conditions.
She hangs on, because her mind's gone completely.

Minute after minute, aeon after aeon,
Nothing lets up or develops.
And this is neither a bad variant nor a tryout.
This is where the staring angels go through.
This is where all the stars bow down.

Hughes attempts to make vocal the inner life, the simple being-thereness, 'the substance, nature and consequence in life' of sea, stone, wind and tree. Blake's pebble and tiger are shadowy presences in the background, as are the landscapes of Anglo-Saxon poetry. And the whole thing is founded on rock, that rock which Hughes presented in his autobiographical essay as his birthstone, holding his emergence in place just as his headstone will hold his decease:

This was the *memento mundi* over my birth: my spiritual midwife at the time and my godfather ever since — or one of my godfathers. From my first day it watched. If it couldn't see me direct, a towering gloom over my pram, it watched me through a species of periscope: that is, by infiltrating the very light of my room with its particular shadow. From my home near the bottom of the south-facing slope of the valley, the cliff was both the curtain and backdrop to existence.

I quote this piece because it links the childhood core with the adult opus, because that rock is the equivalent in its poetic landscape of dialect in his poetic speech. The rock persists, survives, sustains, endures and informs his imagination, just as it is the bedrock of the language upon which Hughes founds his version of survival and endurance.

ANNIE SCHOFIELD

Hughes and the Movement

In June 1954, the month he graduated from Cambridge, Ted Hughes' first published adult poem, 'The Little Boys and the Seasons', appeared in *Granta* under the pseudonym Daniel Hearing. Why did Hughes use a pseudonym? It seems clear that he had already decided to devote his life to writing, so he was not avoiding publicity. If he had been ashamed of the poem it is doubtful if he would have kept it — let alone submitted it for publication. The only conclusion one can draw is that Hughes used the pseudonym to indicate a standpoint. The question then is, why Daniel Hearing?

The reference is to the Biblical Daniel. The canonical *Book of Daniel* is a shamanistic, apocalyptic poem written in a period of a people's spiritual crisis. (It is the only truly apocalyptic book in the *Old Testament*.) It is not, as its apparent narrative would indicate, an account of events during the Babylonian exile of the sixth century B.C., but a poem of the second century B.C. when Israel was undergoing a similar crisis. Under the oppressive rule of Antiochus Epiphanes, the Israelite temple had again been desecrated, the Laws broken and the Covenent defiled. Once more the 'abomination of desolation' was set up on the altar. Jerusalem 'was made an habitation of strangers', 'Her sanctuary was laid waste like a wilderness, her feasts were turned into mourning, her sabbaths into reproach, her honour into contempt'.[1]

The writer of *Daniel* regards himself as having been elected to provide his people with the means of spiritual renewal. The nature of his call is repeatedly described in shamanistic terms. His visions are shamanic flights.

And I Daniel alone saw the vision: for the men that were with me saw not the vision: but a great quaking fell upon them, so that they fled to hide themselves.

Therefore I was left alone, and saw this great vision, and there remained no strength in me: for my comeliness was turned in me to corruption, and I retained no strength.

Yet I heard the voice of his words: and when I heard the voice of his words, then I was in a deep sleep on my face, and my face toward the ground.

And, behold, an hand touched me, which set me upon my knees and *upon* the palms of my hands.[2]

Daniel's visions are invariably preceded by periods of ritual preparation. 'I ate no pleasant bread, neither came flesh nor wine in my mouth, neither did I anoint myself at all till three whole weeks were fulfilled'.[3] Daniel has been chosen because of his 'vehemency of spirit'. He has 'set his heart to understand' and because of this, is privileged to hear the apocalyptic voice: 'Understand, O son of man: for at the time of the end *shall* be the vision'.[4]

The choice of the pseudonym Daniel Hearing, though its use was not continued, indicates that, from the beginning Hughes' poetic intention was that of the writer of *Daniel*: to submit himself to the necessary discipline to hear and proclaim a message of spiritual renewal in a decadent age. It commits him to the idea that the urge towards poetry is a religious urge: to a poetry of inspiration and revelation, to the 'poetic or holy life'. The gesture might seem grandiloquent, but in the context of the 1950's (when book-length manifestos appeared in the guise of literary criticism) it may simply be seen as a statement of attitude: as a spirited reaction against what appeared to be the prevailing poetic climate.

It seemed, at the time, that the poets of the Movement had effected a literary *coup d'état*.[5] Their attitudes to life and art are discussed in Robert Conquest's 'Introduction' to the anthology *New Lines* (Macmillan, 1967), where he attempts to define the aesthetic of their poetry:

I believe the most important general point would be that it submits to no great systems of theoretical constructs nor agglomerations of unconscious commands. It is free from both mystical and logical compulsions and — like modern philosphy — is empirical in its attitude to all that comes.   (p. xv)

In Conquest's view, *New Lines* was a 'standard-restoring anthology'.[6] He, and others, considered that the 1940s had made the mistake of 'giving the Id . . . too much of a say'. The poets he anthologised were '. . . progressing from different viewpoints to a certain unity of approach, a new and healthy general standpoint'. Theirs was to be a poetry of the 'objective imagination'.

The word on the objective breath must be
A wind to winnow the emotive out;
Music can generalise the inner sea
In dark harmonies of a blinded heart;
But, hot with certainty and keen with doubt,
Verse sweats out heartfelt knowledge, clear-eyed art.[7]

This analytical art sought to achieve 'the harmony of science pealing under / The poem's waters like a sunken bell'.[8] This 'new and healthy' standpoint was an attempt to deny any reality but the everyday; it involved (as its paradoxes show) a deliberate shutting-out of intimations of any other. John Holloway warns:

Shun the black puddles, the scrub hedge
Down to the sea. Keep to the wet streets where
Mercury and sodium flood their sullen fire.
Tonight do not disturb the water's edge . . .

I have watched you, as you have visited this house,
And know, from knowing myself, that you will be
Quick to people the shore, the fog, the sea,
    With all the fabulous
Things of the moon's dark side. No, stay with us.
Do not demand a walk tonight
Down to the sea. It makes no place for those
Like you and me who, to sustain our pose,
Need wine and conversation, colour and light.[9]

This quasi-Augustan pose was, ostensibly, a reaction against the poetic trends of the 1940s. It was a repudiation of the 'new apocalyptics' who were thought to have 'opened their Blakes and splashed about in puddles of myth, delighting in portentousness and prismatic effects'.[10] It was an attempt to rid poetry of what were considered the excesses of the neo-Romantics who, according to Conquest, 'were encouraged to regard their task simply as making arrangements of sex and violence tapped straight from the unconscious . . . or to evoke without comment the naivetes and nostalgias of childhood'.[11] Such sweeping condemnation of their predecessors' bad habits carried with it a potential, and frequently actual, rejection of much more than that. Conquest's scientifically harmonic sunken bell is surely a reference to, and criticism of, the musically generalised inner sea of Eliot's *Four Quartets*, and a refusal to hear the 'clamour of the bell of the last annunciation' of 'Dry Salvages'. Holloway's 'warning' appears to be issued against the same kind of dangers. It is given in answer to the forebodings of an old woman, whose prophesy evokes both the warnings and reassurances of the poem: 'Yet shun that dark foreshore [of an "ocean littered with wastage"?] There'll be no sound: except the echoing / Horn of a baffled ship, shut out from home.' Kinglsey Amis' pummelling of the lesser poets in 'Against Romanticism' takes a sideswipe at Eliot:

Over all, a grand meaning fills the scene,
And sets the brain raging with prophecy,
Raging to discard real time and place,
Raging to build a better time and place
Than the ones which give prophecy its field
To work, the calm material for its rage
And the context which makes it prophecy . . .

Better, of course, if images were plain
Warnings clearly said, shapes put down quite still
Within the fingers' reach, or else nowhere.[12]

The 'new and healthy' attitude to life and art wanted no poetic wastelands but neat, well-clipped lawns with no heaps of broken images obscuring the view. Amis' peroration, like Holloway's warning, is really a rejection of any kind of visionary poetry. When Amis 'invokes his muse': 'Let us make at least visions that we need / Let mine be pallid', the lines which follow are revealing. One does not *make* visions. Amis knows this. The 'vision' that he 'makes' lasts only for part of a line before it becomes a defence against the forces which would shatter it:

An afternoon long-drawn and silent, with
    Buildings free from all grime of history,
The people total strangers, the grass cut,
    Not long, voluble swooning wilderness,
And green, not parched or soured by frantic suns
    Doubling the commands of a rout of gods,
Nor trampled by the havering unicorn;
    Let the sky be clean of officious birds
Punctiliously flying on the left;
    Let there be a path leading out of sight,
And at its other end a temperate zone:
    Woods devoid of beasts, roads that please the foot.[13]

If one removes the disruptive elements, Amis' vision is pallid indeed. The whole poem, like many others in *New Lines*, demonstrates an uneasy awareness of these elements. The deliberately cultivated 'urbanity'[14] and blandness of the new poetic diction was an attempt to keep visions at bay. There was a conscious refusal to enter the world which Eliot's poetry inhabits, the world which, by his choice of psuedonym, Hughes indicates will be his too. He is not prepared to assume a nonchalant pose. He will be a Daniel and 'set his heart to understand'.

In the interview with Egbert Faas, Hughes comments on the Movement:

One of the things these poets had in common I think was the post-war mood of having had enough . . . enough rhetoric, enough overweening push of any kind, enough of the dark gods, enough of the id, enough of the Angelic powers and the heroic efforts to make new worlds. They'd seen it all turn into death camps and atomic bombs.[15]

This is not an example of what Hughes' detractors often see as his penchant for hyperbole. The same cause and effect sequence is recognised by Donald Davie. In 'Creon's Mouse' Davie confesses to a 'self-induced and stubborn loss of nerve';

If too much daring brought (he thought) the war,
When that was over nothing else would serve
But no-one must be daring any more,
A self-induced and stubborn loss of nerve.[16]

In the poem 'Rejoinder to a Critic', Davie gives the fundamental reason for this withdrawal from a world and a poetry where the emotional basis of romanticism has any place:

Donne could be daring, but he never knew,
When he enquired, 'Who's injured by my love?'
Love's radio-active fall-out on a large
Expanse around the point it bursts above.

'Alas, alas, who's injured by my love?'
And recent history answers: Half Japan!
Not love, but hate? Well, both are versions of
The 'feeling' that you dare me to. Be dumb!
Appear concerned only to make it scan!
How dare we now be anything but numb?[17]

Davie is well aware that the avoidance of feeling stems from a deeper cause than what Conquest calls a 'negative determination to avoid bad principles'.[18] It is not merely reaction against excess of feeling, the flaw they found in the poetry of the neo-romantics, which underlies the desire for urbanity, but a mistrust of feeling itself. The new poetic was not just resistance to the tendency of their predecessors to see an apocalypse in every sunset, but a visor to cut out the blinding glare of the man-created apocalyptic instrument 'brighter than a thousand suns'.[19] Despite its claim to be anchoring itself in the real world and the real event, the poetry of the 1950s was failing to come to any kind of satisfactory terms with the realest events of its age. Davie appeared to be aware that Hiroshima was not just a causeless physical-historical event but a manifestation of forces operating within the human psyche, but chose not to examine these forces. In a very real sense, every one alive today in the West — if not the world — is a survivor of Hiroshima and the death camps, and must come to terms with their implications. Numbness is evasion.

Someone who has attempted this, though not in poetry, is Robert Jay Lifton. In his book *Death in Life: the Survivors of Hiroshima* (Weidenfeld and Nicolson, 1968) he makes a comprehensive study of reactions to what he calls 'disconnected death': that of Hiroshima and the concentration camp. He analyses what he terms 'psychic numbing'. He suggests that this phenomenon is a pathological extension of a normal, human, adaptive function. In the encounter with death, in the normal human cycle, there is a temporary withdrawal of feeling in order to cope with one's sense of vulnerability. This is followed by survivor guilt, which is expiated by mourning. Unnatural death — that of a child or violent death — disrupts the pattern and the psychic closing-off becomes exaggerated, often leading to an extended withdrawal from life by the survivor . The encounter with death in the concentration camps and at Hiroshima was of such a nature and magnitude as to seem outside any human cycle. The psychic closing-off from these events became psychic numbing. In this condition, the survivor lives at a devitalised level in order to cope with an unmanageable death-anxiety in the face of disconnected death. The state of psychic numbing is a paradox: by detaching himself from events by limiting his emotional involvement, the survivor induces a (false) sense of invulnerability, whilst at the same time offering the devitalised life as a kind of atonement for his survival in the face of his survivor guilt. In Lifton's view, all survivors of 'extreme death immersion' experience the inner command 'Don't dare to feel'. Wilfred Owen is an interesting study here. He provides evidence of psychic closing-off in a letter to Seigfried Sassoon:

The battalion had a sheer time last week. I can find no better epithet: because I cannot say I suffered anything; having let my brain go dull. That is to say my nerves are in perfect order.

It is a strange truth: that your *Counter-Attack* frightened me much more than the real one: though the boy by my side, shot through the head, lay on top of me, soaking my shoulder, for half an hour.

Catalogue? Photograph? Can you photograph the crimson-hot iron as it cools from the smelting? That is what Jones's blood looked like, and felt like. My senses are charred. I shall feel again as soon as I dare, but now I must not. I don't take the cigarette out of my mouth when I write Deceased over their letters.[20]

Section VI of 'Insensibility' provides a comment on those who deliberately choose numbness as a response:

Cursed are the dullards whom no cannon stuns
That they should be as stones;
Wretched are they, and mean
With paucity that never was simplicity.
By choice they made themselves immune
To pity and whatever mourns in man
Before the last sea and the hapless stars;
Whatever mourns when many leave these shores;
Whatever shares
The eternal reciprocity of tears.[21]

Temporary psychic closing-off is a life-preserving mechanism. Its pathological extension — psychic numbing — carries with it the danger that it can destroy the life it seeks to preserve. It can lead to death-in-life: a permanent extension of the state which results in diminished vitality, chronic depression and constricted life-space which cover a rage and mistrust which lie just beneath the surface. The poetry of the Movement exhibits all these symptoms. In addition to the insistence on keeping feeling to a minimum, another aspect of the limiting of emotional and psychic involvement in this poetry is its exaggerated concern with technique. Many of the poems are about writing poems. These poets are seemingly unaware of the dangers here. 'Appear concerned to make it scan' is a 'negative and dangerous' attitude which, translated into the world of medicine, allows the techniques of medicine to become more important than healing — allows, by extension, the experiments in death camps. Translated into the world of nuclear physics it allows the creation and use of a potentially world-destroying weapon without the imaginative, emotional grasp of the consquences. Once the basic stance of detachment is established, the rest can be a matter of degree. Large-scale wars are not continued out of excess emotion; they need propaganda machines to keep the 'hatred' at the requisite pitch. The atom bomb was created by detached scientists and used by tacticians. Racial hatred can only become genocide on the scale of mid-twentieth century Europe's when it has as its instrument a bureaucracy to 'make it scan'. The 'final solution' needed railway timetables.

Conquest claimed that the poetry in *New Lines* expressed the new and healthy attitude: 'empirical' — 'to all that comes'. Its poets were, in this attitude, atempting to emulate the Augustans. In fact, the wide-ranging empiricism of the Augustans had narrowed, in them, to a blinkered selectivity. These poets ignored huge areas of human experience — in particular — that of their immediate past. Had they been less selective they might have seen that the 'urbanity' they sought to achieve was no longer possible. The 'usages of past poets' and the 'tone of polite conversation' which Davie considers 'pure diction' were an inadequate language for a post-Hiroshima, post-holocaust poetry, even if it had been prepared to confront these events. As George Steiner has said, rational humanist poetry is no longer adequate to the situation: 'We cannot pretend that Belsen is irrelevant to the responsible life of the imagination. What man has inflicted on man in the very recent time, has affected the writer's primary material — the sum and potential of human behaviour — and it presses on the brain with a new darkness'.[22] In the·face of this new darkness a 'self-induced and stubborn loss of nerve' was the reaction of the ostrich.

In the conclusion of his book, Robert Jay Lifton offers a more positive response:

Only man, we are often reminded, 'knows death,' or at least knows that he will die. To which we must add: only man could invent grotesquely absurd death. Only man, through his technology, could render the meaningful totally meaningless. And more, elevate that 'invention' to something in the nature of a potential destiny that stalks us all. For, after Hiroshima, we can envisage no war-linked chivalry, certainly no glory. Indeed, we can see no relationship — not even a distinction — between victimiser and victim, only the sharing in species annihilation. Yet we know that great discoveries have in the past been made by survivors — of dying historical epochs as well as of actual catastrophes. By confronting their predicament, they have been able to break out of the numbing and stasis of unmastered survivorhood and contribute to the enlargement of human consciousness. Our present difficulty is that we can no longer be sure of this opportunity. We can no longer count upon survivor wisdom deriving from weapons which are without limit in what they can destroy.[23]

In the book *The Sense of an Ending* (Oxford University Press, 1966), Frank Kermode discusses eschatological literature and disparages the idea that the modern sense of apocalypse is in any way unique: '. . . it would be foolish to argue, in a discussion of how people behave under eschatological threat, that nuclear bombs are more real and make one experience more authentic crisis-feelings than armies in the sky' (p.95). In England in the 1950s there did appear to be a crucial difference. Armies in the sky — even bringing wholesale destruction — imply a deity concerned with the fate of its creation. Nuclear bombs make man his own eschatological instrument. A 'mechnanical parody of the Judgement Day'[24], a Godless apocalypse, is the ultimate absurdity. God had been dumped in the 'myth-kitty' along with all the other mumbo-jumbo. In the face of this absurdity the answer was to deny any potential crisis-feeling. As Kermode points out: 'Apocalypse depends on a concord of imaginatively recorded past and imaginatively predicted future achieved on behalf of us, who remain "in the middest"' (p.8).

The poets of the Movement deliberately refused to travel — imaginatively — in either direction. 'The past is past and the future neuter'.[25]

The art of the past was a dusty museum; its religion only lingered as material for tentative speculations such as Larkin's 'Church Going' when one found oneself in its monuments — its 'accoutred frowsty barn'.

Lifton continues

. . . Hiroshima was an 'end-of-the-world' in all the ways I have described. And yet the world still exists. Precisely in this end-of-the-world quality lies both its threat and its potential wisdom. In every age man faces a pervasive theme which defies his engagement and yet must be engaged. In Freud's day it was sexuality and moralism. Now it is unlimited technical violence and absurd death. We do well to name the threat and analyse its components. But our need is to go further, to create new psychic and social forms to enable us to reclaim not only our technologies but our very imaginations, in the service of the continuity of life.[26]

I cannot say whether Hughes has read Lifton's book, but he shares many of his convictions. 'Karma' in *Wodwo* shows that he too sees now no distinction between victimiser and victim. 'Crow's Account of the Battle' is an account of 'unlimited technical violence and absurd death' where

Reality was giving its lesson,
Its mishmash of scripture and physics,
With here, brains in hands, for example,
And there, legs in a treetop.
. . .

And when the smoke cleared it became clear
This had happened too often before
And was going to happen too often in future
And happened too easily
Bones were too like lath and twigs
Blood was too like water
Cries were too like silence
The most terrible grimaces too like footprints in mud
And shooting somebody through the midriff
Was too like striking a match
Too like potting a snooker ball
Too like tearing up a bill
Blasting the whole world to bits
Was too like slamming a door
Too like dropping in a chair
Exhausted with rage
Too like being blown to bits yourself
Which happened too easily
With too like no consequences.

One of the main preoccupations of *Crow* is the effort to break out of the 'numbing and stasis of unmastered survivorhood'. As early as 1954

Hughes showed that he was aware that some kind of numbing process had taken place; 'The Casualty' was published in *Chequer 7* in that year. The casualty of the poem is not merely the crashed airman but humanity itself. The responses to the airman's horrific death are indifference and voyeurism. Some 'wait with interest for the evening news' where the details will be given along with the cricket scores, and some, their hearts no 'more / Open or large than a fist clenched, and in there / Holding close complacency its most dear / Unscratchable diamond', 'jostle' for a closer view, 'Greedy to share all that is undergone, / Grimace, gasp, gesture of death'.

This poem holds the first of the many images of incineration which appear in Hughes' work. Death by fire — the martyr's death — formerly the death of supreme meaning, has become in the twentieth century the most common form of disconnected — seemingly absurd — death. Incendiary bombs, nuclear explosion, napalm and the crematorium oven have consumed millions, and still:

Russia and America circle each other;
Threats nudge an act that were without doubt
A melting of the mould in the mother,
Stones melting about the root.

The quick of the earth burned out:
The toil of all our ages a loss
With leaf and insect.[27]

It must have seemed to Hughes that the only response to this situation, in English poetry in the 1950s, was the clutching of the close complacency of the spectators in the poem. Instead of openly confronting their predicament the Movement poets were bent on 'sustaining a pose'. Their poetry was the deliberate cultivation of a language and a state of mind that had already been proved inadequate. Hughes holds the view that the implications of the First World War had not been fully realised because the poetic means of expression was not available:

Perhaps Georgian language wouldn't look nearly so bad if it hadn't been put to such a test. It was the worst equipment they could have had —the language of the very state of mind that belied and concealed the possibility of the nightmare that now had to be expressed.[28]

The nightmare that had to be expressed was Western civilisation's first encounter with disconnected death: '. . . the shock of machine guns, armies of millions and the plunge into the new dimension, when suddenly and for the first time Adam's descendants found themselves meaningless'.[29] Forty years and a global war later, with a new nightmare to be expressed — the possibility of the total annihilation of civilisation — and the response of the English poetry 'establishment' was a 'self-induced and stubborn loss of nerve' which advocated a 'chaste diction' and 'urbanity, a civilised moderation and elegance'—as Hughes later said, 'a shrunken, atrophied, suppressive-of everything-under, bluffing, debonair, frivolous system of vocal team-calls'.[30]

In 1954, unlike the Movement poets — not having 'splendidly and ultimately arrived' — Hughes was in no position to issue a poetic manifesto; instead, he chose his pseudonym Daniel Hearing. The implications of the choice are many, some have already been indicated. There is the diverting speculation that since Davie used the hymns of Charles Wesley as models of chaste diction and disciplined emotion, Hughes is thinking of one of those 'geysers of warm feeling' of which Davie disapproves, but which is an indelible part of the memory of a pre-Second-World-War north-country nonconformist upbringing — number seven in Ira D. Sankey's *Sacred Songs and Solos*: 'Dare to be a Daniel, Dare to Stand Alone'. But the choice of Daniel has a more direct reference to the state of English poetry in the 1950s. It points to Blake, of whom Hughes has said 'Blake I connect inwardly to Beethoven, and if I could dig to the bottom of my strata maybe their names and works would be the deepest traces'.[31]

The description of the spiritual wasteland as the *Abomination of Desolation* belongs, in the Bible, to the poet of the *Book of Daniel* and to him alone.[32] Blake appropriates this description and uses it in *Jerusalem* and *Milton*. In *Jerusalem* the *Abomination of Desolation* is brought about by the destruction of the 'emanation' by its 'spectre': the destruction of the Imagination — the Divine in man — by a rigid, rationalist morality.

And in this manner the Sons of Albion in their strength:
They take the two contraries which are call'd Qualities, with which
Every substance is clothed: they name them Good and Evil
From them they make an Abstract, which is a Negation
Not only of the Substance from which it is derived,
A murderer of its own Body, but also a murderer
Of every Divine Member: it is the Reasoning Power,
An Abstract objecting power that Negatives everything.
This is the Spectre of Man, the Holy Reasoning Power,
And in its Holiness is closed the Abomination of Desolation.[33]

In *Milton* he specifically relates the condition to the dearth of Imagination in poetry.

To bathe in the Waters of Life, to wash off the Not Human,
I come in Self-annihilation & the grandeur of Inspiration,
To cast off Rational Demonstration by Faith in the Saviour,
To cast off the rotten rags of Memory by Inspiration,

To cast off Bacon, Locke & Newton from Albion's covering
To take off his filthy garments & clothe him with Imagination,
To cast aside from Poetry all that is not Inspiration,
That it no longer shall dare to mock with the aspersion of Madness
Cast on the Inspired by the tame high finisher of paltry Blots
Indefinite, or paltry Rhymes, or paltry Harmonies,
Who publishes doubt & calls it knowledge, whose Science is Despair,
Whose pretence to knowledge is Envy, whose whole Science is
To destroy the wisdom of ages to gratify ravenous Envy
That rages round him life a Wolf day & night without rest:
He smiles with condescension, he talks of Benevolence & Virtue,
And those who act with Benevolence & Virtue they murder time on time.
These are the destroyers of Jerusalem, these are the murderers
Of Jesus, who deny the Faith & mock at Eternal Life,
Who pretend to poetry that they may destroy Imagination
By imitation of Nature's Images drawn from Remembrance.
These are the Sexual Garments, the Abomination of Desolation.[34]

Bacon, Locke and Newton: the harbingers of three hundred years of
rational enlightenment hardening into scientific objectivity — of
looking with and not through the eye[35] — which according to Hughes,
began by '. . questioning superstitions and ended by prohibiting
imagination itself as a reliable mental faculty, branding it more or less
criminal in a scientific society, reducing the Bible to a bundle of old
women's tales, finally murdering God'.[36]
The result is a 'chronically sick society', indeed, 'a chronically sick
civilisation' — sick as a 'direct result of the prohibition of imagination,
the breakdown of all negotiations between our scientific mental
attitude and our inner life'.[37] Blake's whole artistic effort was directed
to restoring the lost Jerusalem of the English Imagination. Hughes'
work is directed towards the same end. Blake came at the beginning of
the technological civilisation: there is an added urgency for Hughes,
since he comes at what could be its end if the scientific attitude
is allowed to continue its domination of the way man sees his world:
'. . . the last three hundred years in Europe have forgotten, that
without full operation of the various worlds and heavens and hells of
imagination, men become sick, mechanical monsters'.[38] These three
centuries of regarding objective reality as the only reality — the word
on the objective breath winnowing the emotive out — has had
disastrous results. What objective 'scientific' perception of 'reality'
ignores — by 'lucid sophistries of sight'[39] is the inner world of 'the body
and archaic nervous system' — that part of man's make-up which
turns the 'biological craving for water' into 'the precise notion that it is
water that we want'.[40]

. . . every civilised human being, whatever his conscious development, is still
an archaic man at the deeper levels of his psyche. Just as the human body

connects us with the mammals and displays numerous relics of earlier evolutionary stages going back even further to the reptilian age, so the human psyche is likewise a product of evolution which, when followed up to its origins, shows countless archaic traits.[41]

It is the archaic man within — 'the one behind the constructed, spoilt part'[42] — who, in the first version of the poem 'The Jaguar'[43] holds the 'life-prisoners' staring out dumbly through the bars, who, denied existence, becomes 'cannibal murderous with deprivation'.[44] 'The small piloting consciousness of the objective intelligence has steered its body and soul into hell ... The whole inner world has become elemental, chaotic, continually more primitive and beyond our control. It has become a place of demons.'[45]

The threat posed by this inner world is what Movement poetry tries to keep at bay. Amis' poem 'Against Romanticism' is, in fact, against these demands. They are the reason for Holloway's warning against walking at the sea's edge. Hughes argues that these 'dangers' cannot be ignored. The inner world is not a place to be explored or ignored at will, it is 'a region of events'.[46] 'Ghost Crabs'[47] stalk not only the man who 'strolls along the sands' but 'spill inland' and 'press through our nothingness where we sprawl on our beds'. They are not, as Amis and Holloway suggest, the voluntary creations of an intemperate fancy 'They are the turmoil of history, the convulsion / In the roots of the blood'. They are the eruptions of frustrated energy when 'Java Man's bone-grinders' are 'sublimated into chat'.[48] They are manifestations of the split-off parts of the psyche, repressed, disowned by the totalitarianism of consciousness, returning to claim their due.[49] 'And this devil of suppressed life stops making trouble the moment he is acknowledged, the moment he is welcomed into conscious life and given some shape where he can play out his energy in an active part of the personality.'[50] Once this process begins, it is discovered that the Ghost Crabs are not only evils to be shunned. The inner world is not just a place of demons, 'not merely an inferno of depraved impulses and crazy explosions of embittered energy. Our real selves lie down there. Down there, mixed up among all the madness, is everything that once made life worth living. All the lost awareness and powers and allegiances of our biological and spiritual being.'[51] Disconnected from this inner world, life becomes empty, meaningless, sterile.

Hughes sees poetry as a means of finding a way into this 'locked-up life' — a way to *hear* the other creature behind the 'constructed, spoilt' persona (who with the aid of wine and conversation can sustain a pose), who

rarely speaks or stirs at all, in the sort of lives we now lead. We have so totally lost touch that we hardly realise he is absent. All we know is that somehow or other the great, precious thing is missing. And the real distress of our world begins there. The luminous spirit, (maybe he is a crowd of spirits), that takes account of everything and gives everything its meaning, is missing. Not missing, just incommunicado. But here and there, it may be, we hear it.

It is human, of course, but it is also everything else that lives. When we hear it, we understand what a strange thing is living in this Universe, and somewhere at the core of us — strange, beautiful, pathetic, terrible. Some animals and birds express this being pure and without effort, and then you hear the whole, desolate, final actuality of existence in a voice or a tone.

This is Hughes talking about *Orghast* in 1971.[52] In 1967 he used the same concepts in a trilogy, *The Head of Gold*, centred around the 'events' of the Biblical *Daniel*.[53] The first play, 'The Fiery Furnace', deals with the opposition of the 'wise men' of Babylon (a sort of Babylonian Movement) to the threat posed by Daniel. Despite having been assured by these wise men that God does not exist, only atoms and numbers and cash and logic, the king has been converted to Daniel's God. His sanity is doubted. 'After two thousand years' progress' towards rationality — the king has gone back to 'prayers and a bread and water diet'. As in the Biblical account, Daniel's influence arises because he alone was able to interpret Nebuchadnezzar's dream. Daniel has 'unearthed', 'fished-up', 'remembered' the king's dream.[54] The theme of the nature and source of dreams is carried over into the second play, 'The Word of the Holy Ones'. The king is advised by his psychiatrist — who is firmly against romanticism — that dreams are a mere nothing, arising from indigestion, 'a will-o'-th'-wisp from stomach trouble', and that taking dreams too seriously is madness. The conclusion one draws from these plays is that in dreams is heard the 'word of the holy ones' and that if, indeed, the king is mad, he is 'mad as a refuge from unbelief'[55] The third play, 'Daniel in the Lions' Den', again following the Biblical narrative, shifts to the reign of Darius. Here, the lion-keeper talks of his lions in the same terms and using almost the same words that Hughes had used earlier when talking of his poems about animals in *Lupercal*: 'Each one is living the life of redeemed joy. They're continually in a state of energy which men only have when they've gone mad. Their strength arises from their complete unity with whatever divinity they have . . . Animals are not violent, they're so much more completely controlled than men.'[56]

The trilogy ends with the prayers of Daniel — on the same 'wavelength' as the roar of the lions — amplified on a kind of radio-telescope, tuned to 'receive all prayers directed at God'; the 'cries of all wild creatures as well as people's prayers'.

Cries from birds, long ago perfect
And from the awkward gullets of beasts
That will not chill into syntax.   (Epilogue, *Gaudete*, 1977)

Daniel's amplified prayer is not Hughes' poetry. Perhaps because he had not at that time found his own words, perhaps to show that, whatever 'dead spots' it might create for others (see note 25), for him the King James Bible was still 'living language' — the 'greatest poetry in English'.[57] Hughes uses Psalm 104: a voice telling 'what a strange thing is living in this Universe — strange, beautiful, pathetic, terrible', a cry to the Creator: 'Thou hidest thy face, they are troubled: thou takest away their breath, they die, and return to dust. Thou sendest forth thy spirit, they are created: and thou renewest the face of the earth.' In *Gaudete*, Hughes addresses the same deity.

What will you make of half a man
Half a face
A ripped edge

His one-eyed waking
Is the shorn sleep of aftermath
. . .

How will you correct
The veteran of negatives
And the survivor of cease?

He has offered an answer which will at least lay man open to the possibility of correction:

So what we need, evidently, is a faculty that embraces both worlds simultaneously . . .
    The inner world, separated from the outer world is a place of demons. The outer world separated from the inner world, is a place of meaningless objects and machines. The faculty that makes the human being out of these two worlds is called divine. That is only a way of saying that it is a faculty without which humanity cannot really exist. It can be called religious or visionary. More essentially, it is imagination which embraces both inner and outer worlds in a creative spirit.[58]

This has been Hughes' credo from the first. What he felt was needed, in Engish poetry in the 1950s, was a Daniel

To open the Eternal Worlds, to open the immortal Eyes
Of Man inwards into the Worlds of Thought, into Eternity
Ever expanding in the Bosom of God, the Human Imagination.[59]

— a Daniel to cast out those who 'pretend to poetry that they may destroy imagination' — who set up the abomination that maketh desolate on the altar of Jerusalem.

Hughes and the poets of Eastern Europe

The serious writer of verse must be prepared to cross himself with the best verse of other languages, and the best prose of all languages.   (T. S. Eliot)[1]

However rootedly national it may be, poetry is less and less the prisoner of its own language. It is beginning to represent as an ambassador, something far greater than itself. Or perhaps, it is only now being heard for what, among other thngs, it is — a universal language of understanding, coherent behind the many languages in which we can all hope to meet.   (Ted Hughes)[2]

I

Ted Hughes began the 1960s as an extremely accomplished and successful English poet; he ended the decade a major force in European poetry. Through his association with the magazine *Modern Poetry in Translation*, which he co-edited from 1966 to 1971 with Daniel Weissbort, through essays, talks, and, above all, through his poems themselves, he helped to free English poetry and its public from its postwar parochialism, and to develop a sense of poetry as the 'universal language of understanding' during a period of sustained political tension. It was mainly through his personal contacts, and a measure of his literary stature and achievement, that in 1969 a magnificent selection of world poets were attracted to London to take part in a 'Poetry International', including such distinguished figures as W. H. Auden, Miroslav Holub of Czechoslovakia, Janos Pilinszky of Hungary, and Vasko Popa of Yugoslavia.

A crucial influence on Hughes' poetic development has been the poets of eastern Europe, writers such as Holub, Pilinszky, Popa and Zbigniew Herbert of Poland, poets who explore themes of profound immediacy to Hughes — survival, death, war, futility, endurance, the cruel ironies of existence. His assimilation of their work contributed to the poetic fables and myths of *Wodwo* and *Crow*, expressed and energised in the stark, laconic, brutally poignant style that characterises these authors. Learning from their uncompromising honesty and 'unembellished language', he was able not only to articulate more precisely the anguish and epiphanies of his own personal experience during these years, but also to reflect in his verse a sense of the whole European historical and cultural experience, and in so doing joined the mainstream of modernist literature. These Eastern European writers, along with Keith Douglas and Sylvia Plath, helped Hughes to purge his poetry of rhetorical self-indulgence — a process he himself had begun in *Lupercal* — and so realise the kind of poetry Ezra Pound and the early modernists has predicted:

As to Twentieth Century poetry, it will be harder and saner, it will be 'nearer the bone'. It will be as much like granite as it can be, its force will lie in its truth . . . I mean it will not try to seem forcible by rhetorical din and luxurious riot. We will have fewer painted adjectives impeding the shock and stroke of it. At least for myself, I want it so, austere, direct, free from emotional slither.[3]

What Hughes achieved, through his imaginative projection into the worlds of the Eastern European poets, was something which the early modernists could not — an ironic but radiant vision emanating from 'universal compassion' and 'a sense of responsibility, a sense of responsibility for the human conscience'.[4]

II

Yet why should Hughes have been so drawn to eastern European poets in particular? An obvious answer is that they extended and intensified his already acute consciousness of war, which had first been stimulated by his father's anecdotes of the First World War, by Wilfred Owen's poetry, and later, in 1962, by his fascination for the poems of Keith Douglas, who fought in the Western Desert and died in Normandy during the Second World War. Bill Hughes, the poet's father, was one of seventeen surivors in his regiment, which was massacred in the infamous Gallipoli campaign of 1915. On one memorable occasion, he narrowly escaped death, when a piece of shrapnel which should have struck his heart was deflected by a paybook in his breast pocket, an incident alluded to in 'Out' and 'Crow's Account of the Battle'. From the age of four onwards, Hughes' imagination was gripped by war, the casualness of death, the arbitrariness of survival. The remarkably mature and vivid war poems of *The Hawk in the Rain* are the product of a synthesis of his father's experiences, his schooling in the tradition of the English poets of the Great War, and his own imaginative insight.

In Keith Douglas — as later in Popa, Holub, Herbert and Pilinszky — Hughes found a man of words and a man of action, another Major Robert Gregory, who had experienced war at first hand, and whose stark, stripped-down language provided an excellent model for Hughes. It is revealing to compare Hughes' own account of Douglas' poetry — 'The war . . . was his ideal subject, the burning away of all human pretensions in the ray cast by death . . . not truth is beauty only, but truth kills everybody. The truth of a man is the doomed man in him or his dead body'[5] — with Zbigniew Herbert's obsevations on his poetic theme: 'I think that the war has created almost all the problems of my writing: what a man is in the face of death, how he behaves in the presence of a totalitarian threat, what moral values can and should be saved'.[6]

While Hughes was only nine at the outbreak of the Second World War and at the end of the war was writing adventure poems about Zulus and the Wild West, Pilinszky (born 1921), Popa (born 1922), Holub (born 1923) and Herbert (born 1924) were enduring the full horror of Nazism and occupation. Popa fought with the partisans in Yugoslavia, where one and a half million lost their lives. Janos Pilinszky was 'scooped up by the retreating German army' in 1944, and spent the last year of the war 'moving from prison camp to prison camp in Austria and Germany'.[7] Zbigniew Herbert, born in Lwow in the Polish Ukraine, was a member of the Polish Resistance struggling against 'the rascals of history'[8] who murdered six million of his countrymen, and systematically attempted to erase all trace of Polish culture and national identity. At the conclusion of the war with the approval of the Western Allies, his home town and much of eastern Poland was ceded to the Soviet Union, which had originally invaded the area in 1939 in accordance with the terms of the Molotov-Ribbentrop pact. Holub worked on the railways from 1942 to 1945 and by comparison spent the war quietly, yet his poems too are rooted in 'the massacre / of the innocents',[9] the horrendous Revelation of the war years. Three hundred and sixty five thousand Czechs died.

Figures of casualties clearly cannot begin to express the evil of Nazi occupation, for as Herbert wryly comments in 'Mr Cogito Reads the Newspaper',

they don't speak to the imagination
there are too many of them
the numeral zero at the end
changes them into an abstraction.[10]

After such appalling catastrophes as the years 1939-1945 contained, and 1956, and 1968, and 1970, one might expect from the poets silence, intense bitterness, cynicism, desolation, even despair. Instead their work reveals great moral courage and integrity, and how they reacted with compassion and humanity proportionate to the dehumanising political forces arrayed against them, Nazi and Stalinist. Through the medium of a sensitive irony, they have come to terms in their poems in their individual ways with the indescribable suffering of their nations, setting it into a broader historical perspective, yet refusing to diminish the immediacy and reality of the pain.

Like their predecessors, giant figures such as Adam Mickiewicz of Poland and Sandor Petofi of Hungary, these poets embody in their verse 'the consciousness of a people',[11] who through their native languages and through their poetry and music kept ablaze the flame of national spirit, despite centuries of occupation and a 'situation of continual defeat'.[12] While much of Western poetry of political protest rages impotently as much out of 'frustration with the absence of direct experience of atrocities, as deeply felt indignation',[13] the Eastern European poets speak with an authority founded on immediate individual and historical experience. The *Modern Poetry in Translation* editorial of 1969 on Czech poetry makes the point lucidly:

The Western poet perhaps envies his brother in the East, for while he sings of comparative comfort, comparative freedom, comparative despair, the reality of the threat and the disaster is not his. There is a tendency for the Western poet to become isolated and turn inwards, whereas the poet of the East is in tune with the rhythms of his people in a much more direct and dynamic way.[14]

However, it would be simplistic to cast Herbert, Holub, Popa and Pilinszky solely in the role of national spokesmen, since their vision transcends national borders and bloc ideologies, focussing as it does on the universal 'living suffering spirit, capable of happiness, much deluded, too frail, with doubtful and provisional senses, so undefinable as to be almost silly, but palpably existing, and wanting to go on existing'.[15] In them political knowledge has been transmuted into poetic knowledge.

A brief comparison of British and Eastern European attitudes to the Second World War should serve to exemplify many of the points made above, and explain why Hughes felt so imaginatively and spiritually attuned to the latter. For many years following the war, British poets seem to have remained silent on the subject. It is almost as if Britain was still shell-shocked after the First World War, and chose determinedly to close its eyes to more recent history and what it had exposed about 'humanity' in an effort to 'get back to normal' as quickly as possible. Of the *New Lines* breed, Kingsley Amis, born in the same year as Vasko Popa, offers us 'The Last War', while his Movement colleagues remained seemingly indifferent to the subject:

Next day to tidy up as usual, the sun came in
When they and their ammunition were all used up,
And found himself alone.
Upset he looked them over, to separate if he could
The assassins from the victims, but every face
Had taken on the flat anonymity of pain;
And soon they'll smell alike, he thought, and felt sick
And went to bed at noon.[16]

What we are presented with here is nothing of 'the pity' of war, but instead an Olympian overview of human folly. The dead are not actualised, and serve only to illustrate the knowingly clever irony of the author. The horrific absence of emotion this poem displays is never to be found in the poets of eastern Europe. Frequently they adopt a 'cosmic' or historical perspective, but this always provides the medium for an irony of compassion, of humility. As Hughes himself has stated in his 'Introduction to the poetry of Vasko Popa', the individual and collective vision projected by these poets is of a different order from anything to be found in Western poetry: 'The attempt these poets are making to put on record that man is also . . . an acutely conscious human creature of suffering and hope, has brought their poetry down to such precisions, discriminations and humilities that it is a new thing.'[17]

The poetry of Zbigniew Herbert derives its dynamic from the clash of pre-war morality — classical, Platonic idealism, 'splendid and wistful dreams' and the 'savage or abject realities'[18] of existence exposed by the war. The frequent and ironic use of classical and historical characters and references in Herbert in no way parallels their usage in early Eliot or Pound. Their function is not to establish a sublime detachment from which the past may eye superciliously the 'pimply' and corrupt present, but rather to underline the concept of a continuum of human tragedy. Herbert has written 'I turn to history not for lessons in hope, but to confront my experience with the experience of others and to win for myself something which I should call universal compassion, but also a sense of responsibility, a sense of responsibility for the human conscience'.[19] In 'The Rain', for example, a history of human suffering and calamity is compressed into four lines, as an older brother, mortally wounded, returns home:

A splinter of shrapnel
hit him at Verdun
or perhaps Grunwald
(he didn't remember the details)

and the futility and enormity of war are actualized, as it is in 'Crow's Account of the Battle', when the dying man calls out to his long dead comrades:

Roland Jones Hannibal

he shouted
that this is the last crusade
soon Carthage will fall.[20]

The unknown 'Jones', the universal soldier, is placed subtly between the glorious dead, while Carthage is continually besieged and destroyed.

In 'Two Drops', written in 1939, the fifteen-year-old poet depicts a bombardment, and, as the terrible flames embrace them, two lovers become more firmly locked in each other's arms:

So firmly they did not feel the flames
when they came up to the eyelashes

To the end they were brave
To the end they were faithful
To the end they were similar
like two drops
stuck at the edge of a face.[21]

The final image arrests our minds with the beauty and pathos of their dying gesture, its delicacy and intimacy contrasting vividly with the banality and insensitivity of Amis' poem.

Holub's poetry often reflects his scientific background in its courageous experimentalism, and can be seen as an ironic exploration into the 'laws' governing the macrocosm and microcosm. In 'Suffering' our first feelings are of revulsion as we examine the grotesque organisms 'with foam at the mouth / with bristles on their bottoms'[22] under the microscope. Distaste and smug superiority give way to horror, as the reader discovers he is witnessing not the noble advance of science, but instead systematic, callous, pointless murder. The experiments conducted on these creatures suddenly recall those of Ravensbruck and Auschwitz. No longer dispassionate bystanders, we are forced to recognise in ourselves 'the ugly animal god', his unquestioning servants, his victims who 'make love / in between horror and hunger'. Nazism, the eastern European poets repeatedly stress, as does Sylvia Plath in *Ariel*, is not a phenomenon neatly located in the historical past, but a permanent feature of the human identity.

'In a world of malicious negatives'.[23] of grotesque and dehumanising abstractions, Holub's characters strive to retain love, loyalty, dignity, integrity, and refuse to be diminished. In 'Night at the Observatory' a lover's kiss challenges in significance the fall of a meteor. Naively immune to the absurdity of 'A History Lesson' with its evil simplification of events in which

empires rise and fall
at a wave of the pointer,
the blood is blotted out

one inattentive small boy questions

between two victorious wars:

And did it hurt in those days too?[24]

'Five Minutes After the Air Raid' presents a wife and mother, who, with a kind of insane heroism, refuses to accept the annihilation of her world. Although only the stairs and a door remain of her house, she 'locked up carefully'

and settled herself
to wait for the house to rise again
and for her husband to rise from the ashes
and for her children's hands and feet to be stuck
back into place.[25]

Irony in Holub, thus, becomes a medium of compassion, the poem an act of celebration.

While Popa — whom we will examine more closely later — employs the myths, legends and history of the South Slavs or startling poetic fables to communicate his sense of the pathos of the universe, Janos Pilinszky's poetry derives much potency from allusions to the passion of Christ. We are rarely far away from the journey to Calvary and the Crucifixion, his words themselves stretching out towards the silence of the last cry, 'My God, my God, why hast thou forsaken me?'. Despite the frequent moments of cosmic abandonment — 'Suffering cannot redeem me' ('Under the Winter Sky'),[25] 'our hopes / the stars loom dead' ('World Grown Cold'),[27] 'hope / is like a tin-cup toppled in the straw' ('The Desert of Love')[28] — the poems themselves, with their 'terrible beauty', redeem the experience, become incarnate offerings, acts of atonement to the crucified dead. His art, like that of Herbert, Holub and Popa, originates in compassion, in a recognition of moral responsibility. The blood can never be washed away; it stains too deeply the conscience and consciousness

Only the warmth of the slaughter-house
its geranium pungency, its soft shellac,
only the sun exists.

In a glass-cased silence
the butcher-boys wash down. Yet what has happened
somehow cannot even now finish.   ('The Passion')[29]

This poem, written in 1963, prefigures 'Crow Tyrannosaurus', where Man is exposed as

        a walking
Abattoir
Of innocents —
His brain incinerating their outcry.

The phrase 'Abattoir / Of innocents' and the word 'incinerating' telescope two thousand years of brutal history from Herod to Dachau, and perhaps displays the spiritual impact on Hughes of the eastern European imagination.

Hughes first met the work of the poets of Eastern Europe in 1964, but his interest seems to have intensified from 1966 onwards, for in the summer of that year an article of his appeared in *Critical Survey* entitled 'The Poetry of Vasco Popa', and in 1966 he began his co-editorship of *Modern Poetry in Translation* with Daniel Weissbort, a noted translator of Russian poetry. Significantly 1966 was also the year of the rebirth of Hughes' poetry, after the long silence following the death of Sylvia Plath in February 1963. A. Alvarez has written of the 'Plath conception of the adult as a survivor, an imaginary Jew from the concentration camps',[30] and Steiner that 'Sylvia Plath became a woman being transported to Auschwitz on the death trains';[31] it is my contention that her death became Hughes' Auschwitz, the apocalyptic experience that to a major extent determined his poetic development. His discovery of the poets of eastern Europe was crucial at this time in providing models for survival, through whose experience he was able to come to terms with his own experience and his sense of responsibility. Their world is the same world as that of Lady Lazarus, the Sylvia Plath of *Ariel*: 'Like men come back from the dead they have an improved perception, an unerring sense of what really counts in being alive'.[32] In his *Death in Life: the Survivors of Hiroshima*, Robert Jay Lifton describes what turns out to be many of the characteristic stances of *Wodwo* and *Crow*, and equally that of many poems written by poets in eastern Europe, the literal survivors of the Nazi holocaust: 'an extreme vulnerability to danger, a sense of being bound to the dead and guilt at having survived them . . . End of the world imagery is frequent, as is a tendency to assert mastery over death (and assuage guilt) by repeating the process of dying in imaginative form, so that its outcome is a miraculous survival'.[33]

'Skylarks' was one of the first poems composed after the silence, and actualises the Plathian concept of regeneration through self-annihilation, a subject dealt with by Popa in 'Before Play'. The suicidal dive is the price to be paid for the gift of poetic vision. (Writing of Pilinszky's ambivalent vision of joy and anguish, Hughes draws attention to his insistence on 'paying for his words with his whole way of life . . . The moment closest to extinction turns out to be *the* creative moment'.)[34] Rare among the *Wodwo* creations, the skylarks achieve a temporary release from matter and their own 'leaden' physicality, yet almost at the cost of their lives. The narrator, like those of 'The Hawk in the Rain' and 'Acrobats', is overawed by the enormity of the risk the birds take, committing themselves fully to the fury of the elements, and miraculously surviving

My idleness curdles
Seeing the lark labour near its cloud
Scrambling
In a nightmare difficulty
Up through the nothing.

While he remains anchored in his body, the skylarks hurl themselves beyond his sight, hearing and potential: 'my eye's gossamer snaps / and my hearing floats back widely to earth'. The price of such transcendance must be paid in the 'plummeting dead drop', a physical crucifixion which they can withstand, since, unlike Man, they are 'Conscience perfect'. Humanity, living at such a pitch of exposure and commitment — 'Joy! Help! Joy! Help!' — shatters itself, like the violinist and shadow of 'Cadenza', and yet it is to that critical moment that Hughes is irresistibly drawn — 'when all the powers of the soul are focussed on what is final and cannot be altered, even though it is horrible, the anguish is indistinguishable from joy'.[35]

III

In their exposure of the blackest, innermost recesses of Man's being and their questioning of the entire metaphysical structure of the universe which appears to ordain endless, purposeless suffering, and in the startling directness with which the most horrific experiences are confronted, Hughes' poems in *Wodwo* and *Crow* owe much, therefore, to the eastern European revelation.

While in *The Hawk in the Rain* and *Lupercal*, despite the impotence of Man and omnipotence of Death, Hughes held out the possibility of authentic being, *Wodwo* and *Crow* offer no escape, for 'nothing could escape' ('Crow Alights'). Both Man and Nature are now united in ignorance, irredeemably trapped in an inane cycle of brutality, where 'nothing lets up or develops' ('Pibroch'), where 'All is an ugly dream of dust'.[36] Animals, once possessed of the 'angelic eye', and plants, which were previously symbols of pure selfhood and instinct, now appear as doomed as Man, programmed to destroy themselves and each other in a purposeless expenditure of energy. All creation sweats and perishes in 'the dark intestine' — an image probably taken from Keith Douglas' poem 'Time Eating'[37] — employed by Hughes for its diverse and inter-related meanings; a black, airless tunnel, an equivalent of Plath's bell jar; the food apparatus for living on other organisms; a womb, a cave, a grave; the Serpent, the repressed daemonic self, the victim of Calvinism; the source of the ravenous appetite, the materialist and sexual hunger that rips apart inner and outer worlds; the whole universe situated in the entrails of the gods, who at best are blind and incompetent, at worst arbitrary and malevolent like Blake's Urizen.

The 'primitive, pre-creation atmosphere' of these volumes reflects the influence of the poetry of Vasko Popa, as does the immediacy with which Hughes handles his poetic material. In their respective searches of Man's spiritual origins, both poets seek out an ur-language, a language 'below words',[38] a language 'which will not break down',[39] a vocabulary of bone and rock. 'No poetry after Auschwitz' said Adorno; and so Popa and his admirer, Hughes, strive for a poetry of humility and moral vigilance, which will not violate the silence of the camps. 'The Quartz Pebble' is a typical hieroglyph, an attempt to fashion a new Art reconciling innocence and experience, which will endure

> the shameless march of time
> It holds all
> In its passionate
> Internal embrace
>
> A smooth white innocent corpse[40]

like Herbert's 'Pebble', 'equal to itself / mindful of its limits'.[41]

These hieroglyphic poems, with their 'tight knot of image ideas', are 'extremely translatable' and have come to embody a 'universal poetic language'[42] in which poets can meet across the borders. Frequently they take the form of poetic fables and myths, which by means of their 'folk-tale surrealism' probe the eternal, universal situation, forcing us 'temporarily out of the dimension of coherent reality into that depth of imagination where understanding has its roots and stores its X-rays'.[43] Popa's structuring of these fables, these 'provisional little adventures' into poem-cycles also appealed to Hughes, since they offered him the opportunity to tackle a theme from a variety of different directions as he does in most of his latest volumes.

Although written immediately following the death of Sylvia Plath, and before his 'discovery' of the Eastern European poets, 'The Howling of Wolves' (February 1963) and 'Song of a Rat' (March 1963) bear striking similarities in theme and language to many poems of Popa, Herbert, Holub and Pilinszky. The crippled consciousness borne by all animal creation threatens every being sooner or later with the futility of suffering. To obey its instincts 'to feed its fur' leads the wolf into the 'steel traps, clashing and slavering' set by Man. Its hunger, and the instruments by which it satisfies its hunger, its jaws, are its betrayers. Like the rat, it 'comprehends little', until confronted by the moment of death, when it is too late. Only then it acknowledges the reality of iron jaws superior to its own: 'The rat understands suddenly. It bows and is still / With a little beseeching of blood on its nose-end.' The cruelty and pathos of the universe are finely captured here with the vivid juxtaposition of the words 'blood' and 'beseeching'. Hughes' delicate irony echoes that of Popa's 'Kora' collection of 1952, animal fables with resonances for the whole of creation. Like Boxer of Orwell's *Animal Farm*, 'Horse' has been conditioned into absurdity by Man, biting 'his lips to blood' rather than 'chew through that maize-stalk'[46] that belongs to his Master. 'Pig' shares the fate of the rat and the wolf

Only when she felt
The savage knife at her throat
Did the red veil
Explain the game
And she was sorry
She had torn herself
From the mud's embrace[45]

as does Herbert's 'Minotaur' with its 'huge blood-stained head . . . its eyes bulging, where for the first time wisdom began to sprout — which is usually brought about by experience'.[46] Similarly Pilinszky utilises poetic fable to record yet another slaughter of an innocent, in his tale of the 'lonely wolf / lonelier than the angels'. This outcast became so infatuated with the beauty of human beings that he ventured into a house

He stopped in the middle of the room
And never moved from there any more

He stood all through the night, with wide eyes
and on into the morning when he was beaten to death.[47]

Each of these creatures has been maimed from the outset by a callous Creator, smitten with 'imbecile innocence' in a world void of compassion. Hughes' wolf is compelled to wander 'to and fro, trailing its haunches and whimpering horribly', like spiritually dislocated mankind, and while the rat may screech

> threatening the constellations
> The glitterers in the black, to keep off
> Keep their distance

ultimately their emptiness will consume his emptiness.

In this post-apocalyptic world created by Hughes and the Eastern European poets, only the most primitive life-forms seem fated to survive, like the fern in *Wodwo*, Popa's 'Moss' equipped with its 'yellow dust-sheet'.[48] or Holub's sinister mushroom in 'The Forest'

> appearing in this world for the first
> and last time.[49]

Either fungi or the bomb will 'Inherit the earth'.[50]

Hughes' developing interest in surrealism is seen in 'Ghost Crabs', broadcast as 'Nightfall' in October 1965. The poem opens with the sea, the origin and grave of all matter, as in 'Mayday in Holderness' and 'Still Life', described first with the relish of a Gothic novelist, or the playful menace of Popa and Plath

> At nightfall as the sea darkens
> A depth darkness thickens, mustering from the gulfs and the submarine bad-
>   lands
> To the sea's edge.

Although we might be inclined to scorn the 'cowboy/outlaw' world implied by the image 'badlands', any condescension is quickly crushed when the giant crabs themselves appear 'under flat skulls, staring inland / Like a packed trench of helmets'. This last image simultaneously evokes the picture of a Great War battlefield, and prepares us for Hughes' broader presentation of the human predicament. Man is not the possessor of the world, Adam, but a being possessed by dark, vicious, uncontrollable forces embedded in his subconscious, ever ready to emerge like Yeats' Apocalyptic Beast in 'The Second Coming',[51] 'moving its slow thighs' on its remorseless progress towards Bethlehem. Faced by this permanent inner Judas, humanity appears incapable of resistance or any effective articulation, as 'A sliding / Staring / Thickness of silence / Presses between us', like the physical and spiritual fog in a poem by Holub —

I do not understand you:
between us stretches
the enormous body of reality
and from its severed head
bubble the clots
of white blood.[52]

Sexuality, rather than freeing Man from his isolation, becomes a mere 'silent ruthless gymnastics'[53] or plunges Man deeper into a vortex of violence and violation.

All night, around us or through us
They stalk each other, they fasten on to each other,
They mount each other, they tear each other to pieces,
They utterly exhaust each other

like the manic players of Popa's 'Leapfrog' from *Games* (1956):

>   both struggle
> and exhaust themselves and fall asleep from exhaustion
> (This game lasts a long time)[54]

History, whether domestic ('Her Husband') or political ('Karma') testifies to the sovereignty of these forces over human affairs, the callous repetition of pronoun and verb stressing the horror of their demented hegemony. Presiding over this grotesque universe is a God for whom such activity constitutes 'play', for the crabs are 'God's only toys', which exist to torment what we thought were God's only sons. 'Ghost Crabs', therefore, offers us an introduction to the at times sadistic, at times impotent deity who figures so importantly in 'Gog', 'Logos', 'Reveille' and the *Crow* cycle.

Through *Wodwo* and *Crow*, the poetry of Hughes, like that of Herbert, Holub, Popa and Pilinszky, 'strains towards the moment of final silence',[55] the silence of Auschwitz, the most recent crucifixion. 'King of Carrion' takes us to Calvary and Golgotha, and recalls Popa's 'The Tower of Skulls', commemorating a tower built by the Turks in 1809 near Nish in which the skulls of the defeated were embedded.

His kingdom is empty —

The empty world, from which the last cry
Flapped hugely, hopelessly away
Into the blindness and dumbness and deafness of the gulf

Returning, shrunk, silent

To reign over silence.

The insistent images of Christ and Crucifixion — 'the palace of skulls', the crown of thorns, the scaffold, the garments, the last cry — which have permeated the volume *Crow* recur for the last time. Such images and allusions which proliferate in the poetry of Janos Pilinszky provide the core of the emotional charge in *Crow*, since they force us to relate inwards and outwards. As the poets of Eastern Europe had done through their poetic fables, lyrics and myths in an equally spare, naked language, Hughes has universalised and objectified his personal experience, and forced us to acknowledge our own responsibility, emptiness, silence. In 'Myth and Education' he writes: 'To follow the meanings behind the one word Crucifixion would take us through most of European history, and much of Roman and Middle Eastern too. It would take us into every corner of our private life'.[56] Hughes' poetry since *Wodwo* has embodied just such a quest.

Significantly *Crow* concludes on a note of qualified affirmation. 'Littleblood' asserts no despair, but rather continues the struggle towards definition. Like the earlier 'Fire-eater' in *Lupercal*, Littleblood consumes the 'medical earth' and in so doing has 'Grown so wise grown so terrible / Sucking death's mouldy tits', an image which ironically echoes Sylvia Plath's lines in 'Poem for a birthday': 'Drunk as a foetus / I suck at the paps of darkness'.[57] Unable to invoke the Holy Spirit as Milton or Eliot could, Hughes, like his Eastern European colleagues, resolutely carves out a new mythology in this post-Auschwitz world.[58] He summons a fragile wraith — 'little boneless little skinless' — and ends the volume with a prayer as he did in *The Hawk in the Rain*, *Lupercal* and *Wodwo*: 'Sit on my finger, sing in my ear, O littleblood.' As *Crow* has so amply illustrated, all creatures possess such little blood, and what they do possess is so easily, so thoughtlessly squandered.

A number of critics savagely attacked *Crow* for its metaphysics and its style. Like the poetry of Pilinszky, Popa, Herbert and Holub, *Crow* poses questions, offers meditations 'that have been common coin since Job and Sophocles',[59] rather than supplying profoundly original, coherent religious statements. A poet, not a philosopher or theologian, Hughes presents us with an individual interpretation of our fractured universe, a provisional 'bulletin',[60] employing a style wholly appropriate to his subject, the depotentiation of Man and language. Like the works of the early modernists, his books contain a rich synthesis of all that has gone before. Geoffrey Thurley has written that *Crow* 'annihilates and transcends in annihilation, a whole phase of European consciousness',[61] yet the book exhibits as much discipleship as iconoclasm. Dominated by its Christian and mythical allusions and images, it parodies often, but acknowledges throughout the greatness of Christian mythology and language: 'You spend a lifetime learning how to write verse when it's been clear from your earliest days that the greatest poetry is the prose of the Bible'.[62] Just as Vasko Popa in *Earth*

Erect achieves renewal through his re-absorption in Serbian Christian tradition, Hughes thrusts forwards through a consciousness of the spiritual triumphs of earlier generations, and the linguistic triumphs of his own.

IV

The whole sequence operates, with even greater intensity, as an organic sequence of dream-visions, drawing on many sources, charged with personal feeling, an alchemical adventure of the soul through important changes.[63]

This description of Vasko Popa's *Earth Erect* volume could equally well apply to Hughes' *Cave Birds*, and further illustrates Hughes' identification with the spiritual quest of the Yugoslav poet. His introduction to the *Collected Poems of Vasko Popa* encourages us to see the poet's work as a continuum — 'They smoulder along through the years, criss-crossing each other, keeping the character of their own genes, working out their completeness'[64] — and to do full justice to Hughes' achievement it is necessary to view his work as a totality. In his poetic development, the poetry of eastern Europe played a crucial role. The brave experimentation, the drive towards an ur-language, and above all the compassion and humility which pervade the writing of Herbert, Holub, Pilinszky and Popa helped Hughes to lift himself out of the abyss into which he had been hurled by the death of Sylvia Plath, and to quarry 'for himself a little area of light and sense in the engulfing darkness of total war and represssion',[65] 'a small ironic space'[66] in which *his* humanity can respect itself. Having experienced the 'distintegration'[67] — his own personal Auschwitz and Hiroshima — Hughes emerged, annealed,

> a staggering thing
> Fired with rainbows, raw with cringing heat
>
> Blinks at the source.[68]

☰5 GRAHAM BRADSHAW

Hughes and Shakespeare: visions of the Goddess

I

In observing nature, we are apart from it and a part of it; thinking about nature is something the mind does to itself. If nature is all that is undeniably 'out there', our apprehension of it is shaped by the historic moment and by the culture and language we think from or against. In the profoundly challenging essay on Shakespeare that accompanies his *A Choice of Shakespeare's Verse* (published in America as *With Fairest Flowers While Summer Lasts*), Hughes remarks:

It might be said — every poet does no more than find metaphors for his own nature. That would be only partly true. Most poets never come anywhere near divining the master-plan of their whole make-up and projecting it complete. The majority cling to some favoured corner of it, or to remotely transmitted Reuter-like despatches, or mistranslate its signals into the language of a false nature. Shakesperare is almost unique in having unearthed the whole original thing, learned its language, and then found it such a cruel riddle that he could not rest from trying to solve it.

Wordsworth probably provides the greatest example in our literature of the poet who clings to some 'favoured corner'. In the brilliant, ruthless assault on 'the national park of Wordsworthian Nature' that concludes *Angel with Horns*, A. P. Rossiter observes that it is hard 'to see how anyone who *thinks* about Nature can have any faith in the famous lines' from *Tintern Abbey* about how 'Nature never did betray / The heart that loved her'. Rossiter adds, after drily alluding to Annete and Wordsworth's illegitimate daughter and to Dorothy Wordsworth's end as a paralytic imbecile: 'Nature *does*; Nature *did*'. One glimpse of the nature that remained well to the side of Wordsworth's field of vision is provided by a striking paragraph in Hume's *Dialogues Concerning Natural Religion* (part II):

Look round this Universe. What an immense Profusion of Beings, animated and organiz'd, sensible and active! You admire this prodigious Variety and Fecundity. But inspect a little more narrowly these living Existences, the only beings worth regarding. How hostile and destructive to each other! How insufficient all of them for their own Happiness! How contemptible or odious to the Spectator! The whole presents nothing but the Idea of a blind Nature, impregnated by a great vivifying Principle, and pouring forth from her Lap, without Discernment or parental Care, her maim'd and abortive Children.

To the extent that Hume's 'blind Nature' is indeed 'out there' when we inspect, in Hume's sense, and think, in Rossiter's, the limitation of the Wordsworthian perspective is clear enough. Edward Fitzgerald used to refer to Wordsworth as 'Daddy' in his letters, and Wordsworth's Mother Nature is Daddy in a dress — or we might say, remembering Shelley's *Peter Bell the Third*, a shift:

But from the first 'twas Peter's drift
  To be a kind of moral eunuch;
He touched the hem of Nature's shift,
Felt faint — and never dared uplift
  The closest, all-concealing tunic.

Significantly, Hume's passage is both Shakespearean and prophetic. It begins with a vision of Nature not unlike that entertained by the Hamlet Ophelia recalls; then, as in Hamlet's speech on 'this goodly frame', the first, affirming vision is displaced by a vision which, in Hume's formulation, anticipates Schopenhauer's nightmarish world of becoming, and the 'horror of Creation' as envisaged in *Crow*. Replying to the charge that 'Hawk Roosting' celebrated violence, Hughes once remarked, 'Actually what I had in mind was that in this hawk Nature is thinking'[1] — and that vision of Nature as a remorseless, amoral process is very close to Schopenhauer's conception of the Will in Nature, and to Hume's 'idea of a blind Nature'. But such a vision also corresponds with the Shakespearean vision of 'under-nature' that Rossiter discusses so well, and, if Hume's passage seems curiously Shakespearean, this surely has to do with the way in which it opposes two incompatible visions of nature. This happens repeatedly in the great plays: on the one hand there is the sustaining, Humanistic vision of 'great creating-Nature', *Natura naturans;* but there is also the utterly amoral 'Goddess' to whom an Edmund or Iago can appeal, and whose 'multiplying villanies' will, once any 'Devil-porter' opens the gate, 'swarm upon' a Macbeth, Angelo or Othello.

Inevitably, these two conflicting visions yield opposed accounts of value. On the affirmative, Humanistic view, nature itself provides a sanction for human values, which consequently appear to be given or, as some philosophers say, read off. So, for example, in *De con-scribendis* — a work that Shakespeare encountered in Thomas Wilson's *Art of Rhetorike* if not in the original, and recalled in his *Sonnets* — Erasmus writes (in Wilson's translation): 'Now sir (you maie saie) we must follow vertue, rather then Nature. A gentle dish. As though any thing can be called vertue, that is contrary unto Nature.'[2] But the opposed view of Nature allows no such optimistic affirmation; rather, values appear to be created or invented. In the imagery of *Macbeth*, human values are a frail construction, frail as Duncan, raised like a dyke or wall against an encroaching nature that will pour through any 'breach'. The view that values are fabrications gratifies the egoism of the villains and cynics: one thinks of Thersites' habit of explaining everything in terms of the basest instincts and appetites, or of Iago's similarly reductive sneers at 'love and duty'. For others, it is a suddenly apprehended torment: Troilus' crucial question, 'What's aught, but as 'tis valued?', reappears in Hamlet's 'There's nothing either good or bad, but thinking makes it so'. To see how Shakespeare will not let go of Troilus' question is, I think, a good way of recognising the coherence of creative integrity of the *oeuvre*.

One consequence is that Shakespeare is intensely aware of the relationship between the valuer and the valued as something problematic. In one of his best essays, 'Tragedy and the "Medium"', F. R. Leavis writes of the 'tragic experience':

It is as if we were challenged at the profoundest level with the question, 'In what does the significance of life reside?', and found ourselves contemplating, for answer, a view of life, and of the things giving it value, that makes the valued appear unquestionably more important than the valuer, so that significance lies, clearly and inescapably, in the willing adhesion of the individual self to something other than itself.[3]

I am not sure what sense Leavis attaches to the word 'appear', in relation to what he sees as being 'clear' and 'inescapable'. But, in noting how well this passage applies to Shakespeare (and not only his tragedies), we should add that in the plays this creative preoccupation appears in conjunction with the most radical scepticism. In particular, Shakespeare is profoundly aware of what could be called a moral mechanism, through which, once we have endowed someone or something with value, a disjunction takes place, so that the value *appears* to be inherent in the valued and detached from the valuer.

Consider the supposed mixed metaphor to which Dr Johnson objected, in Othello's most revealing speech:

But there, where I have garner'd up my heart,
Where either I must live, or bear no life,
The fountain from the which my current runs . . .

What the metaphor expresses, in a marvellously precise and moving way, is the process of disjunction. The idealistic Othello garners up his heart, and *then* sees his love as the fountain from the which his current flows; this may not be reasonable, but it is natural. The materialistic, nihilistic Iago prefers to regard love as disguised appetite combining with self-love, 'merely a lust of the blood and a permission of the will'; this may be reasonable, but it is not natural. Love is an act of valuing, and we make subtle accommodations between the public and the private realms when we recognise – usually as a matter of course, not reflection – that somebody we love will not have the same value for others. We make a nicely flexible distinction (that could usefully be parallelled in aesthetics) between our sense that somebody 'possesses' unique value for us, and our expectation that other people will have similar feelings about other people. The word 'possesses' itself suggests the peculiar nature of the endowment or investment. Othello is simply not free to reflect that if he was wrong to endow Desdemona with unique value he can do the same with somebody else. The metaphor conveys a penetrating and painful insight not only into Othello's particular case but into the nature of idealism, of the act of valuing. Dr Johnson only sees the mixed metaphor because, for Johnson, values are 'out there'; we might wonder whether, if Leavis had pondered his use of the word 'appear', his reading of Othello's character might have been more sympathetic.[4].

For a supporting contrast we might recall the letter, quoted by Rossiter, in which Wordsworth refers to 'the spirituality with which *I have endeavoured to invest* the material universe, and the moral relations under which *I have wished to exhibit* its most ordinary appearances'. The italics are of course mine not Wordsworth's, and the italicised phrases show a 'disjunction' so blissfully, ingenuously complete as to be altogether immune to irony or doubt. In Wordsworth, the operation of this moral mechanism and the highly selective vision of Nature support each other: every assurance is edited, the vernal woods all whisper Wordsworth. In Shakespeare, the terrible conflict between incompatible visions of Nature gives incomparable urgency to his presentation of the idealists, cynics and nihilists who suddenly began to figure so prominently in the plays that ushered in the new century. As with Othello and Iago, so with Angelo and Isabella, Troilus, Hamlet, Macbeth and the others: questions about human values, about what men live by, prove to be inseparable from questions about the nature of nature.

Yet in Hughes' account of Shakespeare's 'cruel riddle' these questions are separated, split off from each other. How and why this split occurs is the main subject of the present essay, and, if I succeed in showing that Hughes' reading of Shakespeare does raise this critical problem, it should be clear that Hughes' complex creative engagement with Shakespeare illuminates creative tensions in his own poetry. It should be clear, too, that the essay on Shakespeare is *Crow*'s critical twin – as we might expect, on noticing how close Hughes' account of Shakespeare's 'symbolic fable' is to the creative myth in *Crow*.

The problem might be put in this way. There has been – and this suggestion seems more obvious that controversial – no English writer since Shakespeare who is more intensely aware than Hughes of the other nature, the Shakespearean 'under-nature' that speaks in 'Hawk Roosting', makes Crow shiver 'with the horror of Creation', turns the 'great wheel of woe' ('Song of Woe'),[5] and (in a very Schopenhauerean image from *Prometheus on his Crag*) sets the earth leaping 'like a great ungainly top'. The poems repeatedly explore those ways in which, even as we apprehend this nature as something outside humanity – dwarfing the ego and humbling the will – we are brought to recognise something that is also inside us, an inner hinterland that ordinary consciousness excludes. So, although it will be no recommendation to those who warble about Elizabethan word pictures and think that *Macbeth* shows a reassuringly inevitable triumph of good over evil, Hughes is exceptionally alive to the terrifying Shakespearean evocations of an unaccommodated universe. Moreover, his preoccupation with mythology makes Hughes peculiarly sensitive to the long tails Shakespearean comets trail: whatever we think of Hughes' use of the word 'puritan', which I certainly want to question, he sees how the 'quarrel' about the nature of Nature 'opened an archaic mythological dimension beyond the immediate theological one' and 'summoned emotions from the gulf which had very little to do with the often trivial actual points of debate'.

But the difficulty appears here. I take it that the 'other' nature is simply there, when we look and see; whether Shakespeare, Hume, Schopenhauer or Hughes give a 'true account' in acknowledging its reality is not what is in question. The question is whether this true account is complete enough, or needs to be supplemented so as to accommodate *human* nature – that is, the autonomous but natural realm of human values. Shakespeare – the intelligence that shapes and directs the plays – is evidently more sceptical about this than his idealists, and more tentatively affirmative than any of his cynics and nihilists. His preoccupation with the need to 'nurture' nature (to borrow a crucial metaphor from the last plays) intimates that man's moral, imaginatively constructive aspirations might be accommodated in a truly comprehensive vision of Nature. But in Hughes' account of the 'symbolic fable' any such constructive effort actually becomes suspect – a manifestation of 'hardening sceptical intellect and morality', and a hubristic assault on the Goddess.

II

In this, as in other respects, Hughes' reading of the 'symbolic fable' is obviously indebted to *The White Goddess*. Like Robert Graves, Hughes emphasises the conflict between an essentially ambivalent Nature and the 'puritan determination' to 'divide nature, and especially love, the creative force of nature, into abstract good and physical evil'. In the old Catholicism the deposed, pre-Christian Goddess could at least be 'naturalised' as Mother Mary. But during the Reformation – 'as it defined itself from the fifteen-sixties in the gradual rise of Puritanism, together with its accompanying materialist and democratising outlook and rational philosophy' – the 'multiple, primaeval' Goddess was 'dragged into Court by the young Puritan Jehovah'. Venus was viewed through 'Adonis's Calvinist spectacles', and the resulting conflict was catastrophic: 'Nature's attempts to recombine, first in love, then in whatever rebuffed love turns into, and the puritan determination that she shall not recombine under any circumstances, are the power-house and torture-chamber of the Complete Works.'

In this reading, the nature of the conflict is first adumbrated in the two early narrative poems. Whether *Venus and Adonis* and *The Rape of Lucrece* will bear so much interpretative weight might be debated, but then Hughes stresses that they are complementary but as yet *unjoined* 'halves of a single story': 'the story these two halves make is Shakespeare's fable – his major discovery, on which all his work is based. But the most inspired piece of intuition in the whole assembly, the mechanism on which the dramatic development depends, is still absent. It occurs in the gap between the two poems.' This gap 'corresponds to a strange sudden transformation, a frightening psychic event' that is 'the key to the madness of the Civil War' and is 'the mainspring of every play, from *Hamlet* on, in the Complete Works'. The momentous development or closing of the 'gap' occurs when Shakespeare begins to explore the terrifying processes that transform Adonis into Tarquin. So, for example, Angelo is the 'chronic puritan' demolished by his own 'repressed lust', that is, by the rebuffed Venus in her infernal aspect: 'The frigid puritan, with a single terrible click, becomes a sexual maniac - a destroyer of innocence and virtue, a violator of the heavenly soul, of the very thing he formerly served and adored.' In Angelo, 'Adonis has become Tarquin'. In Othello, Hughes sees 'an over-ripe Adonis, at the point of splitting and becoming Tarquin'. In Macbeth, Adonis is 'fully conscious, and dead against his will, understanding just what it means to become Tarquin'. And Hamlet, Lear, Mark Antony, Timon, Coriolanus, Leontes and Post-humus all show, in their various ways, how the 'suppressed Nature goddess erupts, possessing the man who denied her'. The 'mysterious chemical change that converts the resisting high-minded puritan to the being of murder and madness' is the 'occult crossover of Nature's maddened force – like a demon – into the brain that has rejected her'. The 'cruel riddle' is thus compounded of 'four poles of energy' – Venus, Adonis, Tarquin, Lucrece – which appear as 'phrases in a narrative cycle' and are 'rearranged' by the plays in 'all manner of combinations': Venus confronts Adonis, Adonis dies in rejecting her and is then reborn as Tarquin – who destroys Lucrece, himself, and all order. The tragedies resemble the 'revenge fables' in Crow.

I should stress that, although I want to isolate what is Gravesean and unShakespearean in Hughes' conception of the 'puritan', this kind of summarising outline inevitably over-accentuates the broader indebtedness to Graves. The paragraphs on Shakespeare in The White Goddess are too brief and schematic to say much about Shakespeare's poetry, whereas Hughes is marvellously aware of what makes the poetry 'densely peculiar', of the ways in which it works as dialect and has

the air of being invented in a state of crisis, for a terribly urgent job, a homely spur-of-the-moment improvisation out of whatever verbal scrap happened to be lying around ... The meaning is not so much narrowly delineated as overwhelmingly suggested, by an inspired signalling and hinting of verbal heads and tails above and below precision, and by this weirdly expressive underswell of a musical near-gibberish, like a jostling of spirits. The idea is conveyed, but we also receive a musical and imaginative shock, and the satisfaction of that is unfathomable.

Moreover, no summary can suggest how much weight Hughes' account of the 'symbolic fable' gains from the anthology itself. The selection is large enought to clear Hughes of any charge that he is grinding an interpretative axe; yet, after submitting to the salutary shock of re-encountering so many bleeding chunks, it is hard to dissent from the remarks at the beginning of the essay that Hughes modestly calls a 'Note':

Selecting, as I have done, for poetic intensity, length and completeness, has had one result that might surprise some readers. The passages that answer these requirements nearly all have a strong family likeness, especially those coming from *Hamlet* and the plays after. It is impossible not to recognise what looks more and more like a simple fact: whenever Shakespeare wrote at top intensity, at unusual length, in a burst of unusually self-contained completeness, he was almost invariably hammering at the same thing – a particular knot of obsessions.

This seems at once extremely valuable and problematic, and an analogy may help to disentangle the problem. Hughes' comment that in Shakespeare's poetry 'meaning is not so much narrowly delineated as overwhelmingly suggested' might recall Dr Johnson: 'It is incident to him to be now and then entangled with an unwieldy sentiment, which he cannot well express, and will not reject; he struggles with it a while, and if it continues stubborn, comprises it in words such as occur ...'[6]. Both Johnson and Hughes have their eye on the same kind of distinctively Shakespearean effect. Hughes of course approves of it, while Johnson imposes on his description a disapproving tone; but then, as Leavis notes, Johnson's 'description itself, in its lively aptness, implies a measure of appreciation'.[7] To this extent at least, the brilliant description is detachable from the accompanying valuation, the signals of disapproval. And we could – I think, should – make a similar point about Hughes' exposition of the 'knot of obsessions'. We might agree, that is, that the strands of the 'knot', the components of the 'cruel riddle', the *fabulae personae* in the 'symbolic fable', do correspond with Hughes' description – but without feeling obliged to agree that the 'puritans' are as culpable and suspect as Hughes and Graves suppose. Indeed, Hughes himself makes just such a distinction when he follows Graves in regarding the late plays as Shakespeare's own puritanical assault on the Goddess:

Shakespeare's persistence has to be admired. After all his experience of the odds against the likelihood, he did finally succeed in salvaging Lucrece from the holocaust and Adonis from the boar. He rescued the puritan abstraction from the gulf of Nature. He banished Venus, as Sycorax, the blue-eyed hag. He humbled Tarquin as Caliban, the poetry-crammed half-beast. And within an impenetrable crucible of magic prohibitions, he married Lucrece (Miranda) to Adonis (Ferdinand). But what a wooden wedding! What proper little Puritan puppets! And what a ghastly expression on Prospero's cynical face. We know why he wants to drown his book in the sea (where Venus was born – the lap of Creation) – it contains the tragedies, with their evidence.

On this view, Shakespeare has grasped 'the master skeleton-key' but turned it in the wrong direction. Which leaves us free to object, if we find Prospero less frightening than Caliban, that Hughes' attitude towards Shakespeare's idealists does not correspond with out own, just as it clearly does not correspond with Shakespeare's.

Another analogy may suggest how Hughes develops a genuine and important insight in a tendentious way. Hughes sees the Civil Wars as the eventual outward projection of an inner psychic disruption, like the releasing of the 'horrid image' that torments Macbeth. This linking of microcosm and macrocosm has much in common with seventeenth-century habits of thought and feeling. Too much, perhaps: some will reject the idea with impatience. Yet we might well feel, after a reading of Marvell's *Horatian Ode*, that there is indeed an uncanny parallel between the opposition of Richard II and Bolingbroke in Shakespeare's play and the opposition of Charles I and Cromwell. The curious relationship between the *Ode* and *Richard II* has impessed critics not given to wild flights of fancy, and Hughes provides one way of explaining it[8] But then, even if we concede the parallel and agree that it is fascinating, it does not follow, necessarily, that we must identify either Shakespeare's Richard or the real Charles I with Lucrece and 'divine order'. Any such view of *Richard II* would simplify and distort that play's complex perspectives. And my point about Hughes' version of the Civil War is not that it is impossible, but that it is obviously, and perhaps unconsciously, loaded.

The different examples enforce the same point. Apparently, service of the Goddess requires that we see Prospero as 'cynical' and lament the passing of divine order in the revolt against a contemptible king. In each case, the tendentious load is concentrated in Hughes' perjorative use of the world 'puritan'. This brings my argument to a point where it is very likely to be, as Erasmus once said, piddled on by both parties: it will seem equally unsatisfactory to those who feel that Hughes' reading of Shakespeare is merely eccentric and to those who find the reading entirely satisfying. But then I do think that Hughes' reading contains immensely valuable insights, while also thinking that the peculiar, Gravesean ways in which it is tendentious illuminate a powerful creative tension in Hughes' own poetry. Each of these claims requires a fuller exposition than is possible here, so I must content myself with some rapid suggestions.

III

We should try to seize the most obtrusive, crucial strand in Hughes' unravelling of the Shakespearean 'knot of obsessions' – that is, the suggestion that 'the poetry has its taproot in a sexual dilemma of a peculiarly black and ugly sort'. Is that suggestion shocking, impertinent, critically redundant? I suppose it is all these things to the conventional bardolater; yet even the most conventionally respectable accounts allow that the plays frequently project a horribly disturbing, peculiarly comprehensive sex-nausea, a shuddering revulsion from the very springs of life. Perhaps Hughes is tactlessly bald, in eschewing diplomatic obliquities and simply asserting that the 'chronic sexual dilemma' was personal – not merely personal, to be sure, but something known and rendered from the inside. But we know which passages Hughes has in mind, and that's important. How we moralise, rationalise, or negotiate with the imaginatively apprehended crisis is another, later question; we may indeed wish to argue that the plays contain or place the horror, that they are more intelligent about it than the characters who experience it. But those relevant speeches – by Hamlet, Angelo, Othello, Lear, Timon and the others – have already seared our consciousness, as the dramatic stuff with which we struggle to come to terms. If that much is true, the critic who is not shaken by the conflict, who can confidently condemn the sex-horror as 'anti-life' and prate of Hamlet's 'immaturity', is substantially disabled as a reader of Shakespeare or indeed Tolstoy.

But let us ask a specific question: where does Lear's sex-nausea come from? I suspect that the question cannot be answered without opening ourselves to the insensibly humbling approach suggested by Yeats' 'Three Movements' –

Shakespearean fish swam the sea, far away from land;
Romantic fish swam in nets coming to the hand;
What are all those fish that lie gasping on the strand?

or to a line of thought like that suggested by an arresting footnote in Freud's *Three Contributions to a Theory of Sex:*

The most pronounced difference between the love life of antiquity and ours lies in the fact that the ancients placed the emphasis on the instinct itself, while we place it on its object. The ancients extolled the instinct and were ready to ennoble through it even an inferior object, while we disparage the activity of the instinct as such and only countenance it on account of the merits of the object.[9]

It is at least possible to give a narrowly 'realistic' explanation of the sex-horror felt by Othello or Leontes, since both believed they had been abandoned and betrayed by the chosen 'object' – women they loved sexually, and through whom they came to terms with the 'instinct', Eros in Freud's terms and the Goddess in Hughes'. With rather more difficulty, we could also see Hamlet's sex-horror as the result of his disillusion with his mother and Ophelia. We might similarly propose that Angelo's high-minded revulsion from the Viennese sex-sewer has so perverted his imagination that he equates Eros with Evil and consequently never supposes that his feelings for Isabella could be anything but foul, never thinks that he might conceivably woo her; that the responses of the fatherless Isabella are also distorted by her fear of sex suggests why Shakespeare adjusted his sources so as to make Angelo and Isabella perfectly complementary figures – idealistic novices who illustrate the respective strengths and weaknesses that attend on any attempt to nurture Nature, instead of following a Lucio or Claudio by taking Nature as it comes. But Lear is old, and his feelings for Cordelia are not in any obvious sense sexual: where, in that case, is the sex-horror coming from, if Shakespeare is not planting it on his protagonist?

One familiar type of moralising account leaves the comprehensive Shakespearean insight beached and gasping. *King Lear*, we learn from Coleridge (who thought Angelo should be punished) and other more recent 'severe morallers', illustrates the dangers of possessive and egotistical love. So, in this type of reading, Cordelia delivers a public rebuke to Lear in the first scene, for falsifying the emotional accounts. Yet none of the other witnesses – from Goneril to Kent – suggests that Cordelia's replies were other than loving: their responses convey surprise that Lear has misunderstood his daughter's passionate plainness. Although the text of the first scene will submit to both readings, the critic who prefers to have a self-righteously tight-lipped, censorious Cordelia – willing to wound, and not afraid to strike – will have a good deal of explaining to do in the sublime reconciliation of Act IV. Not only does Cordelia reappear as the embodiment of selfless love: Lear's 'gilded cage' speech is as demanding and possessive as ever – yet it would freeze our blood if Cordelia were to respond like one of the severe morallers by observing, 'Sure, I did never marry like my sisters, / To love my father all.' But why *shouldn't* that be her reply, on the moralistic reading?

The answer is surely that the moralists and rationalists are reading another play; and this helps us with the question about Lear's sex-horror. According to the moralistic, book-keeping account, Lear should be preoccupied on the heath with the wrong done to Cordelia. Yet he scarcely refers to her – since his imagination is consumed by a far more terrible and Tolstoyan conflict. Lear's agony, from which even the storm provides a refuge, develops in two directions, each sufficiently comprehensive to account for the comparative neglect of Cordelia. The first imaginative movement occurs with the dislocation of his egocentricity, and involves the horrified repudiation of all the demands – sexual and other – of the naturally predatorial, ego-directed self; Lear projects his lacerating self-disgust on to 'stinking humanity' at large – in the company of the selfless Kent and the selfless Fool. A contrary imaginative impulse begins with a sudden powerful though intermittent compassion, for the Fool ('Proper fool and knave, I have one part in my heart / That's sorry yet for thee'), for Poor Tom, and the 'poor naked wretches'. Then, and only then, can the inner storm begin to work itself out: from projecting onto others his loathing of an intensely demanding, never before confronted self, Lear can begin to feel an inundating compassion that mediates some measure of accommodation to the bare, forked animal. Like Gloucester, he learns to see beyond the self by losing himself − but no such soothing formulation should allow us to forget the cost of the spasmodic regeneration: both men are and remain crippled by their vision. 'Man's nature cannot carry / Th' affliction nor the fear'.

The point I am wanting to establish is that the sex-horror is part of, and an index to, a far more comprehensive horror, precipitated by the debate about the nature of Nature. But the debate has nothing to do with *views*, which might be entertained or modified at will: it is experienced as a divided, rupturing *vision* of the Nature that is both outside and inside the self. The violent dislocation exposes a suddenly naked self to a suddenly transformed world; to borrow a phrase from Milosz, these protagonists are brought to 'contemplate Being'.[10] Because the sex-nausea is the natural quick or nervous centre of a negative, corroding vision, its source is not ultimately more mysterious in Lear's case than in Othello's. Macbeth bypasses the sex-horror, having direct access to the more comprehensive horrors of an unaccommodated universe, while Shakespeare's smaller nihilists and cynics (going down from Iago and Edmund) are spared the sex-horror because their emotional responses are measured, subject to a directing will and ego. The sex-horror only strikes and hurts those who have or have had (and we might think of Tolstoy again) an unusually strong, keen and self-committing sense of life − not those who are the lords and owners of their faces, but those who are, in the broad sense of Bolingbroke's shrewd comment on Swift, 'slighted lovers'.[11] And, even where these 'men of chaos' have been lovers in the more restricted sense, Shakespeare evidently belongs with Freud's 'ancients': the 'object' is a path for the 'instinct', a means of recognising something beyond the self − in Hughes' terms, an access to the Goddess.

My intention in offering these necessarily compressed remarks is to suggest the acuity of Hughes' emphasis on the ways in which Shakespeare 'conducted what is essentially an erotic poetry into an all-inclusive body of political action'. The 'quarrel about the nature of Nature' does indeed seem as central as Hughes suggests, and provides the connexion between the various 'men of chaos'. However, Hughes' attitude towards the 'puritans' − his sense of how the 'quarrel' should have been resolved, if England had not 'lost her soul' − is another matter. Here the indebtedness to Graves is most conspicuous, as is shown by their parallel accounts of *The Tempest*. In Graves' charge against Prospero−Shakespeare there is something unreal, an air of self-mesmerising make-believe, even an exasperating and irresponsible kind of childishness:

Shakespeare in the person of Prospero claims to have dominated Sycorax by his magic books, broken her power and enslaved her monstrous son Caliban – though not before extracting his secrets from him under colour of kindness. Yet he cannot disguise Caliban's title to the island nor the original blueness of Sycorax's eyes.[12]

Sycorax, we are to understand, is Shakespeare's culminating puritanical slander or assault on the Goddess. But what is the substance of this charge, when – and this takes an effort Graves won't make – it is translated back into a real world, where actions and choices have consequences? Should Prospero *concede* Caliban's title? Since Shakespeare's symbolic fable does retain a purchase on the real world, we are in no doubt about the likely consequences of any such surrendering of consciousness and responsibility: Miranda would be raped, and Prospero would be paunched with a stake – long live the Goddess! When Hughes repeats the Gravesean charge he adds that Shakespeare has turned his back on 'the tragedies, with their evidence', but that comment could, after all, be turned on its head by arguing that Shakespeare and Prospero have remembered the evidence – the realities of the 'under-Nature', with its multiplying villainies.

The view of the late plays taken by Graves and Hughes entails a downward valuation: as Hughes writes, 'Shakespeare begins to cheat'. Yet the Shakespearean insight into the nature of Nature is, or seems to me, more subtle, more intelligent, and, necessarily, more ambivalent. The ambivalence registers in a crucial hesitation, when Polixenes speaks to Perdita of the Art that Nature makes. The naïvely primitivistic Perdita sees nature only in *natura naturans*: being young, innocent, 'green', she has no conception of the other nature that swarms through any breach. Her blood has not yet 'thickened'; she has not yet had to 'acknowledge' a Caliban or thing of darkness, a 'dark and vicious place'. This is delightful in her, but a problem for Polixenes: although he does not echo the argument of Montaigne's *Des cannibales* as closely as Perdita (a nice touch), it is Polixenes who has lived through many of the problems raised in that remarkably subversive essay. So, after quickly conceding that Art is indeed in one sense artificial and unnatural – an assault on the Goddess – Polixenes proceeds to argue, with a finely diffident passion, that Nature also 'makes' the Art that builds on Nature. Yet, even as he improves his tentative, paradoxical affirmation, Polixenes has to pick himself up: 'This is an Art / Which does mend Nature: change it rather, but . . .'. The crucial hesitation registers his own uneasy awareness that there is something deeply problematic about appealing to a Nature that is both holy and bestial, that provides a sanction for constructive imaginative and moral effort, yet desperately needs to be 'made better', nurtured, changed not merely mended. Behind that hesitation is the 'evidence' of the tragedies.

Nor are the late plays less concerned to ask what it means, and what it costs, to civilise instinct and nurture Nature. Polixenes struggles valiantly with two images: he wants to see Art – the imaginatively constructive realm of human values that prompts his use of words like 'gentler', 'baser', 'nobler' – as a *graft* that takes, and as a *marriage* to which nature willingly submits. Just as the idea of grafting throws up difficulties, the image of a marriage is a felicitous but no less tricky paradigm for the conflict and tension he would explain to the green girl. Instinct, for a Caliban, means raping Miranda and paunching her father; any attempt to 'mend Nature' is, not only for Caliban but in some degree for all of us, felt as an imposition or deformation or assault. Marriage is artificial, in the sense that Perdita complains to Polixenes that grafting is artificial: it is unnatural, in that it represents a cultural effort to channel, restrain and even deny naturally recalcitrant instincts of the most powerful kind. And yet – as Polixenes' speech implies, and as the moral magus who forcibly constrains Caliban and imposes arbitrary disciplines on Ferdinand very well knows – marriage is a cultural institution that may, although it is unnatural in form, still be said to have a natural sanction in the human need to recognise values. Without some such cultural effort and aspiration, some constructive attempt to foster values by building on Nature, human mating could be no more significant than the mating of animals.

The tentative affirmation is rooted in a profound and radical scepticism: there are no objective values, but the human need to recognise or create values is an objective fact about *human* nature. Man is the animal that makes value judgements. But if the human need to endow life with moral significance and value is itself a reality, it is not a pressing reality for all humans. Antonio and Sebastian leave Prospero's island unredeemed and unredeemable, reminding us that the civilised savage is far worse than the natural savage. Iago kills without compunction or remorse; Macbeth is destroyed by *his* guilt, because his need to invest life with significance was a pressing imaginative reality, that he repressed and denied. Lucio and Pompey Bum find the positive aspirations of Angelo and Isabella unintelligible, very much as Iago finds Othello's idealistic commitment to 'love and duty' unintelligible. Ironically enough, just as Iago would concur with Leavis' hostile account of Othello, Lucio would applaud Hughes' account of Angelo as a 'puritan'.

Or is that unfair? In one sense it is, since Hughes is surely right to observe that the energies which shatter Angelo are, like 'the boar that demolished Adonis' (or for that matter the monster that emerges from the sea, the gulf of nature, to rend Hippolytus in Euripides and Racine), an emanation of 'his own repressed lust – crazed and bestialised by being separated from his intelligence and denied'. Angelo's is indeed 'a mind desensitised to the true nature of nature'. The question is, what would a truly intelligent, sensitised awareness of the Goddess entail? How should a properly apprehended Goddess be served? Some kind of post-Wordsworthian 'wise passiveness' appears to be demanded, yet it remains hard to see what use the Hughesean, Gravesean Goddess would have for a morally, imaginatively constructive intelligence, or for the kind of human aspiration that Lawrence took for his subject in *The Rainbow*.

Paradoxically, *The White Goddess* champions ambivalence against the dualistic abstractions of Christianity and Platonism, but its own schematism is too inflexibly dualistic to admit the Shakespearean ambivalence. *The Tempest* illustrates the point: Shakespeare himself establishes the irony that Prospero is an usurper who has exploited Caliban – but, far from being an inadvertent, give-away slip, this irony is part of a more comprehensive irony, proceeding from the awareness that when nurture will not 'stick' a Caliban must be forcibly constrained. It is not surprising that Caliban's complaint against Prospero looks forward to the Body's complaint against the Soul in Marvell's great 'Dialogue'. Each party in these symbolic conflicts needs the other: the critique of traditional dualism is implicit in this projected interdependence – and that insight goes beyond the recognition that Caliban and the Body each has a strong case. The end of Marvell's poem offers a sudden Shakespearean expansion, in suggesting how any kind of cultural effort is also an attack, or mutilation: 'So Architects do square and hew / Green Trees that in the Forest grew'.

Angelo's idealistic self-denials pervert his natural responses, making him terribly vulnerable and terribly dangerous. Similarly, Isabella's highmindedness, her intense need to transcend the merely animal, makes her vulnerable and dangerous in ways that are unimaginable for a Lucio or Barnardine – those telling paradigms of moral insensibility, who provide the antithesis to the 'Architects' of self. Unlike some critics, Hughes recognises that Shakespeare is sympathetically involved with his idealists – but he then describes that imaginative commitment in adverse terms, short-circuiting the Shakespearan complexity by seeing the idealistic as the brittle, frigid, chronic puritan. Within the imprisoning dualism of the Gravesean schema, any idealistic, morally constructive effort becomes suspect, 'cynical', a hubristic assault on the Goddess. Adonis should have submitted to Venus – but what then?

IV

I have argued that Hughes has a marvellous awareness of the ways in which the plays conduct a quarrel about the nature of Nature, but that he splits this off from what is, in Shakespeare, an inseparable quarrel about the nature of values. That Hughes follows Graves in this respect may seem strange: Hughes could hardly be accused of underestimating the terrors of an 'unaccommodated universe', so in what circumstances could Caliban seem a less alarming figure than the 'cynical' Prospero? Isn't Hughes criticising Prospero and Shakespeare for *not* 'surrendering consciousness and responsibility'? That phrase occurs in the fine essay on Vasko Popa, in which Hughes argues that although the world of Popa, Holub and Zbigniew Herbert is 'as horrible' as Beckett's it 'seems braver, more human, and so more real', since they have 'managed to grow up to a view of the unaccommodated universe' without denigrating or losing sight of 'the living suffering spirit – the only precious thing'.[13] A related contradiction appears when we remark that the *London Magazine* interview – with its vehemently anti-rational insistence on the need for new 'rituals and dogma', its exaltation of the shaman, and its commitment to Jungian notions[14] – seems conspicuously less sceptical, brave, and willing to 'accept the odds' than Shakespeare. The contradictions point to a continuing creative tension in Hughes' own work, and the Shakespeare essay needs to be seen both in a larger critical context and in its creative context, as part of Hughes' developing *oeuvre*.

The creative context is suggested by the way in which, in both *Crow* and the Shakespeare essay – the complementary investigations of Englishness – the 'Shakespearean moment' is seen and diagnosed retrospectively, in the light of a bitterly disturbed understanding of *our* moment: 'The Shakespearean fable, in other words, is really the account of how, in the religious struggle that lasted from the middle of the sixteenth century to the middle of the seventeenth, England lost her soul. To call that event a 'dissociation of sensibility' is an understatement. Our national poems are tragedies for a good reason.' 'The forces that were putting the pressure on Shakespeare' made *The Tempest* a 'tribal dream':[15] in interpreting the dream, Hughes reads back into the dream his diagnosis (at the creative moment of *Crow*) of later nightmares. 'Cromwell took up the fable': because Hughes sees the relevant history as a working out of the rending energies that were imaginatively, prophetically apprehended in the 'Shakespearean moment', Hughes could also write poems that were simultaneously about Shakespeare and England. He could not write in this way about Hopkins and England because, for all the prodigious gifts, there is no comparable pressure behind Hopkins, no sense of a tribal consciousness being divined and defined in the creative achievement.[16].

So, in 'Crow's Song About England' and 'Crow's Song About Prospero and Sycorax'[17] the subject is really the same, and the new 'moment' provides the occasion for reassessing the old: Crow, the contemporary of Zbigniew Herbert's Pan Cogito, picks his way through the post-Cartesian debris and the spiritual insufficiencies of materialistic 'civilisation' – and traces the disease back to its symptoms. In the one poem the sentenced, desecrated 'girl' is the deposed Goddess, Venus branded as Sycorax; in the other, Hughes emphasises the relationship between Prospero and St George, English hero:

She knows, like Ophelia,
The task has swallowed him.
She knows, like George's dragon,
Her screams have closed his helmet.

In one sense this must be seen as an extension of the Gravesean simplification: *The White Goddess* links the *Crow*-fable about the deposed Creatress to Hughes' reading of Shakespeare's own 'symbolic fable'. But to leave the emphasis there would, I think be mistaken, since this would not suggest the scope and urgency of Hughes' continuing creative development. And here, in pointing to a larger critical context, it's worth noticing how the Shakespeare essay also works out a tense creative response to ideas that were very much part of the critical climate of 'Cambridge English' and have few ready parallels in Graves. The important difference shouldn't obscure the connexions, nor should we be too quick to suppose that Hughes' own references to Cambridge as 'a most destructive experience' and an 'ordeal for initiation into English society' tell the whole story.[18] We might even suspect that 'Cambridge English' fostered the conditions in which Hughes' first volumes were not only well received but were almost immediately subjected to sixth-form 'practical criticism'.

The climate of Cambridge English was largely shaped by Leavis, *Scrutiny*, and, through Leavis' advocacy, Lawrence and Eliot (the former supplanting the latter). Doubtless Hughes did not need to be guided to Lawrence or Eliot; that Lawrence's remarks on *Hamlet* in *Twilight in Italy* (frequently recommended by Leavis) anticipated Hughes' reading is no surprise. But Cambridge critics like Rossiter, Traversi and L. C. Knights took a largely unprecedented interest in *Troilus and Cressida* and that play's relation to *Hamlet*. *Troilus* figures prominently in Hughes' anthology, and several passages are tellingly juxtaposed with passages from *Hamlet*: the view that these plays present a kind of pivot in the *oeuvre* has its Cambridge precedents. Moreover, Hughes clearly picks up from Eliot and Leavis in his comments on the 'dissociation of sensibility' and on the fate of 'Shakespeare's English' as it was channelled through the 'crippled court-artifice of Restoration speech' into 'the prose of Addison, which in all essentials is still our cultivated norm'. Nor is Hughes' concern with the great poet's prophetic–creative divination of the historic 'moment' altogether remote from Leavis' preoccupation (especially in his later criticism) with the creative '*Ahnung*' or 'anticipatory apprehension'. The limited edition of *Cave Birds* appeared in the same year as *The Living Principle*: the one book includes a creative critique of post-Socratic and post-Christian dualistic abstraction, while the other argues that 'the Cartesian–Newtonian dualism must be exorcised from the Western mind'. Both Hughes and Leavis revered Blake for his creative onslaught on spiritless materialism; both have developed the insight registered in Lawrence's diagnostic triad, 'ego, will and idea'. The differences are obvious and important, but less important, I think, than the area of convergence and shared concern – particularly the intense concern with a modern *malaise*, and the related idea that something decisive and damaging took place in the latter half of the seventeenth century that had its roots in the earlier period and had consequences that blight our age.

Hughes
and shamanism

Ted Hughes is a poet who is deeply concerned about his culture, a culture where it seems that, in the words of Carl Jung, 'nothing is holy any longer',[1] whose pursuit of material benefit has led to neglect and abuse of both the natural world and the human spirit. Hughes' own response is similar to that of Jung. In his review of Max Nicholson's *The Environmental Revolution* he writes, 'The story of the mind exiled from nature is the story of Western man'.[2] Hughes' poetry is poetry written for a world that has lost its balance, poetry that can vividly portray the crisis, yet which also has a healing force through its emphasis on the holiness of the natural world and the mystery of the human psyche.

In many ways Hughes' poems record the epic journey of Western man returning from exile, and it is in this context that Hughes begins to explore the spiritual technique known as shamanism, which also emphasises restoration of cosmic balance and healing, and which often expresses itself in terms of a journey or flight.

So what is shamanism? There are numerous perspectives on what is essentially a highly individualistic phenomenon, but the basics are clear. Hughes outlines the shamanic experience like this—

Basically, it's the whole procedure and practice of becoming and performing as a witchdoctor, a medicine man, among primitive peoples. The individual is summoned by certain dreams. The same dreams all over the world. A spirit summons him ... usually an animal or a woman. If he refuses, he dies ... or somebody near him dies. If he accepts, he then prepares himself for the job ... it may take years. Uusally he apprentices himself to some other Shaman, but the spirit may well teach him direct. Once fully fledged he can enter trance at will and go to the spirit world ... he goes to get something badly needed, a cure, an answer, some sort of divine intervention in the community's affairs. Now this flight to the spirit world he experiences as a dream ... and that dream is the basis of the hero story.[3]

A fuller description of the shaman's call and practice is given in Hughes' review of Mircea Elaide's major work on the subject.

The shaman is chosen in a number of ways. In some regions, commonly among the North American Indians, the aspirant inflicts on himself extraordinary solitary ordeals of fasting and self mutilation, until a spirit, usually some animal, arrives and becomes henceforth his liaison with the spirit world. In other regions the tribe chooses the man – who may or may not, under the initiation ordeals, become a shaman. But the most common form of election comes from the spirits themselves, they approach the man in a dream. At the simplest these dreams are no more than the vision of an eagle, as among the Buryats, or a beautiful woman (who marries them), as among the Goldi.[4]

More complex forms of this initiatory dream-call contain a 'central episode' which consists of

a magical death, then dismemberment, by a demon or equivalent powers, with all possible variants of boiling, devouring, burning, stripping to the bones. From this nadir, the shaman is resurrected with new insides, a new body created for him by the spirits.[4]

The death experience is a prelude to a number of years of study leading up to the time when the prospective shaman is capable of safely negotiating the spirit realms, realms dominated by 'familiar figures' – 'the freezing river, the clashing rocks, the dog in the cave entrance, the queen of rivers, the holy mountain, and so on'.[4]

The shamanic dance is a performance, and thus always requires some kind of audience, usually having a public purpose.

The results, when the shaman returns to the living, are some display of healing power, or a clairvoyant piece of information. The cathartic effect on the audience, and the refreshing of their religious feeling, must be profound. These shamanisings are also entertainments, full of buffoonery, mimicry, dialogue, and magical contortions. The effect on the shaman himself is something to wonder about. One main circumstance in becoming a shaman, in the first place, is that once you've been chosen by the spirits, and dreamed the dreams, there is no other life for you, you must shamanise or die: this belief seems almost universal.[4]

At the end of the article Hughes suggests that the experience being described is not a shamanic monopoly, being, 'in fact, the basic experience of the temperament we call 'romantic'. He continues,

In a shamanising society 'Venus and Adonis', some of Keats's longer poems, 'The Wanderings of Oisin', 'Ash Wednesday', would all qualify their authors for the magic drum, while the actual flight lies perceptibly behind many of the best fairy tales, and behind myths such as those of Orpheus and Herakles, and also behind the epics of Gilgamesh and Odysseus. It is the outline, in fact, of the heroic Quest.[4]

Both passages link the shamanic and the poetic experiences, a correspondence which the shamanic practitioners also appreciate. The Papago Indians of North America say that 'Only to those who are humble does the dream come, and contained within the dream there is always the song'.[5] The Indian shaman could almost be talking of Coleridge's 'Kubla Khan'.[6] It is thus little wonder that Hughes links shamanic dreams to the 'romantic' temperament. He does not only see this temperament in terms of the song, but also of its content, the harnessing of mythic material to control emotional energy. That is why he can include T. S. Eliot among the 'romantic' candidates for the shaman's drum.

Ted Hughes regards shamanism as a force for equilibrium because it deals with the control and harnessing of energy expressed through ecstasy, energy which can revitalise and empower or bring to chaos and destruction. The poet explains the basis of the dilemmma in his interview with Faas, 'If you refuse the energy, you are living a kind of death. If you accept the energy, it destroys you. What is the alternative? To accept the energy, and find methods of turning it to good, of keeping it under control – rituals, the machinery of religion. The old method is the only one.'[7] Thus it is not surprising that in 'Second Glance at a Jaguar' the jaguar is 'Muttering some mantrah, some drumsong of murder', and is 'Going like a prayer wheel'. He is even, like certain South American shamans, 'making his skin Intolerable' – 'he has to wear his skin out', enabling its replacement by a magical skin to effect a change in sensibility.

But such poems are more than enquiries into the dialectic of elemental energy. They are also 'invocations of the Goddess', and 'invocations of a jaguar-like elemental force, demonic force'.[8] Hughes regards such poems as having 'real summoning force', like 'Gog', which was meant to be a journalistic poem about the Ardennes offensive in the Second World War, until the energy released summoned up the dragon of the Apocalypse, which was only stopped in its rampage through the poet's psyche by the writing of the Red Cross Knight section of the poem.

In keeping with this, Hughes defines energy as 'any form of vehement activity', through which one invokes 'the bigger energy, the elemental power circuit of the universe'.[9] It is this power circuit which both poet and shaman seek to plug into. For the shaman the energy is released in ecstasy, manifested in song and in dance. For the poet the same rites take place in his verse.

Thus, as early as 1957, when *The Hawk in the Rain* was made Poetry Book Society Autumn Choice, Hughes wrote in their bulletin likening his method to that of a musical composer – 'I might say that I turn every combatant into a bit of music, then resolve the whole uproar into as formal and balanced a figure of melody and rhythm as I can.'[10] This establishing of order and restoring of balance is exactly what the shaman is also accomplishing through *his* music.

In 1963 Hughes spoke of a correlation between his interest in music and his writing of poetry – 'my interest in poetry is really a musical interest, I think'. He saw some of his poems as 'musical rhythm – a sort of dance', often initially with no words at all. 'Then I just threw words into them'.[11] The shaman has a similar attitude towards composition. He 'does not fix his or her mind on particular words, nor sing a known tune. In dreams or other dreamlike states, the song comes through the barrier that separates the human being from the spirit world'.[12] Although there are numerous examples of this technique in earlier poems, its boldest application is found in the *Crow* poems. 'Most of them appeared as I wrote them. They were usually something of a shock to write. Mostly they wrote themselves quite rapidly . . .'[13] The experience is very close to that of the Gitksan Indian shaman, Isaac Tens, who declares, 'The songs force themselves out complete, without any attempt to compose them'.[14]

The dance of the gnats in 'Gnat-Psalm' is equally compulsive:

Dancing
Dancing
Writing on the air, rubbing out everything they write
Jerking their letters into knots, into tangles
Everybody everybody else's yoyo.

The figure is carried out upon the dance-floor of the page, as is the rat's dance in 'Song of a Rat'. These dances are also songs, songs of experience like William Blake's 'The Fly', dances which are eventually set to the 'super-ugly' songs of Crow, accommodating his flap and strut and indomitable incomprehension.

In these earlier poems only instinctive insect and animal life can generate the true elemental energy. Man is too much held back by his rationality and his arbitrary taboos. This is why Hughes wants to shift cultural foundations, to 'completely new Holy Ground, a new divinity' replacing Christianity, which he believes is the worn-out religious machinery of a worn-out culture. Hughes is like the protagonist of Carlyle's *Sartor Resartus* who claims that the great need of his age is to replace the 'Mythus of the Christian Religion in a new Mythus'.[15]

This mythus, this 'new divinity', has ancient roots. 'The old method is the only one.' We must tap the primitive impulses at the root of our own minds. As the painter Paul Gaugin put it, 'To achieve something new, you have to go back in time'. Hughes writes in terms of the poet making 'secret flights' into his own mind and becoming sensitized to the 'deeper patterns',[16], as if the further one probes one's own mind the closer to the race's past consciousness one comes.

For the poet a major way of making the secret flight is through dreams. Hughes calls Shakespeare's corpus 'a perfect example of the ancient Universal shamanistic dream of the call to the poetic or holy life.'[16] According to Jung dreams are 'pure nature; they show us the unvarnished natural truth, and are therefore fitted, as nothing else is, to give us back an attitude that accords with our basic human nature when our consciousness has strayed too far from its foundations and run into an impasse'.[17] Dreams are the unconsciousness's equivalent of narrative tales, and like such tales have collective meaning when they have a mythical content. It is not surprising that the dreamlike poem 'Pike' is about fishing in a 'stilled legendary depth', which 'was as deep as England'.

For Hughes, as for Jung, there is a positive effect in just having the dream, particularly in a culture that has exchanged dreaming for aspiration. He sees a story as having the same qualities.

When we tell a child a story, the child quickly finds his rôle; as the story proceeds the child enters a completely imaginative world . . . to some extent he goes into a condition of trance . . . And so whatever happens to him in the story happens under conditions of hypnosis. In other words it really happens. If in a story he is put through a humiliating defeat, the effects on him are of real defeat. If he is put through some sort of victory, the effects on him are of real victory. This is how these early storytellers could claim good fortune and so on for the listeners to their hero tales.[18]

In a later essay on the same subject, that of myth and education, Hughes speaks of stories as a force of reintegration. 'So it comes about that once we recognise their terms, these works seem to heal us'.[19] The narrative poet is like the shaman whose relating of a myth results in 'some display of healing power or a clairvoyant piece of information'. (It is worth remembering that this does not preclude the rituals also being 'entertainments, full of buffoonery, mimicry, dialogue and magical contortions',[20] like *Crow*.

The mythic narrative, the entering of the Dream Time, is central both to the shamanic healer and the 'romantic' poet. Ted Hughes also places great emphasis on this, the poetic experience which is healing because, like the children's story, it 'really happens'. This sense of immediacy is what is being sought in the early poem, 'Childbirth', from *The Hawk in the Rain*, a poem which looks at birth through mythic spectacles.

The poem closely resembles an actual incantation – of the Cuna Indians of Panama, as recorded by Claude Lévi-Strauss[21] – an incantation specifically intended to facilitate childbirth by giving a mythic explanation for the mother's pain. The song is a quest by the shaman for the woman's lost soul, or 'purba', which has been captured by Muu Puklip, the power who forms the foetus. Muu is 'indispensible to creation', and the fight is only against 'her abuses of power'. It is thus a restored balance which is sought. The shaman's task is to help the mother relive her condition by means of an empathic act whereby he too lives through the experience as he chants. To describe the effect upon the patient Lévi-Strauss uses the term 'abreaction' – 'when the patient intensively relives the situation from which the disturbance stems'.[22]. He also points out that the term also applies to the shaman, who is therefore a 'professional abreactor'. (In fact, because the *shaman* abreacts the *patient* abreacts.)

In both the poem and the incantation the treatment of the theme hinges upon the equation of the womb with a hell or underworld:

When, on the bearing mother, death's
Door opened its furious inch,
Instant of struggling and blood,
The commonplace became so strange . . .

In the Cuna chant the uterus is described as 'the dark inner place', and the vagina is inhabited by various creatures of the underworld. In the Hughes poem a similar underworld also lies very close during birth, 'Through that miracle-breached bed / All the dead could have got back'.

Both poem and chant deal with the problem of how a new-born child can come from a place associated with death. This is particularly pressing for the Cuna, who closely link the mother and the earth. The child is therefore an autochthonous being, one truly back from the dead. Hughes' poem reassures us that the cosmos has come back into adjustment after this unnerving miracle. The child has 'Put the skull back about the head / Righted the stagger of the earth'. The shaman calms the frightened mother in a similar way, likewise stressing that the womb-door has been closed and that the dead cannot now escape.

The main difference, besides the fact that the poet treats a condition he himself provoked, is in the degree of identification. The Cuna healing is characteristically shamanic, where the sorcerer too experiences the events, 'in all their vividness, originality and violence'.[22] But the Hughes poem lacks this identification. At this stage of his development he has not yet dealt with a tendency towards curious metaphysical enquiry and a corresponding distancing of the subject from the healing power of the myth.

One begins to be aware that the best poems are where the experience is somehow lived out by the poet himself, while 'Childbirth' and many other early poems seem to have the quality of observations – often striking, but little more. What the poet/shaman does not fully live out cannot be fully appreciated by the reader. Thus, despite Hughes' conscious linking of his craft with that of the shaman, the final test must always lie in the poems themselves.

The shaman's song is based upon three factors; the energy, or ecstasy; the myth, expressed in some form of ritual; and a resulting catharsis or abreaction. These three components combine to produce healing, reintegration and answers to spiritual questions. In his poetic development Hughes deals with each of these elements in turn. In the early work the accent is upon the power, what Mirca Eliade calls the 'Kratophany', the manifestation of force (*Myths, Dreams and Mysteries* p. 126). We are shown the strength of hawk, pike, jaguar, bull, wind, sea. This is why the emphasis is on animal life, since 'Each one is living the redeemed life of joy. They are continually in a state of energy which men only have when they've gone mad'.[23] In *Wodwo* this power is turning inwards and there is danger of destruction. So too in *Crow* the emphasis is put upon the process, the actual machinery of the experience. Thus the volume commences with a kind of catechism ('Examination at the Womb's Door') preceded by a genealogy and a creed ('Lineage' and 'Two Legends'). *Crow* is full of songs, macabre dances and highly compressed rituals, (for example 'A Kill' and 'Crow's Battle Fury') and great emphasis is put upon the search for initiatory experience. The cathartic factor is strongly developed, but it is catharsis and process which are emphasised, not catharsis and reintegration.

It is not until *Gaudete* that Hughes begins to try for answers. The mythic element is made a great deal more accessible by the reintroduction of a human perspective. In the three preceding works the main link with mankind has been the suffering of the protagonists. The events of these volumes are not lived out in a social context. There is no human society present at all in *Prometheus on his Crag*, while in *Cave Birds* and *Crow* human relationships are used more as a counterpoint to the activity of the protagonists than as any kind of background.

In *Gaudete* there has to be a social milieu, since Hughes is now intent upon a poetic living-out of the ritual, believing that if the shaman/poet/reader can even get so far as to ask the vital question of the divine being, that might constitute an answer in itself, as Parzival healed the Fisher-King by asking about his health.

Thus it is possible to see a shamanistic formula being worked out in Ted Hughes' poetic development.

$$\left.\begin{array}{l} \text{energy} - \text{myth} \\ \text{power} - \text{process} \end{array}\right\} \text{catharsis} \quad \begin{array}{l} \text{healing} \\ \text{product}^{24} \end{array}$$

It should be noted that the goal is always interaction with the reader/patient even if the poet is not aware of that when writing. Only the best poems in *Lupercal* and *The Hawk in the Rain* see this formula worked through to a successful conclusion, where both author and reader seem to join together in a sharing of the experience the page provides.

It is with *Wodwo* that Hughes seems to grasp a proper understanding of his goals and begins to take up the call fully. This delay is not surprising, as he points out: 'Poets usually refuse the call. How are they to accept it? How can a poet become a medicine man and fly to the source and come back and heal or pronounce oracles? Everything among us is against it.'[25]

Perhaps one can understand this by making a parallel with the shaman's initial call. Hughes has mentioned the call through dreams, 'the same dreams all over the world'. The potential shaman is usually summoned by an animal or a woman: the summoning by an animal closely parallels Hughes' experience at Cambridge as described by Keith Sagar,[26] which points strongly to a shamanic threshold call. The poem 'The Hawk in the Rain' reminds us of the comment in the Elaide review that in some tribes just to dream of an eagle is to be identified as a shaman, while another common threshold dream, that of the transfigured woman, seems to be behind Hughes' fascination with *The White Goddess* by Robert Graves.

These instances all point towards a shamanic call closely bound in with Hughes' poetic vocation, but at this stage it seems that Hughes had not fully understood the shamanic side of this double call, and is unconsciously seeking to exercise certain atrributes of the shaman without having experienced the necessary deep crisis. This crisis 'has the value of a superior threshold initiation', and gives shamanism, according to Joseph Campbell, 'a quality of general human validity'.[27]

The shaman has four main accomplishments, according to Mircea Eliade in *Myths, Dreams and Mysteries*:

1. The capacity for hierophany – 'Through the strangely sharpened

senses of the shaman, the sacred manifests itself.' The power generated is often 'experienced as a very vivid warmth' (p. 146). The hierophancy is also a 'kratophany' – a manifestation of force (p. 126). It results in:

2. The ability to see spiritually and receive illumination.

3. The ability to journey into the spirit realm, both to obtain answers and to converse with the divine. The climbing of trees or beating of drums are symbolic of the 'mystical flight' into the spirit world.

4. Because the barrier between heaven and earth has been overcome, besides the pre-Fall ability to talk to the Godhead, the shaman can also talk the 'language of the animals' (p. 60) and achieve a renewed friendship with them (this usually includes receiving an animal familiar).

By these attributes the shaman, on behalf of his clan or group, locates them in a spiritual universe where spiritual questions can be answered and healing effected.

Shamanism thus caters for Hughes' doctrine of energy, his love for the world of nature, his metaphysical concerns, and his fascination with animals. It also provides an answer to the twentieth-century poets' problem of whether his work is relevant.

In his early poetry Hughes has a clear understanding of the shamanic call, although much of this is instinctive and not fully developed. He has had the courage to accept the call, but has not yet come to terms with the consequences. The long apprenticeship is just beginning. As has already been pointed out, Hughes has begun to use myth as a means of controlling energy, a technique which becomes a major concern in his later poetry.

Hughes invests his poems with a dream-like quality, a kind of 'reverie'. It is not surprising that such a reverie on a cold winter's night produced 'The Thought-Fox'.[28] In *Lupercal* we see the reverie become dreams, although there is already a strong dream element represented in poems like 'A Woman Unconscious A Dream of Horses' and 'Relic', the last of which is very reminiscent of the eskimo initiate's contemplation of a whale or seal bone, or the Tantric Buddhist meditating upon a skeleton. But the tools of the shaman seem not to be fully developed. Myth and dream *are* used. There *is* the changed sensibility which makes a flower 'Brutal as the stars of this month'. The vision *is* both immediate and convincing. But it is not related to common human experience. Where there is an example of altered vision, of a manifestation of the sacred, the dialectic of myth is missing, blurring the vision; and correspondingly, the dialectic is often cut off from true vision, leaving many of the poems in Hughes' first two collections in a kind of forced metaphysicality.[29]

The integration of vision and dialectic can only come through the initiatory ordeal, which hinges upon the provoking of a profound crisis in the life of the candidate. This is achieved by dislocating the universe of the prospective shaman, usually through isolation and various other forms of privation. In some cultures this might go with an educating process over a number of years. In others, particularly among the Eskimo and North American Indian the ordeal is 'nasty, brutish and short'.

Whatever the case, the crisis is experienced as a symbolic death, by being swallowed, eaten, dismembered or scourged. This mystical return to chaos[30] and destruction of 'normal profane experience'[31] enables a recreation and resurrection. The resurrection brings about a change of sensibility and as a result all experience becomes sacred for the initiate.

In this context it is therefore little wonder that Hughes has called Wodwo 'a descent into destruction of some sort'.[32] The initiatory ordeal emphasises Freud's 'Thanatos', the death-principle within man, death which makes regeneration possible. This emphasis abandons what Freud would see as sanity, the maintaining of the balance between Thanatos and Eros (the life-principle), in favour of a kind of divine madness.

The Hawk in the Rain and Lupercal are part of the balance, since it becomes clear that although the world portrayed is violent in the extreme, it is also a world of life. The 'unselfconscious will to live' is dominant. Death is present but there is no will to die, and without death there is no rebirth. There is indeed a tension between life and death, as a poem like 'Mayday on Holderness' shows. 'The decomposition of leaves' and 'The furnace door whirling with larvae' are both present, but here they are not in competition. What is not present is the tension between the will to life and the will to death, the excruciating competition which begins to fuel Hughes' poetic genius[33] in the mid-1960s.

The poet is now exposed to the full force of his universe with neither shelter nor bearings. This certainly forces him from the limited themes he could have remained chained to, but also commits him to a great responsibility in the use of his gift, and makes him prone to over-reaction when faced with the extremes of numbness and the heights of destructive force.

In Wodwo Hughes descends into depths where true initiation no longer seems possible. The poem 'The Bear' enigmatically says of the bear,

He is the ferryman
To dead land.

His price is everything.

The poem is a shamanic dream, as is the earlier long poem about a bear, 'The Brother's Dream'. Eskimo shamans often dreamed of bears during their search for knowledge. One such dreamer, the apprentice shaman Autdaruta, describes thus how he acquired power over spirits:

I had not been lying there long before I heard the bear coming. It attacked me and crunched me up, limb by limb, joint by joint, but strangely enough it did not hurt at all, it was only when it bit me in the heart that it did hurt frightfully.
From that day on I felt I ruled my helping spirits.[34]

Autdaruta experiences the mythical death which leads to renewal and wisdom, but the bear of *Wodwo* only ferries to 'dead land'. He can take one *to* the Wasteland; but not back again. In 'Out', Hughes' father has in a sense returned from this place, having been dragged from 'The mortised four-year strata of dead Englishmen he belonged with'. The first section of the poem is even called 'The Dream Time', the mythic time the potential shaman seeks to re-enter, but in the second section 'The dead man in his cave' is reborn:

As after being blasted to bits
The reassembled infantryman
Tentatively totters out, gazing around with the eyes
Of an exhausted clerk.

The poet's despairing conclusion is 'Goodbye to all the remaindered charms of my father's survival / Let England close. Let the green sea-anemone close'. This is more than a reminiscence of the poet's juvenile disappointment that his father has not become some kind of super-man as a result of the First World War. Hughes is filled with the suspicion that the initiating experience now only ferries to a dead land.

Eventually Hughes will take up the shamanic tools in a more confident way and seek for a healing of that Wasteland. But at this stage he must explore the possibility that initiation and regeneration are no longer possible for man in a culture where spiritual values have been undermined. In *Crow*, Hughes considers the possibility that if the old body cannot be replaced, maybe Man himself will be.

The final link between the rather disjointed work of the poet's crisis period and *Crow* is *Eat Crow*, a radio play, written in 1964. This piece links the quest for a completed initiation with the crow-figure, the mocking antithesis of that aspiration.

'She' seems to be a kind of midwife to Morgan's initiatory ordeal. First Morgan experiences a tearing apart similar to the Eskimo shaman who is mystically eaten by a polar bear. Afterwards he sleeps – 'When I woke I could hear voices, many voices / It was my bones all chattering together.'[35] This resembles the second stage of Eskimo initiation as outlined by Joseph Campbell and Mircea Eliade, where the prospective shaman contemplates his bones which have now been picked clean. But the great difference is that instead of leading to integration, the ordeal speaks only of dislocation. Unlike Ezekiel's vision of the dry bones coming together in harmony and receiving the breath of God's life – 'the pelvis was shouting. And the bones of the foot / And the bones of the hand, fought.' Instead of a manifestation of the Logos, 'the teeth were screeching something incomprehensible', presaging the many incoherent cries in later Hughes poems.

Morgan is unable to accept the incomprehensible, and that particular task now devolves upon Crow, who is trying to become a man. Hughes says[36] that for this purpose, 'He's put through various adventures and disasters and trials and ordeals' which initially do not alter him at all. Then suddenly Crow's sufferings 'completely transform him, tear him to bits, put him together again, and produce him a little bit changed'. This should bring about Crow's initiation into humanity, but it is not forthcoming.

Whereas in *Wodwo* the initiating patterns are incomplete, and there is even a hint of the possibility of complete annihilation with no rebirth, in *Crow* the spectre is of continual rebirth without initiation.[37] Thus in 'A Kill' Crow is

Flogged lame with legs
Shot through the head with balled brains
Shot blind with eyes
Nailed down by his own ribs
Strangled just short of his last gasp
By his own windpipe
Clubbed unconscious by his own heart.

This is not just part of 'God's Nightmare'. Crow is going through elements of Irish, Scandinavian and Christian initiation of deities through suffering. But here the experience is neither expiatory nor illuminating.

A similar nightmare situation occurs in the *Tibetan Book of the Dead*, the *Bardo Thodol*, a work which underpins the whole schema of *Crow*. In the section entitled the 'Bardo of Karmic Illusions', the dead person comes face to face with the various wrathful deities. 'Have faith in the Blood-drinking Deities too',[38] he is exhorted. In Buddhist terms, if this advice is followed rebirth can be avoided and the true initiation which is Nirvana attained. But Hughes, while greatly utilising this strain of teaching, is far more akin to the Tantric and shamanic influences on the *Bardo*. He says to Egbert Faas – 'the special weirdness and power of all things Tibetan in occult and magical circles springs direct from the shamanism, not the Buddhism'.[39]

Where the Buddhist and shamanic strains are united is in Crow's refusal to abandon his selfhood, his one indestructible desire to live. For the Buddhist this is a tragedy since 'He who hath desire continueth subject to rebirth' (*Brihadaranyaka Upanishad*). Only by giving up the desire to live, which is the essence of selfhood, can Crow escape from the wheel of existence. This same refusal to let go of selfhood also prevents Crow experiencing shamanic initiation since he cannot receive the new self until he has let go of the old.

Also there is the problem of faith. Morgan in *Eat Crow* is far too afraid to 'have faith in the Blood-Drinking Deities'. Crow is far too egocentric to have faith in anything else save himself. By this time Hughes has isolated the two greatest barriers to initiation, fear and lack of faith, both of which are manifested in the desire to remain inside onself, rather than reaching out. Occasionally Crow does manage to look outside himself. One such is the poem appropriately called 'Glimpse':

'O leaves', Crow sang, trembling, 'O leaves —'

The touch of a leaf's edge at his throat
Guillotined further comment.

    Nevertheless
Speechless he continued to stare at the leaves

Through the god's head instantly substituted.

But this is a glimpse and no more. Crow is more truly the 'King of Carrion'.

His palace is of skulls.

His crown is the last splinters
Of the vessel of life.

He presides over what closely resembles a shaman's altar, which is also made of 'skulls' and a 'scaffold of bones'. But his kingdom is empty, and he reigns over silence.

Despite Crow's earlier refusal to allow his suffering redemptive value, eventually he is prepared to attach himself to an Eskimo guide whose function is to give primitive man's answer to the question of mortality and clarify for Crow the nature of his quest. Crow's own perspective is too closely linked to that of twentieth century 'civilised' man, mitigated to some extent by his animal vitality. But the animal is denied initiation because it is not human, and the modern man is denied initiation because he has betrayed his roots. The only hopeful response to the problem of man confronted with his temporality is that of the Eskimo, in 'Fleeing from Eternity':

He got a sharp rock he gashed holes in his face
Through the blood and pain he looked at the earth.

He gashed again deeper and through the blood and pain
He screeched at the lightning, at the frost, and at time.

Then, lying among the bones of the cemetary earth,
He saw a woman singing out of her belly.

He gave her eyes and a mouth, in exchange for the song.
She wept blood, she cried pain.

The pain and the blood were life. But the man laughed —

The song was worth it.

The woman felt cheated.

'How Water Began to Play' repeats the lesson of 'Fleeing from Eternity'. Water, like man, searches the physical universe, meets pain, blood 'maggot and rottenness', and begins to weep uncontrollably. As a result 'It lay at the bottom of all things / Utterly worn out / utterly clear'. If there is any message in *Crow*, this is it, that suffering makes the universe transparent. Poetry is the response to this startling clarity,[40] and is often an expression of the struggle which makes the hierophany possible.

The struggle is particularly evident in *Crow*, where it seems both Crow and his creator are intent upon one thing; to survive the ordeal, knowing that 'The pain and the blood were life' ('Fleeing from Eternity') – 'To emerge is the aim of the Crow poem,' Geoffrey Thurley has said.[41]

After Crow we see a new strand introduced into Ted Hughes' poetry. Suffering is valuable, not only in terms of initiation, but also for expiation. *Prometheus on his Crag* and *Cave Birds* weave these two strands together.

In *Prometheus on his Crag* the initiatory and expiatory elements are linked together in terms of shamanic mediation. Prometheus, like the shaman, is a link between heaven and earth, conversing with both the gods of Olympus and the men of Athens. At this stage he *is* a mediator, but not a true one. He is seeking to deal with divinity on behalf of man, when the problem of guilt has not yet been dealt with. To put things in Judeo-Christian terms, the barrier between man and God requires more than just someone to mediate, but also someone to pay the price for man's sin, which is what put the barrier up in the first place.

As a result Hughes' poetry of the seventies more and more explores the tension between shamanism, which does not deal with guilt, and

Judeo-Christianity, which claims to deal with both guilt and death, yet which seems to atrophy the life of energy which he holds so close. It is this exploration which perhaps most of all establishes Hughes' affinities with the poetry of William Blake.

The major difference between Prometheus' understanding (probably also Hughes') and Christianity, is that one believes in atoning suffering, while Christianity is about an atoning sacrifice-death. So when Prometheus lays himself down in his chains –

On the Mountain,

> under Heaven

> as THE PAYMENT –

He is 'Too far from his people to tell them / Now they owe nothing' (Poem 16). Here we have expiating payment without expiatory results. Prometheus is 'too far' from mankind to communicate the good news, which therefore remains useless. This is not surprising considering the fact that Prometheus is suffering for his own transgression, while Christ died for mankind's. The resulting problem of guilt is most clearly stated in Poem 20, where Prometheus asks, 'Was Life his transgression? / Was he the punished criminal aberration?' The guilt is worsened by the knowledge of his own immortality. Prometheus cannot experience full initiation *or* freedom from sin, since both involve death.

Hughes seems to deal with this problem by focusing upon the initiatory aspect. This is logical, since part of the shaman's repertoire is the ability to return to the pre-Fall state, the Paradise where man, beast and God are in harmony, before the advent of sin. But this raises numerous problems for Prometheus. He has lost any shamanic accomplishments he might have had. He 'has bitten his prophetic tongue off' (Poem 6). He is 'Arrested half-way from heaven / And slung between heaven and earth' (Poem 7).

Prometheus is a prisoner as well as a candidate for full initiation. This situation is repeated in the psychodrama *Orghast*, where the cruel father-figure Krogon victimises Pramanath, who stands for Prometheus. The prisoner/potential initiate correspondence is also strong in *Cave Birds*, where the protagonist is led like a condemned prisoner by the summoner via the interrogator and the judge to the executioner.

In all three works Hughes endeavours to work a poetic solution to a problem which must be solved before his shamanic apprenticeship can end. In *Orghast* this is stated simply in the rising dawn at the end of the performance (it was performed in the open air at the Shiraz festival in 1971). In *Prometheus* it is in the sudden outburst of Poem 21, where the mountain he is chained to 'splits its sweetness', setting him free to tread: 'On the dusty peacock film where the world floats'.[42] This is a beautiful but unconvincingly precipitate release. The same effect is far better achieved in *Cave Birds* where the accent is not so much on the visionary dreams of the candidate, as upon the journey through the spirit-world. These poems bring across a sense of well-deserved nightmare assailing the protagonist, Kafkaesque in its intensity.

The protagonist cockerel, representative of Socratic rationality, tries to argue his way out of the summons to the spirit-world, but:

When I said: 'Civilisation',
He began to chop off his fingers and mourn.
When I said: 'Sanity and again Sanity and above all Sanity',
He disembowelled himself with a cross-shaped cut.
I stopped trying to say anything.
But then when he began to snore in his death-struggle
The guilt came.
And when they covered his face I went cold.[43]

The protagonist deserves the death sentence for his murder of nature through his rationalism and lack of thanksgiving. Nevertheless this sentence is also the hope of regeneration. In 'The executioner' the prisoner says,

You have no idea what has happened
To what is no longer yours

It feels like the world
Before your eyes ever opened.

This is prophetic, but first he must go through the gates of Hell after being equipped with the weapons for the task. He had become the 'warrior', the one seeking to become a 'man of knowledge'.[44] The protagonist enters the Hall of Judgement and his soul is skinned ('A flayed crow in the hall of judgement'). This symbolises his mystical death, as does the image of baptism, taken from Christianity, sleep taken from Gnosticism, burial from Earth-mother cults and eventually the scapegoat image from Judaism. After this, the initiate is given a 'Scarecrow Swift' as his true guide and spirit familiar. He is now 'Walking bare' and like aboriginal shamans whose intestines turn to opal, he has 'the gem of myself'. He can now enter into sacred marriage. 'The violent death is creative',[45] and so the Earth-mother (represented by the Celtic goddess Bloddewydd, in the poem 'The owl flower') is reconciled, and now can be wooed. Immolation and marriage both harness Earth's creativity, whereas in *Wodwo* and *Crow* she has been at enmity with all.

The final vision is of a falcon, 'The risen', 'his shape / Is a cross'. At last there is a vision of divinity, even if it is not the Creator himself.

In *Gaudete* Hughes takes this vision of the divine and puts it in terms of his early fascination with the White Goddess. Now divinity has been discovered the myth does not have to be told, it can be lived. Guilt is at least captured if not actually removed, and has been harnessed to the initiatory experience. In *Gaudete* Hughes can have faith in something, even if as yet it is the 'Blood-drinking Deities' of the *Book of the Dead*.

In both *Cave Birds* and *Gaudete* there is also a greater consciousness of the relationship with the reader, who is encouraged to participate in each poem. Both volumes are cinematic and episodic. The language is far more visual, a long way from the long strings of adjectives in Crow's 'super-ugly' songs. Hughes has found the optimum way of controlling his extravagance of energy. Instead of bald descriptions of what takes place like 'When Crow cried his mother's ear / Scorched to a stump'[46] or the stuttering description of the mother figure as 'Death and death and death' (Gog II) we now see this figure face to face:

A face as if sewn together from different faces.
A baboon beauty face,
A crudely stitched patchwork of faces.

The greater visual emphasis more clearly presents the goal of the *Gaudete* narrative, which is to heal this awful figure, the mutilated Gea Genetrix. Like the hero of Wolfram von Eschenbach's *Parzival* and Peredur in *The Mabinogion*, Lumb is unable to respond from his humanity when confronted with the suffering ruler. He too is dominated by a system based upon denial. He lacks both the compassion which Wolfram extols and the curiosity which the author of *Peredur* emphasises.[47] He is 'The veteran of negatives / And the survivor of cease'.[48] He is a stranger to choice and personal responsibility.

He declares he can do nothing
He protests there is nothing he can do
For this beautiful woman who seems to be alive and dead.
He is not a doctor. He can only pray.   (*Gaudete*, p.15)

The inability to act or enquire is marked by numbness (p. 13), a numbness which is penetrated only by pain,[49] a pain which 'rends him apart, from the top of his skull downwards' (p. 15). Lumb must come to the point where to pray is not the antithesis of to heal, to the fulcrum point of shamanic initiation. Lumb experiences the initiatory effect of pain and crisis, while his double experiences the expiation. One is the hierophant, the other the scapegoat. But as Keith Sagar has pointed out in *The Art of Ted Hughes*, 'the whole story is a psychological analogue, as all the many stories in myth and folklore of doubles, changelings, tanists, twins, weirds and shadows are. There is only one Lumb. He is undergoing a spiritual/psychological crisis.'[50]

The single experience is examined from a doubled perspective. The prologue gives a fairly straightforward initiatory pattern with elements of both the rites of Herakles and of Mithras. The plunge into the wasted otherworld and the return through 'A doorway to daylight' (p. 19) is in itself a mystical death and rebirth. This element of the initiatory experience takes place in the Great Time, while the second element is put in the context of semi-rural England. Perhaps we are being shown two different aspects or levels of the same period of time in Lumb's life. Whatever the case, it is the second strand which is the more complex.

The two are united by the Orphic myth, as modified by its contact with Dionysian religion. The underworld experience in which a female figure is found but not brought back to life parallels Orpheus' quest for Eurydice, while the pursuit and death parody the orthodox Orphic account of their patron's death – hounded by the Maenads for too great a devotion to Apollo. Lumb's devotion to his own deity, enshrined in the sheel-na-gig, is also overweaned, but in this case it is murderous husbands who pursue, rather than Bacchic women.

Nonetheless the major influence on the main narrative is that of the Dionysian rite. Dionysus was brought forth by his father Zeus, after his mother Semele was consumed when she tried to see her lover of the night. As a result he is a deity of inner tension, between father and mother, between exultant joy and pitiful suffering. This tension results in madness. Walter Otto says this of the god: ' . . . he appears among men like a storm, he staggers them, and he tames their opposition with the whip of madness . . . Life becomes suddenly an ecstasy – an ecstasy of blessedness, but an ecstasy, no less, of terror.'[51] He is a god of confrontation, bringing 'A wild uproar, and a numbing silence'.[52] Music often announces his madness, as in 'The scherzo' (*Gaudete*, p. 41). Estridge feels his daughters 'are tearing him to pieces' like the Maenads (p. 42). Music is a 'materialised demon' (p. 44), both an invocation and an announcement of the madness descending.

The madness is health-giving, like the shaman's threshold initiation, a procreative madness, 'inherent in the womb of the mother',[53] and propagated by Dionysus' own sensuality. The problem is that the madness has not been allowed free expression and erupts in an unbalanced form, in a society where very few of the women have children, and in which the youngest, Garten and Felicity, are over eighteen.

The spirit-Lumb is a healer who does not understand the true situation and thus precipitates a corporate crisis. Perhaps there is a degree of release, but Felicity's death is murder, not sacrifice. Lumb must both make atonement and discover the full, true initiation needed to heal the land. The first stage is of alienation, leading to longing—

Me too,
Let me be one of your warriors.

Let your home
Be my home. Your people
My people. (p.190)

The initiand is before the Goddess as Ruth before Naomi, begging inclusion in the chosen people, along with the 'grass-blade', the blackbird and the badger. This mirrors the supplication of p. 53.

He tries to make this ash-tree his prayer,
    reaching upwards and downwards through the capillaries,
Groping to feel the sure return grasp
The sure embrace and return gaze of a listener—

The double's prayer is answered by 'the drowning creature of / mud,' which 'embraces him as he embraces it' (p. 104). The Lumb of the notebooks knows what he is praying for, and to whom he is praying, but the double has not yet reached this stage. The passage which contains this experience strongly emphasises birth. Lumb is buried in primal mud, in a foetal position. He sees himself 'being delivered of the woman from the pit' (p. 105), and is himself delivered. Now, 'He sees her face undeformed and perfect' (p. 106).

It is important to realise that this is Lumb's *individual* initiation. 'The initiand is born again from the womb of Mother Earth',[54] while the descent into the underworld is the heroic and shamanic initiation. The Dionysian element centres upon individual purgation, the use of a victim. Dionysus is both hunter and pursued, and, when pursued, is cast down into a sea, lake or underworld. One of the forms in which he returns is that of a child, the reborn. The Dionysian mystery is also the 'lesser mystery' of the Eleusian rite, performed in the spring – the 'greater mystery' being the celebration of the Great Mother. The Orphic element gives the heroic perspective, descent into the Mother's womb.

Gaudete reminds us that shamaic/heroic initiation must be on a basis of personal rebirth, a personal plugging of our 'energy appeal into the inexhaustible / earth' (p. 163). Throughout the development of this theme, Hughes has been working towards an equilibrium which can be achieved in no other way than through actual experience. The *Moortown* sequence and *Remains of Elmet*, particularly the latter, are heirs to this experience where the initiation of the shaman-poet does not affect poetry alone, but leads to a place in which 'every responsible action is charged with a magico-religious value and meaning'.[55]

7 TERRY GIFFORD
NEIL ROBERTS

Hughes and two contemporaries: Peter Redgrove and Seamus Heaney

Our aim in this chapter is to examine the relationships between Hughes' work and that of two outstanding contemporaries, Peter Redgrove and Seamus Heaney. Both of these poets have shown a keen interest in Hughes, and the interest has been reciprocated. There are close parallels in the three writers' thoughts about poetry, and a detailed comparison of texts will show striking similarities in their poetic procedures. The differences that emerge against this background will we hope illuminate the work of each poet more interestingly than a comparison of more obviously contrasting writers would.

Redgrove, who is two years younger than Hughes, was an early champion of his poetry, before the publication of *The Hawk in the Rain*. He has continued to be deeply interested in Hughes' work, and has recently written, in a letter: 'Hughes had gone further up a road than most of us, and one felt that in being with him; one also felt that he had things that one needed ... The poetry up to *Crow* gave me a working sense (as did Sylvia Plath's) of how much must be done by a contemporary poem, before it *is* a poem.'[1] Hughes indicated his high opinion of Redgrove in an interview in 1965 when, bewailing the stultifying effect of Cambridge, he said, 'only tough poets like Peter

Redgrove ever survive'.[2] And more recently he has praised *The Wise Wound*, the book about menstruation that Redgrove wrote with Penelope Shuttle, in these terms: 'Far and away the most radical and unarguable case for the real dignity and sacredness of woman . . . therefore of the real feminine in spirit and in nature that I've read . . . the most important book about the Goddess since Graves' *White Goddess* and in some essential matters a step or two beyond it'.[3]

Seamus Heaney is nine years younger than Hughes, and by the time he started seriously to write poetry, Hughes was established, with two volumes published. Heaney has publicly acknowledged Hughes' influence on his early work:

Hughes's voice, I think, is in a rebellion against a certain kind of demeaned, mannerly voice. It's a voice that has no truck with irony because his dialect is not that . . . I mean, the voice of a generation – the Larkin voice, the Movement voice, even the Eliot voice, the Auden voice . . . the manners of that speech, the original voice behind the poetic voice, are those of literate English middle-class culture, and I think Hughes's great cry and call and bawl is that English language and poetry is longer and deeper and rougher than that . . . I'm a different kind of animal from Ted, but I will always be grateful for the release that reading Ted's work gave me. I had gone through the education as to Eliot's bringing in irony and urban subject-matter and intelligence, and nothing in that connected with the scripts written in my being. Then I read Hughes, Kavanagh, R. S. Thomas, and I realised it was dealing with my world.[4]

The most significant common factor in these three poets is that they all put their faith in an inward source. The poem, for them, is a psychic or even organic event before it is a conscious artefact. This belief can be perceived in Hughes' comparison of writing poetry with capturing animals, and with fishing: for him the purpose of both writing and fishing is 'to bring up some lovely solid thing like living metal from a world where nothing exists but those inevitable facts which raise life out of nothing and return it to nothing'.[5] *Poetry in the Making*, the book in which this comparison is made, is almost entirely about techniques of imagination bordering on meditation, hardly at all about linguistic skills. Heaney, in a schools broadcast, implied a very similar view of the nature of poetry: a poem is 'alive in an animal, mineral and vegetable way. It comes out of a creature, out of a man's mind and feelings, and it lives and is clothed in the substance of words'.[6] And this is directly paralleled by Redgrove's remark in an interview that 'What you write in a book is only one variety of organic growth, organic life'.[7]

This conception of poetry can be called 'visionary' and is closely akin to those of Wordsworth, Coleridge, Blake and Shelley. It is also related to the influence on all three poets of shamanism and Jungian psychology. Hughes himself made the link with Romanticism when, in discussing the similarity between the phenomena of shamanic vision and poetic imagination, he remarked that the shamanic motif of flight and return was at the heart of 'the literary temperament we call Romantic' – a category which for him includes Shakespeare, Yeats and Eliot.[8]

This conception of the poem having some kind of existence prior to composition can be further clarified by contrasting the thoery and practice of another accomplished contemporary, Geoffrey Hill. Hill has said that he is 'deeply moved' by Milton's description of poetry as 'simple, sensuous and passionate', but that the modern poet who rests in that definition is in danger of debasing it. For Hill the way of avoiding such debasement is 'by an extreme concentration on technical discipline'. This is 'the only true way of releasing the simple, sensuous and passionate'.[9]

Hill's best poems are sensuous and passionate but rarely simple. Moreover they seem so much to be created *by* technique that it is impossible to speak of an inward source of the kind the other three poets describe. His poems throw out an immediate linguistic challenge:

The cross staggered him   ('Canticle for Good Friday')

Undesirable you may have been, untouchable
you were not.   ('September Song')

They bespoke doomsday and they meant it by
God   ('Funeral Music' 3)

Even his most powerfully moving effects cannot be detached, in our response, from the words that embody them:

                    A field
After battle utters its own sound
Which is like nothing on earth, but is earth. ('Funeral Music' 3)

The common technique here is of renewed cliché, and it is the wrenching of a bland phrase into a usually painful meaning that gives Hill's work its savagely sardonic effect.

In this respect, as in others, Heaney is much closer to Hill than either Hughes or Redgrove is. For example, in a poem about a picture of Belfast in 1786 he writes,

It's twenty to four
On one of the last afternoons
Of reasonable light.

This effect could almost have been borrowed from Hill, but such things in Heaney are isolated, not nearly so much a part of the poetic texture.

Puns in Redgrove, as in many of his titles, give the effect of high spirits rather than mordancy, and are often signposts to the metamorphic character of the poems in question.

Comparable effects in Hughes are less intrinsically linguistic, more a matter of 'vision', as when the 'symbol' and the 'symbolised' collapse into a startling literalness in the poem about the vulture-interrogator in *Cave Birds*: 'Some angered righteous questions / Agitate her craw.' As we shall be seeing, Hughes, Redgrove and Heaney are all highly conscious of language, and the contrasting diction of their poetry is one of the features that most significantly distinguishes them from each other. Yet one cannot imagine any of them placing the value Hill places on 'technical discipline' as a thing separately considered, or indeed considering technique as a separate thing at all. In the passages that we have chosen for detailed comparison, it is likely that Hill and many of his admirers would judge that at least two of the writers had debased poetry by a facile reliance on archetypes and myth. The 'visionary', like the 'simple, sensuous and passionate', would be, we suspect; one of the 'beautiful, simple definitions' that Hill believes the modern poet cannot afford to rest in. We believe, however, that our comparison, by bringing out the contrasts in diction and feeling, will reveal something of the intellectual and imaginative discipline with which each poet has discovered and expressed his own meaning in the closely similar archetypal motifs. Parallels that might seem to be evidence of *Zeitgeist* in the merely modish sense, turn out, on close examination, to reveal deeply distinctive qualities in each poet.

The association of the female, mud or earth, and some form of rebirth, is common to all three. None of them, we can safely affirm, would have been written, or would have been quite the same, without the influence of Jung or Graves or both. More generally all of them embody, in varying degrees and proportions, a pervading critique of the masculine intellect, of the Platonic-Christian division between soul and body, and the rape of nature by Western civilisation. Redgrove is a declared Jungian. Hughes is reported by Redgrove to have described Jung, in the 1950s, as 'the philosopher of the next hundred years'.[10] Heaney has described the first of his bog poems as 'an attempt to link, in a symbolic Jungian way, the bog which is in a sense the repository and memory of the landscape with the psyche of the people'.[11]

Heaney's reference is looser, less committed than Hughes' or Redgrove's, but it gives us a more direct access to the particular shaping power that these archetypes have for the poet. In the same interview he goes on to say, of the photographs of sacrificial victims in P. V. Glob's *The Bog People*, 'I saw in these pictures the archetypal symbols of territorial religion and in some ways I think Irish Republicanism is a territorial religion. There's a noumen that presides over the whole gound and she's even enshrined in the Constitution. There's a sacral territory for what used to be called the poor old woman, Cathleen Ni Houlihan, the Aisling figure.' His poem 'Bog Queen' (*North*) begins:

I lay waiting
between turf-face and demesne wall,
between heathery levels
and glass-toothed stone.

My body was braille
for the creeping influences:
dawn suns groped over my head
and cooled at my feet,

through my fabrics and skins
the seeps of winter
digested me,
the illiterate roots

pondered and died
in the cavings
of stomach and socket.
I lay waiting

on the gravel bottom,
my brain darkening,
a jar of spawn
fermenting underground

dreams of Baltic amber.

This poem is based on the only instance in Glob's book of discovery in Ireland. There is no photograph of the woman, since she was found in 1781, another of the 'last afternoons of reasonable light' for Ireland and Europe, by a peat-cutter on the estate of Lord Moira in County Down. The account of the find is written by Lady Moira who, according to Glob, 'paid well' for some of the hair and clothing.[12] This woman, unlike the Tollund Man, the Grauballe Man and the Windeby Bog Girl, is not a victim, either in Glob's book or in Heaney's poem. In Glob she is simply a mysterious well-born lady, possibly a Viking. In the poem she is unmistakably the goddess or 'noumen' herself. Heaney's other Bog People poems, 'The Tollund Man', 'The Grauballe Man', 'Punishment' and 'Strange Fruit', are meditations that begin with the visible evidence and move to and out from the moment of death. It would be unthinkable for the reverent, awestruck writer of those poems to invade the consciousness of the dead people. For 'Bog Queen' on the other hand there is no visible evidence, and no reason for supposing a particularly terrible death. The imagination is therefore freer, the mode more a fantasia than a meditation.

Since the imaginative stimulus in this case does not, like the other Bog People, morally and emotionally demand a contemplation of the death, Heaney can imply, without stating, that she has always been there. 'I lay waiting', she repeats, and the focus is to be on the unearthing, which is ambiguously both a birth and a desecration. She has existed for an indefinite period in a relationship with the earth that has been intimate and natural – 'digested', 'fermenting', and later 'hibernated' – but also slowly destructive of herself – later she tells us that 'My diadem grew carious'. The density and subtlety of the language that conveys this relationship are epitomised in the lines, 'My body was braille / for the creeping influences.' What suggestions of erotic touch, of blindness, and of understanding are combined in the inspired and unexpected word 'braille'.

In one aspect, then, the queen is an earth goddess, at home in the bog: the very goddess, perhaps, to whom the Tollund Man and the Grauballe Man were sacrificed. This is an aspect that she shares with the females of Hughes and Redgrove. But she also has a role in time and history. The moment she is waiting for is an historical moment. 'My diadem grew carious' is not, like the dimming of the diamond in Redgrove's poem, an image of the dissolution of the ego in the collective, of arrogant spirit in benign matter. She must reign above the surface, in human affairs: her burial is a denial of this sovereignty. The line 'between turf-face and demesne wall' is not just a geographical but an historical, social and political location and, characteristically of Heaney, the very diction carries these implications: the local, intimate, benign turf, the foreign, dominating, excluding demesne. The climax of the poem is a condensed three-act drama which is again conveyed in the diction with beautiful subtlety.

My skull hibernated
in the wet nest of my hair.

Which they robbed.
I was barbered
and stripped
by a turfcutter's spade

who veiled me again
and packed coomb softly
between the stone jambs
at my head and my feet.

Till a peer's wife bribed him.
The plait of my hair,
a slimy birth-cord
of bog, had been cut

and I rose from the dark,
hacked bone, skull-ware,
frayed stitches, tufts,
small gleams on the bank.

The sudden incursion of 'robbed', 'barbered' and 'tripped' – the outrage carried in that jarring diction – is, to use Heaney's own word, 'appeased' by the language that describes the turfcutter's atonement for his sacrilege: 'veiled me again and packed coomb softly'. Heaney has said in a letter to Bernard Harrison, 'I used "coomb", a dialect word for turf mould, because I loved the appeasements in the sound, and felt that its benign music would carry it even if its sense were obscure'.[13] Finally the 'bribe' of Lady Moira repeats the sacrilege which is also a delivery, and the queen rises out of the bog to resume a role in history which Heaney leaves for the reader's sense of history to judge.

Whereas, for Heaney, the relevant meanings of the Celtic mythology of *The White Goddess* are immanent in contemporary history, for Hughes they have to be encountered through a more radical imaginative journey. It would be myopic to assert that *Gaudete* has no historical bearings, but for the English poet, unlike Heaney, the essential history that the myth of his poem opens up has not been consciously lived by his people. As Hughes has put it in a letter to ourselves, the 'spirit energy', the 'brilliant real thing', is 'enmired in bodily thickness and ego inertia'.[14] Thus for him the delicate, historically luminous touches of diction such as 'demesne' and 'coomb' are not available. The continuity upon which *Gaudete* draws is underground and has to be processed more thoroughly by the imagination before it can make contact with social reality. In 'Bog Queen' there is hardly any distance between imaginative and social realities. In *Gaudete* the distance is enormous, and this partly accounts for the awkwardness of the poem as a whole. At the same time, to quote the same letter, Hughes is deliberately employing 'a language of enactment, nowhere fine or studied, nowhere remarkable in detail – tolerant of a good deal of vernacular commonplace'. When speaking about Shakespeare and about the dialect of his childhood, Hughes invests the vernacular with a unique power to explore the inner life. This is how the continuity between past and present works in Hughes' language. In contrast to *Gaudete*, the diction and imagery of *Cave Birds* is sometimes strikingly similar to that of 'Bog Queen'. For example, in 'The knight', a meditation on a drawing of a dead bird, compare

He has conquered in earth's name.
Committing these trophies

To the small madness of roots, to the mineral stasis
And to rain . . .

Skylines tug him apart, winds drink him,
Earth itself unravels him from beneath —

with Heaney's

through my fabrics and skins
the seeps of winter
digested me,
the illiterate roots

pondered and died
in the cavings
of stomach and socket.

Or the words of Hughes' goddess/daimon/anima:

      Right from the start, my life
Has been a cold business of mountains and their snow
Of rivers and their mud

with the Bog Queen's

I knew winter cold
like the nuzzle of fjords
at my thighs.

The uses of this motif in *North* and *Gaudete* are the culminations of converging imaginative journeys that begin with the poems that stand at the front, respectively, of Heaney's first volume and Hughes' *Selected Poems*. In 'Digging' Heaney watches, pen in hand, his father digging: 'By god, the old man could handle a spade. /Just like his old man.' The poem, having lovingly devoted some of Heaney's typical early muscular–onomatopoeic diction to the evocation of physical spadework, ends,

But I've no spade to follow men like them.

Between my finger and my thumb
The squat pen rests.
I'll dig with it.

Thus the young poet, with a stated and demonstrated trust in language, attaches what he later calls his 'sedentary trade' to the sanctioned and self-justifying activity of the farmer and his own family history. The motif begins to open up its historical dimension when he returns to it in 'At a Potato Digging', which evokes the Great Hunger, and in 'Bogland', in his second volume, he broaches the symbol whose full potential was to be released by his lucky discovery of P. V. Glob's book.

    The poem 'Toome', in Heaney's third volume, suggests, in a half-playful way, the 'shamanic' parallel to this imaginative process.

This parallel has been there in Hughes from the start, with the emergence of the 'animal helper' spirit from the mind's darkness in 'The Thought-Fox', the awaited rising of a more terrifying dream-vision from the pond at the end of 'Pike', and the invasion of the human world by more fully imagined and articulated spirits from the sea of archaic origins and the unconscious life in 'Ghost Crabs' Interestingly, while Heaney starts with one aspect of farming as his model and subsequently discovers the 'shamanic' dimension, in Hughes this progression is reversed. The vision from which the passage under discussion (pp. 103–6) is extracted begins with Lumb being subjected to the chaos of a herd of frightened cattle: for that, and for the visceral detail which authenticates the rebirth of the goddess, Hughes is surely indebted to the ·experiences so memorably recorded in *Moortown*, particularly 'February 17th', which has its own moments of archetypal vision.

The *Gaudete* episode follows Lumb's discovery of his female parishioners buried alive in a 'drumming downpour'. The rain continues to pour as he sees a being with head, face and hands of mud, but that seems 'almost human', calling to him 'through a moving uncertain hole in the mud face' and reaching towards him.

> The rain striking across the mud face washes it.
> It is a woman's face,
> A face as if sewn together from several faces.
> A baboon beauty face,
> A crudely stitched patchwork of faces,
> But the eyes slide,
> Alive and electrical, like liquid liquorice behind the stitched lids,
> Lumb moves to climb, to half-crawl
> And feels her embrace tighten.   (p. 104)

Lumb's shouting summons sinister 'men in oilskins' who hold him down. After a period of pain, confusion and 'swooning in and out of consciousness' he appears to stand over himself:

> He sees himself being delivered of the woman from the pit,
> The baboon woman,
> Flood-sudden, like the disembowelling of a cow
> She gushes from between his legs, a hot splendour
> In the glistening of oils,
> In a radiance like phosphorous he sees her crawl and tremble.   (p. 105)

Returned in consciousness to his body he discovers himself to be drenched in hot blood. The men are struggling to hold the reborn goddess down, but cannot. Lumb manages to free himself from the entanglement and finally 'sees her face undeformed and perfect'.

What is distinctive about the *Gaudete* passage compared to the

Heaney and Redgrove poems is the nature of the imagined experience and particularly the relationship of the male protagonist to the goddess. The diction is an expression of this. Like the Bog Queen this goddess had a kinship with the mud, but more emphatically than in the Heaney poem her earthboundness is a limitation and suppression of her being, her animal appearance, her stitched, baboon-like face a distortion of her truly human nature. To Lumb, as a man and as an embodiment of the suppression of the feminine in Christianity, she is both a threat and a victim. Having been shown the irremediable fates of the actual women in the story, buried to their necks in mud and screaming, he understands that the 'one creature that he can free' is the feminine in himself. When, to do this, he becomes the mother to his own *anima*, one does not feel that Hughes is drawing on his credit in some 'myth-kitty'. The ritualistic appeasements of the rebirth arche-type are at most glimpsed through a foreground of pain and humilia-tion. The density of the physical experience is a barrier through which each reader must individually pass before he can share in any power the myth might have to bestow order and wholeness. 'Mythical' writing of this order is a world removed from the quaint-sinister antlers and pelts of Lumb's own attempted ritual.

In *The Ironic Harvest* Geoffrey Thurley says that 'Hughes, like Lawrence . . . can never bring himself to submit to the law of the feminine. He is dangerously responsive to the tremors of the ether; he is an agent of the occult. Or is he not a double-agent, one who receives information and uses it for other purposes than the transmitter intended for it . . .?'[15] Peter Redgrove, responding to an essay by one of ourselves which quoted this remark and suggested that the conflict in Hughes is closer to most people's experience than Redgrove's own confidence and serenity, commented:

This is quite possible; yet it is possible also that I am a more feminine personality than Hughes is. It is interesting to me that the more acute reviews of my books have often been written by women. I hope that it may be possible that my vision is closer to most *women's* experience than Hughes' is to date, since I am not a double-agent, but deeply involved with feminine experience as far as I can be as a man. In that case I would see my mission as attempting to arouse the feminine energies in men, and the feminine modes of perception (supposing that I have been able to achieve this in part) and to go some way to confirming them in some public sense so that both men and women may trust them in themselves to a greater extent.[16]

What Redgrove means by 'feminine' is, largely, enjoying comparatively easy communications between the mind and the life of the body. But there is also plenty of evidence throughout his work that his imagination confronts the presence and experience of women without hostility, anxiety or a sense of threat or guilt. The experience of a remarkably large number of his poems is attributed to or shared with a woman, most notably in his later work, but to be seen as early as his first collection, whose best poem, 'Without Eyes', is simply about a woman discovering neglected bodily sensations by closing her eyes:

Sluices her bunched face with closed hands, finds natural grease,
With clinking nails scrabbles for the body of the sprawling soap,
Rubs up the fine jumping lather that grips like a mask, floods it off,
Solving the dingy tallow.
Bloods and pumps her cheeks in the springy towel, a rolling variable darkness
Dimpling the feminine fat-pockets under the deep coombs of bone
And the firm sheathed jellies above that make silent lightning in their bulbs.

In 'The Idea of Entropy at Maenporth Beach' there is, though never stated, an underlying sense of a male observer, but his involvement in the incident is entirely celebratory.

A boggy wood as full of springs as trees.
Slowly she slipped into the muck.
It was a white dress, she said, and that was not right.
Leathery polished mud, that stank as it split.
It is a smooth white body, she said, and that is not right,
Not quite right; I'll have a smoother,
Slicker body, and my golden hair
Will sprinkle rich goodness everywhere.
So slowly she backed into the mud.

If it were a white dress, she said, with some little black,
Dressed with a little flaw, a smut, some swart
Twinge of ancestry, or if it were all black
Since I am white, but – it's my mistake.
So slowly she slunk, all pleated, into the muck.

The mud spatters with rich seed and ranging pollens.
Black darts up the pleats, black pleats
Lance along the white ones, and she stops
Swaying, cut in half. Is it right, she sobs
As the fat, juicy, incredibly tart muck rises
Round her throat and dims the diamond there?
It is right, so she stretches her white neck back
And takes a deep breath once and a one step back.
Some golden strands afloat pull after her.

For a moment the mud 'recoils' over her, then she swiftly re-emerges, all black except for her blue eyes, and runs on the beach, 'sprinkling substance' of mud, as she goes. She laughs aloud and says,

Now that I am all black, and running in my richness
And knowing it a little, I have learnt
It is quite wrong to be all white always;
And knowing it a little, I shall take great care
To keep a little black about me somewhere.

A snotty nostril, a mourning nail will do.
Mud is a good dress, but not the best.

The poem ends with a vision of metamorphosis and matter made articulate.

The black rooks coo like doves, new suns beam
From every droplet of the shattering waves,
From every crystal of the shattered rock.
Drenched in the mud, pure white, rejoiced,
From this collision were new colours born,
And in their slithering passage to the sea
The shrugged-up riches of deep darkness sang.

The female in the poem is not in the first place a goddess, noumen, *daimon* or *anima* but a woman discovering something for herself; secondarily, for the implied male observer, she represents the 'feminine' power in himself to break down the barrier between the 'diamond' of the self-sufficient soul and the 'fat, juicy' organic mud of the body. (In the dimming of the diamond there is perhaps an echo of Hopkins's 'immortal diamond' as well as of the diamond/carbon analogy in Lawrence's famous letter to Edward Garnett.) The effect of the woman's symbolic aspect is entirely one of release, not of challenge, and almost everything about the poem combines to make a strong contrast with the feeling of the *Gaudete* passage. The very title, thumbing its nose at Wallace Stevens' 'Idea of Order at Key West', makes an impression of playful wit which is immediately substantiated by the contrast with Stevens' solemn sonorous diction, and by the incongruity of this woman representing an 'Idea': 'Slowly she slipped into the muck'. The sensuousness of the language is self-conscious; Redgrove draws on a distinct register of mimetic, energetic, colloquial Anglo-Saxon diction with such words as 'muck', 'smut', 'slunk' and 'snotty'. This self-conscious enjoyment of diction is one sign of Redgrove's characteristic high spirits and joviality. It is rescued from preciosity by the energy and variety of the rhythm:

        Is it right, she sobs
As the fat, juicy, incredibly tart muck rises
Round her throat and dims the diamond there?

Who is that negress running on the beach
Laughing excitedly with teeth as white
As the white waves kneeling, dazzled, to the sands?

In the second example the energy is not only of rhythm but of metaphorical conception, reminiscent of Donne or Marvell.

Diction and rhythm however do not disguise the fact that the poem is much more directly metaphysical (in the true, not the literary sense) than either the Hughes or the Heaney. Redgrove's way of imagining the motifs of immersion and rebirth does not erect the barriers, not entail the struggle, that are so integral to the *Gaudete* passage. His mud is not suffocating. The rebirth in his poem does not demand the actual death that Lumb comes close to in this passage, and the protagonist of *Cave Birds* undergoes through the course of several poems. The immersion in the mud is as symbolic as the Christian baptism that it parodies (again, contrast Lumb's baptism in blood in the Prologue to *Gaudete*). Lumb's rebirth and the birth of the Goddess out of himself are a single event; the achievement of this moment finally refutes Geoffrey Thurley's point about submission to the law of the feminine, while the struggle that the achievement entails, indicates how close it is to the truth.

In fact struggle and search have dominated Hughes' poetry. If it is true to say that Redgrove's poetry is the more feminine because he is more in touch at a biological level with his own nature it is conversely true that for Hughes the gulf between consciousness and the natural world has been the dynamic of his poetry. Redgrove's writing on shamanism emphasises the healing effect of 'deepening' the world, of bringing things into relation, of wholeness.[17] Hughes himself has spoken recently of the healing effect of magic in discussing the 'magic'[18] of poetry, but his first references to shamanism emphasised the process of flight and return. Of course Hughes is interested in the vision that results: 'The risen' at the end of *Cave Birds* is an example; but even that poem ends in a question. It is perhaps an oversimplification to say that Redgrove's poems are the results of having come through the fire whilst Hughes is also interested in the tension and pain of the fire. Better to say that Hughes is interested in negotiation and the terms of negotiation, whilst Redgrove re-examines the results.

This difference arises fundamentally from the sense that Redgrove is not searching, exploring in his poems but that they are re-enactments. Redgrove gives the impression of practising his enlightenment in his poetry. Since his vision is so confidently held his humour is relaxed, even throwaway:

I do not like the vicar's dress.
That blank throat needs a pretty bridge.
His chest is black, his pants cut
Apocryphal, without a bulge. I think the vicar
Is always searching for his missing tie:
It would keep body and soul together.
    ('Pictures from a Shirtmaker's Apprentice': *From Every Chink of the Ark*)

Hughes' humour by contrast usually expresses and releases tension and a sense of disharmony:

When men got to the summit

Light words forsook them.
They filled with heavy silence.

Houses came to support them,
But the hard, foursquare scriptures fractured
And the cracks filled with soft rheumatism.

> ('When Men Got To The Summit': *Remains of Elmet*)

These differences are also revealed in each poet's use of what is conventionally called 'pathetic fallacy'. In Redgrove this is so bold as to make us question whether it is in any sense metaphorical. When Hughes speaks of a stone dreaming in 'Pibroch' he is using it as a metaphor for a certain form of human consciousness:

A pebble is imprisoned
Like nothing in the Universe.
Created for black sleep. Or growing
Conscious of the sun's red spot occasionally,
Then dreaming it is the foetus of God.

The irony of that is unmistakable and characteristic. But what is the tone of the opening of this poem by Peter Redgrove, 'Minerals of Cornwall, Stones of Cornwall'?

Splinters of information, stones of information,
Drab stones in a drab box, specimens of a distant place,
Granite, galena, talc, lava, kaolin, quartz,
Landscape in a box, under the dull sky of Leeds —
One morning was awake, in Cornwall, by the estuary,
In the tangy pearl-light, tangy tin-light,
And the stones were awake, these ounce-chips,
Had begun to think, in the place they came out of.

> (*Dr. Faust's Sea-Spiral Spirit*)

The 'thinking' of these stones is unironical. It is a sign of their integration into the living processes of the natural world, of their being what the next line describes as 'tissues of the earth, in their proper place'. As Redgrove has said in an interview, 'I find the conceptual link between mind and matter a very easy one. I find no division between mind and body; I am not a Cartesian man. I find that it is very easy to think of matter as being conscious on a molecular level.'[19] The reader is invited to adopt the vision of the writer in not treating his images as metaphors.

Given Redgrove's vision it is not surprising to find that metamorphosis is common in his poetry and that it 'happens' naturally rather than being 'used' metaphorically, often and easily. In Hughes' poems metamorphosis is usually painful as the whole experience of *Cave*

Birds indicates. In Hughes it is the experience that is important, as much on a moral as a physical level. Indeed here is the source of difficulty in Redgrove's poetry. His freewheeling ability to move through the world in images can become more a skittering across surfaces than a stepping from centre to centre. His poetry seems to us to be at its best when it develops a single image, as in 'The Idea of Entropy'. It is at these times that he is most likely to convey the felt experience. A fine recent example is 'Silence Fiction' *(The Apple Broadcast)*. The protagonists of this poem live in a house built over an early cave dwelling, to which they are admitted by 'a besmirched woman' in 'defiled white'. While they 'Light in the chimney-roots our lower fires, And begin our lives on the unadorned earth floor', the wind and rain can be heard cleansing the upper hearth of its 'soot-flowers'. The poem concludes with their return to the house on the surface, and conveys the calm of the remembered lower levels which are the foundations of the 'chattering' conscious life.

> Then we return
>
> To the sunlit chimneys and the whitened hearths,
> Out of the earth cradle; quenching the flares,
>
> Troop chattering out of the cellar stairs,
> Draw baths and strop to mirror-glass the rusty razors,
>
> Secure the lower doors with their immense keys we hang
> Shining bright in the chimneys; light our upper fires.
>
> The black soot feathers through generations on the long keys.
> We recall wondering, occasionally, that in those cellars
>
> We never spoke, not at any time; once through the door
> We were to keep and breathe the silence
>
> That had gathered there like foundation water
> In the roots of the chattering houses, deep and pure.

'Silence Fiction' exemplifies the way in which Redgrove's most recent poetry, while clearly personal in its origins, retains very strongly an archetypal structure or, to put it another way, the forms of the unconscious life. Hughes and Heaney however have developed, partly alongside and partly subsequent to such work as *Gaudete* and 'Bog Queen', what is for them a more directly autobiographical poetry. In the farming poems of *Moortown* and the love poems of *Field Work* one senses a confidence in each poet of now living through his major themes, the areas of his search; their subject matter at its most universal can now be seen, felt, understood in their own living. And this is not simply a return to the autobiographical mode of such early poems as 'The Hawk in the Rain' and 'Death of a Naturalist'. Whereas the material of those poems is overtly controlled and composed by the writer, poems such as 'February 17th' and 'The Skunk' are much closer to the intimacy and vulnerability of the living moment.

'February 17th', Hughes' poem about delivering a still-born lamb, is a record of a practical activity, with its unreflective and mostly unmetaphorical manner of objective recording, stands in relation to the *Gaudete* vision, both as realistic authentication of its archetypes and as example of the day-to-day engagement that the vision demands. Perhaps its most remarkable feature is that unmistakable archetypal suggestions emerge, without any apparent intention of the poet, from the literal fact: the hacked-off head of the lamb staring at its mother 'With all earth for a body' (an image of literal unity in death); the shift from deadlock to co-operation in the relation between the poet's pushing and the elemental 'birth-push' of the ewe. There is a sense of trial in the poet's entry into the sheep's interior. But such suggestions of vision are firmly subordinated to the sense of practical necessity and, indeed, of practical failure.

Heaney's 'Skunk' is a more artful, reflective and self-conscious poem but its art serves a fidelity to the living moment of extraordinary connection which inspired it and which it celebrates.

Up, black, striped and damasked like the chasuble
At a funeral mass, the skunk's tail
Paraded the skunk. Night after night
I expected her like a visitor.

The refrigerator whinnied into silence.
My desk light softened beyond the verandah.
Small oranges loomed in the orange tree.
I began to be tense as a voyeur.

These opening stanzas recall, not any earlier poem of Heaney's, but 'The Thought-Fox'. The resemblance is probably unintentional but if, as we have suggested, 'The Thought-Fox' inaugurates the visionary quest of Hughes' poetry, the contrast that ensues is a pungent one. In the early Hughes poem, the poet's outer world – the world of 'the clock's loneliness' and his fingers moving on the page – is empty of value and almost of substance. The vision of the fox is hermetically sealed in the poem. Heaney has enough confidence in his outer reality to fuse the image of his animal-spirit visitor with a domestic sexuality that is not only 'intent and glamorous' but ordinary and playful. The poem certainly celebrates both the skunk and the marriage, but above all the living moment in which the connection is made. This connection arises out of the fact that, when he sees the skunk, the poet is away from his wife and 'composing Love-letters again, broaching the word "wife" Like a stored cask'. The poem ends:

And there she was, the intent and glamorous,
Ordinary, mysterious skunk,
Mythologised, demythologised,
Snuffing the boards five feet beyond me.

It all came back to me last night, stirred
By the sootfall of your things at bedtime,
Your head-down, tail-up hunt in a bottom drawer
For the black plunge-line nightdress.

Heaney's skunk is 'mythologised, demythologised', finally revealing the mystery of its ordinariness. Hughes writes about an episode in a farmer's life that seems inescapably to throw up archetypal symbols, but they heighten rather than swamp the solidity and urgency of the lived experience in the outer world. Neither poem, we feel, would be the same if the poets had not explored archetypes and myths as seriously as they have. At the same time their fidelity to the living moment, achieved in such different ways, confirms for us, if we need confirmation, that that explanation was not an aesthetic escape from realities but a quest undertaken with the purpose, in words of Goethe quoted by Hughes, of 'keeping faith with the world of things and the world of spirits equally'.

Chapters of a shared mythology: Sylvia Plath and Ted Hughes

'I need no sorrow to write . . . My poems and stories I want to be the strongest female paean yet for the creative forces of nature.'[1] The words are Sylvia Plath's from *Letters Home* to her mother written during the first few months of her relationship with Ted Hughes. '[H]aving been on the other side of life like Lazarus, I know that my whole being shall be one song of affirmation and love all my life long.' Several poems of the period actually turn this manifesto into practice and the changes in content, style and mood over her earlier ones are remarkable. Still in 'the old style' is a poem she wrote after first meeting Hughes at a 'wild *St Botolph's Review* party' – 'a brilliant ex-Cambridge poet . . . the only man I've met yet here who'd be strong enough to be equal with'. Still, Plath felt hypnotised by 'the simple, seductive beauty' of her own words in evoking a 'symbol of the terrible beauty of death'.

There is a panther stalks me down:
  One day I'll have my death of him;
  His greed has set the woods aflame,
He prowls more lordly than the sun.

In fact, it was Hughes himself who prompted Plath to write 'Pursuit'. But their subsequent love affair and marriage inspired her, at least temporarily, to write poems of a different kind. Most of them are about Hughes himself who, in 'Ode for Ted', has turned, from a symbol of death, into an Osiris-like fertility god.

For his least look, scent acres yield:
each finger-furrowed field
heaves forth stalk, leaf, fruit-nubbed emerald;
bright grain sprung so rarely
he hauls to his will early;
at his hand's staunch hest, birds build.

Another poem from the same period, 'Wreath for a Bridal', shows how nature is reborn from the mating of two lovers who 'bedded like angels . . . burn one in fever'.

From this holy day on, all pollen blown
Shall strew broadcast so rare a seed on wind
That every breath, thus teeming, set the land
Sprouting fruit, flowers, children most fair in legion
To slay spawn of dragon's teeth: speaking this promise,
Let flesh be knit, and each step hence go famous.[2]

Curiously enough, this imagery of bride and bridegroom, love and rebirth is practically absent from Hughes' work of the same period. Nor did it survive in Plath's own. While she continued to rave about the creative forces of nature which, prompted by her husband, she would henceforth celebrate in her verse, poems of more sinister note soon made themselves heard again. And even those from the happy years of her marriage do not return to the simple celebration of a life-giving 'wedlock wrought within love's proper chapel'.[3] As Hughes may have noticed at the time, Plath's poetic genius was not to realise itself in a world of make-believe, into which, although he inspired it, he could not follow his wife himself. No wonder that the defiant opening of 'Wreath for a Bridal' sounds more convincing than the poem's actual message. However strong her desire for rebirth, Plath's sojourn on the other side of sanity and life had left traces not to be erased by a mere new philosophy of life.

It was this season in hell which, when she finally confronted it, inspired her greatest work – 'Johnny Panic and the Bible of Dreams', *The Bell Jar* and the poetry after 'The Stones'. Yet even here, little suggests the rebirth which some of her critics have sought to find in her work. Her poems, in Hughes' words, may well be 'chapters in a mythology where the plot, seen as a whole and in retrospect, is strong and clear'.[4] But to trace this plot from her descent into disintegration towards 'Rebirth, and Transcendence',[5] is to add two chapters which Plath herself left unwritten. Lady Lazarus' transformation into a red-haired vampire who will 'eat men like air'[6] hardly qualifies the poet for a rebirth in mythic terms, and little else in her late work sustains this transformation beyond the occasional yearning in that direction. Her suicide in February 1963 put a tragic end to the possibilities of any such development.

Yet her mythic journey was not discontinued altogether. A sequel, as we shall show in detail, is found in Hughes' work which even more than his wife's is best read as chapters in a continuous mythology. In other words, Hughes' more recent development owes a great deal to Plath, and only if seen in this conjunction, does the plot connecting both appear to us strong and clear in retrospect. A recent poem from Hughes' *Cave Birds*, 'Bride and groom lie hidden for three days', reintroduces some of the symbolism which Plath's 'Wreath for a Bridal' used some twenty years earlier. Here also, bride and groom enjoy a rebirth through love, but their starting point is the nadir of disintegration, so powerfully evoked in many of Plath's mature poems.[7]

I

The opening scenario of the mythic journey in which Hughes' development continues Plath's is 'the city of spare parts . . . where men are mended' from 'The Stones'.[8] Written in late 1959 at Yaddo, the poem, like 'Lady Lazarus', describes a rebirth process *à rebours*. The speaker's patchwork reconstruction with the help of technological medicine ends on a note of grim irony, to which Plath's immediate source, 'The City Where Men Are Mended', a story from Paul Radin's *African Folktales and African Sculpture*, provides the appropriate backdrop. Here the hoped-for rebirth of an ugly daughter who has been killed by her evil mother for this purpose turns into a grotesque disaster. With only 'one leg, one buttock, one hand',[9] the resurrected daughter is far more monstrous than before her death. Plath's poem lacks this fairy-tale directness, but the speaker's final 'I shall be good as new' points up an equal failure.

This is the after-hell . . .
. . .

A current agitates the wires
Volt upon volt. Catgut stitches my fissures.
. . .

My swaddled legs and arms smell sweet as rubber.
Here they can doctor heads, or any limb.
. . .

My mendings itch. There is nothing to do.
I shall be good as new.

Whatever rebirth has been achieved here is as cosmetic as a face-lift.
Not new but good as new.

'The Stones' owes much to the influence of Ted Hughes. Writing
blocks had always been one of Plath's worst problems, but with her
husband she learned to break them by just pouring out 'a few pages of
drivel until the juice came back'.[10] Hughes also encouraged his wife to
sharpen and focus her vision partly by hypnotising her, partly by
setting her daily 'exercises of concentration and observation'. Exploring their dreams helped them discard the conscious use of 'symbols,
irony, archetypal images and all that' as favoured by the New
Criticism. What's more, Hughes taught Plath not to read novels and
poems only, but 'books on folklore, fiddler crabs and meteorites'. As a
result she discovered *African Folktales and African Sculpture* which,
in Hughes' words, worked an 'explosive transformation'[11] in her
poetry. In Radin's collection, which she read at Yaddo, Plath 'found the
underworld of her worst nightmares throwing up intensely beautiful
adventures, where the most unsuspected voices thrived under the
pressures of a reality that made most accepted fiction seem artificial
and spurious'.[12]

Even more crucial was Hughes' role in freeing her imagination and
hence unleashing her worst nightmares. In his own creative endeavours, he had long been familiar with handbooks of Cabbalistic and
Hermetic magic, which Plath learned to use in the same pursuit. While
at Yaddo, they devised 'exercises of meditation and invocation', while
Sylvia, as her husband recalls, started a 'deliberate exercise in
experimental improvisation on set themes'. The result of this
magically liberated imagination, in which Plath fused private nightmares with primitive myth, was 'The Stones'. 'She had never in her life
improvised. The powers that compelled her to write so slowly had
always been stronger than she was. But quite suddenly she found
herself free to let herself drop, rather than inch over bridges of concept.'

As is easily recognised even without Hughes' reminder, 'The Stones'
'is full of specific details of her experience in a mental hospital, and . . .
clearly enough the first eruption of the voice that produced *Ariel*'. As
such the poem has a prelude in Plath's life. In 1958, after a year of
academic teaching, she escaped from a writing block into a job in the
records office for mental patients in the Massachusetts General
Hospital. No doubt the experience brought back all the worst
memories of her life. How she had suffered a nervous breakdown after
her 1953 *Mademoiselle* venture in the glossy world of New York's
literary establishment. How she had been subjected to out-patient

electroshock treatment and how, as a result, she had finally decided to take her life. ECT therapy forced upon her the idea that the only alternative to death 'was an eternity of hell for the rest of my life in a mental hospital'.[13]

I figured that in the long run it would be more merciful and inexpensive to my family; instead of an indefinite and expensive incarceration of a favourite daughter in the cell of a State San, instead of the misery and disillusion of sixty odd years of mental vacuum, of physical squalor, I would spare them all by ending everything at the height of my so-called career.

This had been followed by an unwelcome rescue from death, and further electroshock treatment, by now administered to the hospital-ised mental patient waking up 'in shuddering horror and fear of the cement tunnels leading down to the shock room'.

No wonder that 'Johnny Panic and the Bible of Dreams', a short story prompted by these memories, after first publication in the *Atlantic* of September 1968, found its way into Thomas Szasz' 1973 *The Age of Madness*, an anthology of selected texts documenting *The History of Involuntary Mental Hospitalisation*. In an even more striking way, the story corroborates Szasz' argument in his previous *The Manufacture of Madness: a Comparative Study of the Inquisition and the Mental Health Movement*. Long before the birth of anti-psychiatry, its semi-surrealistic account of how a crew of 'false priests' give the heroine ECT punishment for being a 'little witch' who 'has been making time with Johnny Panic', revealed the Christian inquisitorial implications of electroshock therapy.

The white cot is ready. With a terrible gentleness Miss Milleravage takes the watch from my wrist, the rings from my fingers, the hairpins from my hair. She begins to undress me. When I am bare, I am anointed on the temples and robed in sheets virginal as the first snow.
Then, from the four corners of the room and from the door behind me come five false priests in white surgical gowns and masks whose one lifework is to unseat Johnny Panic from his own throne . . .
The signal is given.
The machine betrays them.
At the moment when I think I am most lost the face of Johnny Panic appears in a nimbus of arc lights on the ceiling overhead. I am shaken like a leaf in the teeth of glory. His beard is lightning. Lightning is in his eye. His Word charges and illumines the universe.
The air crackles with his blue-tongued lightning-haloed angels.
His love is the twenty-story leap, the rope at the throat, the knife at the heart.
He forgets not his own.[14]

Though hardly confessional in content, Plath's mature poetry stems from a clearly biographical impulse which was finally liberated through her work on *The Bell Jar*. The novel was begun in 1960 and completed in the summer of 1962. Crucial to it as to 'Johnny Panic' is what Nancy Hunter, the novelist's room-mate at Smith College, describes as Plath's profound 'horror of doctors and hospitals'. Certain events after Plath's release from the mental hospital struck Hunter 'as if all the commonplace machinery of the profession that had diagnosed and treated her wretchedness of the summer before had somehow absorbed her misery, as if her emotional problems had not been solved but had merely been lifted from her, and hidden away in some antiseptic storage room'.[15] Yet her all-absorbing working partnership with Hughes somehow gave her the courage to enter that secret focus of her anguish. In the surrealism of 'Johnny Panic' this had still been made to appear as if all had merely happened in a nightmare. But now she faced it with the directness of a prose style that has few precedents in Anglo-American literature.

Through the slits of my eyes, which I didn't dare open too far, lest the full view strike me dead, I saw the high bed with its white, drumtight sheet, and the machine behind the bed, and the masked person – I couldn't tell whether it was a man or a woman – behind the machine, and other masked people flanked the bed on both sides . . .

Miss Huey began to talk in a low, soothing voice, smoothing the salve on my temples and fitting the small electric buttons on either side of my head. 'You'll be perfectly all right, you won't feel a thing, just bite down . . .' And she set something on my tongue and in panic I bit down, and darkness wiped me out like chalk on a blackboard.[16]

In describing the results of such treatment, the novelist probably remembered her earlier, mythopoeic account in 'The Stones'. 'There ought, I thought, to be a ritual for being born twice – patched, retreaded and approved for the road.' But as in the poem, expectations of an actual rebirth have been frustrated. 'I had hoped, at my departure, I would feel sure and knowledgeable about everything that lay ahead – after all, I had been "analysed." Instead, all I could see were question marks.'

Even more desperate in tone than *The Bell Jar* are some of the poems from the time during and after the novel was written. 'At twenty I tried to die / . . . But they pulled me out of the sack, / And they stuck me together with glue.'[17] The fact of her desecration has turned into a role which she derisively enacts to herself and others.

There is a charge

For the eyeing of my scars, there is a charge
For the hearing of my heart —
It really goes.

And there is a charge, a very large charge
For a word or a touch
Or a bit of blood

Or a piece of my hair or my clothes.
So, so, Herr Doktor.
So, Herr Enemy.

I am your opus.

The forces of nature which Plath wanted to celebrate, now threaten with annihilation. 'Tulips', in recording another hospital experience, evokes the familiar imagery of mental and physical disintegration.

I am nobody; I have nothing to do with explosions.
I have given my name and my day-clothes up to the nurses
And my history to the anaesthetist and my body to surgeons.

To this fragmented self, the very odour and colour of the flowers have become deadly threats in their vitality. Their redness seems to talk to her wounds, their vividness to eat her oxygen, their mere presence to hurt, upset and depress her. 'The tulips should be behind bars like dangerous animals; / They are opening like the mouth of some great African cat.'

In 'Purdah', even the bridegroom who had promised rejuvenation of both nature and self has joined the rest of the world in treating her like a manipulable parrot of his own needs and desires. The poem was written after the final estrangement from Hughes, a fact which left Plath in the full presence of her most anguishing memories but without the safeguards that had made her dare confront them. In this situation, the urge towards a self-demonisation enabling VPher to destroy her destroyers, offered a specious defence against despair. Instead of being reborn through her bridegroom, she will be transmogrified into a lioness out to murder him.

I shall unloose —
From the small jewelled
Doll he guards like a heart —

The lioness,
The shriek in the bath,
The cloak of holes.[18]

'Don't talk to me about the world needing cheerful stuff!' Plath wrote to her mother less than four months before her death. 'What the person out of Belsen – physical or psychological – wants is nobody saying the birdies still go tweet-tweet, but the full knowledge that somebody else has been there and knows the *worst*.'[19] Yet even before the poet broke down under such knowledge, her poems seem to admit failure in their very defiance. In 'Purdah' as much as in 'Lady Lazarus' or 'Daddy', the attempt to exchange roles with the murderous panther of 'Pursuit' remains a mere gesture, powerful for its self-conscious irony rather than for suggesting fulfilment.

Such irony turns elaborate sarcasm in 'The Applicant' which can be read as the last chapter in Plath's abortive mythological tale of *sponsus* and *sponsa* seeking rebirth in each other's love. Again, there is an attempt to exchange roles. As a worthy partner of his desecrated bride, the applicant bridegroom is supposed to share her patchwork personality.

First, are you our sort of a person?
Do you wear
A glass eye, false teeth or a crutch,
A brace or a hook,
Rubber breasts or a rubber crotch,

Stitches to show something's missing? No, no? Then
How can we give you a thing?[20]

But the right bride for this empty-headed applicant is finally found – 'A living doll . . . / It can sew, it can cook, / It can talk, talk, talk.' Of course, no rebirth can spring from the mechanical union of these robot-like creatures. It simply 'works, there is nothing wrong with it'.

You have a hole, it's a poultice.
You have an eye, it's an image.
My boy, it's your last resort.
Will you marry it, marry it, marry it.

II

It is possible that Elaine, a character in Hughes' 1960 radio play *The House of Aries*, owes part of her insight into her dilemma to Plath's 'Johnny Panic and the Bible of Dreams'. As in the short story, the desecration of the female is related to the Inquisition and Western religious history in general.

I have cried out and become silent at the will of the Inquisitors,
I have drowned in the blood of my family at the Reformation and Counter-
        Reformation,
Every heresy's banner is a strip of skin off my back.[21]

But generally speaking, the continuance of Plath's mythology in Hughes' work owes little to direct borrowing. '[T]his whole business of influences is mysterious', Hughes told me in 1970. 'Sometimes it's just a few words that open up a whole prospect. They may occur anywhere.

Then again the influences that really count are most likely not literary at all.'[22] The sudden emergence of a Lady Lazarus-figure in Hughes' 1962 radio play *The Wound* gives us an instance of such subliminal transference. Here a female Chorus describes the dissection of a living woman conducted under the auspices of an international assembly of scientists including a delegation of 'experimental psychologists of four countries'.[23] Like the play as a whole, this episode is the more or less direct transcript of a nightmare. 'I dreamt the whole thing twice, waking up in between', Hughes recalled in 1977. 'And when I woke the second time I wrote down as much as I could remember.'[24]

THIRD:	Under intense illuminations, they were not in the dark, they did not brave the interior unprepared, their eyes followed their fingers inward.
FOURTH:	And what did they find did they find what they hoped for.
FIRST:	Lusted for.
SECOND:	Sliced me for.
THIRD:	Did they find the gold teeth.
FOURTH:	The plastic gums.
FIRST:	The glass eyes.
SECOND:	The steel skull-plates.
THIRD:	The jawbone rivets.
FOURTH:	The rubber arteries.[25]

Part of the same dream was a later episode in which the play's protagonist, a wounded soldier by the name of Ripley, finds a champion among the Bacchantes-like demon prostitutes at a Queen's château. Ripley at first rejects this 'Girl' but finally, after she has turned into his guide, becomes her bridegroom. Despite the obvious parallels with the Plath mythology, Hughes' version is distinct for its greater display of violence, detailed scenario and ultimately more optimistic orientation. The demonisation of the female which in 'Lady Lazarus' or 'Purdah' remains a largely histrionic gesture, has reached a forcefulness reminiscent of Euripides' *The Bacchae*. Ripley's fellow traveller Sergeant Massey, for instance, is torn apart by the other women at the château. 'One had his leg between her thighs and was trying to twist his foot off. His arms were out of their sockets.' Elsewhere in the play, similar violence is enacted in a setting which reappears in later works like *Eat Crow* and *Gaudete*. A mud pool ('good earth at other times, mother of mankind') turns into a slaughterhouse – 'These women are dragging them all into the ground, it's a massacre.' Despite all this, the play ends on a note of hope. Although a potentially murderous ogress like the rest, the 'Girl', when Ripley throws her away, '*cries out, hurt*', protesting that she loves him. And Ripley, aware of his desecration as much as she is of hers, finally decides to marry her. Hughes avoids the facile rebirth symbolism of poems like

Plath's early 'Wreath for a Bridal,' but there is a hint that in the sequel of their story which remained undreamt and unwritten, Ripley and the Girl might become each other's saviours.

GIRL: Lean on me. Try to walk.
RIPLEY: No, no . . . My feet are stuck in the mud.
            We'd better wait till the rain stops.
GIRL: You can walk. You're walking.
RIPLEY: What's your name? Ah, yes, you told me, didn't you.
            Did you? My memory's been dismantled.
            If ever I get back to streets do you know what I'll do?
            I'll marry you.

Like its beginning, the subsequent chapters of Hughes' mythopoeic quest were inextricably bound up with the destiny of his wife. Her main obsession had entered his imagination through a nightmare. And what transmogrified this obsession into Hughes' own mythic idiom, also suggested to him a way out of the problem. Such hope, however, was cut short by their break-up in 1962 and Plath's suicide in February 1963. After that, Hughes spent over a year working on a verse drama adaptation of *The Chemical Wedding of Christian Rosencreutz* by the seventeenth-century hermeticist Johann Valentin Andreae. At the time, this key text of *sponsa* and *sponsus* mysticism must have appeared to Hughes like a retroactive verification of what otherwise seemed so irretrievably lost to his own vision. Predictably, the effort ended in failure. But at the same time it shows the depth with which some of the nightmare hieroglyphs of Plath's mythology had taken hold of his imagination. The drama was to bear the characteristic title *Difficulties of a Bridegroom*, and its largest published fragment *Eat Crow*, revives some of the basic themes of *The Wound*. Like Ripley, the protagonist, named Morgan, undergoes a shamanistic descent into disintegration amidst the familiar scenario of Hughes' underworld, complete with cattle stampede and lamenting women. Finally, a 'She' emerges from this female chorus to become Morgan's guide. But there is no hint of their sexual or mystical union, let alone salvation. The only sign of hope is communicated through a symbol which was to find its full efflorescence in Hughes' work over the following years.

SHE:
A crow is a sign of life. Even though it sits motionless . . . The crow is composed of terrible black voice . . . But voice that can hardly utter. He looks this way and that . . . resigned to the superior stamina of the empty horizon, limber and watchful.

MORGAN:
The laws are still with the living . . . A crow has come up from the maker of the world.[26]

The Wound and *Difficulties of a Bridegroom* both are attempts in the dramatic mode. But even the poems written since 1962 for the most part are offshoots of a continuous mythic narrative which increasingly focused on the story of Crow. 'It's a way', Hughes explained to me in 1977, 'of getting a big body of ideas and energy moving on a track. For when this energy connects with a possibility for a poem, there is a lot more material and pressure in it than you could ever get into a poem just written out of the air or out of a special occasion'[27] The general framework of this narrative, which is more fully reproduced elsewhere,[28] deals with God's nightmare's attempt to improve on man in a second creation. Its central episode, however, has its roots in the Plath mythology and shows Hughes' ongoing concern with the rescue of a desecrated female at the hands of an equally disintegrated male.

At some point early in Crow's adventures, as related to me early in 1970, the protagonist makes contact with a woman who keeps repeatedly appearing at the nadir of the episodes. She is always in some terrible condition and undergoing some awful torment, so that in a way his whole quest becomes a quest to liberate her. But everything goes wrong until finally, at the very bottom of many different levels of adventure, he is in fact to save her, to lose her again, and to pursue her until she becomes his bride. Like the rest of the story, this part of it, so Hughes insisted in 1977, was 'just a way of getting the poems.'[29] But there was further reason why this particular episode should have remained untapped in *From The Life & Songs of the Crow*. In 1969, Sylvia Plath's suicide of six years earlier found a fatal repetition in the deaths of his companion and their child, and again, as in the case of *The Wound*, a happy conclusion to the poet's central mythopoeic quest was removed from his grasp. Hughes dedicated *Crow* to the memory of Assia and Shura, but whatever poems had a direct bearing on his quest were apparently excluded from the volume itself. Only a few of these surfaced in a small edition after 1970.

One such poem, 'Crow's Song About God', reflects the beginning of the Crow narrative. Man, who has suffered the disintegration familiar in the Plath–Hughes mythology since 'The Stones', has come to the gates of heaven in order to hand his life back to God.

Eyesockets empty
Stomach laid open
To the inspection of the stars
The operation unfinished
(The doctors ran off, there was some other emergency).[30]

Another poem features a female victim of similar desecration, perhaps the one to become Crow's bride:

She tried to keep her breasts
They were cut from her and canned
She tried to keep her cunt
It was produced in open court she was sentenced—[31]

A third describes God's abortive attempt to provide Crow with a bride made up of the burnt carcasses of hags of which cartloads are shipped into the furnaces of heaven.[32] But as in the published fragment *Difficulties of a Bridegroom*, none of these poems deals with the union of this monster bride and bridegroom or with their mutual salvation.

Although his poetic quest for the rescue of the desecrated female remained unfulfilled, the theme widened in significance to Hughes. Talking to me in 1970, the poet described *The Waste Land* as T. S. Eliot's love elegy for a desecrated female. During the same year, we find him pondering the 'subtly apotheosised misogyny of Reformed Christianity' and its 'fanatic rejection of Nature' as well as prophesying something 'unthinkable only ten years ago, except as a poetic dream: the re-emergence of Nature as the Great Goddess of mankind, and the Mother of all life'.[33] In 1971, he diagnosed Shakespeare's supposed 'knot of obsessions'[34] as reflecting the major psychic conflict of his time, the struggle between Calvinistic witch-hunt misogyny and the Celtic pre-Christian Mother worship surviving in the cult of the Queen. 'It was a gigantic all-inclusive trial' which finally, in the seventeenth century, led to 'an upheaval of Civil War and an epidemic of murders of women'. Infected by the sickness of his age like most others, Shakespeare himself, so Hughes argued, joined the same misogynist witch-hunt in finally banishing 'Venus, as Sycorax, the blue-eyed hag'.

Misrepresented as Shakespeare's development may be in this, the poet's own path took a major impulse from the attempt to retrieve Mother Nature from the desecration in which Shakespeare and others were thought to have left her. *Orghast*, a mythic play in a language of pure sound scripted for a 1971 performance in Shiraz directed by Peter Brook, centred on a tale of repression and rebirth which in a way parallels, continues and inverts the victory of the male over the female principle as told in ancient myths like Hesiod's *Theogony* and the Mesopotamian *Enuma elish*. Krogon (the half-brother of Marduk, Kronos and Zeus) imprisons his mother Moa – like Tiamat or Gaia the 'womb of all' – who, along with his father, the Sun, represented the divine harmony of nature. But their repressed energy is finally allowed to resume its flow of creativity with Krogon withering to a 'senile, birdlike thing, croaking empty sounds' before the universe resumes its natural course, undivided and reconciled to itself.[35]

None of all this, however, amounts to a major reorientation of Hughes' thought. *Orghast*, along with the poet's children's books and most of his criticism points up a puzzling split between the poet-prophet of apocalyptic doom and the philosopher-storyteller dreaming up the impossible solution. No personal disasters of the kind involving the deaths of his wife or companion stand between the writing of *Orghast* and *Gaudete* which yet seems to return to the gloomier vision of *Difficulties of a Bridegroom* and *Crow*. Following these earlier books as well as *The Wound*, *Gaudete* continues Hughes' poetic quest in trying 'to bring about this renovation of women and therefore of life in general'.[36] This is the mission of the original Reverend Lumb, alive in a postholocaust North England town turned mass grave. Here the protagonist encounters a female, half animal and half human, whose lifelessness is the appropriate emblem of the waste land surrounding her. She seems to solicit his help, but Lumb merely

> stands in confusion
> And looks round at the shadowed hollow faces
> Crowding to enclose him
> Eyepits and eyglints
>
> He declares he can do nothing
> He protests there is nothing he can do
> For this beautiful woman who seems to be alive and dead.
> He is not a doctor. He can only pray.[37]

Equally ineffectual is the attempt, made by the protagonist's upper-world double, to engender a new, female Messiah by impregnating the women of his parish. It ends with his murder at the hands of the cuckolded husbands. But before that, the protagonist's mission finds an at least dreamlike fulfilment in the phantasmagoric realms of an underworld reminiscent of *The Wound* and *Difficulties of a Bridegroom*. Here the hero's nightmarish counterpart[38] discovers the netherworld doubles of his female parishioners buried alive in mud and screaming in anguish 'As if something hidden under the mud / Were biting into [them]'.[39] In contrast to their helpless agony is the 'horrible reptile slowness' of an 'almost human' creature who 'is calling to him / Through a moving uncertain hole in the mud face'. Despite his failure to save the other women, Lumb feels that 'this one creature . . . he can free'. The face that gradually washes clear in the drumming downpour as he pulls this creature out of the mud is like a Lady Lazarus transmogrified into a nightmarish creature from the land of the dead.

> It is a woman's face,
> A face as if sewn together from several faces.
> A baboon beauty face,
> A crudely stitched pathwork of faces,
> But the eyes slide,
> Alive and electrical, like liquid liquorice behind the stitched lids.

Like the Bacchante prostitutes in *The Wound*, this baboon woman makes real what in 'Lady Lazarus' and other of Plath's poems remains an ineffectual gesture. Encircling him in her spine-cracking embrace, she sends Lumb into a state of paralysis before she saves herself from her own desecration through his deathlike trance. Like the soul of someone recently deceased, Lumb watches this Earth Mother caricature reborn from his own body.

He sees himself being delivered of the woman from the pit,
The baboon woman,
Flood-sudden, like the disembowelling of a cow
She gushes from between his legs, a hot splendour
. . .
He imagines he has been torn in two at the waist and this is his own blood everywhere.
. . .
He sees her face undeformed and perfect.

All this, however, happens in a dream world, while the changeling Lumb's mission to resurrect the Great Mother on earth ends in a total failure. The women he was sent out to save are either murdered, abused or driven to suicide. Asked if this debacle reflected his growing pessimism concerning the task, Hughes, in 1977, wrote to me in a letter: 'The pessimism of the theme is an inevitable part of the working out of the theme.' At the time, I also asked the poet whether what was symbolically implied in the rebirth of the baboon woman might become reality or whether a solution to the problem was as unattainable as a phantasmagorical mirage. Hughes replied: 'You are asking me to explain my riddle, which I should refrain from doing.'

Yet contrary to the pessimism of the *Gaudete* narrative, the book as a whole ends on a note which, for all its obvious irony, seems to be more in tune with the title. The changeling Lumb, champion of the Great Mother, has failed in his mission and been murdered. But the bride of his and the poet's devotions survives in the Epilogue poems. According to the story, they were written by the original Nicholas Lumb who, after the death of his Doppelgänger, reappeared 'in the West of Ireland, where he roam[ed] about half crazy, composing hymns and psalms to a nameless female deity'.[40] In particular, we again and again encounter the suffering, abused and dead representatives of the female divinity worshipped by Lumb.

It was the third time. And it smashed.

I turned
I bowed

In the morgue I kissed
Your temple's refrigerated glazed

As rain-on graveyard marble, my
Lips queasy, heart non-existent[41]

While the speaker is taking 'a few still-aimless happy steps', feeling 'the sun's strength', some female is groaning behind him in a cave, 'In labour — / Or in hunger — / Or in fear, or sick, or forsaken —'. Or suddenly he hears a screech, and running to help finds 'The woman who wore a split lopsided mask—'.

But other poems seem to go beyond the story of Lumb's misfortunes. In 1970, Hughes talked to me about his search for a new divinity which, as he put it, 'won't be under the rubble when the churches collapse'.[42] One lyric, conflating religious with sexual imagery in a new kind of pun-riddled symbolism, points towards the fulfilment of this quest.

Churches topple
Like the temples before them.

The reverberations of worship
Seem to help
Collapse such erections.

In all that time
The river
Has deepened its defile
Has been its own purification

Between your breasts

Between your thighs[43]

By contrast with the Christian god, this female divinity unites the creator and destroyer in one, and in response to Lumb's question 'Who are you?' the implacable cruelty of life spells out the answers.

The spider clamps the bluefly — whose death panic
Becomes sudden soulful absorption.

A stoat throbs at the nape of the lumped rabbit
Who watches the skylines fixedly.

But for the most part, the goddess appears as comforter and protectress. Her kiss of life resurrects the dead and her kiss of death frees us from the 'veils of wrinkle and shawls of ache.'

Yet all such hopefulness is undercut by deep irony.[44] After all, the imagined author of the Epilogue poems is a mere 'survivor of cease',[45] reduced to semi-insanity by his ordeals and errors. In this ambivalence, the ending of *Gaudete* resembles that of *The Waste Land* in which Eliot put the final message of peace from one of the Upanishads – 'Shantih   shantih   shantih' – into the mouth of the mad Hieronimo.

Nowhere are we made to forget that in terms of his original mission Lumb, as much as his Doppelgänger, has proved to be a mere 'veteran of negatives', 'His talents / the deprivations of escape'. A role reversal between saviour and victim adds the final touch of irony, and wisdom, to this story of failure. Instead of Lumb saving the desecrated female, the goddess now comes to the rescue of her helpless warrior champion.

The rain comes again
A tightening, a prickling in
On the soft-rotten gatepost.

But the stars
Are sunbathing
On the shores
Of the sea whose waves

Pile in from your approach

An unearthly woman wading shorewards
With me in your arms

The grey in my hair.

III

All this, I guess, amounts to no less than trying to solve an enigma which Hughes himself prefers to leave unexplained. Yet ironically Hughes' own writing on Shakespeare provides us with a model for this attempt. Here the poet tries to unriddle the playwright's own 'cruel riddle' which Shakespeare, so it is argued, found unsolvable.[46] The results are questionable with regard to Shakespeare but highly interesting in other ways. It may be true, for instance, that a 'sexual dilemma of a peculiarly black and ugly sort' was the taproot of some of Shakespeare's poetry and that it provided the 'skeleton-key fable' to several of his plays. But it seems wrong to me to accuse Shakespeare of beginning to 'cheat' in the romances where 'the young women, murdered by madmen or tempest,' as Hughes argues, 'do not actually die – they reappear to make everybody happy'. Instead, Shakespeare's last plays seem to bring the rebirth theme, which has so far remained abortive in Hughes' work, to their perhaps fullest realisation in Western literature.

Hughes' critique of Shakespeare tells us more about himself than about his subject. The charge levelled against the romances, for instance, may more appropriately apply to Hughes than to the playwright. We have noted the split between Hughes' relative optimism as storyteller-critic and his uncompromising vision as vatic poet. No doubt, the latter voice in his more truthful one, but there are cases in which the two become indistinguishable. This seems to be true of several poems in *Cave Birds: an Alchemical Cave Drama* (1978), the reworking of a volume first published in 1975. Like his predecessor Crow, the protagonist, who is put on trial by an assembly of birds, has incurred the diverse tribulations and culpabilities of man. And in poems such as 'Something was happening' about the death of a beloved woman – the speaker, despite all his grief, continuing in the ruthless routines of life – the tone of genuine experience is unmistakable.

Something was happening

While I strolled
Where a leaf or two still tapped like bluetits

I met thin, webby rain
And thought: 'Ought I to turn back, or keep going?'
Her heart stopped beating, that second.

As I hung up my coat and went through into the kitchen
And peeled a flake off the turkey's hulk, and stood vacantly munching
Her sister got the call from the hospital
And gasped out the screech.[47]

Less convincing to me are the poems in which the dead woman's mythic counterpart is reborn to become the protagonist's enigmatic 'bride' ('A Riddle'). As in 'Crow's Undersong', the eternal Feminine, banished by puritanism and misogyny, has suddenly re-emerged in the hostile surroundings of our civilisation.

After there was nothing there was a woman
. . .
Whose breasts had come about
By long toil of earthworms
After many failures, but they were here now
And she protected them with silk
. . .
Having about as much comprehension as a lamb
Who stares around at everything simultaneously
With ant-like head and soldierly bearing

She had made it but only just, just —

We are not surprised to find that 'His legs ran about', a sequel to 'After there was nothing', is about a love-making session which in its violent intensity recalls 'Lovesong', also from *Crow*. There is something *déjà vu* about these and other poems in *Cave Birds*. Despite its implied narrative, the volume as a whole reads like a collection of poems mixing styles from diverse creative periods and genres. Just as 'The Scream', for instance, recalls 'Hawk Roosting' from *Lupercal*, so 'Bride and groom lie hidden for three days' seems to draw on the lighter and more optimistic tone of Hughes' poems for children. In this way, 'Bride and groom' reads like an almost direct transcript from that ongoing mythological narrative of the gnomic spell maker which, since the early 1960s, has served as the hidden quarry for the poet's lyrical output. Bride and bridegroom have reached the nadir of shamanistic disintegration, but through their love bring about their mutual rebirth:

So, gasping with joy, with cries of wonderment
Like two gods of mud
Sprawling in the dirt, but with infinite care

They bring each other to perfection.

Characteristically, Hughes volunteered to reveal how the poem relates to the Crow story with its quest for the rescue of the desecrated woman. Like 'Lovesong', 'The Lovepet' and 'Actaeon',[48] 'Bride and groom' is one of several answers which Crow gives to the questions posed him by a giant Ogress. Here the question is 'Who gives most, him or her?'

That's right at the end of the story, when Crow is crossing the river and has seven questions put to him by the Ogress he carries across. His answers move from one pole of total disaster in the relationship between him and the female to the opposite pole of totally successful, blissful union. And meanwhile, this Ogress on his back turns into a beauty, before she escapes into the oak forest on the other side of the river. And there are many more episodes in this happy land until the Ogress eventually becomes his bride.[49]

Storyteller fantasies or poetic vision? All one can answer at this point, is that 'Bride and groom', in suggesting a happy solution to the poet's quest, seems to lack the distance from his mythological quarry which Hughes himself claims for his poems for adults.

This also helps to remind us that a poem's message, however positive, has little to do with intrinsic poetic merit. Quite naturally, the works of poets like Hughes invite critics to search for conclusions to the quests they imply. It would be wrong, however, to associate poetic success with such attainment, or poetic failure with the lack of it. Even where the quest reaches its goal, as seems to be the case in Shakespeare, this fulfilment hardly produced the greater poetry. For all one's admiration for the romances, it would be difficult to see these works as superior to tragedies like *King Lear* or *Macbeth*. The same is true of Hughes' development and how it stems from Sylvia Plath's. No doubt their common quest prompted some of their greatest poetry. But perhaps this is so for the very reason that it has remained unfulfilled so far.

PART 2

Works

Oriental mythology in *Wodwo*

Fifteen years after its publication *Wodwo* remains a powerful, yet disquieting, almost forbidding book. Hughes' first venture into surrealism reveals an agitated, tormented psyche locked in a dark night of the soul. But the whys and wherefores of the agony appear occluded. In Part 1 especially imagery of fear, turmoil, blood and death oscillates with imagery of emptiness, silence and libidinal withdrawal from the landscape depicted. The result of the dark night is not less than a loss of faith in the enterprises of Western Christian culture and man's involvement in goal-seeking activity in historical time. But *Wodwo* does not simply express cultural chaos through a chaotic form; Winters' heresy of expressive form does not apply. The reasons for the loss of faith can be specified in the poems, as can organisational patterns within individual poems and in the volume as a whole. Nor is the poetic psyche left helpless: through the agony of the ordeal, Hughes is able to locate new powers within the self, powers deriving in part from Oriental perspectives. These new powers offer important survival strategies for contemporary man.

Before *Wodwo* Hughes seemed eager to applaud participation in temporal experience and cultural advancement. *The Hawk in the Rain* ended with a qualified approval of Bishop Farrar's martyrdom; *Lupercal* concluded with an expression of faith in the Luperci's ritual efforts to reempower man 'age to age while the body hold'. The majority of the protagonists in *Hawk* were heroic, action-oriented figures from England's past, lovers or assertive rural types; they either wrestled, like 'The Dove-Breeder', with experience and invasions of libidinal energies from the unconscious, or were satirized, like 'Egghead', for failing to do so. In *Lupercal* the accomplishments of Dick Straightup, Nicholas Ferrer, Thomas Browne ('Urn Burial') and the Retired Colonel were saluted as admirable; each remained self-assured in life, comfortable in articulating his historical age, and fulfilled in death. The persona of 'Historian' hoped for 'a live brain's / Envying to master and last' the cultural gains such accomplishments produced.

In the early war poetry Hughes seemed confident of his powers to reconcile Eros and Thanatos in the ambiguities and tensions of skilled, aloof New Critical craftsmanship. Here Hughes resigned himself to accepting man's destructive urges and affirmed the worth of the soldier's survival struggle, though he often ridiculed conventional moralisms through paradox and ironic contrast. 'To Paint a Water Lily' typified Hughes' early confidence in matters concerning the destructive aspects of nature. In this poem the persona recognised the meat-eating dragonfly, the 'battle-shouts' and 'death cries' of the insect world above, and the unimproved 'Prehistoric bedragonned times' below, redolent with 'Jaws for heads', yet painted a flower that 'can be still / As a painting, trembling hardly at all', no matter what 'horror nudge her root'.

In *Wodwo* this confidence in man's historical enterprises in Western culture vanishes completely. The personae disdain cultural roots, for nightmarish obsessions with man's destructiveness obtrude. The confident New Critical reconciliation of tensions defers to more confessional modes of surrealistic revulsion against participation in time and human history. The persona of 'A Vegetarian', in summarizing the stages of Western man's odyssey from seduction to pregnancy, birth, wounding and death in the sheep's jaw movement of time, is openly fearful of the entire process. Poems such as 'Thistles', 'Her Husband', 'Ghost Crabs', 'Second Glance at a Jaguar', and 'Scapegoat and Rabies' present expressionistic portraits of weapons, recurring feuds and destructiveness in the blood of the species, a cyclic recurrence of the jaguar's 'drum-song of murder' in man and beast alike. In 'Karma' Hughes despairs of finding any rationale to countenance man's legacy of wartime carnage. Later in the volume, in 'Wings', Hughes argues that even the advancements of twentieth-century philosophy, literature and science attest to contemporary man's complete alienation from any form of ancestral wisdom, for each man is now hopelessly isolated in his own existential agony (Sartre in section I) in a universe the teleology of which man is incapable of understanding (Kafka in Section II) but whose scientific advancements have blasted him to star vapour (Einstein in section III).[1]

The purgatorial process of *Wodwo* is one of disencumbering oneself of failed cultural assumptions and beliefs. The volume closes with its title poem, a meditative piece about a wood sprite whose cardinal axioms are a confidence in the limited but satisfying powers of his own perceiving consciousness as the generator, the 'exact centre' of experience, and a preference for an eclectic, questioning freedom over sitting still and developing any roots or belief systems whatsoever. Quietly and bemusedly the Wodwo will 'go on looking', taking nothing for granted, and establishing his own co-ordinates between himself and nature, as freshly as if he were an alien being just dropped from space.

Of course Hughes' disenchantment with Western culture has biographical reference points. Between the publication of *Lupercal* (1960) and *Wodwo* (1967), Hughes brooded over essays and reviews on the war poetry of Keith Douglas, Wilfred Owen and others.[2] Closer to home, the trauma of Sylvia Plath's tragic suicide (11 February 1963) caused a writer's block, concerning poetry, of at least two years, and certainly a heightened consciousness of the destruction that often attends enticements to act in historical time. Aldermaston marches against the bomb and strontium-90 scares – the legacy of the Cold War in the early 1960s – are possible ancillary influences.[3] Stylistically Hughes outgrew his early New Critical phase, having chafed at what he considered a too figurative language and a consciously crafted form that created a constricted, inauthentic voice, too far removed from objective experience.[4] The departure into surrealism allowed Hughes to acknowledge and explore his personal responses to both private and public catastrophe. Hughes in *Wodwo* is broadly confessional: the dislocation of experience into surrealistic modes is symptomatic of the larger cultural crisis, and the poet's tormented consciousness exists as the moral centre of suffering for both.

The process of cultural divestiture in *Wodwo* is not a facile spurning of tradition, or a simplistic call for personal freedom. In the poems of *Wodwo* one learns that Hughes' disenchantment is personally experienced in private life and analysed through plausible social psychology. The disenchantment is *earned* through the unremitting agony of the poems, and a positive alternative is offered. Through this disencumbering process Hughes opens the door for the emergence of Oriental patterns of thought he had been meditating on throughout the early sixties.

The poem 'Out' is central to *Wodwo*, for it contains the only direct, straightforwardly-told personal experience of man's destructiveness in the volume, and charts the direction of Hughes' meditations on war and Western culture during this period. Here Hughes meditates upon his father, one of only seventeen survivors of an entire battalion from the Gallipoli service of the Lancashire Fusiliers in World War I. In a tone of rueful indignation Hughes considers his father's victimisation and near death by Gallipoli shrapnel (section I), with an eye to the phylogenetic consequences for himself as a more impoverished 'luckless double' of the next generation, the product of an automatic regenerative power in nature (Section II) that simply will not surrender.

But section III of 'Out' presents a new insight into the mass warfare of the twentieth century. Here Hughes reasons that the stark anonymity of amassed millions, insulated from the enemy by machines, militates against even the ability of the psyche to place such slaughter within a larger humanistic retributive scheme. The function of the poppy, emblematic of a remembrance of the sleeping dead from antiquity ·to John McCrae's 'In Flanders Fields' and contemporary Memorial Day customs, is rendered worthless; lost forever are the old ritual intuitions of the potential of the next generation to outlive historical animosities and to repay the debt owed the dead by following their ideals and conquering the foe. Hughes seems to ask McCrae how can we take up our countrymen's 'quarrel with the foe' when the individual soldier's humane responses collapse as he stands in a no-man's land between astronomical body counts and inhuman but terribly efficient machine gun barrels. In a review of I. M. Parsons' anthology of World War I poets (*Listener*, 5 August 1965), Hughes wrote that the four years of World War I were not enough to digest 'the shock of machine guns, armies of millions, and the plunge into the new dimension, where suddenly and for the first time Adam's descendants found themselves meaningless'.

This new dimension of meaninglessness in section III of 'Out' replaces the persona's former faith in nature's cyclic ability (the 'refreshing of ploughs /In the woe-dark under my mother's eye —') to imbue wartime death with value. In the Gallipoli campaign both Turks and Allies lost a quarter of a million men each (eighty per cent of the Allied casualties were British) in nine months of trench warfare issuing in an ignominious retreat.[5] A breast-pocket paybook stopped shrapnel that would have added Hughes' father to the statistics. For Hughes such large-scale carnage transforms the poppy, the emblem of the ideals and courage of the slain, into a 'canvas-beauty puppet on a wire' – a worthless, 'bloody-minded' flower. 'Out' ends with the firm resolve to bid 'Goodbye to the cenotaphs on my mother's breasts' and 'Goodbye to the remaindered charms of my father's survival'. Instead of the affirmation of the 'old spark of the blood heat' in 'Lupercal', Hughes now affirms that he will no longer be constrained by phylogenetic habit to participate unconsciously in repeat performances of the errors of Western cultural history. There is no stronger statement in *Wodwo* of a departure from Hughes' early faith in human potential in historical time.

On the subject of the involuntary transmission of aggressive tendencies Hughes wrote, in a *Wodwo* period review (*New Statesman*, 2 October 1964), that 'The possibilities of what a child might absorb from its lineage . . . are awful, which is what alarmed Freud'. Freud treated violence in his late work as part of Thanatos, the death instinct, which is usually fused with Eros or libidinal energy in the ego, but can be directed outward in aggressive acts. More specifically, when Freud tried to explain the slaughter of World War I, one answer he developed was that of a repetition–compulsion biological urge, like cellular replacement, to regress to an earlier level of evolution. The other concept Freud developed was that of 'archaic heritage' or 'phylogenetic inheritance': inherited memory traces, innately present at birth, of the primordial crime – parricide, the son's first rebellious act against the cruel despotism and sexual covetousness of the patriarch in the primal horde.[6] In *Wodwo* Hughes treats aggression in ways similar to both Freudian theories – the compulsive repetitiousness that breeds hostility, and the inherited phylogenetic predisposition towards violent behaviour. The domestic antagonisms and their 'blood weight of money' in 'Her Husband' are so quintessentially presented that we recognise their daily occurrence in every town; the jaguar in 'Second Glance at a Jaguar' exhibits an inexhaustible power to 'keep his rage brightening', and in 'Thistles' the warriors return to fight 'over the same ground'. The crabs of 'Ghost Crabs' symbolise both the aggressive traits and the repetition–compulsion urge present in the regressive dissolution of the human personality during sleep. 'All night . . . they tear each other to pieces', for 'They are the turmoil of history, the convulsion /In the roots of blood, in the cycles of concurrence'.

Hughes' disenchantment with Western culture is *earned* in the unrelieved torment, communicated through adequate objective correlatives, in the poems of *Wodwo*. Especially in Part I the mood of surrealistic revulsion is so great as to occasion a general libidinal withdrawal from the landscape depicted. The alternate shuddering and silence of the wind-blown trees and the vision of the shadow of the ploughman's bones in 'A Wind Flashes the Grass' mirror the persona's own state of anxiety and fear at the prospect of mortality in the time-bound world of woe. In the last two lines of the poem the conscious use of the pathetic fallacy reveals the persona's fear at the momentary nature of both man and landscape. Similarly, the persona of 'Sugar Loaf', in noticing the hill's time-bound vulnerability to erosion, becomes disconcerted by the hill's ignorance of the process. Unsettling images of naked susceptibility to pain mirror a torment within the psyche of the persona: 'The water is as wild as alcohol — / Distilling from the fibres of the blue wind. / Reeds, nude and tufted, shiver as they wade.' A consciousness of destructive aggression in our culture in the military metaphor of 'Bowled Over' leads to a 'desertion' from the time-bound world after the 'sudden insubordination' occasioned by a realisation of the 'kiss of death' of man's weaponry. This leads to a lapse of attention to the activities of the living – the domestication of farmland and the development of culture ('patched fields, churches'). The military bugle blast of 'Reveille' leads Adam and Eve into historical time and the ashes of nuclear holocaust. In 'Boom' and 'Public Bar T.V.' the personae experience a complete revulsion against what is perceived as a sterile materialism, which fails to satisfy spiritual thirsts, and also leads to the ashes of nuclear holocaust.

One must remember that Hughes' undergraduate studies in anthropology at Cambridge led him to take a long view of history. At the same time it exposed him to alternative cultures in the history of mankind. This fostered a more critical view of our contemporary Western culture. Hughes' nurture in the widowed Yorkshire Pennines, where countrysides are dotted with the cenotaphs of a whole generation of men sacrificed in Asia Minor, is crucial for our understanding of his war meditations. All through his youth Hughes listened to unending litanies of World War I stories from relatives whose chief social chat was the veiled admission that they never fully recovered from the loss of dear friends. By the early 1970s Hughes was able to write essays arguing that eruptions of mass violence in our culture are caused by the complete alienation of mind from nature by our inert scientific empiricism and the total repression of instinct in Reformed Christianity.[7] But in their inception in the 1960s, these theories took a more immediate, poetic form.

In certain poems of *Wodwo* the psychological torment occasioned by the private and the larger cultural tragedy is so great as to cause a complete displacement into the realm of surrealistic nightmare. In 'Cadenza', 'The Rescue', and 'Stations' the personae experience more psychotic states of personality breakdown and libidinal withdrawal. Hughes believes that a descent into surrealism can have therapeutic effects; in an essay on Vasco Popa, published during the *Wodwo* period (1967), Hughes states that he does not approve of the Dadaist 'arbitrary imagery of the dream flow', but favours the temporary retrenchment to the subconscious of folklore surrealism as a vehicle for solving problems and managing practical difficulties.[8] In 'Cadenza' and 'The Rescue' the dissolution of the ego and the abandonment of a normal relationship with the coordinates of our contemporary culture is feared, but taking place nevertheless. In both cases noise is preferred as supportive reinforcement to the security needs of the ego. But in 'Cadenza' the soloist's egocentric refusal to relinquish his dominance leads to an aggressive combat with the orchestra which ends in an explosion. In 'The Rescue' the persona learns that the reality of his psychological state is one of silence, a dying away from the temporal world. The 'five', perhaps the five senses, are too fragile for noises from the world of the living. A mood of surrealistic estrangement is adequately conveyed through images of nightmarish 'sailors white / As maggots', and 'mummies with their bandages lifted off', followed by the soundless 'pouring faces' from the 'ship's dazzling side'. The meditations of 'Stations' present a more complete abandonment of the conscious analytic ego, prized by our empirical culture, as the prime seat of thinking and experiencing. In section III the persona is 'complacent' in his inability to ratiocinate, to make even 'one comparison', and in section IV the abandonment of language is presented surrealistically as a severing of the head by the trainwheels of historical time. The surrealism of these poems is therapeutic to the extent that the personae gradually recognise that they prefer emptiness, withdrawal and absence to participation in goal-directed activity in Western culture.

'Scapegoats and Rabies' is perhaps the quintessential *Wodwo* poem. Though it appeared only in the American edition of *Wodwo*, its first publication in early 1967 (*New Statesman*, 13 January 1967) indicates that it was probably written in mid or late 1966, at the time Hughes was choosing and ordering the poems of *Wodwo*. In 'Scapegoats and Rabies' one recognises a complete surrealistic dislocation into nightmare, the most straightforward analysis of war in terms similar to the Freudian repetition–compulsion biological urge, the extreme moral anguish and sensitivity of the poet to human suffering, and a clear expression of an Oriental way out of this impasse.

Nightmarish images of anonymous dead soldiers obtrude in a garish, surrealistic montage in the first section of 'Scapegoats and Rabies'. Both heredity and the nurture provided by Western culture combine as causes: stares from old women, trembling chins from old men, bow-legs from toddlers, facelessness from 'the mouldering / Of letters and citations / On rubbish dumps'. The funeral parade is endless, for the repetition–compulsion 'drumming /Of their boots' is 'concentrating / Toward a repeat performance' in future generations. The men are 'Helpless in the terrible engine of the boots' and get 'their hopelessness / From the millions of the future / Marching in their boots . . .'

Sections II and III present the poet as General undergoing the psychic shock of having his head torn apart by each memory-trace of the events of war, by a searing, agonized consciousness of human aggresion through the ages, presented as a paranoid sensitivity to every bullet, every shellburst. The General's face is a lantern of light in the darkness of war, its flame blown out and relit in response to the explosive staccato outside.

Sections IV and V present a sardonic, almost misanthropic allegory of a soldier's outfitting for battle, his near-death and resuscitation in the mud of historical time. Since the poet-general, like Diogenes searching with his lantern for an honest man, cannot locate a receptive culture, the only alternative is to exorcise that culture's aggressiveness for the self's sanity. As Christ once exorcised a demon into the Gadarene swine (Mark, 5), so Hughes creates a faceless stereotype as collective cultural scapegoat. This soldier's battledress is woven by some of the most reprehensible elements of contemporary civilisation – its materiality and smug conspicuous consumption, niggard of self-comprehension (IV: stanza one), its petty smallmindedness and selfishness (IV: stanza two), and the poverty and scurrility of its cultural, political and economic products (IV: stanzas III ff.). After being shot while traversing no man's land 'In a shouting flight / From his own stink', the soldier in section V embraces London and the mud of time and human history in a state too hopelessly maimed to muster any resistance. More so than any other passage in *Wodwo*, sections IV and V of 'Scapegoats and Rabies' present an indictment of the enterprises of contemporary Western civilisation, though the specific images are geographically British in reference.

The way out of the impasse presented in 'Scapegoats and Rabies' is through the abandonment of the Western analytic ego – a machine which normally ingests information from the outside and functions as a security-seeking defence mechanism against the outside world – and a retrenchment to a sense of self as the *generator* of one's own perceptions of reality, in a way that *unifies* the perceiving consciousness with external reality. Hughes wrote in a 1970 essay that 'The story of the mind exiled from Nature is the story of Western man. It is the story of his progressively more desperate search for mechanical and rational and symbolic securities, which will substitute for the spirit-confidence of the Nature he has lost.'[9] From the exile of mind from nature, caused, in Hughes' analysis, by Reformed Christianity's repression of the instincts and the cool laboratory analysis of modern science, comes the 'mishmash of scripture and physics' in *Crow* that leaves 'brains in hands' and blown off 'legs in a treetop' ('Crow's Account of the Battle'). To heal the subject—object dualism and the divorce of mind from instinct that leads to cultural schizophrenia, Hughes in *Wodwo* adopts more Oriental perspectives. The poet as General in section II of 'Scapegoats and Rabies' transcends his schizoid

Western culture by opting for an excarnation of the fleshy body and its automatic responses to the environment, and adopting an Oriental subjective monism, a realisation of the self as the creator of its own unitive relationship with nature:

Knives, forks, spoons divide his brains.
The supporting earth, and the night around him,

Smoulder like the slow, curing fire
Of a Javanese head-shrinker.

Nothing remains of the *tete d'armée* but the skin —
A dangling parchment lantern

Slowly revolving to right, revolving to left,

Trembling a little with the incessant pounding,

Over the map, empty in the ring of light.

III

Wit's End

The General commits his emptiness to God.

To leave the instinctual attachments of the fleshy body to its normal, comforting environment, and to abandon the analytic ego and dualistic thinking, is to experience the Buddhist state of *śūnyatā*, a state of complete personality dissolution and a realisation of emptiness, of the fullness of nothingness, where 'nothing' is understood as a non-dualistic involvement in the plenitude of *all* of reality (i.e., no one thing).[10] What is accomplished in the process is a fresh, direct, pre-cognitive perception of reality in its suchness, before the conscious mind labels with Aristotelian categories, semantic descriptions and their underlying cultural assumptions. After this the initiate can experience a fusion of self-as-creator with perceived world, in any of a number of ways: a recognition of the *ātman* or self-soul of the *Upanishads* as the generator of all that is perceived;[11] or the yogic *īshwara pranidhāna*, the God within the self as the creator and ground of all being;[12] or the *satori* sense of ecstatic participatory involvement in the is-ness of all reality, in Zen.[13] Section III of 'Scapegoats and Rabies' begins with a resurrection of the self as creator of reality; the line 'The General commits his emptiness to God' indicates a movement from *śūnyatā* to yogic *īshwara pranidhāna*. By the end of the section the General has realised a new sense of power as the generator of reality-for-the-self as his hand sweeps the battlefield 'flat as a sheet of foolscap' and he affirms a sympathetic commitment to his brethren:

I AM A LANTERN

IN THE HAND

OF A BLIND PEOPLE

In sections II and III of 'Scapegoats and Rabies' Hughes may also have been meditating upon passages in the *Śvetāśvatara Upanishad* (1:14; 2:11–16), wherein the macrocosmic all-space fuses with the soul within the subjective self to create the *ātman* of Oriental monism. In this passage the two concepts fuse into the *ātman* through imagery of fire, God, crystal and inwardly illuminated lantern, similar to that of sections II and III of 'Scapegoats and Rabies'. Both the fire of yogic meditation and the purgative fire at the end of section II of 'Scapegoats and Rabies', the 'slow, curing fire / Of a Javanese headshrinker', lead to a death of the old conscious ego and the attainment of an inner personal godliness. The motif of the willed, self-devouring of the carnal self leading to an excarnation of the flesh, and of the presence of God in all fiery, world-destroyed cataclysms, leaving only the 'Face of Glory' mask, is a prominent motif of Vedic Shivaite mythology. This fiery, self-destructive aspect of Shiva particularly delighted the aboriginal Javanese long after their conversion to Hinduism.[14]

One must be careful to realise that Hughes does not subscribe to a simplistic either/or, Western versus Eastern position; nor is he an ardent devotee of a particular branch of Oriental orthodoxy. Hughes is entirely eclectic, mainly interested in the survival of the spirit and the integrated psyche, and will use, as he once told Egbert Faas, whatever serves: 'You choose a subject because it serves, because you need it'.[15] Like Jung,. Campbell and Lévi-Strauss, Hughes is particularly interested. in conflating the folklore, myth and ritual patterns of primitive man in order to comprehend the psychological and spiritual common denominators operative, and to discover what survival potential these kernels may hold for contemporary man.

From the mid-seventies on, in the epilogue to *Gaudete*, in *Cave Birds*, *Remains of Elmet* and *Moortown*, Hughes can reaffirm, with qualifications, more Western modes of experiencing reality. But during the trauma of the *Wodwo* period Hughes is in need of healing his own split psyche and that of our war-obsessed Western culture. During the *Wodwo* period Hughes believed that an Oriental relocation within the self as the *ātman* centre of all that is perceived, offered potential for psychic reclamation to individuals in a schizoid Western culture. In a 1971 interview with Egbert Faas, Hughes stated that

it's obviously a pervasive and deep feeling that civilisation has now disappeared completely. If it's still here it's here by grace of pure inertia and chance and if the whole thing has essentially vanished one had better have one's spirit invested in something that will not vanish. And this is a shifting of your foundation to completely new Holy Ground, a new divinity, one that won't be under the rubble when the churches collapse.[16]

The new self Hughes alludes to here is a more Oriental concept of the self as the generator of all that is perceived, a mode of perception that frees the self of neurotic dependencies upon expectations and events in the time-bound phenomenal world. With a freedom from such dependencies the self can see reality direct, without the filters imposed by the givens of Western culture – the assumptions, categories and semantic configurations that pre-digest experience for us. In *Wodwo* Hughes argues that contemporary man must heal the divorce between subject and object, between the mind of man and an alienated nature, and that for survival's sake man must locate final authority and assurance entirely within the self, not in the temporal goals, acquisitions, cultural achievements or dependencies that have too often led Western man to destruction. The man capable of the perceptual and psychological revolution of recognising the *ātman* as generator of all that the self perceives, frees himself from bondage to instinctual cravings and attachments, from dualistic thinking and preoccupation with temporality, and becomes the world-all, as in the *Brihad-Áranyaka Upanishad* (4.4.12–13):

If a person knew the Soul [Atman],
With the thought 'I am he!'
With what desire, for love of what
Would he cling unto the body?

He who has found and has awakened to the Soul
That has entered this conglomerate abode—
He is the maker of everything, for he is the creator of all;
The world is his: indeed he is the world itself.[17]

As a final proof of his intellectual preoccupations near the time of the arrangement of the poems of *Wodwo*, one might consider Hughes' review of Constantine Fitzgibbon's *The Selected Letters of Dylan Thomas* (*New Statesman*, 25 November 1966), the only review he wrote during the 1966 and 1967 calendar years. In this review Hughes bemoaned Thomas' failure to destroy the self-conscious 'super-ego stylist', his inability to trust in a 'surrealistic or therapeutic torrent' in order to precipitate 'the delicate cerebral disaster that demolishes the old self for good, with all its crushing fortifications, and leaves the atman a clear field'.

This *ātman* state of union with space exemplifies the 'that art thou' doctrine of the *Chāndogya Upanishad* (6:8–16), where the 'that' is the totality of the perceived environment as it exists for the perceiving consciousness, and the 'thou' is the God, the creator-originator of all that is perceived. In yogic meditation the practised adept can achieve a state of *samādhi*, of agreement or unity with the whole of the perceived object; this union can be achieved either by focusing upon an object of consciousness ('with seed': *samprajnāta*) or without consciousness of an object ('without seed': *asamprajnāta*).[18] In Chinese and Japanese Zen the experience of *satori* or totalistic unity with the infinite is also cognate, though it dawns upon the initiate in an instantaneous and ecstatic epiphanic moment.[19] Through such meditative practises one can obliterate the mental baggage acquired from an over-rational, conceptual culture, and experience reality afresh, direct, without labelling.

In order to liberate the *ātman* the psyche must first experience the *śūnyatā* state of emptiness, of death to the analytic Western ego, and recognise the fullness of nothingness, the fullness of *all* creation. In section III of 'Root, Stem, Leaf' the persona imagines himself as utterly anonymous, as forgotten as a discarded heirloom spoon 'blackening / Among roots in a thorn-hedge . . .'. This leads to a knowledge of the plenitude of *all* of existence wherein 'Everything is inheriting everything'. Of the poems of Part I of *Wodwo*, section III of 'Stations' relates the most completely realised state of *śūnyatā* emptiness; here the poet experiences a queer state of complete dissolution and absence, of estrangement even from his own act of writing:

You are a wild look – out of an egg
Laid by your absence.

In the great Emptiness you sit complacent,
Blackbird in wet snow.

If you could make only one comparison—
Your condition is miserable, you would give up.

But you, from the start, surrender to total Emptiness,
Then leave everything to it.

Absence. It is your own
Absence

Weeps its respite through your accomplished music,
Wraps its cloak dark about your feeding.

'The Green Wolf' and 'The Bear', the concluding poems (except for 'Scapegoats and Rabies' in the American edition) of Part I of *Wodwo*, assist in demolishing the old self as prelude to recognising the sleeping *ātman* within. In 'The Green Wolf' the title allusion to the scapegoat victim of the purgatorial Beltane Fires of Normandy[20] combines with imagery of a cerebral haemorrhage or stroke (the 'dark bloodclot' of line nine) to reinforce a state of deathly neurotic withdrawal. In this state of self-negating passivity, forces in the external environment assist in a destructive process: hawthorn blossom and beanflower symbolise, respectively, forces of erotic seduction and destruction.[21] The frozen left side of the persona is symbolic of a lack of interest in the creative anima's lure of the spirit into activities in the temporal world.[22] 'The Green Wolf' was originally published as 'Dark Women' (*Observer*, 6 January 1963), with only minor differences from the *Wodwo* version. The original poem title contains a cryptic allusion concerning this sundering of the old conscious ego. In cabbalistic lore Ama is the destructive aspect of Binah or Understanding, the third Sephirah in the cabbalistic Tree of Life. Ama attests to the arduous labour needed to achieve any goal, and the necessity of disrupting and destroying the old self-image to create fertile ground for personality growth. She is usually known as the 'Dark Mother', carries a disciplinary bar of wood in her left hand, and is depicted as a gigantic Mother Superior completely shrouded in black.[23]

In 'The Bear', the final poem of Part I of *Wodwo*, the bear represents the 'gleam in the pupil' of the *ātman* hibernating within the self, which can be revealed through opening the *prajñācakṣu*, the Buddhist third eye of transphenomenal wisdom.[24] The bear's 'price is everything' — a recognition of death to the conscious persona, past and present. In return he grants a largesse of comprehension of self-and-world, glueing beginning and end, offering knowledge deeper than a well, wider than the Universe. In 'The Bear' Hughes also draws upon the rich anthropological lore of the bear in primitive cultures, especially its function as a godly regeneration-through-death symbol. Added to the bear's natural attributes of endurance and quiet strength are its symbolic value to primitives as the oldest embodiment of theriomorphic divinity known to man, and its function in shamanic initiation as a vehicle of dismemberment towards the attaining of mystical powers.[25] The bear's abode is 'In the huge, wide-open sleeping eye of the mountain', the principal residence of the gods to primitives.[26] The Ainus of northern Japan practised the earliest form of the 'animal master' ritual known to man, with a bear as its focus; its purpose was to affirm that the process of destruction was only a stage in a recurring cosmic drama of rebirth and regeneration. Hence the young bear, sacrificed with elaborate ritual, was *joyously* sent home to its cosmic abode.[27]

The stories and the radio play of part II of *Wodwo* repeat the Part I process of the dissolution of the Western analytic ego. The central characters exhibit varying stages of neurotic behaviour and personality breakdown based upon the repression of instinct and withdrawal from other-directed libido. Grooby's inability to withstand three hours of harvest heat in 'The Harvesting' leads to an anguished preoccupation with mortality. As ageing victim of the temporal round of birth/death, without capacities to transcend his situation, he himself becomes the hare hunted by the 'big, white bony greyhound', as in the epigraph chant from the seventeenth-century Allansford witch coven.[28] In 'Sunday' what at first appears to be a sexual initiation for Michael results in neurotic flight. The girl is inaccessible, presided over by an 'expert' male companion, and instead of a knowing lure to sexual initiation she offers only 'mesmerised incredulity'. The girl is too much a product of the 'harmless, church-going slopes' to be of aid to Michael's sexual quandary. The only initiation into the birth/death sexual round offered in the story is the sham, degraded showmanship of Billy Red's rat catching. Neither the girl nor Billy Red's grotesquery appeals to Michael, who flees in speechless revulsion at the entire ordeal.

The more severe estrangement from object-directed libido in 'The Suitor' and 'The Rain Horse' leads to more pronounced neurotic behaviour. In 'The Suitor' the estrangement from Eros is presented symbolically, and in a surrealistic landscape – in the continuing darkness and blocked bedroom window of the girl's house, the pummelling received by the man in the trilby (the repressed instinctual component of the suitor's ego), and in the final surrealistic tableau of alienated instinct when the suitor faces away from the flute-playing man in the trilby. Here the flute notes of Pan work their way up the house wall in complete dissociation from the suitor, who has walked five miles in never-used dancing shoes in the hope of an encounter based entirely upon the girl's chance smile in the school corridors. In 'The Rain Horse' the alienation of instinctual life is so total that an eruption of demonised Eros ensues when the young adult businessman returns home after a twelve years' absence. The environment of his nurture elicits only boredom and impatience, and the impatience soon turns to anger at the discomforts of mud and rain. The horse appears *exactly* at this point, and becomes malevolent *only* when the man resolves not to deal with the animal's watchful presence – to repress by banishing from consciousness. Thus the horse symbolises the repressed libidinal energies of the man's own psyche. After a final truce the persona feels lobotomised, but fails to recognise that the cause of this feeling is his having shirked the burden of the experience, of having refused the chance for psychological reclamation.

'Snow' is at once the most psychotic of the short stories and the one which most foreshadows the Oriental conclusion of Part III. Here the normal rational thinking process is equated with the blinding, lifeless snow, the strangling snowdrifts of conscious rationality. In 'Snow' a partly amnesiac survivor of a plane crash in the Arctic wilderness must concentrate and discipline his survival energies, and distrust his tendency to lapse into a muddle-headed optimism. The key to successful endurance provided by the story is to withdraw one's awe, fears and attachments to the temporal world, and learn to awaken a deeper, more essential self at the root of one's inner being. The central character of 'Snow' appears to heed the warning of Patanjali, at the outset of his *Yoga Sutras* (No. 2), that one must control the mind's habitual flow of ideas and conventional choice-making, through concentration and meditation.[29]. The Buddhist chant invoked by the survivor, 'O Jewel of the Lotus', is the mantra of Chenrazee, *'Om Mani Padme Hum'*, used like all mantras as a power charm to focus one's willpower and meditative energies, and to invoke supernormal powers for practical or religious reasons. The survivor remains alive at the conclusion of the story because he trusts his inner powers and disciplines his need for reassurances from conventional rationalisations or from his chair, his one anchor to the phenomenal world. As he develops this meditative control he is even tempted to 'go deep into the blizzard' and leave the chair altogether.

The radio play *The Wound* continues the disenchantment with the Western mythic urge of participation in the temporal round of birth/death. While in combat Ripley learns of the Thanatos that attends Eros as he survives a nine-mile walk for help in a state of unconscious automatism caused by a gaping bullet wound in his head. The play utilises radio's capacity for creating aural, interior space to portray Ripley's experience of near death in terms of a hallucinatory voyage to the underworld. Here the Girl, the anima's believe-it-or-not ability to entice even the near-dead back into further participation in time and history, saves Ripley. The process is not easy, however, for Ripley, like many other Part II characters, is inhibited: he represses his erotic urges even to the point of calling himself 'bitch-proof'.

The mythic superstructure of *The Wound* is entirely Western, but the fruits of the quest are not spiritual enlargement. The dominant images of this radio play are those of horror, of devouring, even of cannibalism, and Ripley's mantra is the unreflective 'Keep going! / Keep going!' Like the soldiers 'helpless in the terrible engine of the boots' in 'Scapegoats and Rabies', Ripley is more the victim of destructive energies than a successful quest hero. Ripley barely survives this initiation into the destructive horrors at the bottom of the self and contemporary Western civilisation; he returns to the wartime world of 'Bleeding mud' in a state of utter helplessness. As soldiers carry Ripley's limp body to camp, the voyage to the underworld ends. The *Wodwo* leitmotif of the dissolution of the conscious Western ego also ends here, allowing the leitmotif of the development of the *ātman* within the self to flower in Part III.

Though Hughes became acquainted with Oriental mythology during his undergraduate work in anthropology at Cambridge, his work on the *Bardo Thödol* libretto immediately after *Lupercal* was doubtless crucial in deepening this interest. While at Yaddo in September, 1959, Hughes met the Chinese composer Chou Wen-Chung, who persuaded him to write the libretto for a large orchestral composition based upon the *Bardo Thödol*, the *Tibetan Book of the Dead*. According to Hughes the work involved a 'Gigantic orchestra, massed choirs, projected illuminated mandalas, soul-dancers and the rest'. Though the project ultimately died for lack of expected funding, Hughes worked and reworked the libretto a great deal after his return to England that autumn, at least through November 1960, later admitting that he 'got to know the *Bardo Thödol* pretty well' during that period.[30] More than deathbed prayers and instructions to the dying, the *Bardo Thödol* is to be used throughout adult life as a meditative guide to the Buddhist art of dying to the phenomenal world.[31] As Carl Jung wrote in his 'Psychological Commentary' to the *Bardo*, the purpose of the meditation is deliberately to induce a psychological state 'transcendent over all assertion and predication', where the initiate realises that 'the "giver" of all "given" things dwells within us' and that 'even the gods are the radiance and reflection of our own souls'.[32]

As the deceased passes from the *Chikkai Bardo* state of the first four days after death into the *Chönyid Bardo* state of the fifth to fourteenth days, the possibility of experiencing the liberating *nirvana* of the Void, the *Dharma-Kāya* of Clear Light, lessens markedly, for *karmic* illusions appear, urging the soul back to participation in the phenomenal world. Here the text constantly exhorts the deceased not to fear or desire such illusions, to abandon egotism and recognise that all thought-forms are 'the radiance of thine own intellectual faculties come to shine. They have not come from any other place. Be not attracted towards them; be not weak; be not terrified; but abide in the mood of non-thought formation. In that state all forms and radiances will merge into thyself, and Buddhahood will be obtained.'[33] For those unable to abandon egotism, the devices of intellect and fears or attachments to objects in the phenomenal world, the final *Sidpa Bardo* state of involvement with animal instinct dawns on the fifteenth day after death; here the deceased are whirled about by *karmic* winds and the play of instinct until reincarnation at the womb door results forty-nine days after death.

The personae of Part I in *Wodwo* fail to recognise that their fears of participation in temporal experience in Western culture are self-caused. The persona of 'A Vegetarian', for instance, is tripped on 'Eternity's stone threshold', by his fear of sundering his automatic instinctual dependency upon the environment. Both 'A Wind Flashes the Grass' and 'Sugar Loaf' contain imagery of wind-driven environments similar to that of the *Sidpa Bardo*, and for similar reasons: in each case the personae fail to recognise that their own winds of instinctual dependency cause the macabre, fearful gusts.

The goal of Hughes' use of Oriental paradigms is not, however, to attain the self-absorbed, world-annihilating state of yogic *samādhi* or the *nirvana* of the Clear Light in *Bardo* thought, but to return to the world cleansed of over-dependence upon a rational analytic ego that divorces man from nature, fortified with the awakened *ātman* within the self as the generative centre of experience, and capable of merging with a nature newly perceived as benign. In a review (*New Statesman*, 6 September 1963) Hughes wrote that we can launch our archetypal journey toward Reality in either of two directions: 'toward the objectless radiance of the Self, where the world is a composition of benign Holy Powers', or 'toward the objective reality of the world, where man is a virtuoso bacteria . . .'. The latter, Western goal-oriented quest in temporality is blocked for Hughes, as we have noted, from the early 1960s until the mid-1970s, after the *Wodwo–Crow* period. The former direction, the Oriental quest to locate a benign nature through an 'objectless radiance of the Self', through an annihilation of the analytic ego's dependency upon a ruined culture, is the direction of the purgatorial progress of *Wodwo*.

A return to a benign nature after the realisation of an *ātman* unity of self and world is closest to the practices of modern Zen. The psychic process in Zen begins with the *Mahāyāna* principle of emptiness, *śūnyatā*, when all impediments of consciousness are annihilitated, and the mind rests in a passive state of personality dissolution, devoid of thoughts, experiencing the fullness of nothingness. The process ends in *satori* as a psychological upheaval occurs wherein the intellect as a primary seat of knowledge is displaced by an intuitive grasp of the totality of Being, a grasp which is periodically realised *within* the world of mundane tasks.[34] The personae of Part III of *Wodwo* look upon life from a newly-won position of self-assurance and self-control, with a calm exercise of judgment. Moods of Oriental serenity (*śānti*) and a Buddha-like compassion and pity for those who cannot transcend the temporal world, predominate in Part III. The personae are often able, especially in the final poems of the volume, to fuse with the landscape, to view nature with a new beatitude of spirit, and thus envision a universe of plenitude, of 'benign Holy Powers'. Poems such as 'Mountains', 'Gnat-Psalm', 'Skylarks', 'Full Moon and Little Frieda' and 'Wodwo' present nature as benevolent, transfigured by a newly-won sense of freedom wherein the psyche of the persona is not subject to an emotional dependency or ego dependency upon the environment or cultural givens, but is rather a bemused spectator who can view nature as a soothing companion because of an already achieved calmness of mind. To view nature as a 'composition of benign Holy Powers' is closest to Japanese Zen's love of nature 'as a friendly, well-meaning agent whose inner being is thoroughly like our own, always ready to work in accord with our legitimate aspirations', in the words of D. T. Suzuki.[35] This is the result of what Thomas Merton has called Zen's 'ontological awareness of pure being beyond subject and object, [its] immediate grasp of being in its "suchness" and "thusness".'[36] In *Wodwo* Hughes finds the serenity of Zen preferable to a culture wherein repressed libido periodically erupts into mass violence, and a necessary healing balm for a distressed psyche.

'Skylarks' and 'Gnat-Psalm' in Part 3 of *Wodwo* are similar in the ability of the personae to revel in a sense of identity with the animal or insect viewed. In a totally absorbed state of mind the personae manifest a sense of psychic participation in the activities of the perceived object. In Zen this is the contemplation of the object in its *sono-mama* state, in the broadest and deepest aspects of the 'situation as it finds itself', in the words of Suzuki; it is an experience of an 'underlying sense of identity' with the perceived object most often found in haiku artists such as the Zen poet Basho.[37] In section IV of 'Skylarks', for instance, the persona's visionary gaze parallels the upward flight of the lark and its downward exhaustion in a sense of communality with the lark's energetic aspirations:

Dithering in ether
Its song whirls faster and faster
And the sun whirls
The lark is evaporating
Till my eye's gossamer snaps
     and my hearing floats back widely to earth

After which the sky lies blank open
Without wings, and the earth is a folded clod.

At the conclusion of the poem the persona attains such a state of sympathy and harmony with the larks' escapades that he recognises in the arc of their efforts a metaphor for the entire joyous agony of life, a paying back with their labour the life-principle that gave them the breath of existence.

Similarly, in 'Gnat-Psalm' the persona's absorption in the frenetic, untiring activities of the gnats inspires him to create a metaphor for the totality of life as an unceasing expenditure of energy:

O little Hasids
Ridden to death by your own bodies
Riding your bodies to death
You are the angels of the only heaven!

And God is an Almighty Gnat!
You are the greatest of all the galaxies!
My hands fly in the air, they are follies
My tongue hangs up in the leaves
My thoughts have crept into crannies

Your dancing

Your dancing

Rolls my staring skull slowly away into outer space.

When one's thoughts have 'crept into crannies' one experiences a fusion of psyche and landscape, a sense of *ātman* self-identity with the fullness of the environment. Hughes may have been meditating upon an often repeated passage of Suzuki's where he contrasts Basho's ability to make his ecstatically absorbed contemplation of a flower a *sono-mama* intuitive experience of the entirety of the situation in which the flower is found, whereas the analytic Tennyson ('Flower in the Crannied Wall') must pluck his flower from its cranny and surround it with abstractions.[38]

In 'Gnat-Psalm' the gnats, environment and persona also fuse with the poet's moment-to-moment activity of writing the poem. All are at work 'Scrambling their crazy lexicon' in an expenditure of joyous suffering; insistent relative clause repetitions reinforce a frenetic tone wherein everybody is 'everybody else's yoyo'. The persona discovers that the gnats 'are their own sun / Their own brimming over / At large in the nothing'. The self-consuming energy of the gnats, congruent with the consuming energy of nature in the poem, is heightened through the use of the solar fire motif. The gnats in their sacrificial energy are 'giving their bodies to be burned'; their wings are 'blurring the blaze' even as the fiery energy of the sun 'blasts their song'. This is similar to the totalistic vision of the world as being a sacrificial fire of energy in the *Chāndogya Upanishad* (5.4–8); Hughes himself once alluded to the 'Heraclitean/Buddhist notion that the entire Universe is basically made of fire'.[39]

'Gnat-Psalm' is an apt illustration of what the ninth-century Chinese Zen master Rinzai called 'sincerity', a placing of one's whole being into action in the moment, holding nothing in reserve. The final image of the gnat's dizzying fury as rolling the persona's skull into outer space approximates Rinzai's 'true man of no-title' who pervades the entire world of time and space.[40] In utter sympathy with the tarantella-like joyous suffering of the gnats, the persona achieves an *ātman* identity with the created universe, a perception so ecstatically and fully experienced as to indicate most properly a state of *satori*.

Both 'Skylarks' and 'Gnat-Psalm' employ the causistical tendency of

Zen to express the transcendence of dualistic thinking through expressions of negations. In section IV of 'Skylarks' the persona views the upward flight of the lark as 'Scrambling / In a nightmare difficulty / Up through the nothing . . .'. The psalmody in 'Gnat-Psalm' is 'of all the suns', of a unitive experience possible because initially the gnats are 'their own sun / Their own brimming over / At large in the nothing . . .'. Their bearded faces weave and bob 'on the nothing . . .'. The monism behind this overspill of the subjective on to the objective is what negates the objective universe into 'no matter' and creates a sea of 'nothing'. The causistical reasoning employed in these uses of negations parallels that used by Nagarjuna in his doctrine of the 'Eight No's', which Suzuki compares to seeing things in their *sono-mama* 'suchness' or 'allness'.[41] According to Suzuki what is accomplished by such negating is a transcendent, godly afirmation of life, for whereas temporality is always becoming, changing or negating itself moment by moment, 'The eternal must be an absolute affirmation which our limited human understanding defines in negative terms'.[42] The complete negation is thus 'no one time' or 'no one thing' – an unchanging, all-encompassing fullness, an allness of benign nature in an absolute present. Through the use of Zen casuistry, the exuberant tone, and the fusion of persona and landscape with the activities of the gnats, Hughes successfully conveys the most fully realised experience of *satori* epiphanic ecstasy in *Wodwo*.

Unlike the worried persona of 'Sugar Loaf' in part I, the persona of 'Mountains' becomes captivated by the mountains' detachment from the world of love, fear, agony, death, and by their ability to possess the days in peace and contentment, without labour. Through another consciously crafted use of the pathetic fallacy the persona of this poem reveals himself in a mood of serenity; here the cyclic world of growth and decay is as decoration to an entity experiencing tranquility. Both mountains and persona are oblivious to all striving or anxious yearning for temporal rewards; they are at home in an essential selfhood that cannot be disturbed by the flux of the phenomenal world. Mountains, often in the history of literature a symbol for the integrated self, here represent an integration of self and cosmos. A fresh ambiguity in the first lines of the poem reinforces this integration. It is impossible for the reader to tell if the configuration of stones, which become a pointing finger, lead the persona's gaze up the mountain's shoulder to the sleeping divinity believed by primitives to be residing in the centre, or up the persona's shoulder to his own eye. A both/and congruence of perceiver and object is intended.

Both 'Full Moon and Little Frieda' and 'Wodwo', the closing poems of *Wodwo*, present affirmative experiences of congruence with a benign nature. In 'Full Moon and Little Frieda' the child is viewed as a 'mirror', a brimming pail of offering, who gazes at the moon, the largest reflecting object in the cosmos available to the naked eye. The resulting astonishment at the recognition of an identity of mirroring artworks is very striking in itself, and describes another experience of *satori*, of the undifferentiated original essence of the cosmos, at times called by Buddhist poets the 'full moon of suchness'.[43] When little Frieda speaks the word 'moon', the first word she ever articulated as a toddler, subject and object, self and environment merge in ecstatic recognition of self-in-another, in the clarity of spotless, mutually reflecting mirrors:

'Moon!' you cry suddenly, 'Moon! Moon!'

The moon has stepped back like·an artist gazing amazed at a work

That points at him amazed.

The cows that loop the hedges 'with their warm wreaths of breath' earlier in the poem convey an almost nativity scene sense of the purity and supportiveness of a benign nature in attendance. The cows, sacred in Oriental symbology as representations of the plenitude of creation, are an apt background for Frieda's offering of self as a brimming pail of youthful purity to an equally pure moonlight.

Hughes has stated that his objective in writing 'Wodwo', the final and title poem of the volume, was to catch this 'half-man half-animal spirit of the forests', originally from *Sir Gawain and the Green Knight*, in a moment of self-discovery, and with a sense of bewilderment as to just what *is* to be its relationship to the world it is in the process of discovering.[44] In the poem the Wodwo discovers itself *as* it discovers the world; both experiences, identical when the *ātman* is awakened in the 'exact centre' of existence, lead to the Wodwo's discovery that it 'can go anywhere' and that it seems 'to have been given the freedom of this place'. As 'exact centre' of existence-for-the-self the Wodwo is the generator, the creator of its own universe, moment by moment. This frees him to inspect, rather than accept unthinkingly, the assumptions and beliefs of different cultures – and frees him especially from acquiescing through habit to the aforementioned destructive alienation of mind from nature, the repression of instinct in Reformed Christianity, and the inert scientific rationalism of our contemporary Western culture. With such freedom the Wodwo becomes, like Hughes himself, the peripatetic, eclectic anthropologist.

Though poems placed earlier in the ordering of Part III of *Wodwo* do not relate experiences of *satori* fusion with the landscape, they usually articulate positions of self-assurance and self-control from personae exercising calm judgment. Moods of Oriental serenity and a Buddha-like pity for those who cannot transcend the temporal world predominate. Only in 'Gog', 'New Moon in January' and 'Karma' do personae express moods of agitation, and in each case the disquiet is resolved, unlike Part I, in the individual poems themselves. Many of the more baffling poems are influenced by Oriental concepts.

In 'Karma' the poet's meditation upon the sufferings and carnage, created by man in his 'hundred and fifty million years' of civilisation, is the Buddhist retracing of time and *karmic* bondage to suffering (*pratilomen*)[45] in order to absorb it and arrive at the timeless, the point before temporal duration where liberation is possible. Then, by wiping away the dust of all earthly objects from the *karmic* mirror, as in the *Sidpa Bardo*,[46] one attains the objectless state. In 'Karma' the poet experiences acutely man's legacy of carnage; his suffering is so intense as to dislocate time and causality on to the plane of surrealistic nightmare. Unable to find a rationale or augury (the 'poulterer's hare' knows nothing) to make this legacy of pain comprehensible, the persona finally achieves a quietude of spirit in a 'seamless' state transcendent of the stitchings of time and causality – an 'objectless radiance of the Self'. By absorbing the pain, instead of refusing the blame, the persona is finally able to stand firm in an assertion that the answer is 'Not here', not available to analytic reasoning. At this point the persona's consciousness has achieved the objectless state of 'the mirror's seamless sand'. Wiping clean the dust of phenomenality from the *karmic* mirror is a favourite Zen simile for the process of attaining the objectless state of transcendence, as in the following verse by the Zen poet Yōka:

The mind is an organ of thought and objects are set against it:
The two are like marks on the surface of the mirror;
  When the dirt is removed, the light begins to shine.
Both mind and objects being forgotten, Ultimate Nature reveals itself true.[47]

Section I of 'Gog' is a meditation on the dragon of Revelation 12:4 who has been awakened by the Christian Logos-God's assumption of total power ('I am Alpha and Omega': Rev. 1:11; 21:6; 22:13) and His expulsion of the world and the flesh to the sphere of the devil. The world of created matter becomes a world of 'motherly weeping' and uncontrolled action, for which the dragon suffers in the form of a consciousness of guilt and fear: 'I do not look at the rocks and stones, I am frightened of what they see'. But the persona of section II (British edition only) no longer suffers from this aversion to the phenomenal world: 'The stones are as they were. And the creatures of earth / Are mere rainfall rivulets, in flood or empty paths.' At this point the persona experiences a *śūnyatā* state of personality dissolution and a recognition of the fullness of all creation: 'The atoms of saints' brains are swollen with the vast bubble of nothing'. Apocalyptic writings of individual converts can no longer harm. In this state of dissolution the persona also recognises that the dust of Eros in the phenomenal world darkens the *karmic* mirror with 'Death and death and death—'. The 'bright particles' of the dust that is 'in power' produce the alluring 'eyes and / Dance of wants' that ultimately lead to the dissolution of the grave. Here the persona gains a new perception of involvement in temporality as self-destructive.

Section III of 'Gog' (also British edition only) is a prayer to the unborn child of Revelation 12: 1–5, who is to 'rule all nations with a rod of iron' and cast the dragon Gog from heaven. But the persona hopes that this quester will accomplish more than the *Revelations* prophecy of a repression of instinctual life; he hopes that the child will be strong enough to penetrate beyond the illusory phenomenal world of love/death and its ultimately destructive energy. Because the tyrant God has banished the instincts from heaven, questing in a Western goal-oriented fashion in the temporal world will only prove destructive: the quester's horse is 'shod with vaginas of iron', the grail is 'fanged' and resides in an environment dominated by the 'salt milk drug of the mothers'. A better path would be to follow the *Bardo* exhortation to regard the phenomenal world as *māyā* or illusion and avoid entering the womb-door into that phenomenal world. By so avoiding the initiate attains a supernormal birth into the transphenomenal world of the Clear Light, the *nirvana* release from rebirth.[48] In section III of 'Gog' Hughes' persona advises the child to pierce the veil of phenomenality. Whereas Coriolanus relented from conquering Rome at his mother Volumnia's request, the child quester is exhorted to be even more non-violent, to pierce with his awakened understanding through the temporal world of *māyā* and refrain from acting. He is exhorted rather to 'follow his weapons toward the light', which in context is an alternative to octopus maw, cradle and womb-wall of *māyā* – perhaps the '*Dharma-Kāya* of Clear Light', the state of *nirvanic* illumination in the *Chikhai Bardo*. A soured attitude toward Reformed Christianity's banishment of instinctual life predominates throughout 'Gog', but in sections II and III the persona is in control of the subject matter, exercising firm judgment.

As with the three sections of 'Gog', the progression of the three sections of 'Song of a Rat' constitute a penetration to a higher comprehension of reality based upon an Eastern model. The situation presented in section I is that of the trapped rats of the short story 'Sunday'. Yet the persona of section I, in contrast to the callow Michael, has compassion and pity for an animal too dependent on its relationship with the physical environment to acquire an Oriental consciousness of the illusoriness of temporality. '"This has no face, it must be God"' and '"No answer is also an answer"' are modernisations of ancient Zen *kōans* designed to destroy human dependence upon logic and objectivity en route to *satori*, as in Eno's *kōan*, 'Show me your original face before you were born', in response to Ming's request for instruction, or Shen-kuang's perfect silence in response to Bodhidharma's request to his pupils to exhibit their greatest insights, or the silent non-lectures on *satori* delivered by Yakusan and Hayakujo.[49] *Kōans* are unanswerable, designed to reveal the limited contexts in which human reason operates, and to promote the realisation that all authority, truth and motivation must come entirely from within the self, not from external authority. By trying to escape its predicament the rat is merely pitiable, until it achieves a sudden moment of understanding, presented in section 11, which differs markedly from the rat's resignation in 'Sunday'.

In 'The Rat's Vision', section 11 of 'Song of a Rat', a moment of insight into the meaninglessness of what is now perceived as a desolate, alienating landscape causes a withdrawal into a subjectively realised personal godliness or *ātman*, a 'Forcing' of 'the rat's head down into godhead'. Paralleling this is a loss of the rat's sense of dependency upon the farmyard environment, due to a new perception of the futility of remaining in a futureless and fatalistic pastoral scene, now an illusory 'Wobbling like reflection on water'.

The imagery and symbolism of section III, 'The Rat's Flight', indicates that the rat has fled the temporal world. The rat supplants hell by casting its material body to the dogs while achieving a state 'Never to be buried' as 'the Shadow of the Rat / Cross[es] into power'. This psychological process is attended by thunder and lightning imagery, standard procedure for instances of *ātman* illumination in the *Upanishads* and of *satori* in Zen.[50] The rat no longer screeches in his trap; he has attained a spiritual body and has freed himself by trusting to inner powers and self-reliance. In Hindu mythology the rat, because of its uncanny ability to overcome obstacles and find a route into the bolted granary, is the theriomorphic counterpart of Ganesha, 'The Lord and Master of Obstacles', son of Shiva and his consort.[51] If Hughes deliberately intends a reference to the Jungian archetype of the Shadow in section III, the reference would be appropriate, for when the Shadow crosses into conscious life in Jungian psychology the formerly unconscious abilities and energies become integrated into a higher state of consciousness, and with a new feeling of power.[52]

Like Gog and the Rat, the persona of 'You Drive in a Circle' recognises the barrenness of temporality. As he careers through sheets of the ubiquitous English rain in a countryside landscape, he realises that roads offer a change of place not worth the taking, that the resistance of the elements is not worth the expense of energy, and that the scenery of sheep-filled moors contains for him but the futility of an unconscious obeisance to animal and vegetable function. With Buddha-like compassion and pity the persona of 'You Drive in a Circle' addresses a bovine, unconscious animal fealty to lockstep instinctual processes going nowhere:

Down in there are the sheep, rooted like sponges,
Chewing and digesting and undeterred.

What could they lose, however utterly they drowned?
Already sodden as they are with the world, like fossils.
And what is not the world is God, a starry comforter of good blood.

A recognition of the yogic *īshwara pranidhāna*, the god within the self as the transphenomenal ground of all being, is the destination abandoned by the persona when he opened his car door. The fact that he does realise this during his journey indicates that he is beginning to acknowledge that inner self as the source of wisdom. The last line of the poem, 'Your destination waits where you left it', echoes a line from *The Zenrin* on the inner location of wisdom: 'If you do not get it from yourself, / Where will you go for it?'[53]

The persona of 'You Drive in a Circle' also recognises the necessity of merging subject and object within the self as he characterizes the low rain-clouds as 'mist-gulfs of no-thinking.' The word 'no-thinking' is a precise term in Buddhist thought: both *munen* and *acintyā* mean literally 'no-thinking' or 'beyond thinking', and are aspects of the experience of Oriental Enlightenment dealing with the merging of rationality and irrationality, subject and object, when the spiritual self penetrates through the analytic thinking of consciousness and an intuitional state of self-identity with the universe is achieved.[54] The persona at the conclusion of 'You Drive in a Circle' realises that 'Everything is already here' – within the subjective self's intuitional powers, which have no necessary 'anchor' in the temporal world.

One final poem influenced by Oriental concepts is 'Theology', the opening poem of Part III of *Wodwo*. Unlike the serpent of 'Reveille' in Part I, the serpent of 'Theology' ends rather than initiates a temporal process by digesting the Adam–Eve historical consciousness and sloping off to another realm, a private 'Paradise' unencumbered by the complaints of a peevish God. The serpent's power to isolate himself from the historical process and the collocation of his smiling with his private paradise suggest that the paradise alluded to is the Western Paradise of Amitabha, the realm away from historical time in the Pure Land School of Chinese Buddhism. In the 'White Lotus Ode', a poem typical of the Pure Land School, and whose title Hughes alluded to in an early poem,[55] the compassionate smile and transcendent abode of Amitabha is available to all those wandering in the depths of temporality who invoke his name. To those confined by 'the body's oppressive sorrows' Amitabha offers 'a spiritual body' in a paradise 'brightened with gladness'; he 'sends his smile out to the dwellings of the suffering' and 'draws every burdened soul up from the depths / And lifts them into his peaceful abode'.[56] The snake of 'Theology', able to slough the skin of temporality, the 'dark intestine' of Western cyclic renewal through temporal birth/death, is Ananta or Shesha, the Hindu cosmic snake, who resides in the supratemporal realm. Vishnu dreams the lotus dream of the universe while reposing on Ananta. As Balarāma, half brother of Krishna, rests lost in thought beneath a tree on the ocean shore, the immortal serpent essence of Shesha crawls out of his mouth and returns to the paradisal Abyss.[57]

The remaining Part III poems, though not influenced by Oriental concepts, are similar in their recognition that goal-oriented striving in the temporal world of Western culture is utter folly. 'Heptonstall', the town whose graveyard houses the remains of Sylvia Plath, is a 'black village of gravestones' in which the only comfort and surety is the meaningless rain of mutability. Viking invaders in 'The Warriors of the North' have tainted Western culture with the anal obstinacy, covetousness and rapacity behind their urge for conquest. The taint affects the future: following Weber and Tawney, Hughes intimates that the intense wordly industriousness, required by Calvinism and other Protestant sects as proof of Election, differs very little from the avarice and rapacity behind the heroic urge for conquest. The wolves of 'The Howling of Wolves' are pitiable; unlike the feared carriers of ancestral evil or re-empowering wolf mask divinities of 'February' in *Lupercal*, these wolves are uncomprehending creatures living by blind instinct. The landscape of 'Pibroch' is destitute, worthwhile only as a veil of materiality to be pierced by the 'staring angels' of one's visionary thoughts. Hughes finds the mind/spirit dichotomy of 'Kreutzer Sonata' to be a laughable, self-castrating process of mutual cancellation, the product of the delusions of unenlightened, analytic reason. The persona of 'New Moon in January' utters the faint shriek of Shelley's 'Epipsychidion' in the hope of transcending the temporal world of blood and death through inner powers. With the single exception of 'New Moon in January' the personae of these Part III poems articulate the folly of goal-oriented involvement in Western culture with self-control and calm judgment.

The work of anthropologists and historians of comparative religion and mythology such as Lévi-Strauss, Eliade, Campbell, Castaneda and Suzuki attest to the fact that the Oriental and primitive minds are by no means uncouth or simplistic, but merely organise reality according to different perceptual coordinates and cultural values. Yet beneath the differing cultural systems man's mythmaking and ordering capacities have basically remained constant in both primitive and literate, Western and Oriental societies; it is only through the insights, inventions and discoveries of men of genius that the field of perception and knowledge widens, after which the average minds reorganise the reconstituted systems. Even language itself serves to systematise man's perceptions and performs as a carrier of embedded assumptions and values; Korzybskian semanticists believe that language imposes a convenient analytic grid upon what remains a mysterious, 'unspeakable' reality. If this is the case, and if our Western Greco-Roman-Christian civilisation is hopelessly bankrupt with scientific abstractions, sterile materialism and periodic explosions of repressed instinctual energy, as Hughes believes, then new capital from non-Western modes of apprehending reality may prove therapeutic. The beauty of the direct, pre-cognitive apprehension of the suchness of reality-for-the-self in Zen can at least awaken the reader to a freedom-promoting consciousness of cultural relativism, and to the elasticity and strength of our perceptive powers.

In *Wodwo* Hughes is not asking us to exchange our bibles and pocket calculators for the loincloths of Oriental asceticism; he is clearing a fresh path for an important revolution in perception that can free the individual from unconscious habituation to the failed values that have blinded us to a bankrupt Western exchequer. He is also suggesting that mind, body and spirit can achieve a self-control that can lead to a reempowering confidence in the gold of our own fresh perceptions, and the treasure of a mastery of our own inner selves and individual destinies. The Wodwo may be a pacifist given to reflection and meditation, but there is much quiet strength and resolve in the decision to live reality according to the clarity of involved, moment-by-moment cognition rather than according to the usual unreflective acceptance of prevailing cultural givens. The Wodwo's opposite is Crow, who expects to achieve wonders through an uncritical and conventional involvement in the landscape, science, language and myths of a culture overflowing with destructive energy. Contrarily, the Zen adept, like the primitive in a shamanising culture, maintains such an exalted respect for nature that aggressive, amoral conduct is far less likely than it is in our Western gospel of materialism.

In the title essay of *The Poet in the Imaginary Museum*, Donald Davie recognises that new research in anthropology is the most significant post World War II cultural event, and that an open-minded cultural relativism is the single most significant attribute of all ambitious, major comtemporary poetry. Yet critics often react stubbornly with charges of obscurantism when contemporary poets are attentive to such research. The problem often lies, however, with the narrowness and rigidity of the critic's education. Though Hughes seldom consciously embeds his poetry with direct references to primitive or Oriental cultures, his mind is imbued with decades of reading in the literatures and mythologies of non-Western cultures, and this inevitably influences the content and subject matter of his poems. Attention to such areas reveals just how carefully organised and lucid are the poems of *Wodwo*. Hughes is not at all desirous of sending critics or readers searching after tarot packs and holy grails, but he is passionately interested in acknowledging and opening up negotiations with the destructive energies of contemporary Western culture, and in redirecting these energies through a mind aware of what modes of perception and spiritual training other cultures have to offer.

The poems of *Wodwo* are carefully articulated stages in the pyschological upheaval from a consciousness of a cultural cul-de-sac to the freedom of the Wodwo, stations in the path the poet creates to extricate himself from the forest of encrusted beliefs to achieve the liberating light of reaffirmation of the self as the generator of one's perceptions and values. The surrealistic landscape of Part 1 of *Wodwo* becomes even more exacerbated in the destructive violence of the landscape in *Crow*, but the Oriental influence achieves more long-lasting, beneficial effects in the clarity of direct perception and involvement with a benign nature in *Remains of Elmet* and *Moortown*.

Hughes and drama

Ted Hughes does not consider himself a playwright. Indeed, he seemed surprised when reminded recently that he wrote at least eighteen plays between 1960 and 1971. He refers to these plays now as 'mere bagatelles'. They 'remained unreal' to him. 'The parts that were interesting became poems.'[1]

Most critics seem now to share Hughes' current view, that what was interesting about his plays was the poems in them, and the poems that came out of them. However, at the time he was writing these plays there was some evidence that he himself and a significant part of the theatre community took them very seriously. For instance, Peter Hall commissioned one for the Royal Shakespeare Company,[2] T. S. Eliot offered to read and discuss them,[3] E. Martin Browne found them 'exciting',[4] and Peter Brook, perhaps England's leading director, established a working relationship with him. Hughes' wife, Sylvia Plath, referred to him repeatedly as a playwright.[5] But the most convincing evidence of his deeply serious commitment to the theatre can be drawn from a close study of the plays themselves. These are not merely situations contrived to give actors an excuse to recite poetry, nor were they simply myth-like structures out of which he could mine for the poems he wished to save, though they did serve these purposes admirably, and that fact is the basis of the rationale that this was their function. They were more. A close scrutiny of the plays themselves reveals an original and exciting approach to drama, an attempt to accomplish something on stage that hasn't been done before, an effort to explore a hitherto uncharted terrain, to open a door for actors and audience into an experience new to them. The plays demand a new kind of theatre, a theatre not truly seen on any stage yet, but implicit in the work. They are visionary plays. One thinks of what it would have been like to read *The Cenci* before the Theatre of Cruelty had emerged to accommodate it.

Major, sweeping changes in the theatre have often stemmed from changes in *mise en scène*, or, in the larger sense, setting, the environment in which a play takes place. An example of this would be the effect of naturalism on the theatre: sets that really look like the places they are supposed to portray, period costumes, actors who could pass on the street for the characters they are playing have a psychological effect on both actors and audience, as well as on the playwright, whose work is limited by what can be realistically depicted on stage. By the same token, the choice of unusual and demanding locales can strain the capabilities of the theatre, and force it to innovate to accommodate the new concept of place. The Poor Theatre, which works with a minimum of props, was a response to the need to develop, in the imagination of the audience, settings which could not be realistically rendered. It has become more difficult to baffle theatre people in this century, as they learned to evoke nearly anything they could imagine, with only a gesture or an attitude to serve as props. However, the netherworld of Hughes' plays, which in this paper will be called the Bardo, proves difficult for the simple reason that it is difficult to imagine.

Another, extremely important source of change in the theatre has been staging, or the way in which a play is presented, and it is here that Hughes' plays seem now to be almost unproduceable. An example of a revolution in staging in the past was when the Elizabethans began to perform the violence left offstage by the Greeks and Romans, that is to say when they made the stage an arena for action as well as for narration. Rather than simply evoking, through dance and poetry, the violent events that had always served as the central focus of the stories they told, actors began to enact them on stage. This development probably occurred out of a misinterpretation of closet writers like Seneca. Not knowing that these plays had been considered unproduceable, they produced them. Not understanding that the ancient could not conceive of a theatre of violence, the Elizabethans, in their naïveté, created one.

With this stroke, the theatre changed in character. It has been a place where only certain kinds of discussions could be held, and became a place where another category of confrontations could occur. Actors were asked to strike each other onstage, to kill each other, to rape and molest, and the discovery that evoking this was no more impossible than evoking the shadow emotions of rage, pity and dread they had been experiencing for centuries led to entirely new and different possibilities.

Another example of a revolution in staging came when actors were asked to become non-human onstage, and in one case even to become a bed-sitting-room. The theatre has found resources to portray a large variety of events and conditions. However, Hughes' work demands an experience that the actor as yet doesn't know how to give: it demands that the actor should become a shaman and perform something like magic onstage, that he should dip into his resources for madness, that he should carry himself and the audience with him into the world between life and death.

In his effort to find a viable alternative to naturalism, Hughes is solidly within the tradition of twentieth-century theatrical movements, such as Expressionism and the Anti-Theatre. Brecht's efforts led him to adopt the stage itself as a setting, and to alienate the actors from the story. Witkiewicz, himself a painter, turned to pure form, and Handke attempted to use language as an environment. Hughes' solution is to make an alternative world, as real as life is, and place the one in juxtaposition to the other. Unlike the dream realms of the surrealists, Hughes' alternative world is taken utterly seriously. It is not to be seen as symbolism, or as fantasy or hallucination. The difference between Strindberg's Dream Plays and Hughes' plays is the difference between declamations through a classic mask and the genuine salt tears of a method actor; it is the difference between symbolism and naturalism. Implicit in Hughes' work is a demand for actors to engage in the spiritual world they have so often evoked onstage, as freely as if they lived there.

Hughes was apparently attracted to the theatre by the dynamism good actors can bring to words with their voices and gestures, projecting personality into passages that might seem cold on paper. He was also attracted by an 'elemental, bottomless, impersonal, perfect quality [in some voices], which seems open to the whole Creation', the 'sort of sound' that makes the spirits listen, a sound that 'opens our deepest and innermost ghost to sudden attention' which he noted actors could sometimes attain. He suggested that the original purpose of drama was to provide occasion for such sounds and gestures.[6] And one might speculate that it was his observation that these spiritual evocations were possible that prompted him to attempt to create a setting in which they would be appropriate.

On another level, he was attracted by the possibilities of plays themselves. He commented that the play, for Shakespeare, was

a wonderfully well organised circuit of interior illuminations, to which all the complexities of the words are aligned with such subtle accuracy it seems miraculous, and which is a bigger poem in bigger language and of greater beauty than any brief isolated passage of verse could possibly bring into focus.[7]

Theatre is like music in that one's understanding of individual words is informed by the theatrical equivalent of melodic line, something actors call 'through line', a thread that serves as plot even when supposedly there is none, and that ignites the story current in a great play.

Even when there are no actors and no stage, and when we are only reading a play, this momentum operates on us to alter the individual definitions of words. 'The play', says Hughes, 'binds the words magnetically, decides their meaning and polarity, seals them off from ordinary life, consecrates and inspires them'.[8] Just as the poet utilises imprecision to his advantage, creating overtones of meaning with the device of charging wildly inappropriate words with the meaning of his context, so the playwright can cast overtones of meaning into his characters, whose existence is coloured by the plots in which they find themselves. It is possible that a careful examination of the plots of Hughes' plays will yield a key to the reality he had hoped to evoke.

Clearly, he did not intend his plays as literature for a reading public, since so few have become available in print. Only seven of his plays have been published in their entirety, and five of these are children's plays. What we have of the rest is fragmentary – odd scenes printed in journals, excerpts appearing as poems in their own right, and sometimes simply the odd review.

His first play was apparently entitled *The House of Taurus*, but it seems never to have been produced or published. *The House of Aries*, his second, is represented only by 'Part 1'.[9] Some excerpts from different drafts of key passages in that Part – 'Speech of the Ouija', 'Wife's Song', and 'The Captain's Speech' – appear in *Two Cities*,[10] and another version of 'The Captain's Speech' and a dialogue, 'The Gibbons', appear in *Texas Quarterly*.[11]

Commentators give totally contradictory descriptions of *Difficulties of a Bridegroom*, which was really only a catch-all title used over and over by Hughes for experiments ranging from a radio drama of 'personal rituals'[12] to 'an outline scenario' for an improvised farce.[13] The ending of the fine press play, *Eat Crow*,[14] has been published separately as a dialogue entitled 'X'.[15] Other parts became such poems as 'Ghost Crabs' and 'Crow Paints Himself into a Chinese Mural'. The beginning of *Crow Wakes* is adapted from a 'monologue by the stuffed father of the Bride'.[16]

The important early play *The Wound* is available in *Wodwo*.[17] The only other play by Hughes which we have whole is his adaptation of Seneca's *Oedipus*,[18] an adaptation that has at least as much Hughes as it does Seneca, focusing on the dual nature of the protagonist rather than his stoicism. *Oedipus* is the one play Hughes still considers 'serious', because it gave him 'an idea of what the level of intensity must be'. Only in the all-but-lost *The Calm* did Hughes feel the same command, and then just in the first scene, after which, he complains, he 'just had to go on and finish it'.[19] *Orghast*, the most innovative and ambitious of Hughes' staged works, is not yet published. The manuscript has recently been found again after being given up for lost. Except for the excerpt 'The Birth of Sogis'[20] we know *Orghast* only by hearsay, though there is a very short plot outline by Hughes himself.[21]

What we have of his work suggests that the topic Hughes has said was uniquely his, the conflict between 'vitality and death' and a celebration of the 'warriors' on either side, was at the centre of each of his plots. One might even say that the phrase 'a conflict between vitality and death' would serve as a plot outline for most of them, and for some, we can even insert the names of characters who personify these forces.

There is some indication that he thinks of this confrontation with the spirit world of death as the original theatrical 'plot'. In this basic story, the young man receives a 'call' to visit the spirit world. Hughes suggests that this sort of call is behind every ancient story. It is a theme that has always been written about.[22]

In his analysis of Shakespeare[22] he points out that the underlying theme in all that poet's work is of a man who suddenly sees the monstrous–divine nature of the woman he loves, and then becomes aware of the monster buried in himself. In Hughes' work this same monster man, deducing from the illogic of the darkness in his own nature another nature, hidden from him, becomes a shaman to enter the underworld and retrieve that warped, demonic psyche which is at the root of this mystery.

Some similar ritual may have been the original purpose of theatre itself. In any case, Hughes evokes this ancient theme with a sureness and literalness that startles us, along with his civilised protagonists, and plunges us into the realm of those transactions. It is as if the poet were working some alchemy, with the play his rite, the magic of contact with darkness his outcome.

Early in his career, after writing *The House of Aries* in 1960, he started working on a verse translation of the Tibetan *Book of the Dead*, the *Bardo Thödol*, to be used as a libretto for an opera by the Chinese composer Chou Wen-Chung.[24]. The *Book of the Dead* was traditionally a guide to the living to help them assist the dead in their passage through the Bardo, the 'between' state, a place where dead souls hover, earthbound but immaterial. It is the place the shaman visits when he wants to speak with the dead, the astral plane, the limbo where dead and living can meet.

Though this translation was never published or produced it seems to have had an enormous impact on Hughes and his development as a dramatist. For it is from this project that we can assume he found his true setting, not simply a Hemingway-like arena of violence to intensify life, but a transcendent zone, the Bardo itself, the 'space between' life and death.

The Bardo is a place that can be entered by the living during certain dreams. In *The Word of the Holy Ones*,[25] Daniel informs King Nebuchadnezzar:

A dream is not like a wild beast
It.cannot be deterred with a strong look.
A dream is not like a flawed glass,
It cannot be demolished with a stout knock.
A dream is not like a brook in a meadow,
You cannot dig it a new channel in a few days.
A dream is not like a bubble or a bubble's shadow,
When it has gone it has not gone: and it stays.
Wishes fly like hail, and melt into the sod,
Or fly like butterflies and wither.
They wet for a while, like the rain's worst rage.
But a dream that comes from God
Comes like a bullet, like a bulldozer, like the breath of an Ice Age,
And lifts a man like a feather.

The Bardo, then, is a place of madness. When he awakes from his seven-year dream, during which he has believed himself to be a wild animal, Nebuchadnezzar says, 'I have paid in pain and blood / For all that can be understood'. 'Happy is the man whom God corrects', we are told by the Narrator. 'The Universe, pestling a man in its mortar, / Smashes him to atoms or perfects.'

Even in the early play *The House of Aries*,[26] though the later recurrent characters from the underworld do not appear, it is not difficult at all to determine who represents vitality and who death. Morgan, the bitter and violent heir of the household, the hero on the side of death, confronts Elaine, his foundling foster-sister, who stubbornly clings to life, and with whom he feels entrapped almost in a marriage of jealous brotherhood and guilt. It is the Lodger, in this play, who is the tourist so frequently found in Hughes' work, the outsider to whom things happen, and whose consciousness is altered by a new awareness of the conflict in the human psyche. He is the protagonist immersed in his civilised concerns. He is neither alive nor dead, but half asleep; living, but only half aware of himself, with the subterranean part of his nature hidden from him. He is adrift in the story, so preoccupied with his studies that he doesn't notice at first the intense struggle between Morgan and Elaine. She is committed to life, and Morgan is as maddened by her optimism as he is by her disgust with him. When he finally assaults her, she suggests that his courage was stimulated by the threat of battle outside (an advancing army is approaching the house) and by his step-mother's sexual advances to him, but we can see that what goads him unendurably is her refusal to see those dark forces herself. He taunts her with the suggestion that the gibbons she sees as a celebration of life will rape her without bothering to take off their boots. It is the Lodger's sudden realisation that this wild attack on her springs out of a frustrated love that triggers his own sudden interest in Elaine, and convinces him that he loves her too.

In Hughes' children's plays, this contest between vitality and death is often very close to the surface. For example, in *Orpheus*,[27] broadcast in the eventful year of 1971, the year that produced *Orghast* and *A Choice of Shakespeare's Verse*, the hero, whose beautiful music had been paid for with the death of his wife, descends to the underworld to bring her back. He is able to flower Persephone's pinched maggot face with his music, and in return Pluto allows him to retrieve his wife's soul. However, he has been seared by the experience, and when he returns to earth with her spirit, which will for ever remind him of the dark realm below, his music is altered. In this play alone of the children's plays, the protagonist comes away from an experience of the underworld scarred and altered, in a pattern as uncompromising as his work for adults. But even in the context of this stern reminder of the irreversible nature of death, the play is a triumphant assertion of the power of love.

Three of the children's plays turn on the image of a father who is helpless to protect his daughter from some supernatural power. But in these works, where Hughes allows himself the luxury of resolution, the daughters are wakened to life. In *Beauty and the Beast*[28] the monstrous shadow which haunts Floreat, and is killing her, turns out to be love, which cures her when it is released. But first she has to tell the bear she loves him. Katy Poppocopolis, in *Sean, the Fool, the Devil and the Cats*,[29] is also miraculously rescued. And in *The Price of a Bride*,[30] that price, which will save the Princess from the Ghost, is the love poem of a defeated suitor. It answers the riddle and wins the wager so the Ghost must 'vanish Forever into the ground' and go to his grave.

In the short poem 'Notes for a Little Play', we see a scenario in which death engulfs life. The horror is let loose, but life will not be vanquished – in the heat, in the pure electrical realm beyond life and death, life asserts itself and begins to make love.

Two survivors, moving in the flames blindly.

Mutations – at home in the nuclear glare.

Horrors – hairy and slobbery, glossy and raw.

They sniff towards each other in the emptiness.

They fasten together. They seem to be eating each other.

But they are not eating each other.

They do not know what else to do.

They have begun to dance a strange dance.[31]

Always, in Hughes' vision, when the monster is released it is seen to be love, and the light it has been inhibited from shedding, and which has become a twisted, killing force, which has made the underworld a place of horror, is love veiled.

The Wound[32] is the first of the plays we have extant to take place actually in the Bardo. The hero is Ripley, a wounded soldier, and the action of the play (taken from one of Hughes' own dreams) occurs in a dream-like place, as he decides whether to join his comrades in the nether world or whether to come back to the mud and horror of the battlefield.

The place is dream-like, but the action is not. Ripley is really *at* the château, and the strange events that form that world are real. We understand him to truly exist there, and to also truly be suffering in the mud somewhere else on some battlefield. And, in the terms of the play, neither reality is compromised by the existence of the other.

Ripley occasionally understands that he is in a place of the dead, but he never truly understands what the women keep trying to tell him: the sergeant and the others are completely dead, but he is different. He is only a guest in the between world, as he isn't quite dead yet. He keeps forgetting where he is, or not quite believing it, though the 'clues' of blood on his boot, the occasional reference to his head wound, and the unreliability of logic in his new environment keep reminding him that he is beaneath the surface of reality, or transcending it. He seems on the verge of guessing that it is within the confines of his own mind that this trick is being played on him. Part of him is creating his dream, as the château mends its own bomb damage and develops a glass floor and ballroom and the beautiful women try to seduce him; but part of him is suspicious and hostile, debunking the pathetic attempts of his mind to mask the horror and corruption in an illusion of vitality. Part of him is Tannhäuser in the Venusberg, part of him contemptuous, resisting even the temptation of the young girl, who he postulates might not be damaged yet, since she shows no signs of the tell-tale greasy mark of corruption around the mouth. It is this girl who prevails. She is an advocate of life. She coaxes him and lures him and gets him walking until, by 'sheer animal instinct' he finds his own lines.

The Bardo is not Venusberg. It does not masquerade as a pretty place. Neither is it precisely hell. Its horror comes in waves, just as its occasional glamour does. We see no malice in the ghoulish women who appear to devour the sergeant.

Although the audience eventually understands what is happening to Ripley, he himself never has to confront the possibilities of the Bardo. But Morgan, in *Eat Crow*,[33] first deduces its existence, and then begins to explore its depths. Morgan is presented incontrovertible evidence by the Prosecutor that somebody else inhabits his body, somebody who has a great deal more power than Morgan does over his body-functions, and over many of his decisions, somebody who remembers everything, who is able to keep track of all the myriad details of his history and his physiology. This other Morgan, Morgan 2, appears to be responsible for that part of himself that Morgan 1 either disclaims or has not competence for. Morgan enters the Bardo in order to meet this double, who then leads him, through guided imagery reminiscent of transcendent meditating techniques, into a realm where he is assured he has been able to murder himself, or his astral self, with the slicing edge of King Lear's 'Never'. However, once he has arrived at the 'other side', he is reminded of the crow, which is a 'sign of life', and like Ripley, he returns to his earthly self, but this time with the intensity of a man who knows, like the crow, the other parts of his nature.

Eat Crow would be a difficult play to produce, because although the format seems on the surface to be expressionistic, it does not make use of symbols as a convention. Rather, it is the expression of a mental state, the sort of expression that is generally confined to the written page. To produce it properly on stage, a vocabulary of movement and sound for that state would have to be developed, or it would in the end remain a reading. In this play, for the first time, we begin to glimpse the challenge of the kind of drama Hughes is writing.

Eat Crow is said to have been a fragment of one version of the radio play, *Difficulties of a Bridegroom*,[34] broadcast several times in 1963, a piece about the vivid dream of a young man preoccupied by his inability to remember what his fiancée looks like. On the occasion of having to slow his car to avoid a hare, Sullivan remembers the death of another hare, whose cry had haunted him. In his dream, a woman places her hand on his arm, and demands that he describe her. The images that come to his mind 'don't fit' and he complains that she is 'putting things' in his mind – terrified fish, animals, a candle flame, none of them like her skin, which is white. He is told that the price of having her is a flat in Soho, a job and parties, and that he dress 'to his convictions', in the skins of animals in honour of the 'flame that leaps the gap'. But he counters by noting that she is unclear to him, a metaphor. Her protests and threats to become a 'maneater' are useless. His contempt for 'metaphysical parallels' is unshakeable. He insists that he will be able to recognise his 'real' bride in a 'platonic blaze of reunion', and he will not be lured by tears or threats to embrace a 'counterfeit'. After a second effort to conjure her image, he is able, this time, to see her body, but this vision too dissolves before his scrutiny, leaving nothing but this 'monumental fact', the 'absolute'. In his third attempt, in a remarkable guide to entering the Bardo, he is instructed to see *through* his images, to free his mind for the task of seeing, not images, but past images. Her dialectical body, the breasts each housing one of the woman's two minds, when seen through becomes 'an assemblage of Universal black, the outer nothing and the inner, electrified with lust, ambition and a nameless raving madness, a God Almighty geometric passion'. In order to perceive her waiting essence he is step by step asked to undergo the kind of transformation Hughes has elsewhere described as the 'central episode' in the classic shamanistic dream, a dismemberment.[35] To reach her he must, in an agonising, violent loss, convert each part of his body, piece by piece, with the help of a ravenous tiger, to abstraction, each to a number. Once he has in this way lost his body to become 'reborn', he is instructed to 'glide in along the sempiternal guides, the grooves worn in the beginning by the hardly awakened angels', and his body, thrice burned, is recovered, and placed in a white bed with and of her. At this completion, a pair of poachers are frightened off, thinking they must have shot Sullivan as well as the hare. Sullivan, after recovering the body of their game, claims to have run over and killed the creature himself, and we are so unclear about which of the events has taken place in the Bardo and which on earth, that we are unable to guess how it died. He sells the carcass and offers his girl friend the money, which she refuses as 'blood money', but which she accepts, reluctantly, once it has been converted 'in heaven' into two red roses.

As with *Eat Crow*, it is difficult to see how a production of these scenes might be mounted without some metamorphosis *inside the actor himself* becoming evident to the audience. External effects, though they would enhance the atmosphere, seem inadequate to express what is going on. In this play, what seems an impossibility is written into the script: an actor, who enters the action in this world, is asked to show us how it looks and sounds when he enters the Bardo.

Sullivan's journey to the Bardo seems almost gratuitously triggered by the memory of a hare's death cry. In *Dogs*,[36] written in 1963 and first broadcast in February 1964, Hughes explores the mind of a man desperately trying to avoid the mental state of being in the Bardo, a state which comes to him, he says, only because of the pressures of his work, and his grief over his mother's death. The pattern of his madness fits what Hughes describes elsewhere[37] as the price of an attempt to repress an irrepressible spirituality. If it cannot express itself naturally, he says, it becomes daemonic. We view Marcus' unwilling shamanistic 'flight', in this remarkable play, both from the outside, studying how it looks to others as he makes the transition, and from the inside, from his own increasingly unreliable perceptions as they filter through the altering state of his mind. We see him through the eyes of his landlady, who is afraid of him because of the violence of his nightmares, and through the eyes of his colleagues, who note that he has 'the sort of eyes people have after some awful disaster' – the right eye quite normal, but the left with a sort of 'unfocussed stare'. Looking out of it, from the right half of Marcus' brain, the part that 'should be more or less dormant', is his double, someone we suppose to be Marcus 2, 'the squatter staring out through the keyhole'. The right eye 'knows nothing about it'.

Marcus himself notes the unreliability of his own brain. At one moment he is looking forward, 'with complete clarity', to killing himself, and then that wish is completely gone. The play becomes a fugue of the two states, the one, when he sees out of his left eye, when he is his animal self, when he is suicidal, when he hears the howling of the dogs, when he is unable to find the connections between the facts of existence; and the other, the left brain-state, when everything makes sense, when even the death camps and the existence of dogs, even the fact that a pretty girl is Chinese and is reading about polyps can make sense to him.

The Bardo, in this play, is no longer a 'place', located on some distant 'terrain', no longer a dream state separated from wakefulness by a total break in conscious states, from waking to dreaming, but a perception of reality which competes for dominance in the mind of a man desperate to retain his 'sane' awareness. The 'double' is no longer a different person inhabiting the body of a man without his knowledge, no longer an 'it' to be examined by him, but has begun to examine *him*. When Marcus cries out for help, he is introduced, by the Defence, to the 'complaints' – voices reminiscent of the Prosecutor in *Eat Crow* – who tell him his body has revolted. 'Your shadow's finished with you, it's sick of your thickness.'

As he slips into his right-brain insanity, Marcus is haunted by the howling of dogs, who represent to him the carnal body in revolution, the Other. Dogs' brains are, we are told, mostly wild, but are contaminated by the 3 per cent of imbecile domesticated cortex which has been grafted onto a missing segment of animal nature. They have eaten the singing 'castaway gilt head', dividing it among themselves. If one listens to their wolf howling, as Bach did, one can perceive a natural fugue. Like men, dogs are neither domestic nor wild, but some bastard mix. It is in the midst of a bar-room row about the virtues of dogs that Marcus finally begins to bark, and kills himself.

Peter Brook had for years been experimenting with the difference that could be effected on stage if the actor himself were to experience some sort of altered consciousness. He had invited the Polish director Grotowski, an innovative researcher along these lines, to work with his company in London, and had involved himself enthusiastically with the philosophy of Gurdjieff, who had spent his life teaching Westerners exotic techniques designed to expand consciousness, culled from such sources as Tibetan monasteries, Coptic teachers and Sufi cults. Both Gurdjieff and Grotowski were interested in sound and movement, striving for a deeply rooted, apparently unmotivated and 'pure' expression, and were able to teach their disciples to control ranges that seemed quite extraordinary. The general idea was that when someone is able to make a genuinely uncomplicated noise or gesture, that is to say, a gesture fully and deeply expressive without the contamination of mannerisms, something about the wholeness of the experience is transmitted to a watcher, so that the interior state is manifest.

It seemed a natural collaboration – Hughes, whose topic was the Bardo, that spiritual 'place' whose expression in reality is a state of mind, and a director whose object was to evoke that state of mind on stage and project it to an audience. The story Hughes had been working on, bit by bit, and that was beginning to emerge, in pieces, from his poetry and his plays, was that of someone outside, someone inexperienced and unprepared for such a reality, first being presented with disconcerting evidence of the existence of the Bardo, and then invited to visit it, which he does, briefly, before returning, altered, to his old pattern. One could imagine that this visitor, a tourist, was like the audience at a play, first coaxed into believing in another reality, and, in some charismatic alchemy, undergoing catharsis, a cleansing visit to that other realm, which sets it back in its seats at the end of the show somehow elevated. Or at least that was the ideal, and must have been the ideal for all the centuries of theatre.

When Brook asked Hughes to do the translation for *Oedipus*, [36] the result was an amazingly compact and musical script, which was staged with Brook's usual brilliance and originality. The set consisted of a revolving cube, which first blinded the audience, then let down its sides to reveal a platform, and finally, at the end, supported a giant phallus. Brook was the master of theatricality, of spectacle. He had just sent around the world on tour his dazzling and flamboyant *Midsummer Night's Dream*, a production that featured trapeze artists and lots of light and confetti, along with a staggering display of human control over voice and body. His actors had learned to make circus gymnastics look natural and easy, and Brook had choreographed them always with the composition of stage-as-picture in mind, as well as the tension between showcase tricks and human sounds of breathing and voice.

In *Oedipus* the problem of duality in a personality is further explored. The Prosecutor returns, in the person of Oedipus himself, who puts forward evidence that, although he knows himself to be innocent, he can prove to himself that he must have committed the crime. He knows himself to be both the healer and the plague, both the detective and the elusive criminal, but he cannot locate the dark process of crime in himself. He ponders the puzzle of how he could have committed an act and be unable to find any trace of it in a concerted search of his own nature, and not until he is given an orientation of names and dates can he recognise with the logic of his own memory that he can embrace the crime as his own. It wasn't the act itself that was committed by the stranger in him, but the arrangement of coincidence to make the act appear innocent to him, so that he couldn't recognise its implications.

In the short play *The Demon*,[39] the contradiction of crime is made explicit:

Female: What is his crime?
Man: There is no crime.
Demon: I am your crime . . . if you live you have to atone.

In *Oedipus* the Bardo remains off stage (as is fitting with the decorum of a classic tragedy). Tiresias and his daughter bring Laius' spirit into Creon, to help unravel the mystery, but we receive information about this trip only through hearsay. Like Oedipus, we are left to deduce what we may about the transactions with the 'other side', but we aren't allowed to witness them first hand.

T. S. Eliot, in his famous criticism of Hamlet,[40] suggested that the emotion of a character in a play must manifest itself in a situation, in a set of objects, in order for the reader or audience to grasp it. This situation which is capable of evoking an emotion he called the objective correlative. He then suggested that there was no objective correlative adequate to signify Hamlet's distress: his mother didn't deserve his contempt and, in general, the situation did not call for Hamlet's response. On this basis, he called the play a failed piece of art.

If Hamlet's horror was, as Hughes suggests,[41] due not solely to his mortal mother's mortal sins, but to some glimpse he had of the underworld in her, then it might be said that the objective correlative for Hamlet's anger and grief could only be discovered on the 'other side', in the spirit world of the Bardo.

Many of Hughes' characters share with Hamlet an inability to find full accounting for their feelings in the surface world around them. Morgan suffers from a disproportionate uneasiness. Oedipus is only satisfied that he knows himself when he discovers the role of fate in his life. For Oedipus, the objective correlative of the uneasiness he had felt all his life was the crime he didn't know he had committed. The knowledge of this crime was hidden in the under part of his nature. And conversely, his disproportionate emotion, and the disproportionate unluckiness of his city-state were the objective correlative of the subterranean knowledge. By that emotion, Oedipus knew there must be a crime, just as we know, by Hamlet's emotion, that he is dealing with something more than his mortal mother. Hughes has taken this principle of equivalence, of correspondence between events and feelings, and has used it as a plot in his plays, as a clue a character can use to unearth his double.

The production was to prove a turning point both for Brook, who then left the commercial theatre and devoted himself to an exploration of the roots of drama, and for Hughes, who worked with Brook's international group, CIRT,[42] developing improvisation and constructing a language, 'Orghast', for the first major experiment, the Shiraz Festival in Iran. CIRT was composed of actors of many nationalities (there was no one language which all of them could speak), and their production, Orghast,[43] was delivered to a cosmopolitan, multi-lingual group of 'jet-setters', directors, journalists, vagabonds and upper-class Persians who made up the audience at Persepolis, the tombs of the great Persian kings, on the occasion of their 2500th anniversary.

The actors in CIRT first made up a language of their own and used it to perform some of Hughes' scenarios under the title of *Difficulties of a Bridegroom* – now a boy-meets-girl, win-the-in-laws, hide-the-body, box-room farce – to peasants in Iran, who probably had never seen a Western play before. Judging from a description of the improvisation written by an assistant director with Brook, the intent of the play as well as the plot seems to have undergone tremendous change in this transition: from one stressing concepts to one stressing theatricality.[44] Hughes' rich language and complex imagery were gone, along with the trip to the Bardo. The attempt now was to find folk elements of plot people anywhere could recognise and respond to.

Orghast was a flamboyantly lighted minimal production. It took the Oedipus story, tangled up along with other myths , into its next stages, where a descent is made into the underworld, of the Bardo, to retrieve the evil nature of the king, the nature that has led him to murder his family, and then to pluck out his own eyes when confronted with the crime. In *Orghast*, the hopelessness of remedying evil so long as it is kept in the underworld is dramatised by the difficulty Moa has in finding a story to enact that will not end in tragedy, until she decides to resolve the problem by embodying the dark nature of the Violator in the child, Sogis, a Promethean figure who must go to the underworld to retrieve the dark father, who becomes a female bird, transmuting the evil through pain as he plucks out Sogis' insides. The implication seems to be that though each individual must go to the underworld for himself, and though the process is dangerous and agonising, it is possible that in this way a resolution between the vital forces of life and death might be achieved.

Despairing of ever seeing 'true' theatre in English,[45] Hughes developed for *Orghast* a guttural and primitive language, designed to express root emotional sounds. The cosmology and the complex story line was worked out together with the cast and Brook in rehearsal into a script. It was a deeply hopeful tale of the descent into the underworld to retrieve evil, the buried husband of life, so that his true nature, that of light, might be released.[46] It was a complex arrangement of symbols and relationships, and there was to be no attempt to make the story really comprehensible to the audience, but only to express, in archetypal terms, a confrontation that might trigger some biological if not psychological recognition in everyone.[47] However, to at least one person – A. C. H. Smith, who wrote *Orghast at Persepolis* – the final rendition seemed, rather than an affirmation of the possibility of change, a suggestion that change was impossible, that the old stories will continue to repeat themselves forever, that the cycle will forever be the same.[48] Since nobody in the audience could have been expected to understand any part of the language of the play, (of the several languages used, none were current among the spectators), misunderstandings were common. But the things which *had* been transmitted were encouraging, and both Hughes and Brook apparently left the experience with the conviction that the natural role of theatre was to convey its message through the humanity and versatility of the actor, nonverbally, through mime and sound.

Both of them had been moving steadily away from an intellectual, expository approach over the years. Hughes had turned to a gut-level, reductionalist approach beginning with his children's drama. He had mixed prose with verse in them (a foreshadowing of the technique he would use in *Gaudete* later) in the way that Richard Howard would characterise as aphorism, like the French *récit*, a blurring of literary distinctions. His translation of *Oedipus* used only three hundred words, the least John Gielgud, who played the part of Oedipus, had ever worked with.[49] With *Orghast* these words became known only to the actors, who used them for clues to find the meaning in the sounds, but with the next project, *The Conference of the Birds*, even this much script was abandoned in favour of Hughes' notes, from which various productions evolved.

Hughes worked with the troup, adapting Attar's metaphysical fable[50] to improvisation situations, sending Brooks 'masses of material',[51] not in script form, but 'plotless and cryptic [tales] without set dialogue and deliberately ambiguous, so that the actors [could] fill in their own psychological logic.'[52] It is unclear why he stopped working with Brook, who, according to John Heilpern, desperately wanted Hughes to join him in Africa. In any case, at that point, everybody agreeing that the theatre belongs to the actor, they appear to have gone their separate ways. Brook, abandoning what Kenneth Tynan called 'the essential thing for a great director',[53] a contemporary author, left the written text behind. He continued to work on *The Conference of the Birds* (CIRT has been improvising on it for nine years) and it played in the spring of 1980 again in New York at La Mama, to mixed reviews. It is still considered an 'experimental' work. And Hughes, who seems never again to have produced a 'script', worked on his own version of *Conference of the Birds*, until it evolved into *Adam and the Sacred Nine*,[54] and influenced *Cave Birds, An Alchemical Cave Drama*,[55] both of them thick and rich with words.

During this eventful year of *Orghast* and *The Conference of Birds*, Hughes wrote an introduction to a selection of Shakespeare's poetry, in which he suggested that the turning point in Shakespeare's art had come when he 'discovered the difference between a poetic drama and a dramatic poem. Instead of using the poetry to explore the drama he discovered how to use the drama to explore his poetry – to explore, that is, his poetic fable'.[56] It is possible that Hughes was writing about himself in this passage as well as about Shakespeare. He has perhaps learned something about poetry during his adventure with the theatre, and if so, then the world of poetry is surely richer for this experience. It could be argued that the best of the plays was the poetry in them, and that Hughes was well advised to concentrate his artistry on the printed page.

However, at a time when the theatre is so clearly at a point of crisis, with actors and audiences alike asking for change, the implications of Hughes' theatrical work seem to call for re-examination. The question is not whether the plays themselves are or are not great plays. This is something that could only be answered once they had found adequate productions, as no one now seems to find that possible. The question is, rather, one of interpretation. What, in fact, is the innovation Hughes has called for?

The great task of twentieth-century playwrights has been to deal with the reality of the subconscious, of the irrational, of the spiritual in a medium which has persistently preoccupied itself with naturalism. Rather than externalising his dreams and expressing them symbolically, Hughes turned to antiquity for the solution, and attempted to revive the holy theatre, in which the actor was himself a shaman, who both enacted and experienced a performance which was both story and ritual.

It may be that in a later time, when actors are able to 'enter' the Bardo as they now 'enter' the life of a character, the theatre will find itself adequate to Hughes. Or perhaps Hughes has decided that the 'empty space' for his words is the printed page, and the 'holy theatre' the mind of the reader.

━━━ *11* JAROLD RAMSEY

Crow, or the trickster transformed

The Chief (Jesus) sent Coyote from above to this land. He had sent crow first, he had him come to see how the people were, how they were then. When that crow arrived, he saw people lying about, dead. He went and ate their eyes, and then he went on, and went above again towards home, to the place of the chief (Jesus). He (Jesus) asked him, 'How did it appear to you?' It seemed to him to be pretty good. Bue he said to him, 'Why, no! You have been eating their eyes. Very evidently you have been doing ill. You are finished, that is as much work as you will obtain.' Then he ceased right there, the chief (Jesus) let him go, he became a crow, he became a black crow.
The chief (Jesus) above spoke, 'I will take another one, and I will send him to go and see.' Coyote said, 'Let me go!' And Coyote came, he arrived there. He (Jesus) had told him, 'That is how you are to be, exactly like myself . . .'[1]

1

In *Crow*, Ted Hughes writes as if the world's mythologies were open and available to his imagination. The title-figure strikes most readers as something new in our poetry, the real thing, an innovation, and so he is – and yet, as I hope to show, Hughes has skilfully fashioned Crow out of bits and pieces of some very ancient traditions from both the Old and the New Worlds. Here is contemporary mythopoesis with a vengeance.

To be sure, T. S. Eliot long ago proclaimed in that famous and very self-conscious review of *Ulysses* that Joyce had brought into modern writing a new 'mythic method', a way of 'manipulating a continuous parallel between contemporaneity and antiquity' that could give shape and meaning to our history – but presumably neither Joyce nor Eliot seriously entertained the possibility of straying, as Hughes has strayed, beyond the Indo-European traditions into the myths and tales of the Eskimos, the Japanese, various North American Indian tribes, and the Persians, and the lore of the Talmud and the Koran, and so on. Nor can it be said, really, that in *his* mythic method Hughes is manipulating parallels between the modern and the antique and/or primitive worlds: instead, he seems to be intent, with help from world folklore, on re-writing portions of Creation itself so that the first story in our book of human predicaments is more consistent with the chapters in which we live. There is a historical perspective in these poems, as we will see, but much of the time it is subsumed in a controlling perspective that manages to be at once mythic, and deeply personal.

In this regard, it is fair to say that Hughes' introduction to the *Selected Poems* of the Yugoslavian poet Vasko Popa (Penguin, 1969) is to *Crow* (1970) what Eliot's review of Joyce was to *The Waste Land* – at least as self-revealing, especially in the careful distinction Hughes draws on behalf of Popa between 'literary surrealism' with its ultimately impersonal surrender to the arbitrary imagery of the dream flow, 'and the surrealism of folklore', which is 'always urgently connected with the business of trying to manage practical difficulties so great that they have forced the sufferer temporarily out of the dimension of coherent reality into that depth of imagination where understanding has its roots and stores its X-Rays' (pp. 14–15). To what extent Hughes himself is 'the sufferer' in *Crow* is not at issue: what such a statement suggests to me about the book is that its author believes in the dream-work efficacy of myth, even today, and unlike Joyce and Eliot ultimately turns to it in Crow for its inherent imaginative sanity, and not just for its ironic bearing on modern history.

For Calvin Bedient, on the contrary, Hughes' conceptions in *Crow* 'fall a little too readily into the mean slots of *nihilism*. In truth he now knows his own mind too well. He needs to pray, like Frost, to have some dust thrown in his eyes.'[2] The 'diagnosis' needs no comment, but it does boggle the mind a little to see the mythic adventuresomeness of these poems, the way Hughes' wit is playing on folklore in them, dismissed so airily as the easy nihilism of a self-imitator. What dust in whose eyes?

II

Speaking to Egbert Faas after the publication of *Crow* about the emergence of certain writers (unnamed but presumably including Popa) who represent a 'post-Christian view', Hughes notes that 'In their world Christianity is just another provisional myth of man's relationship with the creator and the world of spirit'.[3] The observation has been applied to Hughes himself, but erroneously, I think: the central impulse of the *Crow* poems is certainly an ingenious and unrelenting subversion of the Christian mythos, so as to reveal how it has got nearly everything wrong about Man's origins – but the violence of the subversion, the sense of overkill in fact, indicates that for the author Christianity is still much more immediate and formidable that 'just another provisional myth'. Better to say that in these poems, Hughes tries to fight his way free of a still-prevailing Christian–humanistic frame of reference that in its omissions and distortions of human facts makes our inherently bad lot a good deal worse. The impulse appears well before *Crow* in *Wodwo*, in such blasphemous redactions of scriptures as 'Logos', 'Reveille', and 'Theology'; and in *Season Songs*, Hughes' first full collection since *Crow*, there is at least one witty backward glance at an earlier obsession. In a 'Cock Robin'-like poem about the funeral of the fallen leaves, this stanza appears—

Who'll be their parson?
Me, says the crow, for it is well known
I study the bible right down to the bone . . .[4]

Who or what is Crow? In exploring his roots in world folklore, I want to insist that first and last, Crow is Ted Hughes' own astonishing invention, for his own purposes: one might say, admiringly, that he is an addition to folk-literature, not merely something borrowed from it. With this proviso in mind, we can generally identify Crow as a *Trickster*, a member in good standing of that fascinating company of beings which includes Anansi the Spider in African literature; Loki in Norse myths; Coyote, Raven, Crow, Bluejay, Manabozho, Nanabush, and others in North American native mythology (as in the epigraph to this essay); and somewhere more distantly, Hermes in the Greek and Iblis/Satan in the Islamic and Hebraic traditions.

To characterise the Trickster is to characterise the full range of possibilities in the human id and ego; indeed, one of his functions in oral literature is to create narrative possibility in the face of tribal restraints and norms of good citizenship. In Jung's view, he represents the primitive, utterly undifferentiated state of consciousness that societies transcend, perhaps, but individuals don't.[5] A typical Trickster figure in western Indian mythologies is greedy, over-sexed, selfish, covetous, aggressively mischievous, capable of wiliness and cleverness but only on a short-term and over-reaching basis. In short, a creature that is, as we say, 'all too human' in his imperfections; and whose incredible survival despite repeated fatal come-uppances points to the persistence in us of the unreconstructed id, and beyond that, perhaps, to the sheer avid persistence of the race itself. (Can it be that the two are related?)

Clearly the career of a Trickster-figure like Coyote allowed a tribal audience to have its ethics both ways – anticipating with official approval his eventual fall, while at the same time vicariously relishing his freedom from shame-culture morality, before the fall. More generally, as Lévi-Strauss and others have pointed out, the Trickster in his position and actions serves a complex *mediative* purpose – as between the moral ideals of a people's Way, and their naked instincts; as between two modes of survival, hunting, say, and gathering (most Tricksters are animals like Coyote and Crow who as carrion eaters partake of both modes); as between men and their gods. 'Mediation' in this sense, of course, means something more than compromise or reconciliation or a Hegelian middle step: it means, if I understand Lévi-Strauss, a dynamic interposing between polar opposites as a permanent condition, allowing, as in myth and ritual, the mind to hold on to both opposites at once.[6]

Hence, from the point of view of function, the Trickster's unique protean diversity, his predictable unpredictability as a creature metaphysically in the Middle (in all sorts of middles). But there is more to him yet. In many traditions, he has a major role in the primal creation of the world-as-it-now-is. More precisely, he serves as a Transformer: finding the world to be seriously incomplete, disordered, 'crude', the handiwork of a sleeping or absconded Creator, he steps in, takes over, sets mythic precedents large and small, does the best he can to give some shape and order to the available material of the world, before the human race inherits it. Lévi-Strauss' term for the Trickster in his Transforming role is wittily accurate – 'bricoleur', or handyman.

It is important to recognise here that the typical Trickster– Transformer, say, Raven in the mythology of British Columbia Indians, does not invent copulation or arrange for food-supply or procure daylight in a rush of divine or at least promethean philan- thropy. Instead, he generally performs his Transforming deeds *in character* from tricksterish motives of greed or spite or personal convenience: 'the people to come' who know his stories gratefully inherit the world he pieced together, without having any illusions about his motives for doing so, or about a Grand Design in Creation, of which he was Omniscient Designer.

Now we are coming close to Ted Hughes' own Trickster, not just in the lineaments of Crow, but in the teleological and eschatological outlook he seems to represent. The possible wisdom and sanity accruing from the mythic belief that the world was given its present format (which ones takes for better and worse) by a humanly intelligible Transformer is never far, I think, from the poet's mind in these poems, as he follows his quarrel with the Bibilical God. But the Judaeo-Christian account of Genesis with its overwhelming sense of divine teleology and original perfection is what we have inherited, and poor Crow, unlike his tribal counterparts, never really has a chance as a Transformer. His pranks point up some of the most glaring weaknesses in God's design, certainly, but unfortunately God is still around, still meddling in Creation himself. Hughes has spoken frequently in interviews and readings – not always very helpfully – about the imaginative matrix that gave birth to the Crow poems ('From the Life and Songs of the Crow' is the book's subtitle), and according to these premises a malign force mocks God's Creation, especially Man, and when challenged to do better, sends Crow down to earth. But by the standards of primitive myth he is too late and too little as a Transformer. And, as will be seen, he becomes subject to transformation himself.

Why did Hughes choose a *Crow* as his Trickster–Transformer? In one sense the question is silly for anyone who has ever watched a real crow or raven for more than a few moments: if there had been no genus *Corvus*, Hughes or somebody would have had to invent it, as the saying goes, for its raucous intelligence, greediness, and blackness – an image of the human. But beyond the intrinsic appropriateness of the beast as a sort of totem, it is worthwhile noting the kind of crow-lore in world folk-literature that the poet may have assimilated when he was reading Anthropology and Archaeology at Cambridge, or since. There are, of course, the crows and ravens in the Scots ballads, and Noah's Raven, which does not return to the Ark, according to some traditions, because it turns to eating carrion from the Flood. In the Talmud, a crow teaches Adam how to bury his dead, and as a result, crow hatchlings ever since have had white feathers. Another Jewish tradition has it that crows and all other black creatures were created by the Devil in competition with God. In the Alaska Eskimo Creation cycle, Raven finds the first man newly hatched from a wild-pea pod (and behaving strikingly like the unoriented speaker in 'Wodwo'): after helping him find shelter and food, Raven creates the first woman out of clay.

In the Tsimshian and other North Coast analogues of these stories, Raven is a more ambiguous benefactor – finding the world in darkness, he gets himself born to the daughter of the chief who is hoarding the light, and after a series of tricks, carries it off in a box and releases it to men only when they insult him. In the syncretic Cowlitz Indian story given at the head of this essay, Jesus sends Crow down to look after the first people, but, finding them apparently dead, he pecks out the eyes, and is replaced by a more businesslike Transformer, Coyote!

And so on, and on – as Hughes has remarked,[7] crows live nearly everywhere on earth, with a correspondingly rich folklore. Perhaps their traditional associations with human life, and Hughes' own peculiar totemism in these poems, is best summed up in a Hindu saying about the Other World: it is a place 'where no man goes, and no crow flies'.

What Coleridge would call Hughes' 'esemplastic' use of mythologies in *Crow* has distinctive formal and stylistic consequences for the poems: they mostly adhere to a sort of mythic decorum, in fact. The style itself is 'rude' in several senses, colloquially primitive, casual in the manner of transcriptions of aboriginal narratives; and although one might argue against such deliberate flattening of style on the grounds that real native texts are invariably much more artificial in their original languages, still, the effect here is wonderfully appropriate to the point of view: these are crow-songs. Such as it is, the *rhetoric* of the sequence reveals Hughes' commitment to folklore, too, Biblical and otherwise – there are frequent enumerations, as in genealogies and inventories of things; there are formulaic openings ('Once upon a time', 'There was a man'); there are catechisms and magical examinations in the manner of Biblical pedagogy.

As for the action of the book: although David Lodge has plausibly characterised it as deriving from Disney cartoons,[8] in fact it follows very faithfully the typical incidents in a cycle of Trickster-narratives. The wild escapades in series, causes leading to improbable effects that snowball in magnitude, maniacal pursuits, villainous transformations, the periodic Bang! that utterly destroys the protagonist, who then appears in the next scene intact, the wholesale inconsistencies between narratives – all this is standard fare in the Trickster story, as the following synopsis of the beginning of a Transformation cycle from the Tillamook Indians of Oregon will illustrate. The Trickster is named 'South Wind':

He sees a canoe with three people, one a virgin; interested in the virgin, he transforms himself into a baby, lies on the rocks in the water, is picked up by the people, cries until the girl holds him, touches her vulva, exclaims that it is soft like an old woman's. At Bay City he transforms his penis into a clam digger, eats clams with a family, ordains that there shall be but one clam in each shell, and juice instead of oil. He induces the woman to stroke the clam digger and makes sarcastic remarks when she discovers that it is his penis. He avoids Stink Bug women who want to make him impotent, but he copulates with two girls who take him under the ocean with them. He esapes them, asks for rocks to shelter him as he sleeps in the sun, awakens enclosed by rocks, calls Woodpecker who breaks her bill trying to free him, calls Yellowhammer. When she has pecked a hole he reaches up and seizes her leg; she flies away insulted. He takes himself apart, throws body parts out of the hole; Sea Gull and Raven eat his eyes. He feels his way to Bald Eagle's house, pretends to be measuring the house, brags about his eyes, effects a trade with Bald Eagle, who then steals Snail's eyes and voice. South Wind goes on . . .⁹

In fairness to David Lodge's essay, such antic adventures do sound like Disney cartoons, excluding of course the overt sexuality, and unquestionably there is something genuinely mythic in the best cartoons and comic-strips; the Trickster survives amongst us, after a fashion, in the form of Coyote in the 'Roadrunner' TV series, Bugs Bunny, Woody Woodpecker, 'Mr. Natural' in the R. Crumb Comics. But the cartoons are only a useful analogue in our culture to Crow's story – its true source, I hope it is now clear, is Hughes' meditations on aboriginal narratives.

(Another contemporary poet who has made striking use of the forms as well as the content of myth narratives is W. S. Merwin. His uncreation myth, 'The Last One', with its snowballing ecological disaster, is close kin in 'oral' style and apocalyptic vision to many poems in Hughes' book).

The plan of *Crow* itself derives from anthropological sources. Hughes has always aimed at sequentiality in his books: he has noted, for example, that most of *Lupercal* is 'one extended poem about one or two sensations. There are at least a dozen or fifteen poems in that book which belong organically to each other.'¹⁰ The following book, *Wodwo*, he described as 'a single adventure'. In *Crow*, as even the most hostile reviewers have acknowledged, the poems constitute a coherent sequence, with something of a plot; the context accumulates meaning (it would be hard to do justice to the poetry of *Crow* in an anthology), and one has the sense that the whole book adds up to much more than the sum total of its individual parts. Contemporary poetry is in for the Sequence, clearly – Roethke, Lowell, Berryman, Merwin, Kinnell come to mind: what is special about Hughes' book, among other things, is that its loose sequentiality, centring on Crow, is sanctioned by the conventions of Trickster cycles and other serial forms in oral literature.

It is high time for a few of what Wallace Stevens called 'pages of illustrations', but first, I want to outline what the sequentiality of *Crow* turns upon. It seems clear that Hughes' protagonist undergoes a radical transformation in the course of the book: beginning as an avowed meddler who has been created by an opponent of God to 'show Him up' in his Creation, especially with regard to Man, Crow goes through a progress in which he becomes less and less an adversary of Man, and more and more a humanly vulnerable creature himself, sharing helplessly in the human predicament. There is a kind of formula to be seen in the chief mythic identities that Hughes forces upon Crow in the course of his career: beginning as something akin to the Devil, he becomes a Trickster-Transformer whose tricks are nasty for Man; later he is identified with Prometheus and other heroes; later yet he is linked, blasphemously of course, with Christ; ultimately he seems to be approaching 'merely' human status. Crow's devilry gives way very quickly after his incarnation to less confident actions and responses: he peers, mopes, weeps, feels helpless, feels sympathy, is appalled, sings 'trembling', and so on. Hughes' own remark on this question is gnomically definitive: 'He's a man to correct man, but of course he's not a man, he's a crow: he never does quite become a man'.[11] But, we might add, he comes close, too close for Christian comfort.

III

Now to the text, with an eye to its *ordonnance*. The first seven pieces contrive in different ways to get Crow born into earthly life: it is a most reluctant and painful incarnation, as in the Manichean doctrine of the soul, and all expectations of what Mircea Eliade has called 'the prestige of origins' in Western myth[12] are subverted by a poem like 'Lineage', with its mockery of Biblical genealogies. God begets Nothing, who begets Never, who begets Crow. Here and in the following poem, 'Examination at the Womb Door', with its mock-catechism emphasising the primacy of death, Crow is none the less portrayed as somehow circumstantially superior to death:

But who is stronger than death?
        Me, evidently.

Pass, Crow.

The world in these poems does belong to Death, yet Crow, having been begotten by Never, *lives* – like other Tricksters, he carries on with a kind of brute avidity, much like the human race: 'Carrion, Jack!' as Crow might say. Though there is no comfort in asserting mere survival, and indeed no meaning, 'the evidence' supports Crow's assertion, and he passes the exam mysteriously and is sent into life. The last poem in this 'birth sequence', 'The Door', seems to bring Crow into a closer relationship with the poet and his creating vision of things: in the solid wall of a body, there is a black doorway, 'the eye's pupil', and through it Crow is born. In yet a further version of his birth, 'Conjuring in Heaven,' the gods put nothing inside nothing, and drop it from Heaven to Earth: 'There lay Crow, cataleptic.'

With 'A Childish Prank', Crow has fully arrived in life, and takes up his career as Trickster and Transformer with gusto. Here and elsewhere in the book, as Hughes undermines Christian myth, there is a kind of child's naughty delight in blasphemy, in saying forbidden things right under God's nose; the poem is, really, a paradigm of Hughes' sacrilegious use of mythic traditions. God is *deus otiosus* here because, following the *Zohar* and Manichean lore, he can't seem to get Man's and Woman's souls to enter their waiting bodies. The story in the *Zohar* is worth quoting at length (there are analogues in the *Koran*), to illustrate the poet's way with legend:

When the Holy One, praised be He, was about to create the world, the universe was already present in His thought. He then formed the souls which were eventually to belong to man, and they appeared before Him in the very same form they were later to take in the human body. God examined them one by one, and found several which were destined to become corrupt in this world. When the time came, each of the souls was summoned before God, Who said: 'Go to this or that part of the earth and animate such and such a body'. The soul replied, 'O Master of the Universe, I am happy in this world and do not want to leave it for another where I shall be exposed to contamination!'

But God insisted, and 'the soul sorrowfully took the earthly plan and descended among us.'[13]

Crow's solution lacks God's foresightedness and authority, but is perfectly in character, for a *bricoleur*, working with the available materials – he gets the first human bodies animated, and sex invented, along with the precedent for its pains and frustrations. Also in the *Zohar*, there is the Platonic notion that before incarnation all souls are bisexual: 'at the time of marriage, the Holy One, blessed be He, unites them as before, and they become again a single body and a single soul'.[14] Crow's perversion of such a doctrine in 'A Childish Prank' – the consequences of which are more brutally mythified in the following poem 'Crow's First Lesson', and of course in the appalling 'Song for a Phallus' – colours and controls all the 'love poems' in the book. (One uses the label advisedly!) Besides the ones mentioned, 'Criminal Ballad', 'Crow Tries the Media', 'Crow's Undersong', 'Fragment of an Ancient Tablet', 'Notes for a Little Play', 'Snake Hymn', 'Lovesong', 'The Lovepet' – this is fully a sixth of the whole book. To be a consciously sexed being, according to Crow's myth, is to suffer the most exquisite tortures of division and frustration in the name of love: the true fate of that would-be amorous bird of prey in Marvell's poem.

All this, and the view of Woman as Devouring Mother, is familiar enough in Hughes' poetry – what is odd, in a way, is that the poet does not allow Crow himself to get directly involved in sex, despite the

Trickster's tradition of rampant lechery (as in the Tillamook synopsis given above). In a limited edition of the book published in 1973, with twelve crow-drawings by Leonard Baskin, Hughes does include a poem entitled 'Crow's Courtship', in which, following a Talmudic tradition about God's first botched attempt to create a wife for Adam out of raw material, Crow waits impatiently outside the lab as God labours to make him a Frankensteinian bride, and then ruins the work by breaking in at 'the worst moment'. But even here, Crow's sexuality is untested – apparently Hughes wanted to keep his Trickster simple in this respect, even childish, and thus perhaps a sharper perspective on a dimension of the human predicament that (I am guessing) the poet found to be the most terrible of all.

After 'A Childish Prank'; in 'Crow Alights' and 'That Moment', Hughes commences on an intermittent run of poems that are explicitly prophetic and eschatological. Crow, with mounting horror at what he has gotten into, looks ahead to history, to us, from the Creation he is attending. In these two poems, all of God's teleology seems to lead eerily up to a single human face, a hand, a cigarette, which in 'That Moment' are cancelled, apparently by suicide. Typically, Crow, 'stronger than death', surviving at any rate, has 'to start searching for something to eat'. The implications of this detail are at once macabre and eminently practical – the essence of Crow.

'Crow Hears Fate Knock on the Door' and 'Crow Tyrannosaurus' together depict Man, through the distorting lens of Crow, in his predicament as conscious beast, human animal; their chief predecessor in Hughes' early poetry is 'Wodwo'. As in that unforgettable poem, so here, the view of man's condition is *mythic*, the opposite of existential: essence precedes existence, and our essence is hopelessly mixed. On the one hand, Crow – already losing his insouciance as Trickster – cannot resist the Wodwo-like impulse to inspect and try to understand everything, and 'the prophecy inside him, like a grimace' is essentially of Humanism, the concept of Man the Measurer and Measure – 'I WILL MEASURE IT ALL AND OWN IT ALL / AND I WILL BE INSIDE IT / AS INSIDE MY OWN LAUGHTER ...' but in fact the consequences of such an imperative, 'like a steel spring / Slowly rending the vital fibres', will be alienation from Nature and the peculiar ignorance that goes by the names of rational scepticism and scientific inquiry. 'Crow's Account of the Battle', 'The Black Beast' (which owes something, perhaps, to Keith Douglas's poem, 'Bête Noire'), 'Crow's Account of St. George', 'Crow on the Beach', 'Revenge Fable', 'Crow and the Sea' – all dramatise the terrible consequences of Crow's prophecy: we can't help being 'scientific', it deadens us within, and now more than ever threatens to destroy us physically. In 'The Black Beast', Crow the Scientist ransacks all of nature in a final phase of Wodwo's curiosity, but the beast he seeks remains a *bête noire* indeed, hidden in his own self-ignorance.

On the other hand, in 'Crow Tyrannosaurus,' Crow quails before the sheer bloody avidity of Creation and its food-chain hierarchy, and wonders if extreme Manicheeism is the answer: 'Alas ought I / To stop eating / And try to become the light?' But in midst of such elevated human meditations, animal instinct and appetite break in – 'Grubs grubs He stabbed he stabbed / Weeping'. In action now like those 'attent sleek thrushes on the lawn / More coiled steel than living' of an early Hughes poem, in consciousness Crow is still agonised, helplessly other, 'all too human' in his mythic precedent-setting:

Thus came the eye's

>   roundness

>   the ear's

>   deafness.

(Later in the sequence, in 'Crow's Nerve Fails', this helpless guilt becomes a kind of Original Sin for Crow – 'Clothed in his conviction, / Trying to remember his crime / Heavily he flies'.)

At this point, before proceeding with the general career of Crow, his ironic humanising, we should glance at two related themes introduced into the sequence by Hughes once he has gotten the hero established in Creation, and beginning to suffer it. In 'A Disaster', 'The Battle of Osfrontalis', 'Crow's Fall', 'Crow Tries the Media', 'Crow Goes Hunting', 'Owl's Song', and 'Bedtime Story', Crow comes up against the peculiarly human gift-and-curse of language. Significantly, in the logic of Crow's development, in the first two of these pieces he coolly withstands the ordeal by words: in 'A Disaster', in fact, as some sort of demonic Logos runs amok and destroys whole cities (compare Merwin's 'The Last One'), we are told that 'he [eats] well'; and in the following 'Battle of Osfrontalis', although words do turn directly against Crow (one thinks of Stevens' 'The Plot Against the Giant'), he resists them with comical ease. But in 'Crow's Fall', Hughes' contribution to the folklore of corvine blackness, when poor Crow returns 'charred black' from his vainglorious attack on the sun, he must resort to a very human rationalisation: '"Up there" he managed / "Where white is black and black is white, I won" '.

Now our hero is infected by language, like us, it seems. He 'Tries the Media', in the form of a love song, but the available words besmear and corrupt his vision; when he 'Goes Hunting' with words, reality in the form of a hare cunningly eludes them. The poem is a fine example of Hughes' witty adaptation of the logic of oral narratives (and, perhaps, cartoons as well), a goofy chase scene in which the quarry shifts its shape more and more wildly as the hunters, although transforming themselves too, stay always one comic jump behind. The hare escapes: Crow is left empy-handed, 'Speechless with admiration'. This insufficiency Crow discovers in language, the way words fail us, always coming *ex post facto* after experience and blurring it, is an implicit theme in 'A Bedtime Story', in which an everyman, 'out of it' as the saying goes, always comes too late in reality and with a sense of division and distraction. As so often here, one thinks of certain pieces in Merwin's *The Moving Target* and *The Lice*. (Perhaps poems like 'Crow Tries the Media' anticipate Hughes' radical experiments with language in his collaboration with Peter Brook on *Orghast*.)

Crow's trouble with words is, of course, only one part of the burden of human misery that Hughes is trying to name, and although the main imaginative line of the book features the adventures of Crow the Trickster as a kind of mythic displacement of this burden, there is a loose series of poems in which Hughes seems to suggest in direct human terms an emotional stance for bearing it up, I am thinking in particular of 'A Grin', 'Criminal Ballad', 'The Contender', 'In Laughter', 'The Smile', and 'Crow Improvises'. In these pieces there is something of Beckett's grim humour, something of Morgenstern's gallows wit, something of simple hysteria – a terrible comedy beyond tragedy, in which the true funnybone is the skull, and the only smile is its fixed grimace. In 'The Contender', Prometheus on his rock wears a terrifying grin; in 'The Smile', at the moment of death a victim is rewarded by a visit from a disembodied smile, 'for a moment / Mending everything / Before it swept out and away across the earth'. Here and in the following piece, 'Crow Improvises', a sort of apocalypso song in which various human antinomies are conjoined in a man's two hands until the coupling of opposites destroys him, much as Crow is being wracked by his role as Trickster/mediator, the Terrible Smile seems to be at best a provisional stance; if it helps, it comes late in suffering and leaves early, so to speak, belonging to no one alive.

So Hughes follows 'The Smile' with 'Crow Frowns' – the frown coming from Crow's renewed helpless questioning (for us all) of his place and purpose in Creation:

His footprints assail infinity

With signatures: We are here, we are here.
He is the long waiting for something
To use him for some everything
Having so carefully made him

Of nothing.

Who knows the myth, Hughes seems to ask in this haunting and summary poem, that would end such waiting-in-ignorance?

Returning now to the main lines of Crow's career as a prankish mediator in Creation: his drift into the human condition seems to grow more and more unmistakable. To be sure, he continues intermittently to transform God's handiwork, as in 'A Horrible Religious Error', in which it is Crow ('Chrow'?) who vanquishes the serpent that might have served Adam and Eve as a nature-deity; 'Crow's Song of Himself', in which, under God's attempts to destroy it, Crow's body becomes, Whitman-like, the raw stuff of human life, even its Redeemer; and 'Crow Blacker Than Ever'. This last poem, in fact, is a kind of final summary of Crow's original mythic purpose on Earth: Creation is coming a cropper, God and Man have turned away from each other in mutual disgust, but Crow steps in and nails them together forever: 'Then heaven and earth creaked at the joint / Which became gangrenous and stank — / A horror beyond redemption.' And having carpentered our impossible Judaeo-Christian union of divinity and earthly flesh, in his role as bricoleur, Crow exults, 'This is my creation'.

But already in the sequence, in 'Crow's Playmates', our hero has made his own futile anthropomorphic gesture towards divinity, creating the gods for playmates, out of mountains and rivers . . . but, as in the history of man's religions generally, the gods have floated away from their natural, *native* settings, 'gone abstract', leaving poor Crow all the more forlorn in Nature, 'his own leftover', in fact.

And this forlornness in general characterises the last glimpses we get of Crow; he has got involved in Man's estate, it seems, has become in his suffering part of the problem. There is something strangely moving about this (as there is in some authentic Trickster cycles, the Winnebago for example, when the Trickster finally puts aside his pranks and prepares to yield the world to the human race), a sense of wild vitality tamed, and opportunity lost. Reviewers have frequently objected that, as a book, *Crow* falls off in intensity towards the end: I agree that it does, somewhat, but I would wager that Hughes understood the risks and took them knowingly, in his commitment to a significant poetic sequentiality, a progress from origin myths to eschatological images.

In 'Truth Kills Everybody', Crow acts out Menelaus's wrestling-match with Proteus, whose transformations become more and more awesome:

Christ's hot pounding heart – he held it

The earth, shrunk to the size of a hand grenade

And he held it he held it and held it and

BANG!

He was blasted to nothing.

In context, we know that Crow will of course revive; is he not stronger than death? And we know, from context, what Hughes thinks in general of man's alienating, self-obscuring impulse to pursue the truth according to the canons of scientific humanism. But despite it all, despite earth's ultimate BANG!, there is something appealing, even heroic about Crow's sheer childlike persistence; and this note is carried on in the following piece, 'Crow and Stone.' It is another ultimate encounter, but while Crow looks to be a monster of unlimited human 'dominion,' whose eyeblink holds the world in awe, 'still he who never has been killed / Croaks helplessly / And is only just born'. Can this latter figure be Crow the Trickster, the gleeful subverter of God's plan; can it be Crow in the next poem, 'Glimpse,' who sings, yearningly, 'O leaves'? Yes: such is Hughes' refraction of the human image in the evolution of Crow.

The book ends with four summary poems, 'King of Carrion', 'Two Eskimo Songs', and 'Littleblood'. The first of these, coming directly after 'Glimpse', shifts focus dramatically and depicts, as if at a great distance, a kind of terrible final apotheosis of Crow – no longer humanised, a mediator with human impulses, but rather the absolute monarch of the desolation that men now have it in them to create on earth: truly, a place where no man would go, and no crow fly. The special shock of this poem, as a kind of warning, lies in what becomes of Crow: once the image of something 'livelier' than death, now he is death's very totem, immobile, silent.

The two 'Eskimo Songs' which follow are not, to my knowledge, based on extant Eskimo myths or songs: what Hughes seems to be aiming at in the title is an evocation of the quality of Eskimo life – its acceptance of what looks like impossibly minimal conditions of existence, its cultivation of the spirit in song (the Eskimo word for song, *anerca*, is also the word for spirit) and in religion (significantly, in the light of Hughes' treatment of Christianity, there is a popular belief that when Eskimos are Christianised, they die). The title of the first song, 'Fleeing from Eternity', is pretty surely a serious take-off on the title of Yeats' great mordant poem on the pains of this life in relation to the Christian promise of the next, 'Running to Paradise'. Here, man comes 'running faceless over the earth': after several million years of ignorant pain, he cuts himself eyes and a mouth, and when he encounters a woman 'singing out of her belly,' he cuts these apertures for her, too, in exchange for her song. Knowing now that life is 'the pain and the blood', the singing man still feels that 'the song is worth it' – something of a Yeatsian conclusion, in fact, except that the woman (is she a Muse? something of a Great Goddess? something more personal to the poet?) feels cheated in the exchange. At any rate, the retrospective implications of the poem, back over this harrowing book if not over the poet's whole career, seem obvious.

'How Water Began to Play' parallels the faceless man's quest for a viable life in the preceding poem, and indeed Crow's own forays and rebuffs — 'Water wanted to live / It went to the sun it came weeping back' — but what is most crucial, here at the close of the sequence, is the way Water's quest ends. Earlier I spoke of a series of poems seeming to try out a kind of death's head humour as a provisional emotional stance in this world; here, what Water experiences after its very human torments is an absolute purgation of emotions — 'It lay at the bottom of all things / Utterly worn out   utterly clear'. Again the poem has a retrospective effect: this clarity, though gained at such cost as the preceding poems reveal, is good. Will it, as in the title, lead on to 'play'?   In the final poem, 'Littleblood', having attained a measure of calm and even, perhaps, a simple expectancy, and having put aside his mediating Trickster, Crow, the poet turns to appeal to a new bird-totem. Littleblood is one of the very minims of life, it seems: yet being alive it has (like Man himself) 'grown so wise grown so terrible / Sucking death's mouldy tits'. Like Crow, until his apotheosis, Littleblood represents something stronger than death, something older than pain, but the wistfulness and tenderness with which the poet appeals to it dramatises powerfully that the primal agony and rage against the nature of things, through which Crow is so effective a guide, has run its course. 'Sit on my finger, sing in my ear, O littleblood.'

Such, as I think, is the career of Ted Hughes' Trickster Crow. Whether Hughes himself returns at length to him, in *Crow* he has forcibly brought back into our writing a figure from world folk-literature, so compelling, so imaginatively rich and serviceable, so inexhaustible, that other writers, with or without Hughes' gifts, cannot help but pick him up. We have been needing a Trickster, maybe; it is not committing a primitivism to suppose that he may be one of the imaginative things our polarised age demands.

12 ANNIE SCHOFIELD

The Oedipus theme in Hughes

Hero by hero they go —
Grimly get astride
And their hair lifts.

She smiles, smelling the battle — their cry comes back.

Who can live her life?
Every effort to hold her or turn her falls off her
Like rotten harness.

Their smashed faces come back, the wallets and the watches.

('Bones', *Crow Wakes*)

Here come and sit, where never serpent hisses;
And being set, I'll smother thee with kisses. (Shakespeare, 'Venus and Adonis')

In seeking the source of Hughes' creative energy, there is a tendency on the part of some critics to see his work as a problem in pathology. Ian Hamilton's assessment of *Crow* is typical. He feels that there is an 'authorial evasiveness' on Hughes' part in order to find 'a territory and a device which would enable him to unload his obsessions without requiring that he test them out, in any precise way, against reality'.[1]

The 'small psychology' ('Witches') of Freud, which generalises from facts which are relevant to neurotic states of mind only, and reduces everything to the personal, is perhaps the cause of such statements. The 'larger' psychology of Jung might suggest a new stance towards Hughes and towards reality. In his essay 'Psychology and Literature', Jung defines two modes of artistic creation: the *psychological* and the *visionary*.[2] The psychological mode deals with materials from the conscious life of man, 'raised from the commonplace to the level of poetic experience'. However varied and seemingly removed from the level of everyday life, this material 'never transcends the bounds of psychological intelligibility'. The visionary artist's materials are vastly more inaccessible:

The profound difference between the first and second parts of *Faust* marks the difference between the psychological and visionary modes of artistic creation. The latter reverses all the conditions of the former. The experience that furnishes the material for artistic expression is no longer familiar. It is a strange something that derives its existence from the hinterland of man's mind – that suggests the abyss of time separating us from the pre-human ages, or evokes a super-human world of contrasting light and darkness. It is a primordial experience which surpasses man's understanding, and to which he is therefore in danger of succumbing. The value and force of the experience are given by its enormity. It arises from timeless depths; it is foreign and cold, many-sided, demonic and grotesque.[3]

The materials provided by the primordial experiences of the visionary artist are more volatile than those of the psychological mode and their source can be as obscure to him as to his audience. Jung holds that it is this very obscurity which leads to accusations of authorial evasiveness:

We are naturally inclined to suppose – and Freudian psychology encourages us to do so – that some highly personal experience underlies this grotesque darkness. We hope thus to explain these strange glimpses of chaos and to understand why it seems as though the poet had intentionally concealed his basic experience from us. It is only a step from this way of looking at the matter to the statement that we are here dealing with a pathological and neurotic art . . .[4]

Hughes is often accused of other evasions, of what Hamilton calls 'skimped and shallow dealings with the human world', and of escaping into an anachronistic use of myth. Jung argues that the visionary artist, of necessity, uses myth as the only adequate means of expression. 'The primordial experience is the source of his creativeness; it cannot be fathomed, and therefore requires mythological imagery to give it form.'[5]

Perhaps in an effort to rescue her work from the reductive effects of

Freudian criticism, Hughes has offered his account of the background of Sylvia Plath's poems – 'emblematic visionary events' – which he sees as parts of 'one long poem', as '. . . chapters in a mythology where the plot, seen as a whole and in retrospect is strong and clear – even if the *dramatis personae*, are at bottom enigmatic'.[6] Though it cannot yet be seen whole and in retrospect, Hughes' own poetry may be seen in the same way: as emblematic visionary chapters in a developing mythology, where at first he uses the figures of established myth. A central figure in his mythology is Oedipus.

In 'Meet my Folks' in *Poetry in the Making*, Hughes states that 'In writing these poems of mine about relatives I found it almost impossible to write about the mother . . . My feelings about my mother, you see, must be too complicated to flow easily into words' (p. 102). Indeed, in *The Hawk in the Rain* and *Lupercal* there is small mention of the mother-son relationship. In 'Mayday on Holderness' (*Lupercal*), there is the first appearance of a recurring image: the Virgin and the dead Christ – 'The stars make pietas'. What emerges from Hughes' work when he does find himself able to write of the mother in *Wodwo* and in subsequent works – particularly in his adaptation of Seneca's *Oedipus* – is not evidence of an 'Oedipus complex' but an awareness of a Universal dilemma.

Why risk saying too much, too much that is false and inadequate and beside the point, about that human being who was our mother, the accidental carrier of that great experience which includes herself and myself and all mankind . . . a sensitive person cannot in all fairness load that enormous burden of meaning, responsibility, duty, heaven and hell, on to the shoulders of one frail fallible human being . . . who was our mother. He knows that the mother carries for us that inborn image of the *mater natura* and *mater spiritualis* of the totality of life . . . Nor should we hesitate for one moment to relieve the human mother of this appalling burden . . . A mother-complex is not got rid of by blindly reducing the mother to human proportions. Besides that we run the risk of dissolving the experience 'Mother' to atoms . . .[7]

Hughes is not dealing with a familial mother and son, nor even with the wider theme of his emergence from the dark womb of the Calder valley,[8] but with the archetypal love-myth of Mother and Son.

The central theme of the Mother–Son love-myth is the effecting of the union of opposites: matter and spirit, body and soul, feminine and masculine, instinct and reason. Jung's *Mysterium Coniunctionis* is a detailed study of the theme. He sees the symbolism of the Mother–Son love-myth as having been appropriated by Christian ecclesiastical allegory in the mystic marriage of sponsus (Christ) and sponsa (Church), and by the alchemists in the *mysterium coniunctionis* – the alchemical marriage – which was the goal of the alchemical opus. In both of these the dilemma has been brought to a dubious resolution:

The Christian resolution of the conflict is purely pneumatic, the physical relations of the sexes being turned into allegory or – quite illegitimately – into a sin that perpetuates and even intensifies the original one in the Garden. Alchemy, on the other hand, exalted the most heinous transgression of the law, namely incest, into a symbol of the union of opposites, hoping in this way to bring back the golden age. For both trends the solution lay in extrapolating the union of the sexes into another medium: the one projected it into the spirit, the other into matter. But neither of them located the problem in the place where it arose – the soul of man.[9]

Hughes appears to be attempting this task – to be undertaking this psychic journey. He sees the Oedipus myth as central to the Western psyche. In the anecdotes about Crow which accompany his poetry-readings he indicates this. He tells of Crow starting to write plays – rewriting everybody else's plays – because that, it seems, is what everybody else has done.

This thing is a series. And so he only has two characters in his plays – a male and a female of a very crude form – with no speech – and this is a sort of a song that he invents to accompany his dramas, where his two characters – the same old two characters – are performing. He goes through the repertoire picking out stories where these two are the only two that matter. It turns out that there are a great many of these stories, but he finds one particularly attractive tale – treated by Sophocles and again by Seneca and again by Freud – and he thinks, 'There's room for another.'

Crow, at this point in his development 'cribs' his version from Seneca – he writes 'Song for a Phallus'. Hughes' use of the myth starts with Seneca, but does not end there.

A comparison of Hughes' adaptation of Seneca's *Oedipus* with the original, and with Sophocles' *Oedipus Rex*, shows that he makes significant alterations in the role of Jocasta. Sophocles' Jocasta is a rounded – almost naturalistic – portrayal of a woman who is getting on with the job of living from day to day, saying 'A fig for divination' but flinging salt over her shoulder – just in case. Adapting herself to circumstances, she only faces up to reality when it can no longer be avoided. Seneca's Jocasta is not so clearly realised. She has one short 'Pull yourself together' speech at the beginning of the play, appears again to give factual answers to questions about the manner and circumstances of Laius' death, and finally appears to make a short speech accepting her share of the guilt for the crime of incest and to commit suicide.

Hughes' Jocasta shows a prescience completely lacking in the other two. Her opening dialogue with Oedipus starts in the same way but culminates in a long speech – a black Magnificat – for which there is no precedent in the original – but which does parallel 'Logos' and presents aspects of Hughes' vision which are present in 'Crow and Mama', 'Song for a Phallus' and 'Snake Hymn'. This speech of Jocasta's might be regarded as an early Crow poem.

when I carried my sons
I carried them for death   I carried them for the throne
I carried them for final disaster   when I carried my first son
did I know what was coming   did I know
what ropes of blood were twisting together what bloody footprints
were hurrying together in my body
did I know what past and unfinished reckonings
were getting flesh again inside me
did I think that the debts of the past
were settled before I conceived
I knew the thing in my womb was going to have to pay for the whole past
I know the future was waiting for him like a greedy god a maneater in a cave
was going to ask for everything   happiness strength and finally life
as if no other man existed   I carried him for this
for pain and for fear
for hard sharp metal   for the cruelty of other men and his own cruelty
I carried him for disease
for rottenness and dropping to pieces
I carried him for death bones dust   I knew
but I carried him not only for this I carried him to be king of this
and my blood didn't pause
didn't hesitate in my womb
considering the futility
it didn't falter reckoning the odds   it poured on
into him   blood from my toes my finger ends
blind blood   blood from my gums and eyelids
blood from the roots of my hair   blood from before any time began
it flowed into the knot of his bowels, into the knot of his muscles
the knot of his brain
my womb tied everything together every corner of the earth and the heavens
and every trickle of the dead past
twisted it all into shape inside me
what was he   what wasn't he
the question was unasked
and what was I   what cauldron was I
what doorway was I   what cavemouth
what spread my legs and lifted my knees
was he squeezing to hide
was I running to escape
the strength of the whole earth
pushed him through my body and out
it split me open and I saw the blood jump out after him
was I myself   but what was he
a bag of blood   a bag of death
a screaming mouth
was it asking a question
he was a king's son   he was a man's shape
he was perfect

not something monstrous some repulsive accident of wrong limbs and jumbled
   organs
not some freakish half-living blood clot
his eyes were perfect   feet perfect   fingers perfect
he lay there in the huge darkness like a new bright weapon
he was the warrant of the gods
he was their latest attempt
to walk on earth and to live
he only had to live [10]

This is Hughes, not Seneca, speaking through Jocasta. In a text which
he had pared down to the bone – to its 'plainest bluntest form' he has
inserted this lengthy speech. It is parallelled in 'Logos':

God gives the blinding pentagram of His power
For the frail mantle of a person
To be moulded onto. So if they come
This unlikely far, and against such odds —
            the perfect strength is God's.

And if the family features mount yet another
Opportune, doomed bid
To grapple to everlasting
Their freehold of life —
            it is by God's leave.

Logos is, to Heraclitus, the intelligible law of the universe, to the
early Stoics, the rational purpose behind the universe governing the
movement of heavenly bodies and the functions of the natural world
and, coincident with this, the quality in the wisest of men which
enables him to live in harmony with the universe. But the pantheism
of early Stoic teaching was later modified, especially in the cosmogony
of Plato's *Timaeus* where it is combined with a transcendental
monotheism. Hellenistic–Jewish teachers adopted a language appropriate to the Stoic *logos* to describe the Divine Wisdom. In St. John's
Gospel, there is a further development. In Christ – the Son of God – the
cosmological *logos* is Incarnate. The Word is made flesh in Christ.

Throughout its changes *logos* remains a masculine, rational principle and must contend with the female, irrational, creative–destructive
principle. Christ's paternity, for Hughes, is of scant importance; he
will be choked and strangled by the roots which connect him to the
placenta. The medium of incarnation is the umbilical cord. The
fleshed Word has human blood. The foetus, in absorbing blood from
the mother, absorbs also the guilt from the dead which cannot be
absolved,

And within seconds the new-born baby is lamenting
That it ever lived —
      God is a good fellow, but His mother's against Him.   ('Logos')

Her womb has 'tied everything together'. There is no escape from the 'blood-dark womb' ('Gog'). The earlier 'could' of the poem 'Childbirth' when 'Through that miracle-breached bed / All the dead could have got back', has now become a certainty. 'The cords of all link back, strand entwining cable of all flesh'.[11] Descent is matrilineal – 'the grand-mothers / With their ancestral bones' ('Public Bar T.V.). There is no way of escaping, no way of finally severing the umbilical cord, no ending the transfusion of guilty blood, no escape from Mama. Crow makes a last, desperate attempt,

He jumped into the rocket and its trajectory
Drilled clean through her heart he kept on

And it was cosy in the rocket, he could not see much
But he peered out through the portholes at Creation

And he saw the stars millions of miles away
And the future and the universe

Opening and opening
And he kept on and slept at last

Crashed on the moon and awoke and crawled out

Under his mother's buttocks.   ('Crow and Mama')

This inescapable cycle is also the theme of the savagely funny compression of the Oedipus myth in 'Song for a Phallus':

He split his Mammy like a melon
     He was drenched with gore
He found himself curled up inside
     As if he had never been bore
                              Mamma   Mamma

Not only is there no escape; not only is guilt transfused but suffering too. Tormentor and tormented are fed by the same circulatory system. The blood of the victims of past genocides still flows

. . . up the jugular
Smoulderingly
Skywriting across the cortex

That the heart, a gulping mask, demands, demands
Appeasement
For its bloody possessor.

And a hundred and fifty million years of hunger
Killing gratefully as breathing
Moulded the heart and the mouth

That cry for milk
From the breast
Of the mother

Of the God
Of the world
Made of Blood.   ('Karma')

In Hughes' view, God – as *Logòs*, the Rational Principle – is not in control of the world 'made of blood'. If he is to be regarded as the Creator, then he has botched the job so badly and is so helpless to do any running repairs that there is neither hope of alleviation of present suffering nor eventual appeasement. Even if, despite all evidence to the contrary, the Creator were *Logos*, His incarnation is unlikely to have a redemptive effect.

The blood in Eve's body
That slid from her womb —
Knotted on the cross
It had no name.

Nothing else has happened.
The love that cannot die
Sheds the million faces
And skin of agony

To hang, an empty husk.   ('Snake Hymn')

The Incarnation, depending as it must, on the moulding of the 'blinding pentagram' of spiritual perfection on to a frail and vulnerable body,[12] saturated in guilt and torn by suffering cannot, in Hughes' view, result in *the Resurrection* and a once for all *Redemption*. For Christ, as for Prometheus

        . . . all his preparations
For his humanity
Were disablements   ('Prometheus 8', *Moortown*)

In the last chorus of *Oedipus*, Seneca only implies what Hughes overtly and emphatically states:

the good luck the bad luck everything that happens
everything that seems to toss our days up and down
it is all there from the first moment
it is all there   tangled in the knotted mesh of causes
helpless to change itself
even the great god lies there entangled
helpless in the mesh of causes
and the last day lies there tangled with the first
a man's life is a pattern on the floor   like a maze
it is all fixed   he wanders in the pattern
no prayer can alter it
or help him to escape it   nothing

then fear can be the end of him

a man's fear of his fate is often his fate
leaping to avoid it   he meets it   (*Oedipus*, pp. 52–3)

Oedipus tries to avoid his destiny and ends mangled by fate: Macbeth
tries to avoid the fate of being only a king when he would be a dynast –
he too is mangled by fate. In Hughes' work, the links between Oedipus
and Macbeth are strong. Comparison of the final dialogue between
Oedipus and Jocasta reveals that, consciously or unconsciously,
Hughes is linking Oedipus with Macbeth. 'Let the vast sea roll
between our impious selves, / let remote lands separate' is all that
Seneca says, but Hughes adds

the salt bottomless
ocean should be washing between our bodies   not to
cleanse them   nothing can cleanse them

The image of a guilt so vast and deep that an ocean could not wash it
clean is Senecan, but it is used in the *Phaedra* and *Hercules Furens*, it
is not used in *Oedipus*. Shakespeare used it in his most Senecan play,
Macbeth:

Will all great Neptune's Ocean wash this blood
Clean from my hand? No: this my hand will rather
The multitudinous seas incarnadine,
Making the green one red.   (Act 2, scene 2)

We are reminded of Macbeth in 'Song for a Phallus':

O do not chop his winkle off
His Mammy cried with horror
Think of the joy will come of it
                    Tomorrer and Tomorrer

which echoes Macbeth's

Tomorrow, and tomorrow, and tomorrow
Creeps in this petty pace from day to day,
To the last syllable of recorded time;
And all our yesterdays have lighted fools
The way to dusty death . . .   (Act 5, scene 5)

Men's fate is his humanity – his mortality. In leaping to avoid his fate,
Macbeth meets it. One way to avoid mortality – to assert a claim to
everlasting life – is in the founding of a dynasty. Macbeth, the
would-be dynast, is tormented not by the ghost of the murdered
Duncan, but by the ghost of Banquo – the destined begetter of kings.
The dynast sees life in terms of linear time only, of generation upon
generation. To him immortality is a succession of begats, a succession
of tomorrows holding out infinite possibilities of redemption. When

Macbeth hears of the death of the co-founder of his dynasty he utters his cry of despair. All he sees now is a recession of hopeless yesterdays. He does not have the resilience of Oedipus Crow who 'wins' the first few rounds of his battle with mortality and time:

And he ran, cheered by the sound of his foot and its echo
And by the watch on his wrist

One-legged, gutless and brainless, the rag of himself —

So Death tripped him easy
And held him up with a laugh, only just alive.

And his watch galloped away in a cloud of corpse-dust.

Crow dangled from one claw – corrected.

A warning   ('Oedipus Crow')

Macbeth cannot let go of his watch which ticks away the linear time, measuring the hopeless tomorrows and yesterdays. He cannot look steadily at his fate – his mortality. He is blinded by corpse-dust and lapses into a despairing nihilism; life becomes 'a tale / Told by an idiot, full of sound and fury, / Signifying nothing.'

But Macbeth's *nothing* is not Hughes'. For Hughes *nothing* is not zero. Zero is a void. *Nothing* is the flux – no *thing* – chaos – the Heraclitean fire, where everything is born out of the death of something else. Hughes paraphrases Heraclitus in 'Ghost Crabs': 'Mortals are immortals, and immortals are mortals, the one living the other's death and dying the other's life' becomes

They are the powers of this world.
We are their bacteria,
Dying their lives and living their deaths.

Hopkins contemplates on mortality in the poem 'That Nature is a Heraclitean Fire and of the Comfort of the Resurrection':

. . . Manshape that shone
Sheer off, disseveral, a star, death blots black out; nor mark
          Is any of him at all so stark
But vastness blurs and time beats level. Enough! the Resurrection,
A heart's-clarion! Away grief's gasping, joyless days, dejection.
          Across my foundering deck shone
A beacon, an eternal beam.   Flesh fade, and mortal trash
Fall to the residuary worm; world's wildfire, leave but ash:
          In a flash, at a trumpet crash,
I am all at once what Christ is, since he was what I am, and
This Jack, joke, poor potsherd, patch, matchwood, immortal diamond,
          Is immortal diamond.

Hughes can find no such comfort.

Adam

Lay defeated, low as water

Too little lifted from mud
He dreamed the tower of light.
. . .

Wrapped in peach-skin and bruise
He dreamed the religion of the diamond body.

His dream played with him, like a giant tabby.
Like a bitten black-wet mouse . . .   ('Adam')

Diamonds are not immortal, imperishable. They only appear so in a
limited conception of time. (Crow contemplates nature's stupor and an
oak tree grows out of his ear.) They are as much a part of the
Heraclitean flux as flesh and bone, and must, too, be subject to the
recycling process. If Creation is not to fail, the only answer to death is
continuous resurrection: every death must result in rebirth,

and yet you cannot possibly pay
not in this lifetime
you need to be born again   suffer for everything again
and die again   over and over   lifetime after lifetime
every lifetime a new sentence
and length of penalties   (*Oedipus*, p.50)

There seems then, a terrible irony in Jocasta's words about the birth
of Oedipus: 'he only had to live'. He *only* had to live in a world which it
seems is rendered almost uninhabitable by the forces militating
against life. He *only* had to live when (if one looks at the 'evidence'
offered by Hughes) love seems an empty husk, laughter a criminal, science a ceremonial sword with which maniac man will butcher his
children, a grin is a grimace of death whose repository is the skull, and
the death-dealing guilty genes are transfused from generation to
generation in a cycle which can never be broken. He only had to live
when the new-born are 'wounded-fatal'. But, Jocasta knows all this,

        I knew
but I carried him not only for this I carried him to be king of this
and my blood didn't pause
didn't hesitate in my womb
considering the futility
it didn't falter reckoning the odds
. . .

he was a king's son   he was a man's shape
he was perfect
. . .

he was the warrant of the gods

Oedipus is potentially capable of making a successful Heroic Quest – 'one of the main regenerating dramas of the human psyche',[13] the 'archetypal journey to the bottom of the soul'.[14] The Heroic Task is that of the theme of the Mother-Son love myth, the reconciliation of matter and spirit; reconciliation of the spirit with the Great Mother.

In his book *The Hero With a Thousand Faces*[15] Joseph Campbell outlines the hero's deed. His objective is to achieve complete union with the 'Cosmic Mother' – the source of all being.

The mystical marriage with the Queen goddess of this world represents the hero's total mastery of life ... And the testings of the hero, which were preliminary to his ultimate experience and deed, were symbolical of those crises of realisation by means of which his consciousness came to be amplified and made capable of enduring full possession of the mother-destroyer, his inevitable bride. (pp.120–1)

To achieve this union with the goddess, however, the hero must be capable of seeing the Mother-Goddess in both her benign and malevolent aspects: to look directly at the evidence of her power, and accept what he sees without revulsion – to accept the challenge.

By deficient eyes she is reduced to inferior states; by the evil eye of ignorance she is spellbound to banality and ugliness. But she is redeemed by the eyes of understanding. The hero who can take her as she is, without undue commotion but with the kindness and assurance she requires is potentially the king, the incarnate god of the created world. (p.116)

Hughes' Oedipus believes himself capable of meeting the challenge, 'the high law of nature   I respected that   determined / to guard that', but like Macbeth he cannot; the inevitable biological cycle is meaningless sound and fury. The high law of nature is 'death rottenness dropping to pieces'.   It is the swift's body

Pulsating
With insects
And their anguish, all it had eaten   ('Crow Tyrannosaurus')

Oedipus is unable to look at and beyond 'the core / Of an eternal fierce destruction'[16] to see the flux as anything but desolation. 'Though he bends to be blent in the prayer' he sees only the 'orgy' of the world of blood:

the shark's mouth
That hungers down the blood-smell even to a leak of its own
Side and devouring of itself.   ('Thrushes')

Like Melville's Ahab, (Melville is another of Jung's primordial adventurers) he sees only the side of nature which impels the sharks;

he does not find the 'enchanted calm ... at the heart of every commotion'[17] or see the nursing whales in the maelstrom of killing. Oedipus sees the 'orgy' but does not hear the 'hosannahs'.

The blinded Oedipus comforts himself:

> I like
> this darkness   I wonder which god it is that I've
> finally pleased   which of them has forgiven me for all
> that I did   he's given me this dark veil for my head
> pleasant
> the light   that awful eye   that never let me rest
> and followed me everywhere   peering through every
> crack   at last you've escaped it

but he is mistaken. When Jocasta (the Mother) comes again to claim kinship, Oedipus spurns her as the cause of his pain and the author of his guilt. The Goddess is only redeemed by the eyes of understanding, and Oedipus prefers his blindness.

> The crux of the difficulty lies in the fact that our conscious view of what life ought to be seldom corresponds to what life really is. Generally we refuse to admit within ourselves or within our friends, the fulness of that pushing, self-protective, malodorous, carnivorous, lecherous fever which is the very nature of the organic cell ... But when it suddenly dawns on us, or is forced to our attention, that everything we think or do is necessarily tainted with the odour of the flesh, then, not uncommonly, there is experienced a moment of revulsion: life, the acts of life, the organs of life, become intolerable to the pure, the pure, pure soul.   (Campbell, p.122)

Campbell sees Hamlet, who wishes that his 'too, too solid flesh' would melt, as the supreme spokesman of this moment. (Eliot can find no 'objective correlative' for the emotions of Hamlet – perhaps there is one here.) Hughes sees Hamlet in much the same way: he comes in 'staggering Mother-wet, weak-eyed, horrified'.[18] Campbell continues:

> Where this Oedipus-Hamlet revulsion remains to beset the soul, there, the world, the body, and woman above all, become the symbols no longer of victory but of defeat. A monastic-puritanical, world-negating ethical system then radically transfigures all the images of myth. No longer can the hero rest in innocence with the goddess of the flesh; for she is become the queen of sin.
> (p.123)

Hughes' comment on Hamlet comes in his essay on Shakespeare's *poem*: Shakespeare's attempt to resolve the conflict. When reading this essay one is continually aware that what he says about Shakespeare may equally apply to himself. Hughes, too, sees himself as answering the 'ancient Universal shamanistic call to the poetic or holy life'. He, too, has a preoccupying concern with the resolution of the conflict between the 'biological polarity of the life of the body and archaic nervous system and the life of the reflective cortex' (p.199) – that 'flying malevolent custard', the conflict between the beast and the angel in man. Its resolution will be to *live* – to reach a satisfactory 'state of negotiation' with 'his idea of the Creator' (p. 184). The theme runs through his work as surely as he sees it in Shakespeare's. In the early 'animal' poems there is almost invariably an implicit, if not overt, contrasting of the animal with man. There is an explicit and pessimistic statement of the conflict in 'Fair Choice'. The 'fair' of the title is bitterly ironic since no possibility of reconciliation is offered – no chance of rearing both twins of man's cloven psyche 'fairly' — 'Your every glance shall see one of your twins / An Abel to the other's bloody Cain'. In *Wodwo* in the poems already quoted; the theme is still being explored. By the time Crow appears, perhaps because his work on Seneca's play had released the imagery, Hughes is using the Oedipus myth to examine the conflict.

The poles of energy, as he sees them in Shakespeare's *poem*: Adonis and Venus, become, at this stage in Hughes' work, Oedipus and Jocasta.

Jocasta is the Mother – Nature – the blood root – love; Oedipus is the opposite pole: the Spirit – intellect – reason – rigid moral law: the opponent and suppressor of that which, in many, and especially in the poet answers the call of the White Goddess, 'who was the goddess of natural law and of love, who was the goddess of all sensation and organic life – this overwhelming powerful multiple, primaeval being, was dragged into court by the young Puritan Jehovah' (*A Choice of Shakespeare's Verse*, p.187). A seminal influence on Hughes' work, particularly on this essay on Shakespeare and the poem 'An Alchemy' is Robert Graves' book *The White Goddess*. Graves traces the development of Middle Eastern and European myths and legends and their relationship to each other. An extremely simple and incomplete account of his theories would be that, in all these myths, there is in the beginning, an all-powerful female goddess – Mother of all things – Creator, who is usurped by a male god. In the Babylonian myth she is Ishtar, an emanation of whom – Tiamat – is hacked in two by the upstart godling Marduk (whose predecessor was Bel who usurped the Sumerian Mother goddess Belili). It is this Goddess who 'calls' the poet, and whom he must celebrate.

In Graves' view, the developments in Judaeo-Greek mythology which changed the concept of the nature of the godhead and introduced a false duality were instigated by Ezekiel. He considers that the the idea of a God of Light, disembodied from the physical Universe, and all-powerful, is initiated by Ezekiel, who has 'edited' the Genesis Creation myth and repudiated the White Goddess, turning her into the Whore of Babylon – with disastrous result:

The new God claimed to be dominant as Alpha and Omega, the Beginning and the End, pure Holiness, pure Good, pure Logic, able to exist without the aid of woman; but it was natural to identify him with one of the original rivals of the theme and to ally woman and the other rival permanently against him. The outcome was a philosophical dualism with all the tragi-comic woes attendant upon a spiritual dichotomy. If the True God, the God of the Logos was pure thought, pure good, whence came evil and error? Two separate creations had to be assumed: the true Spiritual Creation and the false material Creation . . .

(p.465)

There are undoubted links between the Book of Ezekiel and the Book of Revelation: Gog appears in both.

Hughes' poem 'Gog', though it started as a poem about the German push in the Ardennes' (the death throes of Hitler's Reich), 'ended by being a poem about the Dragon in Revelation'. In Ezekiel, Gog is the protagonist of the Whore of Babylon in the war between good and evil. In Revelation, Gog and the Dragon are merged in the symbolism. Gog is the Dragon, the beast which cannot be killed and wages continual war with the God of Light. Though it is not dead, the beast is at least asleep. In Hughes' poem, Gog is awakened by God's shout of omnipotence: 'I am Alpha and Omega'. A battle ensues, perhaps the beast is beheaded, but, like the beast in Revelation, is not killed but becomes a darkness – a living darkness, a perpetual challenge to the God of Light. The horseman of the poem is the horseman of Revelation 'who shall rule with a rod of iron', he is God's protagonist. The horseman of iron gallops forth from a stone womb 'shaking his plumes clear of the dark soil'; like Mr. Kurtz in Conrad's *Heart of Darkness*, he thinks he has 'kicked himself clear of the earth'. But the granite womb is, 'blood-dark' and its lintel 'Overwritten with roots'. The horseman trusts to his iron will to bring him clear of the

. . . softness of the throat, the navel, the armpit, the groin.
Bring him clear of the flung web and the coil that vaults from the dust.

This 'Holy Warrior' finds his enemy: the grail, the female – the living darkness.

The unborn child beats on the womb-wall.
He will need to be strong
To follow his weapons towards the light.

The unborn child will need greater strength than the iron horseman who finds shelter and consolation in the 'law and mercy of number' (because if we read 'Crow's Account of St. George' we learn that in killing his beast he has murdered his wife and children). He will need other strengths than Melville's 'iron horseman' of God – Ahab – in his monomaniac pursuit of his beast Moby Dick:

The path to my fixed purpose is laid with iron rails, whereon my soul is grooved to run. Over unsounded gorges, through the rifled hearts of mountains, under Torrent's beds unerringly I rush! Naught's an obstacle to the iron way (p. 171).

Ahab's God is the God of 'Gog'. The irony of *Moby Dick* is that, in his attempted defiance of this God, Ahab serves Him. He senses and seeks his true Creator as something greater and beyond this God:

I own thy speechless, placeless power; said I not so? . . . Yet blindfold will I walk to thee. Light though thou be, thou leapest out of darkness; but I am darkness leaping out of light, leaping out of thee . . . But thou art but my fiery father; my sweet mother I know not. O cruel! what hast thou done with her? There lies my puzzle; but thine is greater. Thou knowest not how came ye, hence callest thyself unbegun. I know that of me, which thou knowest not of thyself, oh thou omnipotent. There is some unsuffusing thing beyond thee, thou clear spirit, to whom all thy eternity is but time, all thy creativeness mechanical. (p.447)

Ahab's quest is to find this Creator. His 'Sphynx' is the whale which 'contains the constituents of a chaos' – contains the secret of Creation. Ahab senses this but makes the mistake of the Oedipus of 'Song for a Phallus'; he seeks an answer by main force. He pursues the whale 'darting barbed iron from one side of the world to the other'. The 'harpooner of Nantucket' is in good company, he is 'enrolled in the most noble order of St. George'. Whaling is 'a Scandinavian vocation'. Ahab is fulfilling his destiny as one of Hughes' Vikings,

Bringing their frozen swords, their salt-bleached eyes, their salt-bleached hair,
The snow's stupified anvils in rows,
Bringing their envy,
The slow ships feelered Southward, snails over the steep sheen of the water-globe
. . .
To no end
But this timely expenditure of themselves,
A cash-down, beforehand revenge, with extra,
For the gruelling relapse and prolongeur of their blood

Into the iron arteries of Calvin. ('The Warriors of the North')

In *The White Goddess*, following Graves' argument, it is possible to trace a direct descent from Ezekiel, through the Essenes and Christ to Calvin: a genealogy of an increasingly repressive puritanism with a concommitantly increasing resistance to and detestation of material creation. It was Calvin's Puritan Jehovah who was attempting to dethrone the Goddess in Shakespeare's England and it is this conflict which Hughes sees as being the source of Shakespeare's *poem*:

Adonis's Calvinist spectacles ... divide nature, and especially love, the creative force of nature, into abstract good and physical evil. Nature's attempts to recombine, first in love, then in whatever rebuffed love turns into, and the determination that she shall not recombine under any circumstances, are the power-house and the torture-chamber of the Complete Works.

And the vital twist, the mysterious chemical change that converts the resisting high-minded puritan to the being of murder and madness [Adonis into Tarquin], is that occult cross-over of Nature's maddened force – like a demon – into the brain that had rejected her. (p. 192)

The Goddess cannot be usurped completely, finally. Sooner or later 'this suppressed Nature goddess erupts, possessing the man who denied her, and creating this king-killing man of chaos' (p. 194) For Shakespeare, this man is Hamlet, Macbeth, Othello and Lear successively. For Hughes it is usually Oedipus though he also uses Tolstoy and St. George as the arch-puritan oppressor. Links between Macbeth and Oedipus have been demonstrated. Othello appears (indistinguishable from Tolstoy) in 'Kreutzer Sonata':

Now you have stabbed her good
A flower of unknown colour appallingly
Blackened by your surplus of bile
Blooms wetly on her dress.

'Your mystery! Your mystery! . . .'
All facts, with all absence of facts,
Exhale as the wound there
Drinks its roots and breathes them to nothing.

Vile copulation! Vile!——etcetera.
But now your dagger has outdone everybody's.
Say goodbye, for your wife's sweet flesh goes off,
Booty of the envious spirit's assault.

A sacrifice, not a murder.
One hundred and forty pounds
Of excellent devil, for God.
She tormented Ah demented you . . .

Hamlet and Lear appear, unambiguously linked with Oedipus, in 'Prospero and Sycorax'.[19]

Shakespeare's attempted resolution of his dilemma in *The Tempest* does not satisfy Hughes,

After all his experience of the odds against the likelihood, he did finally succeed in salvaging Lucrece from the holocaust and Adonis from the boar. He rescued the puritan abstraction from the gulf of Nature. He banished Venus as Sycorax the blue-eyed hag. He humbled Tarquin as Caliban, the poetry-crammed half-beast. And within an impenetrable crucible of magic prohibitions, he married Lucrece (Miranda) to Adonis (Ferdinand). But what a wooden wedding! What proper little puritan puppets! And what a ghastly expression on Prospero's cynical face. (p. 198)

In the poem 'An Alchemy', Hughes reiterates this argument,

Then black Venus
                    double-tongued
Swine-uddered Sycorax
                        Lilith the night-crow
Slid from the Tree
Released the Rainbow
                    Breasted Dove
With a leaf of light
                    Miranda with a miracle
To Adam Adonis

And sank
        In the crucible
                        Tiamat
                            The Mother
The Scales
        The Coil
                Of the Matter
                                Deeper
Than ever plummet
                With Prospero's bones
And the sounding Book

Crow's version of *The Tempest* – of Prospero and Sycorax – is Hughes' summary of Shakespeare's *poem*:

She knows, like Ophelia,
The task has swallowed him.
She knows, like George's dragon,
Her screams have closed his helmet.

She knows, like Jocasta,
It is over.
He prefers
Blindness.

Prospero repudiates Sycorax – Hughes' Oedipus repudiates Jocasta:

        you are spoiling
my comfortable darkness   forcing me to see again
go away   we must not meet

He has 'found / Something / Easier to live with — / His death and her death'. Oedipus is a failed hero: 'The adventures of the hero represents the moment in life when he achieved illumination – the nuclear moment, when, while still alive, he found and opened the road to the light beyond the dark walls of our living death' (Campbell, *Hero with a Thousand Faces*, p. 259). Oedipus cannot face the 'nuclear moment'. He chooses the living death rather than facing the world as it is; he prefers blindness. The true hero is 'he who re-opens the eye – so that through all the comings, delights and agonies of the world panorama, the One Presence will be seen'. In the successful heroic quest the hero penetrates the dark chthonic maternal womb in active incest, and emerges in triumphant rebirth because the light of spirituality survives the union – he re-opens the eye. He does not suffer a dissolution of consciousness, but unites the conscious with the unconscious – the masculine and feminine halves of his cloven psyche.

We can see why Oedipus was only half a hero . . . though Oedipus conquers the Sphynx, he commits incest with his mother, and murders his father, unconsciously.
  He has no knowledge of what he has done, and when he finds out, he is unable to look at his own deed, the deed of the hero, in the face. Consequently he is overtaken by the fate that overtakes all those for whom the Eternal Feminine reverts to the Great.Mother: he regresses to the stage of son, and suffers the fate of the son-lover. He performs the act of self-castration by putting out his own eyes.[20]

The latest overt reference to Oedipus in Hughes' work is in 'Prospero and Sycorax' (1971). Up to this point there had seemed no possibility of a solution to the conflict - no reconciling of polarities. Though Oedipus, himself, does not appear, the Oedipal dilemma appears in later poems – with a difference. Something has happened on Hughes' psychic journey. He is now creating images of an integrated psyche. One of these comes in *Prometheus on His Crag*,[21] perhaps, too abruptly. The creation, by Prometheus, of a mandala from images of the possible nature of his tormentor in 'Prometheus 20' comes too suddenly. The language of the poem indicates that the 'horror' has not been truly assimilated. Prometheus is, perhaps, as he imagines 'mutilated towards alignment'. In the process of *individuation* – the creation of an integrated *self* from a divided psyche 'every experience must be lived through. There is no feat of interpretation or any other trick by which to circumvent this difficulty, for the union of conscious and unconscious can only be achieved step by step'.[22]

  In *Cave Birds: an alchemical cave drama*, 'a mystery play of sorts', there is a step by step transformation. The original version of *Cave Birds*[23] appears to have two parallel dramatic sequences. In one there is 'a man who is a kind of a cockerel' and in the other a male and female, perhaps the male and female of Crow's dramaturgy. The cockerel-hero is faced with an Oedipal situation:

A sphynx
A two-headed questioner

First, a question
The simple fork in the road.

Then an answer. So this is what I am finally

Finally horror

But this is not the final answer. The alchemy of *Cave Birds* offers other possibilities.

The cockerel-hero, who has 'corrupted the pure light / To put it to work', has created a religion of 'the reflective cortex' with a 'bonfire unconcern for the screaming in the cells' – the 'body and archaic nervous system', is arraigned for all the crimes committed by Western civilisation:

What Herod
Crosses himself in the careful lines of your brow.

What Rome
Amuses itself in the irony of your mouth.

What autos-da-fe crack and spittle
In your sigh

What death-camps
Sweeten beneath the civet of your voice.

What Stalin
Draws the curtain of your solicitude.

As he 'comprehends some contradictions of his guilty innocence and innocent guilt' he is 'possessed' by a Raven and subjected to a new series of trials in the Underworld. 'Stripped bare' and in complete darkness, he has to seek a new way to the light – to be, in effect, reborn. The cockerel-hero's moment of subjection to the powers arraigning him, appears to be the moment when the male and female are able to move towards each other. In the linking narrative of the drama, it is suggested that the accused is 'guilty of some error in the use of his life': 'The hero's cockerel innocence, it turns out, becomes his guilt. His own self, finally, the innate nature of his flesh and blood, brings him to court.' When summoned, he is surprised, and when the nature of his crime is indicated, he is puzzled: 'He is confronted in court with his victim; it is his own demon, whom he now sees for the first time. The hero realises he is out of his depth. He protests, as an honourable Platonist, thereby re-enacting his crime in front of his judges . . .'

In Hughes' work, in addition to and combined with the Ezekiel-Calvin genealogy, there is the 'lineage' stemming from Plato and continuing through Descartes; a lineage which has made a 'beast-death of the body' a 'sacrifice to the god-head' of the mind.

I knew that I was a substance whose essence or nature is only to think, and which, in order to be, has no need of any place, and depends on no material thing; so that this I, that is to say, the soul by which I am what I am, is entirely distinct from the body, and is even easier to know than the body, and although the body were not, the soul would not cease to be all that is.

(Descartes, *Discourse on Method*)

One 'Oedipus' descended from this lineage is Sartre in 'Wings'. There is small hope of him 're-opening the eye' so that 'the One Presence will be seen' (Campbell). 'M. Sartre Considers Current Affairs' and his Cartesian ego-consciousness 'regrows the world inside his skull'.

He yawns, tilting an extinct eyeball
To the fly asleep on the lampshade.

Yet his heart pounds on undeterred . . .

The skull-splitting polyp of his brain, on its tiny root,
Lolls out over him ironically:

Angels, it whispers, are metaphors, in man's image,
For the amoeba's exhilarations.

Sartre's eyeball is extinct. The 'archaic nervous' system is sending messages to a brain no longer capable of receiving them: the 'skull-splitting polyp' – the pineal gland, believed to be the remnant of a third eye, still functioning in some lizards - tells him of 'the impulse that first moved the world' (Campbell), but he stays helpless in double-darkness. Sartre's reaction to Nature is that of Oedipus to Jocasta – 'So this is what I am finally / Finally horror'. In *Nausea* we can see what current affairs have made of Plato's Perfect Forms in Roquentin's anti-epiphany:

If anybody had asked me what existence was, I should have replied in good faith that it was nothing, just an empty form which added itself to external things without changing anything in their nature. And then, all of a sudden, there it was, clear as day: existence had suddenly unveiled itself. It had lost its harmless appearance as an abstract category: it was the very stuff of things, that root was steeped in existence. Or rather the root, the park gates, the bench, the sparse grass on the lawn, all that had vanished; the diversity of things, their individuality, was an appearance, a veneer. This veneer had melted, leaving soft, monstrous masses, in disorder – naked, with a frightening, obscene nakedness . . . I realised that there was no half-way house between non-existence and this rapturous abundance. If you existed, you had to *exist to that extent*, to the point of mildew, blisters, obscenity. In another world, circles and melodies kept their pure and rigid lines.[24]

In 'Revenge Fable', we have an anonymous hero, another beneficiary of the Platonic legacy – the scientific rationalist, the technocrat – who cannot cope with Nature except as an abstract category:

There was a person
Could not get rid of his mother
As if he were her topmost twig.

So he pounded and hacked at her
With numbers and equations and laws
Which he invented and called truth.
He investigated, incriminated
And penalised her, like Tolstoy,
Forbidding, screaming and condemning,
. . .

With all her babes in her arms, in ghostly weepings,
She died.

His head fell off like a leaf.

In his review of Max Nicholson's book *The Environmental
Revolution*[25] Hughes gives a prose account of the effect of these
combined inheritances on Western civilisation:

> The story of the mind exiled from Nature [both inner and outer nature] is the
> story of Western Man. It is the story of his progressively more desperate search
> for mechanical and rational and symbolic securities, which will substitute for
> the spirit-confidence he has lost. The basic myth for the ideal Westerner's life
> is the Quest. The quest for a marriage in the soul or a physical re-conquest. The
> lost life must be recaptured somehow. It is a story of spiritual romanticism and
> heroic technical progress. It is a story of decline. When something abandons
> Nature, or is abandoned by Nature, it has lost touch with its creator and is
> called an evolutionary dead-end. According to this, our Civilisation is an
> evolutionary error.

In *Cave Birds*, when the 'honourable Platonist' has been disabused of
'all that civilisation has amassed in the way of hypotheses',[26] the male
and the female 'formerly dead to each other', find and begin to recreate
each other. It is at this point that Hughes creates his images of an
integrated psyche.

His legs ran about

Till they tangled and seemed to trip and lie down
With her legs intending to hold them there forever

His arms lifted things, groped in dark rooms, at last with their hands
Caught her arms
And lay down enwoven at last at last
. . .

And so when every part
Like a bull pressing towards its cows, not to be stayed
Like a calf seeking its mama
Like a desert staggerer, among his hallucinations
Seeking the hoof-churned hole

Finally got what it needed, and grew still, and closed its eyes

Then such greatness and truth descended . . .

What follows, in the male–female dimension of the drama, is a joyous Creation myth – totally different from Ezekiel's Genesis edition – and a new account of a resurrection, which is, in fact, a recreation. In 'Bride and groom lie hidden for three days' the Oedipal journey does not end in entrapment in the dark womb of the mother and a blinded Oedipus: 'She gives him his eyes, she found them under some rubble'. With new eyes and new hands,he fashions for her 'new hips / With newly wound coils, all shiningly oiled'. The newly wound coils of the Serpent are no longer Anathema to the Light – 'They keep taking each other to the sun, they find they can easily / To test each new thing at each new step'. Next, 'She smooths over him the plates of his skull', so that his frontal bone is no longer the 'carapace of foreclosure' that has brought the cockerel-hero to court, to longer the braggart-brow of the egg-head who 'Must stop the looming mouth of the earth with a pin- / Point cipher' ('Egg-Head'). In this step by step re-creation of each other

. . . gasping with joy, with cries of wonderment
Like two gods of mud
Sprawling in dirt, but with infinite care

They bring each other to perfection.

The theme of the Oedipus myth – the Mother–Son love-myth – the reconciliation of opposites: spirit and matter, male and female, conscious and unsconscious – the alchemical opus 'worked out in the soul of man' – is Jung's process of *individuation*. The *unio mystica* – the alchemical marriage – is the creation of a *self* from the divided halves of a psyche. This realisation of a *self* is, at the same time, a realisation of the totality of the nature of the Godhead.[27]

There is no suggestion in *Cave Birds* that Hughes has reached any final answer to the Sphynx. The alchemical marriage is a 'costly, precarious condition': 'The dynamics of man's resistance to demoralisation and confusion, the techniques of 'creating' God and Holy Joy where there seemed to be only emptiness, never change, but they demand a man's whole devotion. And they can be abandoned in a day, whereon the world becomes, once more, Gehenna.'[28] Whilst the mutual recreation of each other is occurring in the male–female dimension of the drama, the cockerel-hero is undergoing an apotheosis into what looks suspiciously like the god of a religion of the 'diamond body'. Hughes is not offering global solutions to the problems of Western Civilisation. Like Eliot's *Waste Land*, Hughes' Oedipus myth is 'the chart of his own condition'. 'I can't believe that he [Eliot] took the disintegration of Western civilisation as a theme which he then found imagery and a general plan for. His sickness told him the cause. Surely that was it. He cleansed his wounds and found all the shrapnel.'[29] Like Eliot, Hughes is recording his quest for a wholeness which man in this civilisation has lost. He is not even offering a *final* answer to his own 'sphynx'. The Sphynx is asking a dilemma question: one to which there is no final answer: 'We go on writing poems because one poem never gets the whole of the account right. There is always something missed. At the end of the ritual comes up a goblin'.[30] This goblin appears at the end of *Cave Birds*. But, it does seem that, in this *mystery play of sorts*, Hughes has reached a new stage in his negotiations with his 'idea of the Creator'.[31]

Creative mythology in *Cave Birds*

Since Hughes is a major poet, and since the volumes that followed *Wodwo* confirmed that creative mythology had assumed a central importance in his poetry, we must expect a torrent of exegesis of a kind already familiar to students of Blake and Yeats. This will be welcome in some ways, distracting in others; one reason for beginning the present essay by recalling some of the critical dangers is my fear that I may not succeed in avoiding them.

I

I do not doubt that the 'she' of 'Crow's Undersong' evokes the figure of the Great Goddess, Robert Graves' White Goddess; nor that similar figures recur in most mythologies; nor that the symbolic figure connects, more or less mysteriously, with deep inner needs, so that Hughes is right to direct attention to the cultural and psychological importance of the fact that Catholic countries could surreptitiously accommodate the Goddess as the Virgin Mary, while Protestant countries suppressed her. (Milton made much of the analogies between Osiris, 'Thammuz yearly wounded', and Christ, but he could hardly develop the complementary analogy between Isis, Ishtar and the Virgin.) But then, supposing that this is all true, what questions would it answer, and what would it tell us about Hughes' magnificent poem? After all, similar observations would be in place in a discussion of Keats' 'La Belle Dame Sans Merci' or Lucio Piccolo's 'Veneris Venefica Agrestis', of the Lorelei poems of Brentano, Heine or Eichendorff, or of the presentation of Circe in Homer. Pope's Homer, Joyce's *Ulysses*, and Stuart Montgomery's fine poem *Circe*: how could this advance our understanding, and in what direction? If we suppose that our apprehension is not predominantly literary, then what are we apprehending? And, supposing that the Goddess is some kind of figuring forth of deep inner needs, what needs are satisfied by reading or writing a poem about her?

Taking an example from *Cave Birds*: there is clearly some connection between the falcon in 'The risen' and Horus and Osiris. But it would be critically evasive to assert the connection without asking what kind of imaginative reality it has for us. Any lover of Egyptian art will know that the falcon and vulture had a special significance for the Egyptians, partly determined by the stark contrast between the territories of the Lower and Upper Nile, the dramatic collision of arid desert and fertile valley. But this makes it unlikely that the symbols could ever travel without being transformed – just as we would expect the moon and stars to figure more prominently in the mythologies of nomadic tribes than in those of agricultural countries that depended on the sun, rain and harvests; nor should we forget the great difficulty intelligent foreign contemporaries like Herodotus and Plutarch had in trying to understand Egyptian religion. Similar worries occur, when the separation is temporal but not geographical: we might well ask, for example, how far the Celtic raven or crow could be available for us, today, as an 'autochthonous Totem', while the reader who assumes that some ready access to the Goddess is, happily and mysteriously, plumbed into the psyche will find it harder, not easier, to understand why *Gaudete* moves to a painful crisis and conclusion.

The power and imaginative reality of Hughes' greatest poems depends on an achieved miracle of language within a rich cultural and literary tradition (which his work is also extending), rather than on obscure mechanisms and psychic imprints, like the so-called innate releasing mechanism that tells birds what to eat or hide from, and where to fly when they migrate. To make that distinction is not (necessarily) to deny the reality of archetypes, but merely to remember that they are, for critical purposes, elusive entities. The distinction is more easily made than applied, since in practice one naturally wants to mention, say, the Goddess, in tracing continuities within Hughes' poetry, in indicating its range and human relevance, and in understanding how the poetry reflects Hughes' passionate interest in mythology and folklore. Jungian exegesis tends to dissolve the distinction altogether, in a way that is encouraged by Hughes' own emphasis on the poet's shamanic role[1] – which analogy needs, in turn, to be mediated by Jungian ideas and assumptions. For it seems evident that the power and efficacy of the utterances of an Australian or Siberian shaman do not depend on considerations of literary quality, whereas (to borrow some of Hughes' own examples) the supposedly shamanic character of *Ash Wednesday* or *Venus and Adonis* does; moreover, since the shaman's role and function within his community is defined in relation to a body of communal beliefs, any analogy with 'the basic experience of the poetic temperament we call 'romantic' ' is bound to seem loosely metaphorical unless it is harnessed to Jungian assumptions. *Cave Birds* can be interpreted as a representation of the shamanic 'magic flight', dismemberment and reconstitution; but such a reading would offer assumptions as explanations, shackle Hughes' poem to a tendentious, or at least controversial, analogy, and alienate at least as many readers as it excited.

While it is entirely proper that writers like Rasmussen should not interpose Western attitudes when reporting accounts of shamanic experience, critics have other responsibilities. These include being ready to ask practical questions, before accepting the shaman as a symbol of psychic integration that exposes Western inadequacies. For example, do we belive that shamans fly, or that their intestines turn to opal after death? What do we actually know about the incidence of neurosis and schizophrenia in primitive societies? To adapt Goethe, one cannot keep faith with the world of the spirit by breaking faith with the world of things.

'Crow's Undersong' is a poetic evocation, not a functional invocation: that would be a shorthand way of making the point that Hughes' creative mythology is an imaginative creation, differing in form and function from myths that are rooted in communal beliefs and in rituals on which the life of the community is thought to depend. The term 'creative mythology' is ungainly, but implies some important distinctions. Works like *Paradise Lost, Ulysses, The Waste Land,* or *Joseph und seine Brüder* cannot properly be regarded as myths; rather, they treat mythic themes and material. A further distinction appears when we consider, on the one hand, the versions of *Tristan* by Béroul, Thomas, Gottfried and Wagner, and, on the other hand, different Greek dramatists' versions of Greek myths: all are individual creations, but the Greek myths were also communal and rooted in ritual. To do critical justice to Hughes' achievement, such distinctions need to be pressed, not relaxed, since the creative mythology is itself critical, in an important sense. This is seen, for example, in the ironically diagnostic opposition, in *Crow* and *Gaudete*, between the suppressed Goddess and the usurping God, or Logos; in *Cave Birds* there is a similarly critical contrast between pre-Christian and post-Christian, pre-Socratic and post-Socratic, modes of thought and feeling. Precisely because Hughes' creative mythology embodies a profoundly serious critique of Western culture and modern civilisation, it is also more analytically diagnostic and less purely inspirational than the analogy between poet and shaman suggests.

It might even be said that one important function of Hughes' creative mythology is to dramatise the lack of a sustaining communal myth. It is clear from Hughes' essays and reviews that what gives his preoccupation with mythology its especial urgency is his belief that, as he wrote in a 1964 review, the 'realm of mythologies' is 'the realm of management between our ordinary minds and our deepest life'. Like the American cultural anthropologist Joseph Campbell, Hughes finds profoundly suggestive similarities in the various mythologies, which on this view comprise a vast body of elemental lore dating back to the earliest period of man's recorded history.[2] The idea that some common interpretative principle might be formulated, to provide that Key to All Mythologies for which poor Casaubon laboured in *Middlemarch*, appears to have a Romantic origin. We find it towards the end of the eighteenth century, in Charles-François Dupuis, and in Jacob Bryant, who influenced Blake. In our own century, anthropologists of the Myth and Ritual school have argued, much more rigorously, that the Near East provided a kind of culture cradle or basin from which different Occidental and Oriental mythologies and cultural institutions developed. There has been disagreement about the prominence of supposed correspondences, and about whether the agreed resemblances were the result of independent evolution or 'culture spread'. One may concede the similarities and still account for them in different ways: Jung's account would not resemble that of Freud or Lévi-Strauss. Modern man has lost contact with the old myths without finding generally acceptable new myths that might perform a similar function; both Hughes and Campbell attempt to diagnose what they take to be an unprecedented crisis, that is manifested as a failure to render modern life spiritually significant.

II

Hughes provided an excellent outline of his own creative mythology when he summarised the story of *Orghast* a decade ago.[3] Whether or not he intended to prophesy, the fact that the different parts of his synopsis correspond very strikingly with different cycles and sequences that were to appear in the 1970s would probably not surprise

Hughes, since he believes that 'at the level of generalisation, on which this myth works, the writings of most poets are one system and the same'. Actually, my own purpose in wishing to call attention to this continuity is somewhat paradoxical, since I shall go on to argue that *Cave Birds* also shows a significant (and deeply moving) development – in directions that the 'myth' may obscure or even distort.

The first part of *Orghast* presented 'the story of the crime against material nature, the Creatress, source of life and light, by the Violator, the mental tyrant Holdfast, and her revenge'. This gives us the mythic nucleus of *Crow*, with its various revenge fables involving the deposed Creatress. Hughes went on to explain that, after making various unsuccessful attempts to revenge herself on the tyrant who deposed her, the Creatress in *Orghast* eventually succeeds by creating a 'Prometheus figure' who 'includes the elemental opposites, and in whom the collision and pain become illumination, because it is the true account'. This provides the nucleus of *Prometheus on his Crag* (as Keith Sagar brings out very well in *The Art of Ted Hughes*), and of other poems that show pain transforming itself into some kind of spiritual revelation; if Ezra Pound had not given us a superb version of Sophocles' *Trachiniae*, Hughes might have done so. Part Two of *Orghast* then took up 'the story of the tyrant Holdfast in the Underword'; and when Hughes added that it showed the 'decomposition of the fallen ego among the voices of its crimes, oversights, and victims', he might have been describing *Cave Birds*, where the figure of the dying Socrates links the 'mental tyrant' to the decomposing, 'fallen ego'.

Even in outline, this creative myth is distinctly Blakean; the 'mental tyrant Holdfast' sounds very like Blake's Urizen, just as the ineffectual but dangerous presumptuous 'God' of *Wodwo* and *Crow* recalls Nobodaddy. D. H. Lawrence provides a still more pertinent literary analogy, since both Lawrence and Hughes arrive at a similar diagnosis of Western civilisation and its discontents. Indeed, one way of characterising Hughes' development would be to say that Lawrence's *The Fox* prefigures the early Hughes, while the later, mythologising Hughes has been steadily reworking *The Man Who Died*. In that late tale Christ survives, like the escaped cock (on loan from Melville's great short story *Cock-A-Doodle-Doo!*), realises what is fundamentally disabling in Christian attitudes to Nature and sexuality, and returns to the worship of Isis, the Egyptian mother goddess. In *Cave Birds* there is a parallel return to Egypt and the mythological motifs of the pre-Christian, pre-Socratic 'culture cradle' of the Near East. In Egyptian mythology, that part of the self that can be reborn after death is reunited in a Sacred Marriage with the part of the self that corresponds with the source of all life; the living Pharoah is Horus the

Falcon, son of Isis and Osiris, while the dead Pharoah is Osiris , who fuses with the sun-god Re. In *Cave Birds*, what survives of the protagonist is returned to the source, the sun, and, after an alchemical Sacred Marriage, is reincarnated as Horus the Falcon, 'The risen'.

Besides being highly personal and literary, Hughes' myth has an assumptive basis that is historical and corresponds with his critical diagnosis of a series of cultural disasters. So, for example, the deposition of the Creatress by the Violator parallels the replacement of the mother goddess Anath by Jehovah. More generally, the first disaster occurred as the religions of the Near East – Sumer, Mesopotamia, Egypt – were gradually subjected to a frightful process of patriarchal 'correction': the suppression of the Mother Goddess entailed the suppression of Nature and sexuality, and radically altered man's apprehension of the world and his place in it. That disaster was compounded by the fatal convergence of Socratic and Christian attempts to isolate dualistic, abstract conceptual principles of Good and Evil. Finally, Hughes sees these cultural disasters entering a new, peculiarly demented stage during the Reformation and Counter-Reformation: this is a major preoccupation in *Crow* and in the remarkable essay on Shakespeare, and in the later *Crow*-poems about Shakespeare and England.

The effect of Socratic idealism is barely treated before *Cave Birds*, although the attacks on hubristic and dualistic rationality prepare us for the pointed allusions to Socrates in the poems concerned with the strutting cockerel ego; the relationship is clearly indicated by Baskin's title for the drawing that accompanies 'The Accused' – 'A Tumbled Socratic Cock'. Hughes' diagnosis of the effects of the Christian dualism is implicit or explicit in countless earlier poems, essays, reviews, and even in some of the stories for children. So, for example, both *The Iron Man* and 'Gog' in *Wodwo* 'correct' the legend of St. George, which, as Hughes remarks in his essay 'Myth and Education', is deeply suspect since it advocates 'the complete suppression of the terror': 'It is the symbolic story of Christianity. It's the key to the neurotic-making dynamics of Christianity. Christianity in suppressing the devil, in fact suppresses imagination and suppresses vital natural life.'[4] In striking out at 'the womb-wall', 'the root-blood of the origins', 'the rocking, sinking cradle' of the presumed dragon 'whose coil is under his ribs', the hooded horseman of iron and self-styled Holy Warrior is making the same 'Horrible Religious Error' that Crow makes in the poem with that title.

The emergence of the creative 'myth' in *Wodwo* suggests why *Cave Birds* includes so many counter-images that evoke a pre-Christian, pre-Socratic era. The idealistic attempts to isolate abstract conceptual principles involve identifying Good with God as Logos. 'What is not the world is God' (*Wodwo*: 'You Drive in a Circle'); and, necessarily, whatever is not God is the World, Evil, Satan, the serpent. 'Logos' ends 'God is a good fellow, but His mother's against Him', and at the end of 'Reveille' we see dispossessed Nature becoming the serpent, spreading over the whole of Creation:

> out beyond Eden
>
> The black, thickening loops of his body
> Glittered in giant loops
> Around desert mountains and away
> Over the ashes of the future.

In 'Gog', the Nature that is roused to malevolence by the cry of God as Logos – 'I am Alpha and Omega' – had slumbered for ages before God's arrival on its scene, and the very same ironic point appears, as lightly as could be, in the lovely story for children, 'How the Bee Became'.[5] The presumptuous cry creates and releases the problem of Evil (with the abstracting capital) that confronts all Christians, since they are committed to the belief that God is, somehow, both benevolent and omnipotent. The pain and abundant horror that fills creation has to be seen as a privation, a withdrawal of God from material Nature, a tenuously metaphysical absence that actually corresponds to everything that *is*: 'I ran and an absence bounded beside me'. One effect of the perversion of reality is man's isolation from the rest of creation: man becomes hybrid, straining to be released from the body of this death.

An obvious contrast here is provided by the Egyptian pantheon of gods with the bodies of men and the heads of animals or birds. The wonderful art repeatedly conveys a view of creation in which man belongs with every other created, animate being. Indeed, the motif of the man with a bird's head is still older, and appears in what is probably the earliest known artistic composition: in the inmost cave at Lascaux is the famous picture of a man falling back after apparently being wounded by the great bison he has killed; he has the head of a bird (something like the ibis, sacred to Egyptians), and has dropped something like a shaman's stick, with another bird-head for its handle. The man has four digits on each hand; in other cave paintings we find pictures of hands with missing digits, and we know of societies where cutting off fingers is an accepted sign of grief and bereavement. Turning to 'After the first fright' in *Cave Birds*, we see Baskin's drawing of a strange hybrid bird, with a head very like that of the Lascaux shaman, while Hughes' poem includes these lines;

The disputation went beyond me too quickly.

When I said: 'Civilisation,'
He began to chop off his fingers and mourn.
When I said: 'Sanity and again Sanity and above all Sanity,'
He disembowelled himself with a cross-shaped cut.

In our civilisation it would not seem 'civilised' or 'sane' to cut off one's fingers, while *hara-kiri* seems · unspeakably alien – although the Japanese ritual suicide is part of a culture that is certainly not 'primitive', and the need to give inner anguish a concrete, physical reality is, I assume, intelligible.

'After the first fright' is not one of the best *Cave Birds* poems, but it does indicate the relativity of different cultural responses to the facts of existence. (This will commend itself, for the wrong reasons, to those who like to criticise our culture from the standpoint of other cultures, while steadfastly refusing to criticise other cultures – and truly barbaric practices like clitoridectomy – from the standpoint of our own.) For Hughes, as for Nietzsche, the question to put of any mythology or religion is, how well does this help us to manage our lives – and, in this poem, to cope with that 'stopping and starting Catherine·wheel in my belly'? (In Baskin's picture the bird's belly is severed from its head above and its wings below, so that it looks like a lopped, half-stripped tree.) And Hughes' answer is that, far from helping, post-Socratic and post-Christian civilisation has suppressed the archaic sense of a morally ambivalent nature in which men could feel more truly at home. *Cave Birds* explores this sense of displacement, but in a peculiarly original and moving way – which may send us back to earlier poems with increased understanding but could hardly, I think, have been predicted when Hughes outlined the *Orghast* myth. If I succeed in suggesting what is new and unexpected in *Cave Birds*, and have already gone some way towards suggesting the continuity within the creative mythology, it should become clear why I have so far hesitated to attempt any summary description of *Cave Birds*.

III

In his first interview with Ekbert (then Egbert) Faas, Hughes mentioned that 'the only philosopher I have ever really read was Schopenhauer'; I suggested, in an earlier essay on *Crow*, that the Schopenhauerean connection (we need not posit an 'influence') helps us to characterise the sense of Nature as a nightmarish *process* that is so strong in Hughes, and the corresponding pessimistic sense that in man, too, the will is primary, while intellect is secondary and adventitious.[7] The voice heard in 'Hawk Roosting' is that of nature, conceived as Schopenhauer's 'Will in Nature'. Constructive imaginative and moral effort is, in the terms of this nature, a 'falsifying dream' and 'sophistry'. Indeed, any morally compassionate impulse, any empathy with another creature's suffering, represents a weakness, something unnatural and indeed criminal. This paradoxical concept of criminal empathy – and the sense of moral guilt at being implicated in an amoral creation – will be crucially extended in *Cave Birds*.

In two of the best poems in *Crow*, 'Crow Tyrannosaurus' and 'Crow's Nerve Fails', Crow feels moral guilt at being part of 'the horror of Creation' but cannot get beyond this: he too is locked into the nightmarish world of process by the implanted mechanism that makes his 'trapsprung' head jerk to each grub. The 'weeping' that elicited Crow's first, wondering use of the word 'ought' includes his own weeping, when he realises that there is no escape. In the later poem the guilt revives, when there is a momentary relaxation of the implacable natural process: 'Crow, feeling his brain slip, / Finds his every feather the fossil of a murder.' 'Crow's Nerve Fails' then develops the grisly ironic theme as a series of questions that clearly look forward to *Cave Birds* and the 'flayed crow in the hall of judgement':

How can he fly from his feathers?
And why have they homed on him?

Is he the archive of their accusations?
Or their ghostly purpose, their pining vengeance?
Or their unforgiven prisoner?

We should note, however, in order to bring out the contrast with the later work, that just as Crow cannot get beyond these intimations of existential guilt, there is no attempt to develop the implications of this grim theme for man, who is also 'a walking / Abattoir / Of innocents'; the poetic method is surreal, gnomic, elliptically oblique. We recognise, in 'Crow Hears Fate Knock on the Door', that we too are 'Fastened to this infinite engine', but the main effect is to concentrate the sense of metaphysical helplessness:

He imagined the whole engineering
Of its assembly, repairs and maintenance —
And felt helpless.

The moral possibility presents itself to be denied, in the image of 'a steel spring / Slowly rending the vital fibres' – without opening up the possibility that the word 'vital' could point towards a vision of nature that would include the autonomous world of human values. The *Crow*-world includes nothing to correspond with Schopenhauer's positive insistence that the intellect *can* wrench itself free from the bondage to the will and the Will – through the disinterestedness of artistic creativity, and through the ethical struggle to ensure that epistemological egoism does not turn into moral egoism (this being the Schopenhauerean idea that mattered most to the author of *Middlemarch*).

Although it is still somewhat schematic, another *Crow*-poem, 'Criminal Ballad', moves closer to the creative preoccupations of *Cave Birds* by taking the idea of 'criminal' empathy further. The relationship may be suggested by setting these lines from the 'Criminal Ballad' —

And when he ran and got his toy squealing with delight
An old man pulled from under the crush of metal
Gazed towards the nearby polished shoes
And slowly forgot the deaths in Homer
The sparrowfall natural economy
Of the dark simple curtain

— alongside some lines from the first poem in *Cave Birds* that convey the unreflective, all too 'natural' callousness of the ego, before the invasion of moral guilt and horror:

Flesh of bronze, stirred with a bronze thirst,
Like a newborn baby at the breast,
Slept in the sun's mercy.

And the inane weights of iron
That come suddenly crashing into people, out of nowhere,
Only made me feel brave and creaturely.

Clearly, 'the man' who is born at the beginning of 'Criminal Ballad' does not know that, at the moment when he was toddling after his toy, an elderly lover of the classics was dying after a road accident. But the constant accompaniment of horror impinges, gradually and remorselessly, on his consciousness, while details in the poem remind us that it is delineating a problem that has become peculiarly urgent in our age. When Tolstoy deliberately absorbed a pressing issue of the day into the final book of *Anna Karenina* by making Levin decide that the Slav war did not figure among his nearest concerns, Dostoyevsky was appalled: his enraged response is recorded in his *Diary* under the significant heading, 'Does Humaneness Exercise Influence At A Distance?', and, after cataloguing various reported atrocities (to make the point that Tolstoy/Levin would feel differently if Kitty were having her breasts lopped off in the next field), Dostoyevsky went on to put some of the same arguments, almost *verbatim*, into the mouth of Ivan Karamazov.[8] Today, technology has shrunk the world, and the media do Dostoyevsky's work for him, battering us daily with close-up technicolour images of horror that steadily erode the ability to distinguish nearer from more distant concerns. In 'Criminal Ballad' the 'man' grows up, and passes that crucial stage when he has fulfilled the biological function of the species by having his own children:

And when he walked in his garden and saw his children
Bouncing among the dogs and balls
He could not hear their silly songs and the barking
For machine guns
And a screaming and laughing in the cell
Which had got tangled in the air with his hearing . . .

Because he cannot 'shake his vision to splinters' and dissociate himself from the surrounding, contingent horrors, the man becomes part of them, finding 'his hands covered with blood suddenly' when he has slaughtered his children.

Precisely because I think that the problem this poem presents is profoundly important, and because it is part of Hughes' claim to greatness that he is intensely aware of it, I find the ending facile: that the man becomes 'criminal' in a more conventional sense diverts attention from the deeper irony, that his empthy – the poet's empathy, in antithesis to the conception of what is 'natural' in 'Hawk Roosting' and in the Schopenhauerean conception of Nature – is unnatural and criminal. Like Ivan Karamazov, like Stevie in Conrad's *The Secret Agent*, 'the man' is disabled by his empathetic sense of the horror and absurdity that barely impinges on the supposedly normal, 'brave and creaturely' response.

In *Cave Birds* 'the man' reappears - but presented in the first person, very much from the inside, as in the eighth poem:

How close I come to a flame
Just watching sticky flies play

How I cry unspeakable outcry
Reading the newspaper that smells of stale refuse

How I just let the excess delight
Spill out of my eyes as I walk along

How imbecile innocent I am

So some more perfect stranger's maiming
Numbs me in freezing petroleum
And lights it, and lets me char to the spine

Even the dead sparrow's eye
Lifts the head off me – like a chloroform . . .

Because this 'criminal' empathy resembles a poet's negative capability, we are hardly prepared, if this poem is detached from its context, for what follows – which is more disturbing than the ending of 'Criminal

Ballad'. The first and third poems in *Cave Birds* had hinted at a crisis, that occurred when the death of 'a mate' released a deep sense of guilt at being a 'brave and creaturely' part of the remorseless natural process. In this poem, the empathy and imbecile innocence are associated not with an excess of life, but with its opposite – the lack of any sustaining meaning, the sense that the self and the world to which it related have been emptied of significance, and the terrible slide into *anomie* that is conveyed in the images of slipping scree and snow 'cutting deeper / Through its anaesthetic', until finally

The whole earth
Had turned in its bed
To the wall.

The 'mate with his face sewn up' was male; in the thirteenth poem a woman dies

While I strolled
Where a leaf or two still tapped like bluetits.

There is no suggestion of guilt of an ordinary, consequential kind, involving intentions or negligence; the obscure disturbance has much more to do with the lack of consequence, the failure to establish a relation between the death, the surviving self, the contingent world and the lapsing of time until new leaves appear:

And when I saw new emerald tufting the quince, in April
And cried in dismay: 'Here it comes again!'
The leather of my shoes
Continued to gleam
The silence of the furniture
Registered nothing

The earth; right to its far rims, ignored me.

Although there is a discernible relation to earlier themes, and, as I've suggested, to that part of the mythic outline that is concerned with the mental tyrant Holdfast in the Underworld and 'the decomposition of the fallen ego among the voices of its crimes, oversights, and victims', the fallen ego is not that of a Hughesian 'egghead' but that of an unusually sensitive, suffering man; nothing in the 'basic outline' promised the personal urgency of this intensely compassionate, inward dramatisation.

'Imbecile innocent' would be a good translation of *parsi-fal*; remembering Schopenhauer's greatest declared disciple and the importance of '*Mitleid*' in his final drama, we might even say that *Cave Birds* is Ted Hughes' *Parsifal*. The starting point of the imaginary spiritual journey is a lapsing of the Will, and in the fifth poem, 'She seemed so considerate', this lapsing of the biological, predatorially self-affirming urge is seen as the necessary precondition of a possible spiritual development:

I felt life had decided to cancel me
As if it saw better hope for itself elsewhere.

Then this bird-being embraced me, saying:
'Look up at the sun. I am the one creature
Who never harmed any living thing.'

Poem and picture here support each other superbly. The once 'brave and creaturely' ego, represented as a cock, collapses like the 'pet fern' that appears in Baskin's drawing as a visual pun (the fern is the collapsed cock). After the fern's death, 'I was glad to shut my eyes, and be held. / Whether dead or unborn, I did not care.' Here, in the fullest possible sense, is the antithesis to 'Hawk Roosting'; and it is the point of *growth*, as the breakdown and collapse of the cherished fern-self at last allows something else to emerge with the mysterious, tender 'bird-being'.

The unifying theme is indeed an extraordinary one, bringing together several related creative (and critical) preoccupations. Joseph Campbell once observed, in a discussion of human sacrifice in *The Masks of God*, that for the West 'the possibility of . . . an egoless return to a state of soul antecedent to the birth of individuality has long since passed away';[9] but *Cave Birds* actually attempts to project, in mythical and poetic terms, just such a vision of an 'egoless return', in which the soul or inner self undergoes a process of 'alchemical' purfication. But, as the poems already quoted should suggest, it would be misleading to speak of a mythic bird-fable supported by a human narrative, since there are several poems in which the two mingle.

Indeed, the richness of *Cave Birds* depends on this to-fro movement between a bird-centred symbolic journey and the correlative human crisis. The bird-fable frequently reminds us of the stages or stations of a symbolic progress like that of Bunyan's Christian or that of the birds who journey through the Seven Valleys in Attar's Persian *Mantiq Ut-tair* (on which more in a moment). But it should be clear enough that the relevance of such symbolic demarcations is not to be apprehended literally: Wordsworth's concern with the 'spots of time', T. S. Eliot's with the redeeming 'moments', are sufficient reminders that real life is more disordered, its illuminations more fitful and spasmodic. In *Cave Birds* the escape from the ego and a constraining rationality is presented, symbolically, as a death or execution (with allusions to Socrates' enforced suicide), but also corresponds with an attempt – rooted in the personal crisis – to rediscover 'the realm of management between our ordinary minds and our deepest life'. Our knowledge of what it is or might be to escape from the ego isn't likely to be final and definitive in the way that death is, but comes, if at all, in rare moments of heightened awareness before an inevitable relapse – and this is true of the end of *Cave Birds*, where the vision of the reborn bird is immediately followed by the return to the human world in which it is hard, in Goethe's phrase, to keep faith with the world of things and the world of spirits. Between each stanza of Keats' *Ode to a Nightingale* there is a silent reference to the continuing human dilemma that gives urgency to, and prompts the shifts of direction in, the imaginative flight, and at the end this gives depth to the poignant questioning of the status and value of the vision or waking dream. *Cave Birds* is similar, in that the magic flight issues from the unresolved personal crisis as a dramatic projection of the human protagonist's tensions, intimations and aspirations. This gives the poem a human urgency that is lacking in the very austere *Prometheus on his Crag* or the concluding poems in *Gaudete*, where I feel that only a very singular reader could breathe that air and command those heights (Dr. Sagar admires both greatly, but may be such a reader); and the poems that comprise *Cave Birds* comment on each other, without seeming, like *Crow*, to need a supporting narrative.

This suggests, I hope, how we might understand the strange genesis of *Cave Birds*, and the presumably final form the sequence takes in the Faber edition. As Dr. Sagar explains, *Cave Birds* began when 'Leonard Baskin showed Hughes a set of nine drawings' and Hughes, 'not suspecting that there were to be more, made a complete cycle of poems to go with them'.[10] The nine poems were as follows, and their place in the final sequence is indicated in the brackets:

A 1. 'The Summoner' (2)
A 2. 'The Advocate'
A 3. 'The Interrogator (4)
A 4. 'The Judge' (6)
A 5. 'The Plaintiff' (7)
A 6. 'The Executioner' (9)
A 7. 'The Accused' (once called 'Socrates' Cock') (10)
A 8. 'The Risen' (28)
A 9. 'Goblin' or 'Finale' (29)

Then, Sagar reports, 'Baskin became enthusiastic and produced another ten birds', and 'to accommodate them Hughes had to invent a whole series of further stages between execution and resurrection':

B 1. 'The Knight' (12)
B 2. 'The Gatekeeper' (14)
B 3. 'A Flayed Crow in the Hall of Judgement' (15)

B4.   'The Baptist' (16)
B5.   'A Loyal Mother' (now 'A green mother') (18)
B6.   'Incomparable Marriage' (now 'A riddle') (20)
B7.   'The Culprit' (now 'The scapegoat') (21)
B8.   'The Guide' (23)
B9.   'Walking Bare' (25)
B10. 'The Good Angel' (now 'The owl flower') (27)

Finally, Hughes wrote a dozen more poems, and Baskin subsequently produced eight more drawings to go with eight of the poems:

C1.   'I was just walking along' (now 'The scream') (1)
C2.   'After the first fright' (3)
C3.   'She seemed so considerate' (5)
C4.   'Your mother's bones wanted to speak'
C5.   'In these fading moments' (8)
C6.   'First, the doubtful charts of skin' (11)
C7.   'Something was happening' (13)
C8.   'Only a little sleep' (17)
C9.   'As I came, I saw a wood' (19)
C10. 'After there was nothing' (17)
C11. 'His legs ran about' (24)
C12. 'Bride and groom' (26)

Any adequate study of the various, sometimes radical, revisions would need to be very long.

In outline, this complicated history would seem to promise a very loose sequence. If the A group had appeared on its own, it might have seemed remote from what Dr. Johnson calls 'human interest'; on the other hand, the C group contains the personally urgent, introspective poems that suggest a striking development, of a sort easily ignored in any schematic outline of the myth. The original 'bird-drama' would have been, as Sagar tellingly puts it, 'a sort of static mystery play'; but it now becomes part of a larger, more involved and involving human drama – and this development was essential to Hughes' more subtle conception. So, of course, is the extraordinary final sequence, following the *resumé* in 'The scapegoat': the last four poems – which span the three groups – are as original and powerful as any Hughes has written. The B group would seem to be more occasional, and Dr. Sagar suggests that 'the story, seduced no doubt by Baskin's drawings, seems to lose its way' (p. 179) in the sequence from 'The gatekeeper' to 'The scapegoat'; actually, although I think there is some truth in this, the place of these poems becomes more evident if we remember that *Cave Birds* is neither 'static mystery play' nor 'story', but is a 'drama'.

A passage in Jung's *Mysterium Coniunctionis* may remind us that *Cave Birds* is a peculiar and original drama for which there are, none the less, more familiar analogies. Jung is describing the 'process of coming to terms with the Other in us' by concentrating on a dream or fantasy-image, until a 'chain of fantasy ideas develops and gradually takes on a dramatic character':

... the passive process becomes an action. At first it consists of projected figures, and these images are observed like scenes in a theatre ... If the observer understands that his own drama is being performed on this inner stage, he cannot remain indifferent to the plot and its dénouement. He will notice, as the actors appear one by one and the plot thickens, that they all have some purposeful relationship to his conscious situation, that he is being addressed by the unconscious, and that it causes these fantasy-images to appear before him. He therefore feels compelled or is encouraged by his analyst, to take part in the play and, instead of just sitting in a theatre, really have it out with his alter ego. For nothing in us ever remains quite uncontradicted, and consciousness can take up no position which will not call up, somewhere in the dark corner of the psyche, a negation or a compensatory effect, approval or resentment.[11]

Jung provides one way of understanding the 'bird-being' and 'she' who appears in 'She seemed so considerate', 'The plaintiff', 'In these fading moments' and 'A riddle', when he observes that 'The self is the hypothetical summation of an indescribable totality, one half of which is constituted by ego-consciousness, the other by the shadow', adding that the shadow 'usually presents itself as the inferior or negative personality' but 'forms, as it were, the bridge to the figure of the anima, who is only partly personal, and through her to the impersonal figures of the collective unconscious' (pp. 107–8). Moreover, Jung's concern to trace the connection between the 'private theatre' and the alchemist's laboratory should help us to understand why *Cave Birds* is subtitled 'an alchemical cave drama'. But I hope that this section of my argument has suggested that Jung isn't an indispensable mediator in any attempt to grasp Hughes' main conception: the mythologising poems are placed against the dramatised crisis.

IV

There are still problems, arising from Hughes' characteristic treatment of mythic material. The visionary intensity of the best poems in *Cave Birds* depends very closely on Hughes' manipulation of an eclectic, complex body of mythological material. The organisation of this material is impressive and subtle but also highly contrived, so that it is hard to reconcile the impression that the sequence is an erudite poetic fantasia with the urgency and power of the best poems, or indeed with the seriousness of Hughes' diagnostic, critical concern with the consequences of Socratic and Christian dualistic abstraction. A similar difficulty recurs in all the long works and sequences, where they result from the kind of welding process Hughes described when discussing

Orghast with Tom Stoppard (*Times Literary Supplement*, 1 October 1971): 'We started with a fairly complicated narrative using several myths which we blended together into one cosmology. The Prometheus myth was one, and also the mythology and cosmology of Manichean writing.'

If we set aside local allusions and echoes that don't become structural, such as the resemblance between 'A green mother' and Matron Clay in Blake's *Book of Thel*, or the echo of the *Bardo Thödol* (a very important book for Hughes) in 'A flayed crow in the hall of judgement', there appear to be five main strands of allusion that are 'blended together' in *Cave Birds*: (1) Plato's account of the death of Socrates, and his cave parable in *The Republic*; (2) cave art and so-called primitive art; (3) Near Eastern mythology, especially that of Egypt; (4) Attar's Persian poem *The Conference of the Birds* (*Mantiq Ut-tair*), on which Hughes worked for over a year with Peter Brook's actors, apparently using C. S. Nott's translation from the French, rather than the abridged but poetically attractive version by Edward Fitzgerald; (5) literature relating to alchemy, notably Johann Valentin Andreae's *The Chymical Wedding* (*Chymische Hochzeit: Christiani Rosencreutz*, 1616, translated by Foxcroft, 1690), Jung's *Psychology and Alchemy* and *Mysterium Coniunctionis*, and Mircea Eliade's *The Forge and the Crucible*.

I have already indicated the relevance of the first three 'strands'; the fourth and fifth are linked, in an important way, through the Sufi idea of the alchemisation of the soul in a process of purification. Idries Shah discusses this (in relation to Attar, Rumi and Ghazali) in his book *The Sufis*, which Hughes reviewed in *The Listener* (29 October 1964) with understandable excitement and a measure of indulgence: Hughes didn't question Shah's largely undocumented claims about the extensive influence of Sufi doctrines on European writers, including Roger and Francis Bacon, whom Shah confused, and Bunyan, whom Shah took to be Catholic. As for *The Chymical Wedding*, Hughes mentioned in his second interview with Egbert Faas that it had influenced his unpublished radio play *Difficulties of a Bridgegroom*, and described it as 'a crucial seminal work —like *Parzifal* or *The Tempest* — a tribal dream'.[12] Jung refers to Andreae's haunting work several times in *Mysterium Coniunctionis*, where his chief concern is to show that the practical operations of the alchemists expressed

a psychic activity which can best be compared with what we call active imagination. This method enables us to get an active grasp of things that also find expression in dream life. The process is in both cases an irrigation of the conscious mind by the unconscious, and it is related so closely to the world of alchemical ideas that we are probably justified in assuming that alchemy deals with the same, or very similar, processes as those involved in active imagination and in dreams, i.e., ultimately with the process of individuation.[13]

That Hughes would agree with this is fairly clear from that reference to *The Chymical Wedding* as a 'tribal dream'; it should also be clear, from the discussion of his critique of Christian dualistic abstractions, that he would be attracted to Jung's suggestion in *Mysterium Coniunctionis* that the 'arcanum of alchemy is one of these archetypal ideas that fills a gap in the Christian view of the world, namely, the unbridged gulf between the opposites, in particular good and evil' (p. 473). In general terms, the projected bird-beings in *Cave Birds* and the hallucinatory psychic landscapes correspond with a healing, psychotherapeutic process that takes place in the cave of the creative imagination, rather than on the analyst's couch.[14]

In assessing Hughes' creative achievement in *Cave Birds*, an appropriate touchstone is provided by *Anthony and Cleopatra* – that truly miraculous example of creative mythology, in which Shakespeare's development of the Egypt/Rome antithesis assimilates specific and telling historical data into a compellingly symbolic, richly coherent poetic vision. The best poems in *Cave Birds* also achieve a highly original imaginative fusion, which I would attribute largely to the 'formality' and poetic concentration that Dr. Sagar tends to regret; he finds the 'crush of images' in 'The owl flower' too packed, and wishes the poems had generally been 'a little more ragged, and with more of the directness and urgency of letters and bulletins'. But we might rather speak of an advance on the formal and linguistic 'raggedness' of *Crow* – and speak, indeed, of a Shakespearean density of suggestion.

So, for example, in the concluding lines of 'The accused', 'annealed' clearly includes the sense of 'aneled'. This pulls together the different suggestions of metallurgical vitrification, primal guilt, shamanic initiation procedures, rituals of purification and self-sacrificial atonement – while powerfully concentrating the central idea: the submission to the first stage of an 'alchemising' process of spiritual refinement, corresponding to the First Valley in Attar's poem, where the questing birds must detach themselves from the 'clay', 'mud' and 'ordure' of this world and learn that 'God's mercy is a burning sun which reaches to the smallest atom'. Hughes' bird – the 'fallen ego' of Western rationality – 'confesses' his body's parts in a series of kennings, and then

On a flame-horned mountain-stone, in the sun's disc,
He heaps them all up, for the judgement.

So there his atoms are annealed, as in x-rays,
Of their blood-aberration —

His mudded body, lord of middens, like an ore,

To rainbowed clinker and a beatitude.

The last line, we note, picks up both suggestions in 'annealed' while providing a very powerful contrast with the preceding 'lord of middens'.

None the less, the poem as a whole doesn't suggest that Hughes is in full control, poetically, of the range of associations he wants to plant. The awkwardly deliberate similes – 'as in x-rays', 'like an ore' – suggest the difficulty of the welding process. In *Anthony and Cleopatra* Shakespeare has an uncanny – an anthropologist might say, clairvoyant – intuitive grasp of the significant contrast between Egypt's agricultrual matriarchy, centred on the queen and Isis, and the partriarchal, imperial pantheon of Rome: the one is presented in images of sun and slime, elements and humours, fertility and barrenness, the other in images of assertive male power and dominance, the arched empire, the bridge that *won't* melt into the Tiber, autonomous, human constructions and institutions that buttress the controlling social and imperial order. But Shakespeare could at least assume a schoolroom grasp of the enabling historical data; much of Hughes' raw material, is inescapably alien and unfamiliar – unless we accept the Jungian assumptions about psychic imprints. One result is that it's harder to know what to make of specific details, like that 'sun-disc'. The winged sun-disc was an important symbol for the Egyptians and travelled to Assyria, Persia and Cappadocia, but need not have symbolised the same things: should its appearance here be regarded as chiefly atmospheric? Such problems recur: for example, is it relevant or distracting to remember , when reading 'The gatekeeper', that the Sphinx near the pyramids of Gizeh represents Heru-khuti, 'Horus of the two horizons', who is depicted as a man with two hawk-faces pointing in opposite directions?

But such difficulties are easily exaggerated. It seems less important to try to attach precise significance to that 'sun-disc' than it is to register the intense contrasts between the cruel desert glare in this poem and the enveloping black wet darkness in the preceding poem, 'The executioner'. (The extremity of that contrast suggests alchemical 'opposites', while the inundating darkness is, as Jung put it, the 'irrigation of the conscious mind by the world of the unconscious'.) And these violently expressive shifts of imagery involving heat, light and space contrast with subtly disquieting, introverted images like those in 'The summoner':

The carapace
Of foreclosure.

The cuticle
Of final arrest.

Among crinkling of oak-leaves – an effulgence,
Occasionally glimpsed.

Shadow stark on the wall, all night long,
From the street-light. A sigh.

What might be called Hughes' Senecan aspect – his mastery of
intensely forceful effects – has probably been too much stressed; these
early poems in *Cave Birds* work on each other in a wholly original
way, endowing familiar images with a mysterious presence that
corresponds with unsuspected, luminous potentialities in the self. The
images in 'The summoner' establish the discrepancy between our
sense of ourselves as bodies and our sense that we inhabit our bodies,
which thus define but also constrain and 'arrest' our being. The image
of a queer light in fallen oak-leaves is unexpected, but leads to the lines
that follow:

Evidence, rinds and empties,
That he also ate here.

Before dawn, your soul, sliding back
Beholds his bronze image, grotesque on the bed.

The images quietly coalesce as a series of disquieting correspondences:
the soul, the spectral summoner; the body, rinds and empties, autumn
leaves, ominous hints of a mysterious quasi-legal process; behind all
this, the obscure guilt and lapsing of the ego.

As the sequence progresses, Hughes can co-ordinate these diverse,
potentially centripetal allusions, while their cumulative force allows
ever more rapid and powerful conflations. Sometimes the success
derives from a willingness not to try to keep too many balls in the air
in the same poem – here I think of assured poems like 'The
executioner' or 'The knight' – or from a very concentrated wit, as in
the opening lines of 'The interrogator': 'Small hope now for the
stare-boned mule of man / Lumped on the badlands, at his concrete
shadow.' 'Stare-boned' is marvellous, conveying the man's conspicuous exposure to the approaching vulture in ways that are both visual
and empathetic. It suggests how the man appears from a height, with
his rigid limbs (cf. the German *starren*) but this is also the rigidity of
horror: it's as if the whole body watches as the vulture descends and
ruffles 'the light that chills the startled eyeball' (which is staring in the
more obvious sense).

The lawyer-vulture will soon carry its 'dripping bagful of evidence'
back to the 'courts of the after-life', and a different kind of wit appears
in the way that Hughes picks up suggestions from Baskin's picture,
referring, for example, to the bird's 'humped robe' and its 'prehensile
goad of interrogation'. Man is a 'mule' not only in his obstinate,
uncomprehending attachment to self, but also because, in Platonic and
Christian thought, he is the hybrid thing, the great amphibion

described in Pomponazzi's *De immortalitate animae*: 'Just as the mule, halfway between the ass and the horse, participates in both yet does not truly possess the properties of the horse or the ass; so also the human soul, halfway between material and immaterial things, aspires to eternity, granted that it cannot perfectly attain it . . .'[15] Such associations are picked up again in the reference to the man's 'concrete shadow': this reinforces our sense of the exposure to burning light, while also wittily playing on Plato's cave-parable, where the 'shadow' corresponds with the material rather than the spiritual or ideal, and is mistaken for reality.

Such associations run through *Cave Birds* as a whole, so that our reading of this and other early poems is enriched by our reading of the poems that follow. The way in which this happens can be illustrated from the next lines: 'This bird is the sun's key-hole / The sun spies through her . . .'. The powerful evocation of a black bird seen against blinding light is immediately complicated by the dizzying, paradoxical reversal of the light/dark opposition, in the suggestion that the sun spies (and can be spied) through the black spot, the keyhole in the sky. This is metaphysical in a way that might have delighted Donne, since sun-spots are the result of a particularly intense concentration of energy (so, light). But on a first reading we are unlikely to realise that more is involved. In *Cave Birds* as in Attar's poem (which has several references to shadows on the sun), the sun is the source and crucible, the refining fire: God's mercy burns – and the vulture is its instrument. So, we understand later, but not at once, why the vulture-interrogator is also God's spy: it is part of the positive development as the ego-directed self dies and the other, mysterious self emerges as the supplanting plaintiff.

'The plaintiff', which I would have liked to quote in full at this point and trust that the reader will know or consult, is one of several extraordinary poems which probably yield only a welter of intense but baffling sensations, until we come to understand its place within the sequence. Indeed, Hughes' very extensive revisions suggest how, for the poet too, a difficult, necessarily heuristic and non-discursive process of 'thought-fox' thinking was required, before the inner 'drama' of creative solicitation could take a satisfactory form. The early version of this poem, as it was performed at the Ilkley Literature Festival in May 1975 (and later broadcast, already with a few changes), bristles with distracting images and allusions – for example, to 'that steady face on Veronica's cloth', to 'easeful Bach', and to a 'hound-pack' (an awkward echo from a poem that originally preceded this one but was omitted from the published sequence). The original, formally loose central section, with its references to Herod, death-camps and Stalin, illustrated the dangers of Hughes' *penchant* for improvisatory lists: a couple of lines on 'autos-da-fe' were thrown in and then pulled out, without making any significant difference to the poem's accretive, loosely co-ordinated structure. But in the published version which first appeared in *The Listener* on 12 February 1976, there is not a wasted word. The haunting invocation of 'the bird of light', the 'wise night-bird' that is also 'your moon of pain', is now both concentrated and firmly integrated within the sequence: that suppressed, suffering part of the protagonist's own nature which had surfaced in 'The scream' is now emerging to 'supplant' the established self – the cockerel self in its ego-directed desert. 'Your moon of pain' powerfully evokes an inner, psychic landscape, now under the sway of night and a more accusingly importunate, female 'moon'-self. This emergent self is mysteriously, deeply rooted ('the life-divining bush of your desert'); the change from 'your blood-red flower' in the Ilkley text to 'your heart's winged flower' points the connection with poems like 'A riddle' and 'The owl flower' while adding to the Shakespearean density of suggestion in the word 'supplant'. There are no awkward similes, as there were in 'The accused', and, far from seeming schematic, the amazingly rapid poetic conflations in the vivid shift from feathers to leaves, tongues, mouths, wounds and flames typifies the imaginative fusion that occurs in the best poems. Such a fusion depends on there being an imaginative sequence, within which intense local effects can acquire a deeper, more extended significance. 'The plaintiff' was originally part of the A group, and a more abstractly schematic sequence. The revised poem belongs in a far more ambitiously extended sequence; it gains enormously from being placed within a representative but personal crisis, so that it emerges as a tentative but imaginatively all the more compelling 'projection', and its effect is truly dramatic, rather than didactic or schematic.

A similar point may be made of representative poems from the B group, like 'The baptist' or the preceding poem, 'A flayed crow in the hall of judgment'; the essential definition is poetic and dramatic. On other occasions, when Hughes is less than wholly engaged, he can bombard the reader with images as if he expects them to work like thrown switches; or his references to a 'system' (as in the *Orghast* summary) may provoke similar doubts. But here the imaginative definition takes place within the poems, and the wealth of allusions and associations don't distract from or stand substitute for the creatively apprehended meaning. We may indeed find 'A flayed crow' still more richly rewarding, if Jung's *Mysterium Coniunctionis* has helped us to recognise that there are alchemical references to the *caput corvi*, the *caput Osidiris*, and the 'Moor' of *The Chymical Wedding*, or that in one Orphic hymn the black, creative night (the spagyric *nigredo*) is described as a raven that was fertilised by the wind and produced a silver egg, and so on. But, although I look forward to a more competent exegesis of the alchemical allusions than I can provide, an intelligently responsive reading of this poem wouldn't so much depend on our grasp of these and other details as on our involvement with an unfolding psychic drama, in which such 'projections' dramatise unsuspected potentialities in the self.

In 'The baptist' the 'winding waters' may release a great many associations, for example with the *aqua divina* in which alchemists dissolved the imperfect body; with the *prima materia* that is associated in so many myths with the moon, Isis and healing wisdom; with Christian and other forms of baptism where the body is spiritualised; with the Jungian 'irrigation' of the conscious by the unconscious – and so on, again. Sun and moon, Logos and Eros: such contrasted psychic states are projected in the contrasted image clusters and inner landscapes throughout *Cave Birds*. But the poetry itself controls and concentrates such associations, as it projects the central idea of some mysterious healing process. Before it eventually issues in the firmer hint in its concluding images, of some spiritually positive outcome, 'The baptist' unsettles us like a pregnant, haunting dream or elusive memory – evoking the sense of submitting to, being lapped by, then enfolded, embalmed and even bandaged in, primaeval waters whose 'cool wholesome salts' dissolve the familiar material self like a 'hard-cornered grief'. An elaborate exegesis may uncover *analogies*, in helpful or off-putting ways, but can no more explain the ultimate source of the poem's unnerving power than we can explain Ariel's songs in *The Tempest*, which provide one of the more obvious analogies.

None the less, the images work on each other, in the poetry, so as to allow subtle and necessary discriminations. 'A green mother' provides a good example of this, since some of its images project the comfort of the various 'heavens' in a way that recalls Blake's tender Matron Clay and, more generally, the innumerable presentations of an Earth Mother in art and mythology. But Hughes' images also hint at spiritual dangers: 'the city of religions', evoked in ways that movingly remind us that the impulses registered here are deeply rooted in human needs and aspirations, is also 'like a city of hotels, a holiday city'. The poetry intimates that to succumb to these ever-tempting consolations would be regressive, and would involve (to recall a phrase from Hughes' essay on Popa) 'surrendering consciousness and responsibility'. What is apprehended in poetic terms as a cautious inner prompting away from the offered solace corresponds with Jung's warning, in *Mysterium Coniunctionis*, that the projections of the 'soul', of the 'anima and Shakti', are often 'delusory' 'wish-fantasies'. But I need not dwell further on this, since it is discussed in Dr Sagar's pioneering chapter on

Cave Birds and I want to say more about the astonishing final group of poems, which projects the protagonist's culminating vision and relapse.

Here that process of 'blending together' which Hughes discussed with Tom Stoppard results in an extraordinary imaginative fusion. Just as Jung's *Mysterium Coniunctionis* provides a psychosomatic reading of Andreae and other alchemical literature, these poems are the creative issue of Hughes' analytic concern with the *correspondences* between ideas and motifs that reappear in different myths and in alchemical and psychological works; richly diverse, potentially centripetal echoes and allusions are welded, imaginatively, as the culminating vision of the psychic drama. I can best try to bring this out by taking the final poems out of sequence, in order to trace some of the chief correspondences.

The relationship with Attar's poem becomes particularly important in the final stage of the protagonist's progress. 'His legs ran about' suggests Attar's sixth stage or station – the Valley of Astonishment and Bewilderment, in which a man does not know how to 'continue his way' but can say with certainty, 'I am in love, but with whom I do not know'. The next poem, 'Walking bare', no less clearly corresponds with Attar's seventh and final station, in the Valley of Deprivation, and it's interesting to compare Hughes' poem with Fitzgeralds's impressive version of the corresponding passage in Attar. Before Attar's birds set out on their quest for the creative source, or *Simurgh*, the psychopomp hoopoe warned them that the final Valley would bring *fana*, utter loss of self, after which (and here I quote from the translation given in Cyprian Rice's *The Persian Sufis* since Nott's version is less clear, perhaps because it was translated from a French version) 'there is no deliberate advance: going is foregone, henceforth one is *drawn*'.[16] This sense of being drawn is vividly present in 'Walking bare' – with its 'progress beyond assay', as 'one gravity keeps touching me'. In Hughes as in Attar it represents an advance on 'His legs ran about' or the Valley of Astonishment, but, significantly, the advance has ceased to be in any sense purposive.

The parallel with Attar's poem is then momentarily interrupted, since 'Bride and groom' has no direct counterpart in Attar, but 'The owl flower' very obviously has. At the end of Attar's poem only thirty birds have survived the ordeals of the quest for the source or *Simurgh* – and the point of this depends in part on an irreproducible pun, since *si-murgh* means *thirty birds*. The birds themselves realise as they confront the sun of majesty and source of life that 'they and the Simurgh are one and the same being'. In Hughes' poem the protagonist at last confronts the source of life in which he will be consumed: this source is – all at once! – sun, flower, alchemical crucible, 'cauldron of tongues', 'brimming heaven-blossom', Attar's *Simurgh* and the Egyptian *Re*, or sun-god. An extraordinary sense of foreboding and mystery precedes this culminating vision, and here Hughes draws in an extremely powerful way on suggestions that have accrued from earlier poems in the sequence. So, for example, the 'owl' is 'the wise night-bird' of 'The plaintiff' in its most majestic metamorphosis, and when we remember how 'the sun spies through' the female vulture in 'The interrogator' or how, in 'She seemed so considerate', the 'bird-being' who embraced the collapsed cockerel-self told him to 'look up at the sun', we realise with an imaginative shock how the earlier bird-figures or projections are being transformed and subsumed. Images collapse into each other: the imaginative shock comes first, and the critical, detective mind trails after. Earlier poems had been dominated by opposed images: here, 'in the maelstrom's eye', sun and moon, desertscape and nightscape, male and female, are all confounded or rather integrated in the single but diverse image of the source and crucible of creation. 'Walking bare' had finished with a concealed or tacit pun on the flower's 'corolla' and the sun's corona; here we confront the 'heaven-blossom' itself. In 'The baptist' the 'winding waters' were the 'mummy bandaging' of a 'seed in armour'; here, the 'mummy grain is cracking its smile / In the cauldron of tongues' as the 'wounds flush with sap' and 'the dead one stirs',

And a staggering thing
Fired with rainbows, raw with cringing heat,

Blinks at the source.

Once again, I wish it were practicable to quote the whole poem; but that regret is tempered by the realisation that what makes 'The owl flower' so astonishing is the intensity of its imaginative integration of so many accumulating suggestions – one would have to quote most of *Cave Birds* too.

In Attar, when the tattered remnant of the original parliament of fowls confronts the source, the Simurgh invites them to annihilate themselves gloriously and joyously in the divine crucible, whereupon 'the birds at last lost themselves for ever in the Simurgh – the shadow was lost in the sun, and that is all'. But it is not all in Hughes' psychic drama, since the various parallel allusions to Egyptian mythology culminate in an Egyptian sequel: following the Sacred Marriage and the immersion in the source, the protagonist is reincarnated – which is to say that the human protagonist's 'projection' of the journeying, questing part of his self now takes shape in yet another form – in 'The risen': he is Horus the Falcon. Moreover, the Sacred Marriage has special significance in alchemy as the *mysterium coniunctionis* – Andreae's 'chymical wedding' – and this, on a Jungian reading, corresponds with the process of individuation; unless we have some sense of how these other strands of suggestion are figuring in the final poems, we may find it hard to account for the presence of the 'bride', who, as I've already remarked, has no counterpart in Attar.

'Bride and groom' is a magnificent love poem, and, like 'The knight', its claims to being considered as one of Hughes' finest poems appear even when it is read in isolation from its context. It might be compared with Donne's 'The Good Morrow', in that both poems express the wondering sense of renewal in love by recreating *clichés*, and pressing familiar metaphors in witty, quasi-literal ways: in Donne's poem the lovers are reborn, in Hughes' poem they are created and recreated for and by each other:

He oils the delicate cogs of her mouth
She inlays with deep-cut scrolls the nape of his neck
He sinks into place the inside of her thighs

So, gasping with joy, with cries of wonderment
Like two gods of mud
Sprawling in the dirt, but with infinite care

They bring each other to perfection.

Read in context, the poem also works at other levels. Within the psychic drama it realises, creatively, the glimpsed imaginative possibility: the wound of being is closed, miraculously, in a healing union of the opposed elements within the psyche – of the 'he' and 'she' that had previously advanced only at the other's expense, as in 'A riddle':

As your speech sharpened
My silence widened.

As your laughter fitted itself
My dumbness stretched its mouth wider

As you chose your direction
I was torn up and dragged . . .

And the crucial idea of the mystic union of opposites has, of course, a very rich background in myth and in the alchemical *coincidentia oppositorum*: at a conceptual level, the poem corresponds with the spagyric marriage of sulphur and mercury, the cabalistic union of the *absconditus sponsus* and *abscondita sponsa*, the mythological union of Sol and Luna, Rex and Regina, and, in the terms of Jungian psychology, the union of Logos and Eros in the process of individuation. Andreae's *The Chymical Wedding* works, in a somewhat similar way, at several levels, assimilating arcane alchemical processes to a Christian, Lutheran development of the familiar analogy between Christ as groom and Church as bride; so does the extraordinary fifteenth-century *Cantilena* by George Ripley (we never learn the first name of the protagonist in Hughes' *The Wound*), which Jung analyses at length in *Mysterium Coniunctionis*; and one might well think, in this connection, of the conclusion of Goethe's *Faust, Part II*, which shows that Goethe knew Andreae's work.

Jung himself explores the relationship between the Union of the Rex and Regina in the thalamos, and that of sulphur and mercury in the alchemist's retort. Alchemy intervenes in, and hastens, that process that would in time make all ores 'ripe' metals, bringing them to 'perfection'; and, as Eliade shows in *The Forge and the Crucible*, in the mythology of metallurgy such processes are closely bound up with motifs of ritual union and sacrifice. Hughes' lovers are reforging each other – whether we want to be reminded of the alchemical reference in the last line is another matter; in a still more important sense they are not lovers at all, but hitherto opposed aspects of the psyche. Although a Jungian reading is so readily available and would probably have Hughes' approval, it's worth remarking that *Cave Birds* is linked to Jung by way of the shared subject-matter, but this does not necessarily commit us to a rigidly Jungian reading. David Lindsay's *A Voyage to Arcturus* is centred on the idea of a quest in which the protagonist meets strange creatures who misrepresent the source of life for which he is searching; moreover, the protagonist, Maskull, is eventually replaced by a supplanting shadow-self called Nightspore, after learning that illumination is achieved only through pain – and the vulture's significance in *Cave Birds* and in *Prometheus on his Crag* is closely akin to that of Krag, or Pain, in Lindsay's masterpiece. The overlapping in the creative mythology isn't a reflection of Jung's influence (*A Voyage* appeared in 1920), although Lindsay owed much to Schopenhauer and Nietzsche. The comparison is also instructive in relation to a point made earlier in this essay. Lindsay may be a visionary seer, but he is not a great writer; moreover, the disturbing strength of his work lies in its conceptual ruthlessness, and in the thoroughgoing lack of the compassion that is so striking in *Cave Birds*. If attention to the creative mythology brings out a resemblance, attention to Hughes' poetry reveals a far more profound difference.

The risks taken in *Cave Birds* are commensurate with the original-ity of the creative undertaking. As Philip Rahv remarks in *Literature and the Sixth Sense*, the greatest danger in literary mythologising is that it very easily becomes 'a kind of nebulous religiosity, a vague literary compromise between scepticism and dogma, in essence a form of magico-religious play with antique counters in a game without real commitments or consequence'.[18] This may at least remind us that Hughes' achievement in *Cave Birds* is impressive in two ways that are not easily reconciled. His command of his poetic resources is more impressive than ever; and the synthesising of mythological material – as seen in the multiple levels on which 'Bride and groom' and 'The owl flower' work – is brilliant and fascinating in itself. The danger is that the latter achievement represents a *tour de force* that might cast doubt on the authenticity of the experience the poetry conveys, and leave one uncertain whether *Cave Birds* is more than a highly original fantasia on mythological themes and motifs. Moreover, Hughes' mythologising can seem primitivistic in worrying ways, when the saving 'primitive' message depends, for its creative advancement, on a highly elaborate and 'intellectual' ideology of romantic retrospection.

However, although my feeling that these dangers are present – they will worry some readers more acutely, and others not at all – made me want to approach the creative mythology in *Cave Birds* in a somewhat circumspect fashion, the positive reason for this circumspection is that Hughes himself has projected a highly critical awareness of such dangers into his 'alchemical cave drama', which is tentative and heuristic – not vatic – in ways that might remind us of *Four Quartets*. This is brought out most dramatically in the conclusion to 'The risen', where Dr. Sagar complains that by introducing a 'distinction' between the symbolic Horus and a real falcon Hughes seems 'to make nonsense of the whole conception'. In the early poem 'The Dove Breeder', Hughes made the falcon on the wrist an image of achieved harmony and control; 'The risen' follows the culminating imaginative vision with a question (if not a question mark) that returns us to the human protagonist of the psychic drama: 'But when will he land / On a man's wrist.' We might be reminded of the ending of Keats' Nightingale Ode, as I suggested earlier, or even of the ending to Ripley's *Cantilena* with the moving prayer 'Wherefore, O God, graunt us a Peece of This': the problem that Hughes acknowledges in this wry, poignantly ironic return is that of sustaining the imaginative vision, so that it informs and transforms daily existence. As Jung writes near the end of *Mysterium Coniunctionis* (p. 544): 'transformation into the psychological is a notable advance, *but only if the centre experienced proves to be a spiritus rector of daily life*'. And *Cave Birds* ends with the sardonic, quizzical 'Finale': 'At the end of the ritual / up comes a goblin'.

Far from making 'nonsense of the whole conception', this return to the human protagonist is an integral part of the 'drama' as Hughes finally conceived it. The 'Finale', itself a verbatim quotation from the *London Magazine* interview, reminds us that the problem confronts the poet as well as his protagonist; this suggests how Hughes has avoided or at least contained the danger of romantic retrospection and sophisticated primitivism, by recognising it within his 'alchemical cave drama'. The protagonist is so evidently a modern man, sensitive

to the strains and insufficiencies of contemporary life. By harnessing
the creative mythology to this psychic drama, Hughes provides a
creative commentary on the world we have lost and on the difficulty or
impossibility of recovering it, unless in a precarious and provisional
way. The creative mythology dramatises the lack of a sustaining
communal myth, and the need to find some 'realm of management
between our ordinary minds and our deepest life'. In this respect, as in
others, *Cave Birds* seems to me Hughes' most subtle and compelling
achievement to date.

Hughes' poetry for children

Ted Hughes' artistic mission has always been to open our eyes to the power and mystery of the universe we inhabit. He is equally concerned with the mysterious inner world of our imagination. Hughes' poetry is often propelled by a restless, urgent energy, for the need to regain contact with the powers without and within is of crucial importance. If Hughes' vision sometimes seems extreme, this is because extreme measures are necessary to awaken us, given the debased, technological times we live in.

Hughes blames much of the situation we find ourselves in on the 'scientific style of mind'. The scientist's understandable need to 'record the facts accurately' is all well and good, but unfortunately the scientific attitude has infiltrated – and damaged – the lives of all of us. The result: 'passivity in the face of the facts, this detached, inwardly inert objectivity, has become the prevailing mental attitude of our time'.[1]

Hughes singles out photography and television as especially characteristic of our mental passivity. To Hughes, 'photography is a method of making a dead accurate image of the world without any act of imagination'. Television is even deadlier, for we sit paralysed before the insidious box, 'our imagination ... immobilised', 'fixed in a condition of pure observation and all our inner activity ... suspended'.² The deadness is not in the stars but in ourselves.

It is striking but not surprising that Hughes has become an important and prolific writer of children's books. Often enough a poet will write a few children's books as a sideline, sometimes as a cure for writer's block, often because of encouragement from the poet's publisher, who is keen for books that might sell better than poetry. But Hughes has demonstrated a sustained commitment to children's literature from the early stages of his career. He has published ten books for children. There are six books of poetry, two of fiction, one of plays (though several of his children's plays for radio have never been collected), and *Poetry in the Making* (entitled *Poetry Is* in America), an introduction to poetry for young readers.

Hughes cannot feel that the older generation is a totally lost cause, or else he would not continue to be a poet. But if there is real hope, it is with the children. As he has said, 'every new child is nature's chance to correct culture's error'. The child to Hughes has a chance to recover 'the lost awareness and powers and allegiances of our biological and spiritual being'.³ Hughes' children's books are dedicated to this process of recovery.

Hughes has written a beautiful broadside poem about the force contained within childhood:

In the little girl's angel gaze
Crow lost every feather
In the little boy's wondering eyes
Crow's bones splintered

In the little girl's passion
Crow's bowels fell in the dust
In the little boy's rosy cheeks
Crow became an unrecognisable rag.

Crow got under the brambles, capitulated
To nothingness eyes closed
Let these infant feet pound through the Universe

It is as if the child and Crow are the two sides of Hughes' imagination. Note too that the side of childhood, of innocence and wonder, is in no way sentimentalised. That angel gaze, those rosy cheeks contain a power capable of annihilating evil and darkness. It is easy to understand that Hughes has written so many children's books, for the power of those pounding feet must be preserved.

In this essay I will be discussing the six books of poetry for children.⁴ I will concern myself only briefly with *Meet My Folks* and *Nessie the Mannerless Monster*, both picture books to be read to younger children, both written early in Hughes' career. *Moon-Bells and Other Poems* is a recent small anthology; most of these poems have previously appeared in other books by Hughes. I will be drawing briefly on a few of the *Moon-Bells* poems in my conclusion. Of greatest interest are the three other collections, *Moon-Whales and Other Moon Poems*, *Season Songs*, and *Under the North Star*, and these books will receive most of my attention. I will also be considering what I take to be the most interesting question about Hughes' children's poetry, that is, the relationship between this poetry and his poetry for adults. I am convinced that the children's poetry forms an integral part of Hughes' oeuvre, and that is a conviction with interesting implications.

In *Meet My Folks*, Hughes' first book of poems for children, the poet introduces us one by one to the members of his extravagantly fantastic family. The book exists in three different versions, each of which contains a slightly different assortment of relatives, and there have been two different illustrators.[5] As so often happens with Hughes' poems, the formal stopping-point that a book represents is no guarantee that his imagination has reached its own final stopping-point. He was adding new 'folks' and dropping others long after the book's first appearance in 1961.

The idea behind *Meet My Folks* is appealing. A child's family of course looms large in its perceived sense of the world. Hughes stretches the boundaries of the child's imagination by transforming a family into a wild, strange collection of eccentric persons and odd creatures. Father is 'Chief Inspector of HOLES', Mother has baked a cake / As huge as a palace that architects make', Uncle Dan is an inventor of useless things such as 'the toothless saw that's safe for the tree', Aunt Dora grows a great weed that devours her, the very ordinary Aunt Flo nightly becomes a witch. Granny, in a poem that suffers from excessive whimsicality, is an octopus who weeps when she tries to say a word but fails: a poet's grandmother indeed. Sister Jane is 'a great big crow', wearing a huge pair of spectacles 'to cover her very crowy stare'. As Hughes has said, 'If you are bored by your relatives, it is very amusing to re-invent them'.[6]

The problem with *Meet My Folks* is in the poetry. As Keith Sagar has observed, 'Few lines have the inevitability that would make them memorable. The poems are fresh and engaging, but shapeless'.[7]

'My Own True Family', one of the additions to the American edition of *Meet My Folks*, suffers from this poetic looseness, but it is fascinating nonetheless, revealing as it does how Hughes' most pressing concerns find their way into a book for young children. Indeed the seriousness of the poem makes it seem a little out of place in *Meet My Folks*. Instead of presenting one more warping of a child's assumptions about parents, siblings, uncles, and aunts, Hughes offers a concise fifteen-line fairy tale dramatising his abiding concern with man's place in the created universe. The narrator, looking for a stag, creeps into an oak wood, where he meets an old woman who informs him that she has his 'secret here inside my little bag'. When she opens up the bag, the narrator comes 'twice awake' as he enters the world of vision. He finds himself tied to a stake, and the oak trees inform him that they are his 'own true family'. He must pledge to plant two oak trees whenever he sees one chopped down unless he wants actually and permanently to become an oak tree. When the boy returns to 'human company', his 'walk was the walk of a human child, but my heart was a tree'. The boy achieves his true human identity only in discovering his identity with the trees. As with so many of Hughes' best works, the poem aspires to the condition of myth.

Like *Meet My Folks, Nessie the Mannerless Monster* (entitled *Nessie the Monster* in the U.S.A.) is a picture book for young children. The book first appeared in England in 1964 and in America a decade later, again with different illustrators.[8] Nessie is the Loch Ness monster. Her story is told in flat, loose doggerel with lines of uneven length. The manner is that of the Scottish poet William McGonagall. Serious readers of poetry find McGonagall irresistibly though unintentionally comic. But Hughes reasoned that McGonagall's unforced but strongly rhyming awkwardness, which sounds inept to an adult, would be delightful to a young listener. Furthermore, this is doggerel which is as amiable as Nessie herself:

'They are taking me to the Queen,' thinks Nessie,
'And the Duke of Edinburgh will say "Now there's a bonnie lassie! "
Then I shall be all right, I shall have class,
And everybody will say, "Oh, everybody knows Nessie; she's a grand lass.'
And all these good people are bringing this to pass.'

The argument behind the poem is worth noting, for it illustrates Hughes' critique of contemporary society as articulated in his 'Myth and Education' essays. Nessie is 'sick with sorrow' because 'nobody thinks I exist', and indeed no one believes in anything not measurable or scientifically explicable. *Nessie the Mannerless Monster* tells the story of her successful campaign to 'make myself known or bust'. The less than ferocious Nessie is rather like Puff the Magic Dragon, but at least she is a monster, ancient and immense, emerging from the prehistoric darkness of Loch Ness.

On her way south Nessie visits 'Yorkshire, the greatest shire', but the streets are empty since everyone is 'indoors in front of the TV with a dead stare'. A Ban the Bomb group wants her to be their mascot, but the demonstrators cannot appreciate what she really is, categorising her as a 'peaceful beast, beautiful and dumb'. The scientists at the

Kensington Museum tell her to go away and stop bothering them since their books tell them that all Plesiosaurs 'have been dead a million years'. Tourists believe she's 'another famous London sight'. Londoners think she's an advertisement for a circus.

Nessie is recognised only by Willis, a 'wretched Scots writer of verses'. Willis may be penniless, but, like Ted Hughes, 'he knows a monster when he sees one'. The poet is the only person whose imagination has not been destroyed by the modern world. In the end the Queen appoints Nessie 'vice-regent of Scotland, Wales and Northern Ireland'; England is apparently beyond redemption. Willis becomes a civil servant charged with the responsibility of making sure Nessie is well fed. When scientists come in droves, 'Nessie invents stories about her ancestors and they write them all down in their book'. *Nessie the Mannerless Monster* has both wit and charm. It is an altogether pleasing book of poetry for the young.

Moon-Whales and Other Moon Poems is intended for older children, adolescents. *Moon-Whales* has a lengthy compositional history. *The Earth-Owl and Other Moon People*, containing twenty-three poems and illustrated by R. A. Brandt, was published in England as long ago as 1963. In 1976 the Rainbow Press published a limited edition of *Earth-Moon* with illustrations by Hughes himself. *Moon-Whales*, published in the United States, also appeared in 1976. *Moon-Whales* collects all the poems in the two other moon volumes, and this time the illustrations are masterful pen-and-ink drawings by Leonard Baskin. I mention all this not out of bibliographical pedantry but to point out that Hughes' moon creatures have had remarkable staying power in his imagination. During this period of some fifteen years, creating new inhabitants for his moon must have become something like second nature to him.

Hughes has remarked, partly tongue-in-cheek, that 'the number and oddity of the creatures which inhabit the earth or the planets, are nothing to those which inhabit our minds, or perhaps I ought to say our dreams, or the worlds from which our dreams emerge, worlds somewhere out beyond the bottom of our minds. Now it is a fact, deny it as you may, that one of the worlds from which our dreams come seems to be very like the moon'.[9] Hughes' moon is a strange alternative world of the imagination – or, as he suggests, of somewhere even deeper than the imagination.

These poems have also been criticised for looseness and casualness, but I do not believe that such a criticism is justified, especially as it pertains to the full-scale *Moon-Whales* version. Truly the poetry is simple and straightforward; it is never insisted upon. But the very offhandedness of the poems is essential to their effectiveness, for no matter how violent and nightmarish the creatures described, the poetry never wavers from its neutral, deadpan manner. Keith Sagar offers a description of Hughes' 'bedtime stories' which could serve as a perfect description of the power of the moon poems:

These bedtime stories . . . have a wide-eyed childlike simplicity, eschewing all 'effects', just recording the elementary facts. This matter-of-fact unadorned style generates a remarkable tension between the linguistic innocence and the horrific content of the stories. . . . The dispassionate, understated narrative seduces the reader to give his total attention and credence. It is only a fairy-tale, about the once-upon-a-time world which is not our world. It is too late to draw back when the realisation comes that it is very much our world.[10]

Like the poetry of Vasko Popa, the poems of *Moon-Whales* combine 'surrealism' with a 'down-to-earth, alert tone of free enquiry'.[11]

   Moon-Whales is a book in which the whole is far greater than the sum of its parts. The book possesses an imaginative wholeness and an eye-opening visionary quality. Hughes has succeeded – and rather effortlessly it would seem – in populating an entire alternative world. On the moon anything goes: each creature is a law unto itself. The poor, limited earthling must leave behind his earthbound assumptions, 'for over the moon general madness reigns'. The poems are at once wry and frightening, and their cumulative power is undeniable.

   Needless to say, Ted Hughes' moon isn't a nice place to live or even to visit. The laws of terra firma are quite terrifyingly suspended, as a poem called 'Visiting the Moon' makes clear. Try the 'bell-pull — /But what use is the silk-tassel tail of a white bull?' If you open the 'little door', you only discover 'space' sitting 'smiling there'. And then the attempted journey becomes even more treacherous:

I looked into the mirror—
It escaped, leaving a big-eyed feather.

I looked into the inkwell
Which still hadn't set sail.

When I met her in the dark
She jabbed me with a bent hypodermic.

Was I juggling with hoops?
Was I hanging from a hook through my lips?

The speaker wakes up in a tower,

And there the moon, molten silver in a great cauldron,
Was being poured
Through the eye of a needle

Spun onto bobbins and sold to poets
For sewing their eyelids together
So they can sing better.

The moon visit described in the poem may seem nightmarish and surrealistic, but Hughes is suggesting that it is no less real for all that. This harrowing moon exists within us all. We try to escape it at our own peril.

Terror lurks everywhere on Hughes' moon. The burrow wolf lives in the moon's holes 'with a huge grin of ferocity' and with eyes that 'start clean out of his head on eleven-inch stalks'. Moon-nasturtiums are 'giant, jungles of them, and swarming with noisy gorillas'. On the moon a silent eye the size of a large owl 'flies about the sky', staring, peering, and weeping until 'you begin to wish it would stop it and just go'. On the moon 'bodiless heads drift and bump among the moon's / Volcanoes', 'made of astral light colder than any snow' and hoping for the bodies that will allow them 'to be properly born'. The moon-witch sucks her victim empty and steals and swallows his signature; and on the moon, foxes hunt men. Even more brilliantly terrifying are the 'Moon-Horrors', all predatory, the 'hideous number nines', the 'fearful horde of number sevens', the 'horrible number three', and worst of all, the 'flying strangler, the silent zero', 'that specialises in hunting down the great hero'. A danger even lurks 'in every moon-mirror', for 'look in it – and there glances out some stranger / Who stares at you astounded and goes pale'. Furthermore, moon-thirst is the worst, and moon-stroke makes you croak.

Clearly Hughes' moon creatures are nightmares with a comic dimension. Indeed the poems would hardly seem safe for children without this strongly whimsical element. If Hughes loves to make your flesh crawl in *Moon-Whales*, he does so almost as much for the fun he can evoke as for the fear. Moon-roses are each the size of a turkey, and of course moon-hops really hop. If you catch cactus-sickness on the moon, you will grow ten or fifteen extra heads. But don't worry, when you cough the heads will all fall off and you will be cured. Sometimes the whimsy gets rather thick, as in the account of musical instruments on the moon: bassoons that blow not notes but huge blue loons, harmonicas whose tunes produce German measles, violins so violent that they have to be sunk in deep wells, and so forth. Still, it is hard to resist the crab grass on the moon, which controls the moon's badlands and which spells certain death to a 'benighted tourist':

You know a crab-grass is about to attack, by its
   excited hoot.
It has no eyes, so do not wait to see the whites of
   those before you shoot.

This mixture of the fantastic, the horrific, and the comic is the hallmark of *Moon-Whales*. In this mixture may be discerned the appeal of the poems to the reader and to their author as well. It goes without saying that most of Hughes' major poems, from 'The Hawk in the Rain' to 'Earth-Numb' in the *Moortown* collection, seem to be produced with extreme artistic intensity. At the same time it mustn't always be entirely pleasant for Ted Hughes to have the experience of confronting the darker side of his vision of earthly experience – and as we know, that can be a very dark side indeed. Therefore *Moon-Whales and Other Moon Poems*, which allows him on one hand to reduce the poetic pressure and relax and on the other to domesticate the horror by making it comic. The moon poems have served as a marvellous artistic release for their author.

As often as not it is in the best of these poems that Hughes' imagination expresses itself in directly mythic terms. I am thinking for example of the moon-bull who 'thinks Night is his cow':

There he stands now
Licking the glossy side
Of his infinite bride.

Similarly vivid and mythic is the account of the perpetual civil war on the moon between the soldiers of the Moon-Dark and the soldiers of the Moon-Light, a dialectical struggle of particular interest to readers who come to Hughes by way of Lawrence. I would place the scarifying 'Moon-Marriage' in the same fully mythic category. This poem bears comparison with Hughes' many other evocations of the female as monster. It may be that a

smiling wolf comes up close
While you doze off, in your chair and gives you a kiss,
A cold wet doggy kiss, and then you know
You have been CHOSEN, and it's no good flailing awake bawling, 'No!'
Wherever the wolf is, she just goes on smiling . . .

After all it is not far to travel from the moon creatures to the eerie, sinister 'Ghost Crabs' of *Wodwo*. The imaginative intensity and the mysterious quality are very much the same.

Season Songs, first published in the United States by Viking in 1975 and in England by Faber & Faber the following year, is one of Ted Hughes' most accessible and most obviously pleasing books. *Season Songs* enjoyed an enthusiastic critical response upon publication, which has been rare for the works of Ted Hughes. Indeed the reviewers seemed relieved to be able to praise Hughes for a change.

Season Songs is aptly named, for it consists of poems about the four seasons, each capturing and celebrating some aspect of the organic life of nature. The poems originated in the *Five Autumn Songs for Children's Voices*, published in 1968, but more importantly they grew out of Hughes' experience of farming in Devon in the 1970s. In Thomas Lask's phrase, the book is 'a kind of modern shepherd's calendar'.[12] The cycle of life is here, death as well as renewal and new life; throughout the mood is one of acceptance, even serenity. Once again Leonard Baskin is Hughes's illustrator, and the collaboration is remarkable. Baskin has contributed both line drawings and rich, sumptuous watercolours. As Geoffrey Wolff has commented, 'like the paintings and drawings – bright, vivid, misty, broody, violent, loving – that Leonard Baskin has created for this book, Hughes' performance is varied and his intention capacious'.[13]

The appeal of *Season Songs* is broad. Hughes' description of his aims in writing the poems provides a sense of his intended audience: 'My only concern was to stay close to simple observation, directing my reader's attention to things which had interested me and keeping myself within hearing of children'.[14] The poems must be accessible to children, but this does not mean that they cannot speak to adults as well. Indeed *Season Songs* is crucial to Hughes' unfolding poetic career. The sequence from *Crow* to *Prometheus on His Crag* contains superbly strong and original poetry, but it also represents motion toward something like a nihilistic impasse. For Hughes at this point in his career, *Season Songs* offered a path back toward life and wholeness of being. And as J. M. Newton has remarked, the 'composition of [these poems] couldn't have taken place without the idea of a young audience'.[15] The childhood vision was liberating and led the poet to a renewed vision of life's sacredness and harmony. Hughes 'needed to refresh himself at the source';[16] with *Season Songs* he was able to do so.

Ted Hughes has always been praised for his ability to capture and evoke nature. As with D. H. Lawrence before him, critics who are willing to grant him very little at least grant him that. In *Season Songs* the panoply of the seasons is spread out before us. The poems share an ease of manner and a delicacy of touch that are uncanny. Lawrence's *Birds, Beasts and Flowers* is a marvellous book, but the reader is all too often aware of Lawrence straining for effect. In contrast all the poems of *Season Songs* seem simply to be there. Once Hughes had relaxed and opened up his senses, the poems seemed to create themselves – or at least that is how they read. The poems bring to mind Hughes' comments on how to capture animals in words: 'Imagine what you are writing about. See it and live it. Do not think it up laboriously, as if you were working out mental arithmetic. Just look at it, touch it, smell it, listen to it, turn yourself into it. When you do this, the words look after themselves, like magic'.[17]

Though the *Season Songs* blend together harmoniously and seem all of a piece, the book is actually made up of a variety of different kinds of poems. For example, consider the flight of the swifts, there before us in the language and the nervous, stuttering, jagged lines of 'Second Glance at a Jaguar':

> And here they are, here they are again
> Erupting across yard stones
> Shrapnel-scatter terror. Frog-gapers,
> Speedway goggles, international mobsters —
>
> A bolas of three or four wire screams
> Jockeying across each other
> On their switchback wheel of death.

This poem is one of many that demonstrate what Hughes learned from Gerard Manley Hopkins. As in 'The Windhover' and 'God's Grandeur', the aim of the poet is not to paint a picture but rather to create the natural world as a living presence and to put the reader into it, to break down the barrier and distance between art and reality.

In contrast to 'Swifts', 'A March Calf' is like a Blakean song of innocence, a poem of rare simplicity and gentleness:

> He shivers for feel of the world licking his side.
> He is like an ember — one glow
> Of lighting himself up
> With the fuel of himself, breathing and brightening.
>
> Soon he'll plunge out, to scatter his seething joy,
> To be present at the grass,
> To be free on the surface of such a wideness,
> To find himself himself. To stand. To moo.

Here is life in all its vulnerability, but here is also the power of those 'infant feet' that 'pound through the Universe'. 'New Year Song' near the end of the book has the same delicacy and simplicity in its celebration of the Christmas rose and the 'tight-vest lamb / With its wriggle-eel tail / and its wintry eye' and the 'weak-neck snowdrops' and the 'brittle crocus'. Hughes sings a song of renewal and of life triumphant though the 'worst cold's to come'.

'Leaves' in the autumn section is a revised nursery rhyme, a version of 'Who Killed Cock Robin?' Some of the poems seem part of a verse diary, while 'Snow and Snow' is built around the fanciful conceit that snow is 'sometimes a she, a soft one' with 'her kiss on your cheek, her finger on your sleeve' but 'sometimes a he' with 'muffled armies' that 'move in all night'. 'The Warm and the Cold' is even more richly imagistic:

> Freezing dusk is closing
>   Like a slow trap of steel
> On hills and roads and hills and all

That can no longer feel.
But the carp is in its depth
   Like a planet in its heaven.
And the badger in its bedding
   Like a loaf in the oven . . .

Season Songs is remarkably, perhaps blessedly, free of humankind, but 'The Stag' is an exception. This poem, like others Hughes has written throughout his career, is built out of the contrast between the dignity and purity of nature and the blind stupidity and destructive- ness of people. The stag in hemmed in in his forest

While the rain drummed on the roofs of the parked cars
And kids inside cried and daubed their chocolate and fought
And mothers and aunts and grandmothers
Were a tangle of undoing sandwiches and screwed-round
   gossiping heads . . .

This familiar Hughesian dichotomy is angrily and heavy-handedly present in 'Work and Play' as well.

Many of the *Season Songs* become beautiful little myths and fairy tales. Keith Sagar has observed that 'The Golden Boy' is an 'asto- nishingly fresh and vivid reworking of the John Barleycorn story'.[18] The journey of the chestnut to the ground to take root or be devoured is presented as the story of a 'tall armoured rider' riding to 'fight the North corner' and 'win a sunbeam princess'. The advent of autumn is a 'day that caught the summer / Wrung its neck / Plucked it / And ate it'. This day, called autumn, has a mouth 'wide / And red as a sunset. / His tail was an icicle'. He is succeeded by another mythic figure, 'the warrior of winter'.

Though I have been cataloguing the kinds of nature poems that make up *Season Songs*, in a sense such an endeavour is beside the point. Like *Moon-Whales*, *Season Songs* is a book whose whole is greater than the sum of its parts. Each poem is appropriate to its season and its subject, each is based on precise observation and a masterful, flexible command of the resources of English poetry. But the element which holds the book together is not one of technique or method. Rather the overarching unity of *Season Songs* is a unity of vision.

All the poems of *Season Songs* have a wonderful openness to life and its processes. This is an important quality to discover in a poet whose nature poems in the past, for all their wonderful vitality, have had something fixed and unyielding about them. In contrast to the openness of the *Season Songs*, many of the earlier nature poems seem almost like anatomies. This is not even to consider *Crow*, where the poems are fixed within rigid, cartoon-like lines of definition.

The *Season Songs* are in no way prettified or sentimental versions of nature. The brute facts of life are not omitted, and there are moments of violence. The crow will be parson in Hughes' version of 'Cock Robin', and the crow also puts in appearances in 'Autumn Nature Notes' and 'The Defender'. 'A March Calf' includes the recognition of 'butchers developing expertise and markets'. Furthermore, Hughes refuses to end the book with spring; instead it ends with the inescapable fact of winter and

Such a frost
　The freezing moon
　　Has lost her wits.

　　A star falls.

The sweating farmers
　Turn in their sleep
　　Like oxen on spits.

Hardly a cheering note on which to end the book, even if revelation may be discernible in that falling star.

And yet always there is acceptance of and even reverence for the process. Though death and life seem at opposite extremes and sometimes at daggers drawn, in *Season Songs* they comprise a 'single world of being'.[19] Even the darkest of the poet's intuitions about life are perceptions about a process that is sacred. 'Every living cell is sacred to each other, and all are interdependent'.[20]

It is also worth noting that these nature poems are called songs by their creator. They are not the first of Hughes' songs, but these are no harsh, ugly, grating songs of the crow. In *Season Songs* the music is genuine and beautiful. If the music becomes more muted in the autumn and winter poems, if it becomes stiller and sadder, it never ceases to be music. Three of the poems in the American edition actually have the word *song* in their titles, including the 'Solstice Song' when the sheep are starving and

Your anklebone
And your anklebone
Lie big in the bed.

Even in the dead of winter 'A song comes into the storm-cock's fancy', and 'the robin and the wren / they rejoice.' In the dead of winter the snowdrops appear:

Such a too much of a gift
　　　　　　　　for such a mean time
Nobody knows
　　　　　how to accept them
All you can do
　　　　　is gaze at them baffled

These are things worth singing about, and in *Season Songs* that is what Hughes does. Some of the book's most memorable moments are little litanies, as in the song in celebration of the mackerel or in the appropriately glowing conclusion to 'The Golden Boy':

With terrible steel
  They slew him in the furrow
With terrible steel
  They beat his bones from him
With terrible steel
  They ground him to powder
They baked him in ovens
  They sliced him on tables
They ate him they ate him
  They ate him they ate him

Thanking the Lord
Thanking the Wheat
Thanking the Bread
For bringing them Life
Today and Tomorrow
Out of the dirt.

In the words of the poet, 'such a too much of a gift for such a mean time'.

Hughes' latest book of children's poetry is *Under the North Star*, published in both England and America in 1981. This book is another collaboration with Leonard Baskin, with visual results that are glorious. *Under the North Star* could be called Hughes' *Birds, Beasts and Flowers*, for after 'Amulet', an introductory poem, it consists of separate evocations of twenty-three different creatures: mammals, birds, and fish. *Under the North Star* began as a poetic birthday present for Baskin's small daughter Lucrece. Hughes has said that all the creatures live near the Arctic circle, though this seems to stretch the range of such animals as the puma. At least they all live under the North Star in the sense that they reside in the Northern Hemisphere, but there is larger significance to the title. The North Star is the popular name for the Pole Star or Polaris, which is situated above the North Pole and which the earth's axis points toward. From our perspective it seems like a fixed star, and because of this, it has always been used for ocean navigation. It is difficult to find the kingdom east of the sun and west of the moon, but the North Star is the centre of things.

Hughes makes unobtrusive use of these associations. His creatures, blessedly unconscious, live in harmony with the forces and energies that order the universe. Like the sailor at sea, they have a star to steer by. It almost goes without saying that the divided, fragmentary lives lived by human beings are no longer in alignment with the North Star. The creatures are so powerfully alive partly because they do live in the axis of the star. Like Shakespeare's Julius Caesar, they are 'constant as the northern star, / Of whose true-fix'd and resting quality / There is no fellow in the firmament.' These ideas subtly unify the collection.

The ideas are reinforced by the cosmic imagery that figures so importantly in most of the poems. Almost all the creatures are presented as larger-than-life, and they relate directly to the sun, moon, and stars. The loon is 'Hatched from the Moon', the wolverine 'bobs up in the Northern Lights', the snowy owl stares 'the globe to stillness', the muskellunge is an 'interplanetary torpedo'. Similarly, though the snow-shoe hare wants to hide, 'the starry night is on his track', and the wolf 'Licks the world clean as a plate'. The goose 'Turns the globe in his hands', and the eagle has 'a continent' for his 'trapeze'. Most impressive of all is the birth of the mosquito, emergent from the 'slow millstone of Polar ice, turned by the Galaxy':

The lake that held him swelled black,
Tightened to granite, with splintering teeth,
But only sharpened his needle.

Till the strain was too much, even for Earth.
Winter sank to her knees.

The stars drew off, trembling.
The mountains sat back, sweating.

The lake burst.

The Mosquito

Flew up singing, over the broken waters—

A little haze of wings, a midget sun.

It is as if in *Under the North Star* Hughes is creating his own poetic constellation.

By now we have come to expect Hughes to be masterful at evoking the living presence of birds and beasts and fish, and from this perspective *Under the North Star* is a brilliant success. The poems seem effortlessly and uncannily to bring the creatures to life. The seal is 'a serpent of crestings— / As she unscrolled a long gash / In ocean's ripe flesh'. The snow-shoe hare is 'his own sudden blizzard', the moose is a 'walking house-frame', and the Arctic fox is a 'fur of breath / Empty as moonlight' with a listening ear that is a 'star-cut / Crystal of silence'. The brooktrout, when it leaps, is 'gorgeous as a jaguar, / But dropping back into swift glass / Resumes clear nothingness'. The poems are richly sufficient simply as evocations of the twenty-three creatures, for Hughes has never been better at his special sort of literary legerdemain.

The poems are written from the same poise and equilibrium, the same inner stillness, that is discernible in *Season Songs* and the *Moortown Elegies*. They seem part of the overflow of the creative breakthrough represented by the nature and farming poems. As usual there is more than enough bleakness and violence to go round, as Hughes underscores by beginning the collection with 'Amulet', which takes an incantatory path from the wolf's fang by way of the ragged forest and the North Star – and also by way of the wolf's fur, foot, tongue, blood, and eye – before culminating back with the wolf's fang. It is this fierce, predatory energy that governs the universe. And yet Hughes is calm even in the contemplation of his frightening vision. He is no longer too insistent; he doesn't seem to need to prove anything. The poems are all the more effective because the language is so relaxed.

Though the creatures are strikingly conjured up, the poems are simple and accessible. As in *Season Songs*, the poems have a simplicity that has been hard-earned. There is strength and substance behind the simplicity, there is even complexity on the other side of the simplicity. The central themes – of life and death, of the power and mystery of the cosmos – can be traced back twenty-five years and more to the beginning of Hughes' career as a poet. But now he has worked through the struggle and inner turbulence, now he has refined his technique down to a direct, unforced, but still powerfully poetic method. The simplicity of *Under the North Star* is resonant with all that has come before, as the marvellously vivid 'Eagle', which concludes the collection, demonstrates:

His spread fingers measure a heaven, then a heaven.
His ancestors worhip only him,
And his children's children cry to him alone.

His trapeze is a continent.
The Sun is looking for fuel
With the gaze of a guillotine.

And already the White Hare crouches at the sacrifice,
Already the Fawn stumbles to offer itself up
And the Wolf-Cub weeps to be chosen.

The huddle-shawled lightning-faced warrior
Stamps his shaggy-trousered dance
On an altar of blood.

The images of violence and destruction are balanced and tempered by images of harmony – for hare, fawn, and wolf-cub are eager 'to be chosen' – and ecstasy. The depiction of cosmic process and the sharply focused images are familiar, but now the poetry seems effortless. It is almost as if Hughes has moved beyond technique.

A few of the poems are less successful. 'The Loon' and 'The Wolverine' are both lighter, even a little frivolous, and seen more in the manner of *Moon-Whales*. The song of the 'gleeful evil Wolverine' – 'I am coming to swallow you all, Hiya!' – is rather disconcerting in the context of the volume. In poems like 'Mooses' and 'Puma' Hughes seems to be forcing metaphorical meaning. For example, the 'goofy Moose', crashing 'into a lake' and wondering where he belongs is amusing but unconvincing. But there are few such relative failures, and they are more than offset by small treasures like the portrait of the skunk, the 'King of Stinkards!':

> And only the Moon knows
> He is her prettiest, ugliest flower,
> Her blackest, whitest rose!

One creature after another parades before us, complete and self-contained, allowing us to prove Hughes' darkly vitalistic vision on our own pulses. How marvellous it must be to be a musk-ox:

> He's happy.
> Bowed beneath his snowed-under lean-to of horns,
> Hunched over his nostrils, singing to himself,
> Happy inside there, bent at his hearth-glow
> Over the simple picture book
> Of himself
> As he was yesterday, as he will be tomorrow
>
> While the Pole groans
> And skies fall off the world's edge and the stars cling together.

It has been my aim to demonstrate that *Moon-Whales, Season Songs* and *Under the North Star* are striking and successful volumes of poetry. Even though they were written for children, they figure significantly in Ted Hughes' poetic career. I believe that these books demonstrate another important fact about Hughes' children's poetry: in recent years the adult and children's poems have drawn closer and closer together. The themes and the visionary intention are absolutely the same, and often so is the subject matter. Even the style is not dissimilar, though of course the children's poems are simpler, less elliptical, less freighted with external mythic reference. It is fair to say too that the children's poetry is less *in extremis*, for one of the functions of the children's poetry for Hughes is to bring him back from those extremes. The children's poems do not need to be so urgent, for after all children are easier to reach than their parents: Hughes doesn't need to shout. Though there is nothing else in the canon exactly like the moon poems, those poems nevertheless emerge from an unmistakably grown-up region of Hughes' imagination.

The point is that it is no longer Hughes' practice to write down to children, as he did in *Meet My Folks* and *Nessie the Mannerless Monster*. Instead all his children's poems are now poems that are written 'within hearing of children'. That phrase reveals a belief that children are – within necessary limits – capable of comprehending and responding to adult poetry. Indeed nearly all the samples of poetry presented in *Poetry in the Making* are adult poems. Hughes pays tribute to the capacity of children to take poetry seriously. There is no need to give them a simplified substitute. Conversely, poems written within hearing of children are poems that their parents will want to listen to as well.

Moon-Bells and Other Poems, published in the Chatto Poets for the Young series in 1978, is filled with such poems. The book is a miscellaneous gathering of previously published poems, both collected and uncollected. Apart from several moon poems and a monologue by Nessie the Monster, the poems are mostly about the natural world. The birds and beasts will seem exceedingly familiar to Hughes' adult readers. For example, the tigress is cousin-german to Hughes' jaguar:

She is moving, in her hanging regalia
Everything in her is moving, slipping away forward
From the hindward-taper, drawing herself
Out of the air, like a tail out of water

A bow on the war-path, carrying itself
With its dazzling and painted arrows

The same fierce, untamable life-energy is discernible in poems like 'Pets' and 'A Mountain Lion'. Even the bullfinch is able to 'pack a summerful of apple-power / Under his flaming shirt'. 'Fox-Hunt' is also familiar, for it plays off the barbarous mechanical destructiveness of man against the purity and beautiful brute force of the natural world.

An essay remains to be written on the relationship between *Crow* and children's literature. Suffice it here that that relationship is unmistakable, and a full-fledged Crow poem, 'Horrible Song', shows up in *Moon-Bells and Other Poems*. Indeed *Moon-Bells* contains poems collected in *Recklings*, *Crow Wakes*, and *Moortown*, none of them books for children. And for that matter *Season Songs*, a book of children's nature poems, many of which centre in the agricultural cycle, has led naturally to the 'Moortown' sequence, an adult cycle about cattle and sheep farming. It is not always easy to discriminate between these two versions of pastoral, and 'Sheep' in *Moortown* is but an abbreviated version of 'Sheep' in *Season Songs*.

One of the implications of my argument is that Hughes' critics need to pay greater attention to the children's poetry. His most recent books of children's poetry are an integral component of his artistic achievement. At the same time it is clear that Hughes has a basic and abiding need to write children's poetry. The act of addressing an audience that contains children is both relaxing and liberating to his imagination. Prometheus can come down from his crag.

However, in claiming Hughes' best children's poems for old as well as young, I in no way mean to deny them to the children. If we adults are able to appreciate the poems written 'within hearing of children', at least there is more hope that our children will really be able to respond to them. The effort to reach the child's imagination with poetry, to nurture it, to preserve it and keep it whole, must be recognised as being of paramount importance to the literary faith of Ted Hughes.

The good shepherd: *Moortown Elegies*

In October 1978 the Rainbow Press published a limited edition called *Moortown Elegies*. The fly-sheet described it as 'a sequence of thirty-five mostly hitherto uncollected poems and passages from a verse journal about the author's experiences farming in Devon'. Perhaps it was the project of gathering together and editing these journal entries from a phase of his life that had closed with the death of his partner and father-in-law Jack Orchard that suggested to Hughes the word 'elegies'. But, though several of the poems are about the deaths of animals and some about Jack Orchard himself, the atmosphere of the collection is not principally elegiac. It may be, therefore, because 'elegies' raises expectations of a mournful or lamenting mood inappropriate to the entries themselves that Hughes dropped it when, the following year, he made these poems the title section of the Faber volume *Moortown*. This trade edition contains much else besides the farming poems, and so, for the sake of convenience, the word *Moortown* is here reserved for the Faber volume as a whole, whilst the earlier title will be used when referring specifically to the farming poems. The two printings of these contain the same poems and there are no substantial alterations in the text. In the Faber the order of

'Struggle' and 'Poor Birds' is reversed, and 'Roe-deer' is moved further into the collection. Three poems can also be found in *Season Songs*: 'March morning unlike others' and 'Sheep, 1 and 2'.

Hughes has expanded elsewhere on the account of the genesis of these pieces given in the fly-sheet:

While I farmed I kept a journal of sorts. Whenever some striking thing happened (and on a stock-farm, as in a hospital, something is always happening) I made a diary note of it[1] . . . The idea of such notes is to get the details down fresh, to make an archive of such details . . . To begin with I used the ordinary journal prose, a short-hand sort of jotted details, relying on these things to bring the memory back. Then I happened to write one in rough verse, and at once discovered . . . that . . . not only did I seem to move deeper and more steadily into reliving the experience, but every detail became much more important . . . After that I stuck to verse.

To try reworking an entry into more orthodox poetic form was to discover 'that no matter what I did I destroyed the thing I most valued, the fresh simple presence of the experience'.[2] A similar conventionalising and staling could occur another way:

If I let the event go past, four or five days, and then made my note, even though I remembered every detail perfectly, those details no longer seemed important . . . I'd no wish to make a subjective synthesis of these external details, all I wanted was the record, the externals neat. But only a very few details seemed worth setting down. The rest hadn't gone, but their charge of importance had gone. Very curious. The result, I found, was already imposing patterns and half-way to a poem that I recognised as familiarly my own.[3]

Much of Hughes' reputation amongst the poetry-reading public rests, rightly or wrongly, on poems displaying the results of careful, acute, empathic observation of nature. Any reader aware of this will have clear expectations raised by the criterion of freshness of seeing he brings into play here. Such a reader will look for concentrated perceptions issuing in 'words which belong directly to one of the five senses'. Hughes once had occasion to introduce pupils to some poems about rain, the last of them being 'After Rain' by Edward Thomas:

This is the soaking, coming and going, day after day kind of rain, which is one of our national prides . . . He uses simple language, and takes microscopic visual close-ups of one thing after another, till the scene gradually fits together as we read, and the atmosphere begins to soak into us.[4]

These words might serve equally well to introduce the first poem in *Moortown Elegies*, which could scarcely begin with simpler registrations:

Rain. Floods. Frost. And after frost, rain.
Dull roof-drumming. Wraith rain pulsing across purple-bare woods
Like light across heaved water. Sleet in it.   ('Rain')

The rain 'goes on and on, and gets colder', and the poem mimes this
continuance by renewing itself with more and more observations of
rain-affected things. By often small and subtle shifts of language
freshness of vision is conveyed. Calves stand, for instance, not in shiny
mud, but 'in a shine of mud'. The more obvious adjectival formulation
would be inferior, because it implies (in however small a way) an
ideational insulation from reality. It presupposes a scientific explanation saying: the mud is the abiding fact, over which an ephemeral and
less important effect of light plays. Hughes' words are more accurate,
and draw attention to what is actually seen, not to what is thought to
be present. Similar reasoning can explain the hyphenation of nouns
here:

                    A raven,
Cursing monotonously, goes over fast
And vanishes in rain-mist.

What is actually seen is neither rain and mist, nor misty rain, but an
independent entity somewhere between the two for which we have no
single word. Language has again been subjected to a small alteration to
make it more accurate and vivid in embodying the observed reality.

Valuing freshness of vision, Hughes tries to use words to recreate the
reality he sees for his readers. The poems in *Moortown Elegies* show all
his customary mimetic skills. Here, in 'Rain': 'The fox corpses lie
beaten to their bare bones, / Skin beaten off, brains and bowels beaten
out'; whilst, a lighter effect: 'Magpies / Shake themselves hopelessly,
hop in the spatter'. Such local effects are not merely decorative
felicities in Hughes' nature poems. They are the substance and *raison
d'être* of the poetry. 'Rain' is a single long verse paragraph. It has no
imposed form at all. It continues as long as there are enthralling things
to observe in the rain and evoke for the reader. Hughes' attitude to
form implies his attitude to life. Where the use of fixed stanzaic
divisions, rhyme schemes and metres implies that the life dealt with is
a meaningless chaos until it is redeemed and ordered by art, Hughes'
free verse implies that life has a pre-existing significance which it tries
to discover, celebrate and make available. This is especially true
where, as here, he is attempting to get 'the externals neat'.

Since his earliest nature poems Hughes has greatly increased the
range of moods and effects open to him. Situations of obvious power
and elemental vigour are the subject of the early poems, and they
continue to find their place in *Moortown Elegies*. But now Hughes has

developed a language capable of offering other gentler or less turbulent atmospheres too. In 'Snow smoking as the fields boil' he adopts shortish end-stopped lines, preventing his words from generating an inappropriate rhythmic momentum. The poem itself is short, as though it also has been shrunk by the cold and the clogging snow:

The bull weeps.
The trough solidifies.
The cock pheasant has forgotten his daughters.
The fox crosses mid-field, careless of acquittal. . . .   (*Moortown*, p. 26)

Where the coruscations of his early language and its Hopkins-like wrenchings of syntax, associated with the evocation of a particular zone of vitality, sometimes seem now to be themselves formal and stylistic devices. Hughes' recent work seems to make a deliberate abasement or renunciation of stylistic concerns. His account of his aims in these pieces implies as much. It is as if he were saying that the observed world (or, more accurately, the observed world plus the instant lively pattern of the observing mind) is of sole importance. The poetry, all stylistic devices and prepared expectations of wrought complexity, are allowed to come about only in so far as they serve the world.

These are the virtues suggested by Hughes' account of the making of his journal and found throughout *Moortown Elegies*. But his concern for freshness of seeing, for recording the details of real events, and for preventing himself gravitating back to the writing of poems 'familiarly my own' cannot obscure the fact that even such pieces as are printed as unaltered journal entries (and many of them are not) are clearly the work of a poet with an established way of seeing. Perhaps the very notion of his being able to come in from a long day's farming and set down his impressions, already in a kind of verse, suggests as much.

This produces both advantage and disadvantage for the reader. If Hughes, in a particular entry, lights on a metaphor which fits well with his deepest convictions, for instance the idea of the ewe's dangling afterbirth as a tattered battle banner, or the idea of life as flame carried within, the reader can be sure to find it elsewhere in the collection. As in *Remains of Elmet*[5] some readers will find the repetitions claustrophobic rather than reinforcing. This applies to the subject-matter of the poems too. Most of the more memorable pieces deal with the birth, death-at-birth, or infancy of lambs and calves. Also, although the sequence runs roughly through the seasons (from November to midsummer) until the poems about Jack Orchard are reached, there is a heavy bias towards winter.

And yet the same narrowness of focus, that might disconcert some, is the source of the collection's deepest virtues. The journal from which Hughes has taken these entries was not, as some nature diaries are, an extensive collection of largely superficial and fragmentary notes. Hughes has said at public readings that, although he kept his journal for several years, he made only about as many entries as the number of pieces contained in *Moortown Elegies* itself. It seems, then, that even in keeping a diary Hughes has directed his attention only to scenes of prime importance for his imagination. The result is a collection which stands on all fours with the major themes and concerns of his other works.

It seems best to begin, therefore, by trying to place *Moortown Elegies* in relation to Hughes' career and the aims he has set himself. Two sides to his enterprise might be distinguished. On the one hand there is his concern to invoke and prove the reality of natural energy. And on the other the seeking after human, religious, orientations towards energy. The division corresponds to that between Hughes the author of individual nature poems, using mimetic language to realise a particular creature or scene, and Hughes the author of sequences of inter-related mythic poems. At first reading, when the startling vividness of individual poems impresses, *Moortown Elegies* would appear to stand firmly on one side of this division. It has no obvious mythic ramifications. But when it is possible to stand back and review the premises and overall shape it has, then it comes to have relevance for the totality of Hughes' effort.

The rough divisions just proposed are the real embodiment of the problem to which Hughes has addressed himself. He believes in the necessity of human access to an energy found at its purest in nature. He believes too in the existence of societies where such access is or was available (the closer to home one looks the further back in time they recede), whereas in the West today life seems to him structured on the very principle of insulating men from energy. One mode of access still available is the writing of poetry. But no society can be made up wholly of men wholly devoted to the imagination. So Hughes' poetry bears the signs of a search for a more everyday practical access. Now and again he can be found trying, like Wordsworth, to approach the problem of picturing the accommodated man. Yet none of the character sketches he has made until recently provide a picture of orientations which might be other than peripheral to the body of a society. It may be that the task is, as F. R. Leavis suggested in relation to Blake, ultimately impossible, and that the Romantic poet ought to confine his efforts to fighting for the imagination instead of trying to conceive the results of its restoration:

The telos in view, the goal and upshot he posited as the end that gave the battle its meaning, was the reversal of the Fall . . . But Blake can no more know, or imagine, what follows the reversal of the Fall than he can what preceded it. . . . In postulating a telos, a terminus ad quem, Blake was involving himself in a fundamental contradiction.[6]

Leavis' point might be of greater relevance to the conclusion of a completed *Crow*, with its marriage in the Happy Land, but it serves here to alert us to difficulties Hughes is already facing. The immense difficulty involved in realigning the two worlds, in bringing the human into fruitful conjunction with the natural (part of the Hughesian reversal of the Fall), stands attested in the early poetry. At the same time that his representatives of natural energy, the hawk, jaguar, and pike, portrayed that energy at its purest and most rousingly intense, they portrayed it also at its farthest remove from man, especially social man. A man and a jaguar have only two obvious relationships: mutual ignorance, or predator and prey. This makes it hard for the beast to function as a directed symbol of communion between man and nature. The very wildness of the energy invoked in the early nature poems made it difficult to deal with.

Further, most of the poems in the early books which explore human access to energy have a negative outcome. In other words they are the stripping away and rejection of false orientations. In terms of human life at its most practical levels, Hughes' poetry has until now discovered only a very few categories of men who seem to have any success in dealing with energy. Among these are saints, poets, tramps, men of action. Commitment to any of these or other types is more or less heavily qualified. To see this is perhaps an austere realisation for those of his readers who understand how far Hughes intends his work to help in the business of living.

With *Moortown Elegies* a new and important category is opened up: the farmers. The rationale of farming draws together previously divergent strands in the pattern of Hughes' thinking. For it is the farm, *par excellence*, that is the meeting place of the two worlds, natural and human. And the meeting is not a confrontation, since the farm can be seen as a working laboratory of co-operation between man and nature. Hughes has discovered in these poems the utility of a real situation perfectly apt for expressing practical ecological awareness, the sanctity of nature, and the value of man's being in touch with natural energies. Where the independent and exotic predator, the jaguar, seems likely only to ignore or attack (or be attacked by) man, cows and sheep, because domesticated, stand in need of man's supervision. Nor is this situation, so suitable to Hughes' central meanings, one of his own devising. Farms of the non-industrialised kind he writes about really exist, representing a way of approaching nature sanctioned by long usage. Better still, this farm is English – an oasis of relatedness within the urban malaise, a seed all the more hopeful for being indigenous.

Even the negative features of the farm's situation have their uses. It will be clear to all his readers that Hughes' farm, Moortown, is not only set over against an increasingly dominant urbanisation, but also against the drift of contemporary farming, which is moving away from the paradigm he offers, becoming more and more characterised by a side he does not mention. There are no battery chickens, insecticides, A.I. men, or factory-reared veal calves here. So the invitation Hughes extends becomes the more urgent because such farms as his are dwindling and stand for a way of life once central to England but now pushed to the peripheries.

The question which seeks an overall valuation of *Moortown Elegies* frames itself like this: Has Hughes found a solution to his problem which can bear the test of the stringent standards he has set himself in his previous search for human orientations, or has he, temporarily, relaxed his frame of reference so as to produce a pseudo-solution? Under this question will be subordinate ones: is he compromising himself by showing one side only of farming, and by writing now about domesticated not wild animals? Does the situation he begins with, the farm, already imply the answers he is searching for? Although I return, briefly, at the end of this chapter, to the consideration of how these poems relate to the problem Hughes has always addressed his work to, it should be pointed out here that the answer to these questions lies as much in the reader's cumulative response to the felt reality of individual poems as it does in the validity or otherwise of the schematic context I have set up so far in order to relate this collection to Hughes' others.

Those readers who decide that *Moortown Elegies* is a compromise on Hughes' part will do well to formulate clearly what it is they think Hughes has compromised with. For the poems make it obvious that his disenchantment with urban industrialised secularism is as strong as ever. In presenting the farm as one variety of relatedness to nature, *Moortown Elegies* is offering an open invitation to the alienated and dissatisfied to make a change. But the change proposed is thorough-going and does not entail the amelioration of rural values to suit outsiders. The change must come from the outsiders. *Moortown Elegies* is the opposite of Country Park and Tourist Board ruralism. Its invitation is to commitment, of one kind or another, not to holiday.

The invitation is implicit in the use Hughes makes of the journal form itself. Because there is no public readership in mind at the time of making an entry, there is no need for explanatory background material. So a diary entry, written for its author, is in notes and phrases that say only what is necessary. If, as here, the subject matter is interesting, this can produce a concentration of significance equivalent to the density found in more public and formal kinds of poetry. But it is a special kind of concentration and economy. Coupled with the diarist's tones (he need not pitch his material to fit any orthodox notion of how things sound when they are important) it takes the reader into the poem's confidence. There are no apologies, qualifications or withdrawals. Each poem says: 'the things I notice and feel you too would grasp; what I don't mention is left out because you too will know it or be able to work it out'. This serves the purpose of progressively bringing the reader into Hughes' way of seeing things, into complicity with his perceptions.

The thoroughgoingness and stringency of the invitation can be found in Hughes' tactics with language at the most local level. In 'Foxhunt' the hounds are likened to squeaking and groaning rolling stock. It is one of the handful of occasions in the collection where Hughes seeks to make plain the rural by reference to the urban. Almost invariably the metaphors and similes are as rural as the subject matter: a calf is 'black as a mole' (p. 47), Jack Orchard's hands are 'lumpish roots of earth cunning' (p. 65), another calf is 'wet as a collie from a river' (p. 44), faces at an auction are 'like pulled-out and heaped-up old moots' (p. 66). Hughes is devoting his language to the recreation of an autonomous rurality, and so, necessarily, avoiding drawing the rural away from its own centre of gravity. The two environments, rural and urban, remain separate, whilst the poems initiate the reader's moving away from the one set of associated values and towards the other. It is essential therefore that the poems should provide as few opportunities as possible for the doctoring of the rural to suit the urban mentality.

The separateness of the rural world is carried to its furthest extent here in 'Tractor'. Because many of the collection's readership will have experience in towns of trying to start a car with a flat battery on a cold morning, the poem runs the risk of assimilating rural experience to urban, of too easy an attractiveness. This could not happen with the poems of midwifery, because they automatically carry with them an inconvertible atmosphere. In the event, the poem not only avoids this risk but uses the situation to create a miniature triumph of rural homogeneity. Hughes makes the tractor incomparably realler than it could ever be in its own terms, by treating it as though it were living. In effect, he ruralises it, by the use of theriomorphic imagery and the pathetic fallacy. The tractor is an intrusion from the urban dimension remade by subjecting it to the strong and open combination of feeling and imagination Hughes associates with country life. In the course of the poem it gains so much vitality that, in becoming almost independent of its master, it voluntarily

           lurches towards a stanchion
Bursting with superhuman well-being and abandon
Shouting Where Where?

                                                       (*Moortown*, p. 30)

And by the end of the poem it is 'streaming with sweat, / Raging and trembling and rejoicing'. Powerful as the poem is in this theriomorphism it would be the poorer if it sought to obliterate all awareness that this is after all a machine and not a living creature. So Hughes is careful to maim his creation and evoke the hell it necessarily inhabits:

> Power-life kneels,
> Levers awake imprisoned deadweight,
> Shackle-pins bedded in cast-iron cow-shit.
> The blind and vibrating condemned obedience
> Of iron to the cruelty of iron.

The reader realises that the vitality Hughes attributes to his machine must really be that of his own imagination. The poem, though it shares the vehemence of feeling found in the pieces about life and death issues, cannot share their depth of feeling. The attempt to feel from the inside the life of an animal can never cease to be relevant to the human reader, however deep into instinct and primal behaviour it penetrates, because, as Coleridge put it, we are all one life. Not so with the tractor. Any attempt to bridge the gap between the living on the one side and the inert or merely mechanical on the other serves only to finally emphasise its unbridgeability. The pathetic fallacy remains just that, and for a more straightforward statement of the real allegiance of the tractor as a symbolic participant in the war between the rural and the urban resort must be had to R. S. Thomas' 'Cynddylan on a Tractor'.[7]

None of the limitations inherent in the tractor apply to the poems Hughes devotes to the birth, death-at-birth, and infancy of lambs and calves. Though written before *Moortown Elegies* was published, Denis Donogue's words provide a useful introduction to this group of poems at the core of the collection:

American feeling is concentrated upon forms of life that have resisted the official categories ... American readers are skilled in contemplating preconditions and beginnings, they are not embarrassed by aboriginal motifs. English readers are regularly embarrassed by such motifs. History, time and the public categories are entertained by English readers as the only terms of reference they want or need: daily life is what they know, and they want to make the best of it, so they are embarrassed and resentful when invited to start further back or further down or to hold themselves available to novel forms of feeling, not yet accepted in the schools. This is where Hughes's poems come in.[8]

The birth–death poems take the technique of microscopically detailed registrations into an area most poets would regard as taboo, approaching issues directly and with a candour Donoghue would call American. In an introduction to one of these poems Hughes has implied that his candour and anatomical explicitness are adopted not to shock his audience by exposing it to unsustainable harshnesses, but because he believes men can face the facts in birth and death and live all the more fully for doing so. Indeed it is in our dealings with birth and death and sex that we reveal our capacity or lack of capacity for allowing into our lives the natural energy Hughes sees as essential:

Once I read this in a hall full of university students, and one member of the audience rebuked me for reading what he called a disgusting piece of horror writing. Well, we either have a will to examine what happens, or we have a will to evade it. Whatever your judgment may be, in my opinion the piece can be justified. Throughout it, I might say, I was concerned not at all with the style of writing, simply to get the details and steps of the event for the record.

Of all the mistakes a lamb can make the worst is, having got himself conceived inside a rather small mother, then to grow too big before being born. He can compound this error, in the crucial birth moments, by neglecting to keep his front feet up under his nose so he can dive out slowly and gracefully into the world. If his feet trail behind, his shoulders come up behind his mother's pelvis, and are trapped, and he will end up with his head born but his body unborn and stuck. His mother can't help. And if the good shepherd isn't nearby, it's the end. If he is nearby then he catches the mother and with a gentle hand feels-in past the lamb's neck to find maybe a crooked leg or a half-way hoof, so with this he can help the lamb out . . . But if the good shepherd's a little bit late, the lamb's head, trapped at the neck, will be too swollen to be pushed back in . . . and the lamb is dead. This happens now and again, and then the lamb has to be got out of its mother.[9]

The poem, 'February 17th', tells of this last possibility, when the rescue operation has failed. It is perhaps the most harrowing poem Hughes has written. And yet the response of the student he mentions, misinterpreting the poem's explicitness and seizing on the fact of the lamb's death, misses a great deal in it. Hughes describes what 'happens now and again':

> Laid her, head uphill
> And examined the lamb. A blood-ball swollen
> Tight in its black felt, its mouth gap
> Squashed crooked, tongue stuck out, black-purple,
> Strangled by its mother.   (Moortown, p. 39)

This is a real situation into which, as is often the case in his recent work, Hughes has introduced himself as agent of his own morality. Presumably, at this point in real life, those who 'have a will to evade . . . what happens' would be found wanting. Hughes is not found wanting, and the rest of the poem, beginning with the sentence 'I felt inside' is an example of how the courage to face facts can result in helpful action.

In this poem, as throughout the collection, the second subject, after the event or animal that occupies the foreground, is the good shepherd himself, man as custodian and helper of nature. It is partly through this figure that the radicalness of the poems is achieved. So much in the long tradition of English nature poetry stops short, leaving the reader in a still detached contemplative sympathy. Hughes here does not. His invitation is that of a farmer, and it is to some kind of true involvement. The reader is moved towards this partly through his growing identification with the human figures seen in the background of most poems performing a variety of tasks.

It is a commonplace about animal poems that the energising effects they have on a reader are not limited to the sphere of the poem's ostensible subject-matter. Because unconscious contents are frequently imagined theriomorphically, they find themselves associated with and activated by animals in powerful poems. This can happen even when those contents have no obvious connections with the poem's immediate setting and subject. Thus, even someone who in his conscious mind would feel not at all disposed towards accepting the burden of the didacticism I've imputed to Hughes might, deeply and against his will, find himself moved by a suitably affective animal poem. The exact effect the poem has on the imagination of such a reader will depend less on the subject of the poem and more on the pattern of action it carries through. That is, on whether it moves the component with which the reader has consciously identified towards a successful or unsuccessful outcome. Hughes believes that this influence applies not only to the poem's readers:

I have a superstition that the writer, even more than the reader, is affected by the mood and final resolution of his poem, in a final way. In each poem, the writer to some extent finds and fixes an image of his own imagination at that moment. But if the poem concludes in a down-beat mood, his imagination is to some degree fixed and confirmed in that mood. In the ordinary way his imagination would heal itself, move on to new moods. But the poem stands there permanent, vivid, and powerful, and tries to make him continue to live in its image.[10]

In assessing the birth–death poems care must be taken not to make too simplistic an application of this principle. It does not follow, as Hughes' student critic may have felt, that the reader's psychic health is promoted by those poems in which the lamb or calf survives, whilst being damaged by those in which it does not.

For, cutting across any simple equation, is the epic–tragic dimension, in which, though death occurs, it is not finally depressing:

It's extremely difficult to write about the natural world without finding your subject matter turning ugly. In that direction, of course, lie the true poems, the great complete statements of the world in its poetic aspect. I mean that catalogue of disasters and miseries the *Book of Job*, or that unending cycle of killings and grief *The Iliad*, or the great tragedies. What all those works have in common, of course, is not exactly a final up-beat note; but it is a peculiar kind of joy, an exultation. For that's the paradox of the poetry, as if poetry were a biological healing process. It seizes on what is depressing and destructive, and lifts it into a realm where it becomes healing and energising . . . And to reach that final mood of release and elation is the whole driving force of writing at all.[10]

There is no need to claim tragic status for 'February 17th'. It is enough to point to the mechanisms by which a 'final mood of release and elation' is created. The poem builds towards a crisis of unrelease:

> Then pushed
> The neck-stump right back in, and as I pushed
> She pushed. She pushed crying and I pushed gasping.
> And the strength
> Of the birth push and the push of my thumb
> Against that wobbly vertebra were deadlock,
> A to-fro futility.

And then moves towards its close:

> Till I forced
> A hand past and got a knee. Then like
> Pulling myself to the ceiling with one finger
> Hooked in a loop, timing my effort
> To her birth push groans, I pulled against
> The corpse that would not come. Till it came.
> And after it the long, sudden, yolk-yellow
> Parcel of life
> In a smoking slither of oils and soups and syrups —
> And the body lay born . . .

When this last passage is seen in isolation it becomes clear how far it represents a release. The rhythms quicken, and the vocabulary is that of birth. The deadlock has been resolved, and even though the lamb produced is not alive the process is still a birth: the ewe will live, whereas, without the intervention of custodial humans, she as well as her lamb would die; Hughes himself has been freed to go about his next task; even the dead lamb might be said to have been made available as sustenance for ravens or other scavengers. Indeed it may be with some surprise that the reader who feels this comes on the reminder in the final words of how such release has been achieved: 'And the body lay born, beside the hacked-off head.'

If release is so clear, then it may be that the objection of Hughes' student rests on how that release is achieved. This point again relates to the symbolic affectiveness of the poem on the reader's psychic economy. The lamb must die for the ewe to live. Perhaps the implied notion of necessary sacrifice is what irks. With such fears for the safety of the ego (which probably identifies with the lamb) we move into the zone of the pattern of spiritual growth explored in *Cave Birds* and *Gaudete*, where it is the ego that must be sacrificed for the new growth to take place. Many of the poems in *Moortown Elegies* have such resonances, linking them with those mythic works of Hughes' which are more obviously concerned with the psychology of making a self adequate to modern reality. Everything explored in this commentary on the farming poems, about the nature of perception, relatedness, the attempt to place and give meaning to death, has its counterpart in the mythic sequences. In *Moortown Elegies* the meanings are approached without any loss in the vivid presence of real life. This is the collection's finest virtue. Of course, there are things that could not be said in these poems, and the territory of the mythic sequences remains open.

In other birth poems Hughes moves towards 'release and elation' by other means. 'Birth of Rainbow', which again has the good shepherd in the background, tells of the successful birth of a calf. The poem has a tripartite movement. It begins with a general scene setting, taking a widish field of vision, from which the main centre of attention emerges. The main body of the poem describes in detail the birth of the calf. Then the last seven lines open out again into a general vista. This movement is found in several other poems. It implies that no event or creature exists in isolation, that the world is ultimately a unity. The tripartite movement is thus useful when a poem has to deal with a death at birth. The supervening, at the close, of the general scene can place an individual death in a potentially redeeming perspective. It also leads towards an acceptance of natural processes. In this it is a moment-by-moment equivalent for the tripartite time-scale found in many poems in *Remains of Elmet*, which moves from a pre-industrial nature, through the ambivalent hiatus of the mill culture, and on towards a return to nature.

'Ravens', beyond the qualities it shares with the other birth-death poems, utilises the tripartite movement to make a dialogue of youth and experience. Hughes has introduced the poem like this:

here is another, a record of a disaster, which I tried to turn up-beat at the last moment. A sheep farmer must expect to lose five per cent of his lambs. In this poem, the sheep are lambing on a high field. I visit it every two or three hours to do what has to be done to new lambs, or to any accident that might have happened. On this particular day — on this particular spring — a gang of ravens made this hill-top their H.Q. for the lambing season. I have with me a three-year-old boy.[10]

They enter the field together, and after a few lines of scene-setting, a newly-born lamb engages both their attentions. The adult Hughes soon shifts his elsewhere, but the child remains engrossed:

Over here is something else. But you are still interested
In that new one, and its new spark of voice,
And its tininess.   (*Moortown*, p. 37)

The poem might at this stage have become a contrast between childish freshness of perception, its capacity for seeing miracle in the commonplace as yet unsullied, and the jaundiced eye of adulthood, habituated and bland. But it actually swings in the opposite direction, and the turning of the poem up-beat that Hughes mentions is the product of an experienced mind. For what takes the child's attention next is a dead new-born lamb pulled open by scavenging or preying ravens. Hughes tries to explain to his young nephew 'That it died being born. We should have been here, to help it. / So it died being born.' This is deliberately flat and inadequate in the face of the child's puzzlement. Repeatedly the child now asks '"did it cry?"'. Confronted by the child's incapacity to alter its involuntary absorption with the corpse, Hughes finds himself uttering a token reply: '"Did it cry?" you keep asking, in a three-year-old field-wide / Piercing persistence. "Oh yes" I say "it cried".' These words, ambiguous to the point of meaninglessness, close the main action of the poem. The final separate verse paragraph which follows is the third part of the tripartite movement, but it is not part of the exchange of child and adult. It is addressed straight to the reader who can accept its wisdom where the child could not. In 'Ravens' Hughes has assigned two parts of his vision, that of the instant registration of life, and that of the more recently developed longer perspective, to two characters, and enacted something of their confrontation and interrelationship.

Several poems make use of the notion that the body is a mechanism which needs a spirit to animate it. In 'Struggle' the death of a newly-born calf is described:

We tucked him up
In front of a stove, and tried to pour
Warm milk and whisky down his throat and not into his lungs.
But his eye just lay suffering the monstrous weight of his head,
The impossible job of his marvellous huge limbs.
He could not make it. He died called Struggle.
Son of Patience.   (*Moortown*, p. 21)

This implies a further way of placing death, of making sense of the puzzlement of the child in 'Ravens', and hence of moving towards 'release and elation'. If the first way is to present death as a necessary sacrifice, and the second is to subsume it in the wider perspectives in which the individual is revalued, then the third is to make oblique resort to the spirit of life who is the goddess of *Gaudete* and *Orts*. This goddess is at once transcendent of and incarnate in her creatures. Her symbol in outer nature in *Gaudete* is the sun, the source of all energies, and in inner nature that fragment of sun the flame of life. Those characters who struggle against the facts of their existence have a harsh self-consuming flame, whilst those who are at one with the facts have a soft lambent flame. The decline of Lumb's energies in the main narrative corresponds with the setting of the sun. In the birth–death poems in *Moortown Elegies* Hughes uses the same nexus of symbols, but here so as to express not the quality of the life flame, but whether it can be fanned into existence from the tiny spark found, for instance, in the first lamb in 'Ravens'. The stove in 'Struggle' is an attempt to help nature by stimulating the flame from outside. Variations are made on the flame of life image in a number of poems. It is even used of Jack Orchard in 'Now you have to push'. Perhaps the cleverest reworking, particularly appropriate to the wobbliness of new-born lambs, is in 'Sheep 1', where one dies even before its flame can begin:

> Then his rough-curl legs,
> So stoutly built, and hooved
> With real quality tips,
> Just got in the way, like a loose bundle
> Of firewood he was cursed to manage,
> Too heavy for him, lending sometimes
> Some support, but no strength, no real help.   (*Moortown*, pp.59–60)

In *Orts*[11] there are several poems which show that with the failure of one of her creatures the goddess, strong through transcendence, moves elsewhere. But one poem there suggests that the agency of the human poetic imagination can strengthen the goddess even more than her own transcendence of the individual. In that poem, 'Searching, I am confronted again', Hughes says to her

> That third, the Creation, will end us two
> Unless we twist together quickly
> A knot of the one iron
> Of non-existence.   (*Orts*, poem 21)

In speaking of his 'Thought-Fox' in *Poetry in the Making* Hughes makes a related suggestion:

every time I read the poem the fox comes up again out of the darkness and steps into my head. And I suppose that long after I am gone, as long as a copy of the poem exists, every time anyone reads it the fox will get up somewhere out of the darkness and come walking towards them.

So, you see, in some ways my fox is better than an ordinary fox. It will live forever, it will never suffer from hunger or hounds. I have it with me wherever I go. And I made it. And all through imagining it clearly and finding the living words.
(pp. 20–21)

The notion of poetry's immortality, perhaps more usually associated with classicising poets, has been revised to fit Hughes' idea of the poem as a means of invoking life energy: a good poem can do this whenever it is read, but one could go for a long time without happening on circumstances so effective in real life. The notion finds a touching embodiment in 'Orf'.

On one occasion, I had a sick lamb. Its malady was orf, a horrible disease of the feet and mouth. After months of treating this lamb, and getting to know it very well, I decided it could not live. I wrote out an account of what happened, but not as a diary entry: I left it too late, and it wasn't for a week or two that I sat down to try and record it. Already the incident had mingled with memory and conscience, and it tried to become a poem. It took quite a while to get it into shape.[12]

Hughes decides to shoot the lamb, and the poem, like both the account above and the other pieces in *Moortown Elegies* where he is associated with the death of animals, makes it plain that the shooting is the opposite of the Ancient Mariner's mindless violence. The act is really just the least pleasant part of the human custodial role, the worst task the good shepherd has to carry out. The lamb's reaction seems to confirm the appropriateness of Hughes' decision. Its life-blood is almost pleased to be given the chance of abandoning too difficult a task:

He lay down.
His machinery adjusted itself
And his blood escaped, without loyalty.
(*Moortown*, p. 46)

This is the end of the lamb's purely physical part. But the informing spirit, the goddess, here called 'the lamb-life', cannot simply pass elsewhere. Such has been Hughes' involvement over the months that the energy remains attached to him, seeking a new pathway, through his art:

the lamb-life in my care
Left him where he lay, and stood up in front of me

Asking to be banished,
Asking for permission to be extinct,
For permission to wait, at least,

Inside my head
In the radioactive space
From which the meteorite had removed his body.

The idea behind waiting is that the period of corpsehood and physical decay is an interim between lives, between being a lamb and having the flesh reabsorbed by nature and reused (see *Orts*, poem 27). But here the waiting will take place at a higher level, in Hughes' imagination and his poem.

'Surprise' is a description of the painless, natural, and wholly successful birth of a calf. It is also another essay in the quality of perception – this time not the sudden attention-grabbing rearing of a dramatic event out of the surrounding landscape that is often built into the tripartite movement in these poems, but instead a relatively unspectacular event that almost passes unappreciated: a surprise rather than a shock. The first nine and a half lines are a general scene setting. Though they are not unvivid, these lines, broken medially by pauses to prevent impetus growing, and settling back on the word 'hay', generate the required mood of half-sleepy peace that envelops both cattle and farmer. The second part, that of the birth, begins without Hughes' full awareness:

> Looking at cows
> Sharing their trance, it was an anomalous
> Blue plastic apron I noticed
> Hitched under the tail of one cow
> That went on munching, with angling ears.   (*Moortown*, p. 34)

These lines are more flowing than their predecessors, but in a rather unexcited way. His drowsiness wants to make Hughes find some suitably unstirring explanation for this apron. But events overtake his cogitations:

> Crazily far thoughts
> Proposed themselves as natural, and I almost
> Looked away. Suddenly
> The apron slithered, and a whole calf's
> Buttocks and hind-legs — whose head and forefeet
> Had been hidden from me by another cow —
> Toppled out of its mother, and collapsed on the ground.

It might seem that Hughes had been deceived, out of touch with the real mood of the shippon that afternoon. But this is not the case. The birth doesn't cancel the trance. Instead it crowns and completes it, elevating a seemingly idle peace into unspectacular fulfilment:

> Leisurely, as she might be leisurely curious,
> She turned, pulling her streamers of blood-tissue
> Away from this lumpish jetsam. She nosed it
> Where it lay like a still-birth in its tissues.
> She began to nibble and lick. The jelly
> Shook its head and nosed the air. She gave it

The short small swallowed moo-grunts hungry cows
Give when they stand suddenly among plenty.

Perhaps no other poet has captured precisely this atmosphere, or its implications of what constitutes normality. However modest his intentions, Hughes has opened, or maybe reopened, a stratum of feeling previously closed to many readers. No poem, however skilful and technically excellent, which seeks to rework the standard poetic postures (nostalgia, cynicism, ambivalence, wit etc.) can claim as much.

'Surprise' illustrates an important development in Hughes' verse. The increased flexibility of his language and range of mood have already been noted. This is not only a matter of responsiveness to a wider variety of subjects. It also reflects his growing capacity for showing in his poetry the turns and changes in the mind of the poet in the act of observing. In the nature poems of his early books he was concerned largely with capturing and proving the vital essence of the creature observed. The newer capacity for showing the quick of the thinking mind is a significant addition.

Hughes has sometimes been adversely criticised for the hyperbolic quality of his language, and for his flouting of the orthodox canons of feeling. With these suggestions goes the further one that he dwells too much on the ultimate issues. 'Surprise' is one of the many poems that might be used in arguing against these points. It seems to be the case that Hughes needs the big subjects, so that his concern, which he limits to getting the details for the record, may, without the imposition of formal techniques, naturally carry connotations of real depth and significance. There is a group of poems in *Moortown Elegies* which have not been discussed in this paper, which deal with more mundane farming matters such as 'Feeding out-wintering cattle at twilight', 'Bringing in new couples' and 'Turning out'. Though these poems have virtues, they are mostly less memorable than those dealing with matters of life and death. Some subjects are slighter than others, and the quality of Hughes' language reflects this. Even poems that are about important events can get drawn-off into what cannot carry weight. Take this passage, from 'Last Night'. It describes the attempts of two rams to mate with a ewe which has just lost a lamb:

Confusion of smells
And excitements. She ran off. They followed.
The greyface squared back and bounced his brow
Off the head of the surprised blackface, who stopped.
The greyface hurried on and now she followed.
He was leading her away and she followed.
She had stopped crying to her silent lamb.
The blackface caught them up on the steepness.

The greyface shouldered her away, drew back
Six or seven paces, dragging his forelegs, then curling his head.
He bounded forward and the other met him.
The blackface stood sideways. Then the greyface
Hurried to huddle with her. She hurried nibbling,
Making up for all she'd missed with her crying.
Then blackface came again.   (*Moortown*, pp. 35–6)

This is surely inferior writing, conveying little charge. It may be that
for once Hughes has allowed the journal-keeping imperative, the need
to record every detail, to override the real issue that grasped his
imagination: the fact that the ewe, soon after her bereavement, was to
be mated again. The hillside manoeuvrings of the three sheep, which,
as he watched, must have seemed to Hughes stages in a drama moving
to a climax, here only clog the poem with facts.

Perhaps Hughes became aware, as he prepared the collection for
publication, that over and against the advantages the farming situation
provided, had to be set certain dangers of habituation and routine. If so,
this may account for his including a number of very fine poems about
non-routine matters, which, though rural, are not strictly about
farming. Two of these pieces are specifically addressed to the problem
of habituation: 'Roe-deer' and 'Coming down through Somerset'. Both
are epiphany poems, concerned with some special moment that
separates out of habitual mundane reality and the usual levels of
consciousness. The latter has claim to consideration as the finest poem
in *Moortown Elegies*.

   Dawn features in several recent poems of Hughes' as a time which
offers an exceptional opportunity for seeing the sacredness of nature. In
'Roe-deer', though it comes to provide an epiphany of the naturally
sacred, dawn itself features only as a grey snowy backdrop for that
event: 'In the dawn-dirty light, in the biggest snow of the year / Two
blue-dark deer stood in the road, alerted'. (*Moortown*, p. 31) As in
Lawrence's 'Bavarian Gentians' dark blue connotes a majesty and
other-worldly mystery, here intensified by the repetition of the vowel
sound at the start of the second line. The colour contrast too enhances
the feeling that the deer have come from another world. Or rather, as
Hughes puts it, that at this moment two realities have intersected:
'They had happened into my dimension / The moment I was arriving
just there.' The weather and light have added an ethereal, visionary
quality to a meeting of the human and the natural. Hughes is so taken
by the deer that the snow seems to be completely rubbing out the usual
world for him:

They planted their two or three years of secret deerhood
Clear on my snow-screen vision of the abnormal

And hestitated in the all-way disintegration
And stared at me.

His sense of time becomes dislocated, and what almost supervenes is a higher reality which men and animals share, a united life where there are no barriers of incomprehension. It is as though the deer, at once messengers and message, were about to disclose their 'secret' and so summon Hughes to the naked presence of the usually veiled goddess:

And so for some lasting seconds

I could think the deer were waiting for me
To remember the password and sign

That the curtain had blown aside for a moment
And that where the trees were no longer trees, nor the road a road

The deer had come for me.

But as other poems of Hughes' show, the goddess never sheds all her veils, and the meeting does not reach its wished-for climax. Yet even the departure of the deer reinforces their specialness. They don't simply run off, but make a ghostly numinous ascension like that of the visionary figure in 'Ballad from a Fairy Tale' (*Wodwo*) and 'The Angel' (*Remains of Elmet*):

finally
Seeming to eddy and glide and fly away up

Into the boil of big flakes.

A moment of creative potential has passed, but though the old world returns, some of the reverence and readiness for miracle Hughes shows here will remain with him in his everyday dealings, as is seen in other poems.

'Coming down through Somerset' again portrays the meeting of two worlds or dimensions. Hughes on the one side, and a badger on the other, are the representatives of the two spheres, and each is on a journey. Hughes' journey, though it covers many miles, is confined to the tasteless, touchless, muffled interior of a car. In other words it represents an intensification for poetic purposes of the flat, limited, unrelating normality any reader will often find himself operating within. The badger, on the other hand, being dead is journeying to its underwords. But though it is dead, the poem cannot be understood unless the beast is taken as first of all a representative of life, and the meeting as an epiphany of the sacredly alive.

In the course of the poem Hughes goes through all the striking qualities of the badger, and they appear so intensely vivid that he cannot bring himself to believe they will disappear as the body decays.

In fact, but for the memory and the kind of recreative art of 'The Thought-Fox' and 'Orf', they will disappear: the animal's unique vivid presence is one with its physicality. People sometimes complain when they visit dead relatives in a chapel of rest that the corpse 'looked nothing like him', as though the undertaker's functionaries had cheated them of a final leavetaking with the person they knew. It might perhaps be worse still if the dead looked exactly as they were when alive, as this badger with its 'perfect face' seems to, for then there would be no visible sign of the difference between life and death to help us place and accept death; a corpse would be even more inexplicable, and death as puzzling to all of us as it is to the child in 'Ravens'. Hughes explores the idea of a physical change marking death in 'Hands', not feeling cheated, but instead thinking of that change as the revelation of a new level of being in Jack Orchard. The alternative of a continued unchanged physical presence after death is explored in 'Coming down through Somerset'. The poem offers us the contradictory feelings, the anguish that Hughes felt anterior to the writing of any poem seeking to rescue and make available a reality that would otherwise fade and disappear. The anguish comes directly from the unspoken realisation that it is the badger's very death which has given Hughes access to its life. At the start of the poem the badger's deadness operates as its exact opposite: its death has made available to Hughes all those lively qualities (warmth, rankness, thrillingness, strength, the flow of the blood) that would have remained hidden and remote had this secretive nocturnal creature remained alive. Because dead and approachable the badger begins as an epiphany of life:

> Beautiful,
> Beautiful, warm, secret beast. Bedded him
> Passenger, bleeding from the nose. Brought him close
> Into my life.
>
> (*Moortown*, p.48)

But, as the deadness begins to move into decay, it takes on its more usual meaning: it becomes the destroyer of life. Decay and time are here synonymous, so the decomposition of the badger comes to stand for any of those time-borne forces which wipe out the substance of an epiphany. Revulsion at the temporariness of epiphany follows the initial absorption in the epiphany: 'A grim day of flies / And sunbathing. Get rid of that badger'. And this feeling is itself followed by the desire to rescue something:

> I want him
> To stop time. His strength staying, bulky,
> Blocking time. His rankness, his bristling wildness,
> His thrillingly painted face.
> A badger on my moment of life.
> Not years ago, like the others, but now.

Though Hughes only mentions, and rejects, physical remedies for physical decay, like skinning the beast and preserving its skeleton, and though the feelings he describes are anterior to the act of writing, he is clearly moving implicitly towards the idea that it is in this poem, if anywhere, that time will be blocked. For, at the same time that he has been offering us the pith of his own changing feelings, he has also preserved in words this just-dead beast. The present tense used takes on its full import in relation to the poem's final plea:

I stand
Watching his stillness, like an iron nail
Driven, flush to the head,
Into a yew post. Something
Has to stay.

The nail and post image stands for the badger's painful reality, but also perhaps for the poem itself, recording and recreating the badger and its associated anguish with a nail-like permanence.

I hope it will be plain from the discussion of these last two poems how, in approaching the theme of a changed type of perception and consciousness, they possess both virtues and limitations when set beside the mythic sequences in which that theme is so central.

Epiphany is one means of renewal at the creative source, through a stepping out of ordinary time into an individualistic heightened experience. The two poems just examined are in the general direction of Hughes' poetry through the years, which is, at one level, more often about the individual's quest for spiritual salvation than about man in society. As has been suggested, there is a hint in *Moortown Elegies* of a shift in the opposite direction. This appears at its most obvious in 'Last Load', where Hughes celebrates shared communal farm labour as a means to a kind of grace. In *Season Songs* there is a poem in which he writes of hay-making as the marriage of man and nature:

Happy the grass
To be wooed by the farmer, who wins her and brings her to church in her beauty,
Bride of the Island.
Luckless the long-drawn
Aeons of Eden
    Before he came to mow.   ('Hay', p. 30)

Of this activity he has said: 'Growing grass and making hay of it and bringing the loads in across a land crawling with slow loads is one of the deepest ceremonial satisfactions in farming, and every farmer feels it, no matter how mechanised or exhausted he might be.'[13] The idea of cooperation between man and earth joins with that of ritual or ceremony to provide the wedding image. The same idea of fruitful union stands at the back of 'Last Load'. It begins with an urgency it

maintains, stating the two colliding facts of the situation: 'Baled hay
out in a field / Five miles from home. Barometer falling'

(*Moortown*, p. 55)

In contradistinction to the experience of epiphany, the urgency does
not abrogate ordinary time, but makes it seem all the more precious.
And the preciousness does not exclude a sense of joy and fun:

You feel sure the rain's already started —
But for the tractor's din you'd hear it hushing
In all the leaves. But still not one drop
On your face or arm. You can't believe it.
Then hoicking bales, as if at a contest. Leaping
On and off the tractor as at a rodeo.

Hurling the bales higher. The loader on top
Dodging like a monkey. The fifth layer full
Then a teetering sixth . . .
                          And if a bale topples
You feel you've lost those seconds forever.

Like the air charging with electricity before a storm, every agent in
this scene seems alive and alert, directed and participating. Perhaps the
meaning of this ritual is first of all to do with farming: the satisfying
culmination of previous efforts in the production of needed fodder. But
Hughes chooses to draw our attention not so much to this as to the
quality of being of those taking part. The completion of the task,
bringing 'release and elation', crowns this. It is not only time that has
been made more precious for the farmer and his helpers by their
cooperative activity, but also the earth itself, even the rain that
moments ago was the enemy. A new unity fills the scene at the poem's
close, signified in the word 'whole':

Softly and vertically silver, the whole sky softly
Falling into the stubble all round you

The trees shake out their masses, joyful,
Drinking the downpour.
The hills pearled, the whole distance drinking
And the earth-smell warm and thick as smoke

And you go, and over the whole land
Like singing heard across evening water
The tall loads are swaying towards their barns
Down the deep lanes.

It is a unity of the elements, of man with the elements, and, unusual
for Hughes, of man with man. 'Last Load' stands as foil for the
microscopically intimate dealings in the birth–death poems. It is a
summer of fruition to set beside the winter's difficult beginnings.
    'Foxhunt' is the antithesis of 'Last Load'. It is satire rather than

celebration, and Hughes is a detached observer of a very different communal activity. In the radio broadcast 'Crossing Lines' he speaks of his first meeting with the power of poetry:

When I was six, perhaps even a bit younger, I heard my brother declaiming a phrase from, I think, some book of Rider Haggard's, about tribal war in South Africa. The phrase evidently intrigued him. But its effect on me was unlike anything I had known up to then. It came as a bewildering physical shock. The phrase was: the blessbok are changing ground. For years, well into my twenties, I could reproduce that first reaction, at will, simply by repeating the phrase. The effect was: my whole body would freeze, then with one shiver I would experience an explosion of wonderful joyful energy. I could make this happen at any moment of the day. And I could never exhaust its effects. I was afraid to go on repeating the phrase because I felt there was no limit to where it might take me. What I was experiencing in my reaction to these particular words, of course, was a poetic frisson of the first order. And I was responding to what still seems to me a phrase of immense poetic force and beauty: the blessbok are changing ground.[14]

So strong has Hughes' liking for this phrase remained that he has included a variant of it at the start of 'Foxhunt'. But though the phrase itself is attractive, the hounds it is used to describe are not. Indeed they suffer the indignity of one of the collection's rare urban similes:

Two days after Xmas, near noon, as I listen
The hounds behind the hill
Are changing ground, a cloud of excitements,
Their voices like rusty, reluctant
Rolling stock being shunted.   (Moortown, p. 23)

The simile suggests that the hunt is a mechanical activity, and that the hounds themselves would not engage in it without the driving engine of human will; it suggests too a ridiculous unsubtlety and noisiness that could never succeed as a mode of hunting; above all it suggests that this particular way of hunting is alien and unrural. A crow and a blackbird join Hughes in protest, but the pursuit continues, for 'the hunt / Has tripped over a fox'.

From this point the poem moves more into the fox's vision of things. As in Tarka the Otter, a book Hughes admires and has drawn on before when describing the hunted (e.g. at the close of the main narrative of Gaudete), the purpose of showing things from the animal's point of view is clear:

For the animal they hunt to kill in its season, or those other animals or birds they cause to be destroyed for the continuance of their pleasure in sport — which they believe to be natural — they have no pity; and since they lack this incipient human instinct, they misunderstand and deride it in others. Pity acts through the imagination, the higher light of the world and imagination arises from the world of things, as a rainbow from the sun.[14]

(Puffin edition, Harmondsworth 1949; revised, 1963, p. 163)

To have the fox's sense of things, through an imaginative leap, is to have pity awakened. So Hughes gives us the fox's ears:

> Lorry engines
> As usual modulating on the main street hill
> Complicate the air, and the fox runs in a suburb
> Of indifferent civilised noises. Now the yelpings
> Enrich their brocade, thickening closer
> In the maze of wind-currents.

Hughes suspends his poem before the conclusion of its event. The fox may yet escape or perish: 'As I write this down / He runs still fresh, with all his chances before him.' There is still time for the fox to make his getaway, and time too to call off the hunt which has lost any of the ritual satisfaction it may have had in the distant past and dwindled to 'A machine with only two products: / Dog-shit and dead foxes'.

Moortown Elegies comes to a close with a section of six poems which crystallise the human component in rural life. These poems share much with the generous celebrat ons of folk-life in *Remains of Elmet*. Five of them are about Jack Orchard. With these pieces, the farmer, who has been in the background of the previous poems as helper to nature, is now made the centre of attention, and in an almost Wordsworthian enterprise, his moral qualities extracted. Over the course of the poems he appears tirelessly strong, selflessly devoted to his role, precise, capable of great gentleness, stubborn, savage, quick tempered. This mixture of qualities serves a double purpose. Its initial effect is to remind us that this is a real individual Hughes is describing, and so to prevent the portrait he draws being an example so ideal as to rob itself of all human reality. Later, however, it may appear that the qualities once placed on the debit side of the account cannot be so easily separated off, that they may be the essential corollary of the more convenionally praiseworthy qualities. This is why the two sides of the character are presented in words which go some way towards the language of paradox. Hughes does not write: 'despite his general clumsiness, Mr Orchard was capable on occasion of a subtle craftiness', but instead describes his father-in-law's hands as 'lumpish roots of earth cunning'. By such means Hughes hints at an alternative, more accepting and inclusive, moral standard than the residuum of Christianity by which we usually judge. In one way, therefore, these poems mark the climax of the didactic effort of the collection to reorientate the reader.

In 'A Monument' Hughes recalls Jack Orchard putting up a barbed-wire fence in difficult conditions of terrain and weather. Of the various qualities he shows in doing his fencing it is the self-consuming dedication to land and beast that strikes Hughes most forcibly:

And that is where I remember you,
Skullraked with thorns, sodden, tireless,
Hauling bedded feet free, floundering away
To check alignments, returning, hammering the staple
Into the soaked stake-oak, a careful tattoo
Precise to the tenth of an inch,
Under December downpour, mid-afternoon
Dark as twilight, using your life up.   (*Moortown*, p. 62)

Hughes is aware that the qualities he is celebrating are some way from any contemporary heroic norm. Indeed to call this fence a monument is to draw attention to the disparity between civic and rural virtues. For it is the exact opposite of a conventional monument: informal, useful, anonymous, self-erected, hidden. Few of us would think of the fence as a monument at all without the prompting of Hughes' poem, just as few would know the import of the pile of stones at the head of the ghyll in Wordsworth's 'Michael'.

'The day he died' pushes the motif of the good shepherd, man as nature's helper, to its zenith. The poem begins in steady building rhythms suggesting the improving weather. But in the fifth line this effect is cut short:

The day he died

Was the silkiest day of the young year,
The first reconnaissance of the real spring,
The first confidence of the sun.

That was yesterday. Last night, frost.   (*Moortown*, p. 64)

The earth has retreated into the sickness of winter because of the loss of Jack Orchard, and (though today is St Valentine's day, a day of love and a hopeful look to the future, not mourning)

The bright fields look dazed
Their expression is changed.
They have been somewhere awful
And come back without him.

The badger in 'Coming down through Somerset' had flies to 'bejewel his transit ... / Towards his underworlds'. Jack Orchard has been escorted to his underworlds by the land he served, which only on its return realises its loss. In the following poem, 'Now you have to push' this journey is described on behalf of the traveller as a staying on in darkness after the last embers of the fire of life fade and die. But here Hughes concerns himself with those left behind. He shows how much a farmer can mean to his land by describing his absence's effect. Because he is dealing with domesticated, dependent animals, he can create a special pathos:

The trustful cattle, with frost on their backs,
Waiting for hay, waiting for warmth,
Stand in a new emptiness.

This trustfulness is another theme that has run in the background of the collection and is now brought to the fore. It is an important sign of their dependence on man, the quality which provides man with a niche and role closer to nature than in the cities. Anyone who reads the accounts of the early explorers will see that it is a quality that once had its parallel in many more wild animals than today.

Though, at its close, the poem must take up the hint given in the mention of St Valentine that the land will in the end continue without Jack Orchard, Hughes makes it do so in words which at the same time intensify the motif of the good shepherd into an image of parenthood, making the farm a newly orphaned child:

From now on the land
Will have to manage without him.
But it hesitates, in this slow realisation of light,
Childlike, too naked, in a frail sun,
With roots cut
And a great blank in its memory.

In 'Hands' the paradox of Jack Orchard's character, the mixture of seemingly opposed characteristics, is resolved in his demeanour after death. His hands, a focus of attention in all five poems,

      lie folded, estranged from all they have done
And as they have never been, and startling —
So slender, so taper, so white,
Your mother's hands suddenly in your hands —
In a final strangeness of elegance.   (*Moortown*, p. 68)

It is as though death, bringing to an end the life's task, has freed in him a delicate beauty that had previously often been hidden or run unnoticed. This is the collection's final piece, but its immediate predecessor, 'The Formal Auctioneer', takes some of the qualities attributed to Jack Orchard in other poems and generalises them into a picture of the rural Devon character, as shown by the bidders at an auction. Every metaphor and simile is rural, enforcing the traditional cohesion of man and nature in this environment:

      All eyes watch.
The weathered, rooty, bushy pile of faces,
A snaggle of faces
Like pulled-out and heaped-up old moots,
The natural root archives
Of mid-Devon's mud-lane annals,

Watch and hide inside themselves
Absorbing the figures like weather.   (*Moortown*, p. 66)

The tree metaphor is appropriate not only for the picture it offers of
complete mute passivity and wrinkled wornness, but also for the
connotations it has of indigenousness and belonging. Hughes adds to
traits like these a canny stealthy secretiveness:

Or if they bid, bid invisibly, visit
The bidding like night-foxes,
Slink in and out of bidding
As if they were no such fools
To be caught interested in anything,
Escaping a bidding with the secret
Celebration of a bargain, a straight gain
And that much now in hand.

This bidding and buying, though it takes a different form, is truer to
the spirit of hunting than is the 'Foxhunt', being one expression of an
immemorial way of life Hughes has throughout this collection been
reminding us of.

That life is, of course, rural, not natural. That is why the paired
terms 'rural' and 'urban' have been used here, rather than any others.
Whilst there is much in *Moortown Elegies* to suggest that Hughes
would attach positives to the former which he wouldn't to the latter,
in doing so the poems never suggest that rural life can be for man the
natural life. The idea of the human custodial role depends on the
presence of consciousness in man, and with it a capacity for choice
which he will necessarily exercise over his own way of life. In other
words, these poems imply that there is no obvious and natural life for
man, and that all human lives are to a degree artificial, chosen, made.
The key issue is not then artifice versus nature, but the much more
relative one of a choice amongst artificialities: hence urban versus
rural.

At the same time that the collection implies a preference for the
latter of these terms, it also makes clear that the presentation of the
rural cannot provide the complete answers to Hughes' quest for
accommodation. The vividly present life of the farm is exemplary in
the ways suggested, but can only hint and imply when it reaches the
borders of what can be more directly and fully dealt with in the mythic
sequences. Hughes has set the farming poems at the beginning of the
carefully structured *Moortown* because they offer a touchstone and
base for the mythic sequences that follow it in that volume. It is out of
the soil of the farm that the spiritual quest grows.

Fourfold vision in Hughes

I

My purpose here is simply to take a central idea of Blake's – his concept of single, twofold, threefold and fourfold vision (with some of the attendant ideas) and see to what extent it can serve as a paradigm for Hughes' poetic development. I am going to be highly selective, leaving out of account important aspects of Blake which do not fit into my scheme. And I am going to make Blake's ideas seem more simple, consistent and systematic than in fact they are. If I did not take these liberties, I should end up with a chapter on Blake, not on Ted Hughes.

Single vision is fallen vision, fallen, that is, from an assumed original, primal, unified vision, symbolised by Eden. At the Fall, which is both a curse we inherit and a process we reenact in every life, man is assumed to lose his ability to perceive anything in the spiritual dimension, anything as holy or miraculous. Hence it is a fall into sterile materialism and rationalism. He is assumed to lose his innocence, which is not simply his ignorance and inexperience but his flexibility, openness to experience, good faith, capacity for spon-taneous authentic living; to lose his access to the Energies, either within himself or without. Fallen man lives a second-hand life, a living death, in a self-made world of false rigidities and mechanisms of thinking and feeling and seeing. Single vision cannot see wholes, only fragments. It is analytic, compartmentalising. It cannot see relationships and patterns and wholes, and is therefore solipsistic, reductive and dehumanising, at the mercy of time and chance and death. Single vision is alienated, hubristic selfhood, and the achievement of twofold, threefold and fourfold vision are therefore stages in the annihilation of the self. The purpose is to regain Paradise – but it will not be the same Paradise. The new Paradise will be 'organised innocence' and atonement on the far side of experience and suffering and many inner deaths.

Single vision has been Western man's common condition throughout historical time. Artists and prophets have always cried out against it. Only the symptoms change from age to age, and the artist must diagnose them afresh, for the new symptoms are usually hailed as signs of 'progress'. Blake saw the symptoms in the late eighteenth century as the deification of reason and the five senses (Locke), mechanistic science (Newton), the increasingly repressive Puritanism of the churches, and the first mills of the Industial Revolution.

It is not assumed that every artist is born with fourfold vision and never loses it. What he can never lose is the sense of something lost, and the obligation to struggle to recover it. The artist is but a man and has to live in the world of men. His attacks on single vision in others are also attempts to purge it in himself. He is a healer because he recognises the need to heal himself, and the methods which work, being an artist, he is able to make available to others.

Blake's use of the suffix 'fold' implies that each stage depends upon and then subsumes the former. That is, the recovery of true vision, whereby we shall see things as they really are, can only be achieved by passing through all four stages, and in this order.

Stage one is the recognition of the all-pervading symptoms of single vision as such, of the need to undertake the psychic or spiritual journey out of its dark prison, and to engage it in a lifelong battle. Stage two is the release of the energies which will be needed for this battle and this journey, energies which, denied and repressed, have become 'reptiles of the mind'.[1] Stage three is the recovery of innocence. Stage four, the recovery of unified vision, will be a vision of the holiness of everything that lives.

What I am suggesting here is that Hughes' career has taken him this very route – not in a straight line, not without temporary diversions and retreats – there are endless recapitulations. The vision once achieved is not subsequently 'on tap': it has to be won again every time. If it is taken for granted, if short cuts are taken, it loses its validity. Every insight must be paid for. Nevertheless, looking at Hughes' work to date, the paradigm fits.

II

The Hawk in the Rain is about man, imprisoned in single vision as in his own body, looking out through the window of his eye at the surrounding Energies, the 'wandering elementals'. He is, in this book, making no effort to come to terms with them, as though that were inconceivable, but is cowering, hiding, peeping through his fingers in fear, gripping his own heart, or running for dear life. In 'Wind', 'this house' is the insulated human world, the world of books, thoughts, human relationships, and a blazing fire creating a magic circle the beasts cannot enter. It contains all human bearings and assurances, yet is as tiny and flimsy as a ship in a storm (the title poem was originally 'The Hawk in the Storm'), and has been 'far out at sea all night'. Wind, sea, darkness and 'blade-light' are images of what it cannot contain or cope with. The wind dents the balls of his eyes, but is itself the lens of a mad eye. He is eyeball to eyeball with everything that what we call sanity cannot cope with, perhaps with

The huge-eyed looming horde from
Under the floor of the heart, that run
To the madman's eye-corner.   ('Childbirth')

protected from it by nothing more than a delicate membrane, a window which 'trembles to come in'.

Castaneda's Don Juan calls what is inside the house (that is, inside the personality – its grip on its own identity and its subtle relationships and adjustments within the world of ordinary, mundane, visionless reality) the *tonal*. What is outside the house, 'where power hovers', he calls the *nagual*:

As long as his *tonal* is unchallenged and his eyes are tuned only for the *tonal's* world, the warrior is on the safe side of the fence. He's on familiar ground and knows all the rules. But when his *tonal* shrinks, he is on the windy side, and that opening must be shut tight immediately, or he would be swept away. And this is not just a way of talking. Beyond the gate of the *tonal's* eyes the wind rages. I mean a real wind. No metaphor. A wind that can blows one's life away. In fact, that is the wind that blows all living things on this earth.[2]

The *tonal* 'would rather kill itself than relinquish control':

Everyone's obsession is to arrange the world according to the *tonal's* rules; so every time we are confronted with the *nagual*, we go out of our way to make our eyes stiff and intransigent . . . The point is to convince the *tonal* that there are other worlds that can pass in front of the same windows . . . *The eyes* can be the windows to peer into boredom or to peek into that infinity.[3]

Men with the courage to confront the *nagual* and 'peek into that infinity' Don Juan calls sorcerers; we call them poets.

The poet is one who has

> dared to be struck dead
> Peeping through his fingers at the world's ends,
> Or at an ant's head.

('Egg-Head')

One of the 'world's ends' Hughes describes is the 'whaled monstered sea-bottom'. Perhaps he is remembering, consciously or unconsciously, that passage in *Moby Dick* where Melville gives us most overtly his version of the *nagual*:

By the merest chance the ship at last rescued him; but from that hour the little negro went about the deck an idiot; such, at least, they said he was. The sea had jeeringly kept his finite body up, but drowned the infinite of his soul. Not drowned, entirely, though. Rather carried down alive to wondrous depths, where strange shapes of the unwarped primal world glided to and fro before his passive eyes; and the miser-merman, Wisdom, revealed his hoarded heaps; and among the joyous, heartless, ever-juvenile eternities, Pip saw the multitudinous, God-omnipresent, coral insects, that out of the firmament of waters heaved the colossal orbs. He saw God's foot upon the treadle of the loom, and spoke it; and therefore his shipmates called him mad. So man's insanity is heaven's sense; and wandering from all mortal reason, man comes at least to that celestial thought, which, to reason, is absurd and frantic; and weal or woe, feels them uncompromised, indifferent as his God.

This is the madness of the Ancient Mariner, of Blake himself, of every genuine poet, and the world in which Hughes has had to pursue his vocation is no more receptive than Blake's was: 'Poets usually refuse the call. How are they to accept it? How can a poet become a medicine man and fly to the source and come back and heal or pronounce oracles? Everything among us is against it.'[5]

The man who defends his *tonal*, his single vision, at all costs, Hughes calls 'Egg-Head':

> Long the eggshell head's
> Fragility rounds and resists receiving the flash
> Of the sun, the bolt of the earth: and feeds
> On the yolk's dark and hush
>
> Of a helplessness coming
> By feats of torpor, by circumventing sleights
> Of stupefaction, juggleries of benumbing,
> By lucid sophistries of sight.
>
> To a staturing 'I am'.

Our attachment to single vision is a mixture of arrogance and complacency, a willed blindness and deafness. It is hubristic and solipsistic, needing to reduce and degrade the universe to the point where man can feel himself to be a god in it:

> it is a role

In which he can fling a cape,
And outloom life like Faustus.   ('Meeting')

It is not enough to purge ourselves of arrogance and complacency. The protagonist in most of the poems, the poet himself, has got that far, but finds himself left with only the utter helplessness, the sense of his own fragility and mortality. This is why he looks with such fascination at other creatures which seem to be able to live permanently in the *nagual*, plugged in to 'the elemental power circuit of the Universe'[6] and drawing their vitality from it. And he is representative enough in this, for this, surely, is why we are all drawn to zoos and wildlife parks and wildlife programmes on television, and why the Esso tiger is the most potent of all advertisements.

In a late poem 'Flowers and Men', Lawrence asks: 'Oh what in you can answer to this blueness?' He saw that every bird, beast and flower faces us with a similar challenge. Hughes was later to write of the blueness of the harebell, and many other softer qualities of the non-human world. But in *The Hawk in the Rain* he is asking the more urgent questions: what in us can answer to the power of the jaguar, the poise of the hawk, the patience of the horses?

Hughes is also fascinated, in this volume, with those moments when man is involuntarily exposed to the Energies – when he is born: 'Miracle struck out the brain / Of order and ordinary.' ('Childbirth'), when love strikes into his life like a hawk in a dovecote, and when he is dying. Hughes, like the onlookers in 'The Casualty' or 'The Martyrdom of Bishop Farrar', is 'Greedy to share all that is undergone, / Grimace, gasp, gesture of death.' But of *chosen* or achieved strategies for dealing with the Energies, he has, at this stage, little to say. There is the crudely-imagined grandeur of the Ancient Heroes, the gracious but remote, tapestried chivalry of 'A Modest Proposal'. The most affirmative lines in the book are the ending of 'The Dove Breeder': 'Now he rides the morning mist / With a big-eyed hawk on his fist.' But Hughes was soon to learn that Love is an Energy not so easily tamed. For the bird-protagonist of *Cave Birds* there is a hard-earned rebirth as a Risen Falcon; but the poem and sequence ends with the lines: 'But when will he land / On a man's wrist'.

An early poem, 'Quest', pictures the Energies as a many-headed cosmic dragon, and interprets the hero's role as sacrificial:

My victory to raise this monster's shadow from my people
Shall be its trumpeting and clangorous flight
Over the moon's face to its white-hot icy crevasse
With fragments of my body dangling from its hundred mouths.

It seems impossible that human vision could ever be reconciled to such Energies: the equivalent of the hawk landing on a man's wrist would be the dragon laying its head on a man's shoulder or a woman's breast. But this is precisely what happens in Blake's *Jerusalem*.

III

In *Lupercal*, though still very much in awe of the Energies and their destructive manifestations, Hughes is wholly committed to the attempt to evoke and control them:

If you refuse the energy, you are living a kind of death. If you accept the energy, it destroys you. What is the alternative? To accept the energy, and find methods of turning it to good, of keeping it under control — rituals, the machinery of religion.[7]

Again the title poem is carefully chosen, for the Lupercalia were precisely religious rituals to tap and control and turn to good energy in its primary manifestation − fertility. The barren women are living a kind of death until their frozen bodies are touched by the Maker of the world, not directly, which would destroy them, but through two sets of intermediaries. First the dog and the goat provide a spark of God's fire, which is then transmitted to the women through the 'flung effort' and 'poise' of the racers.

These racers are not the only human figures in *Lupercal* who are in control of potent energies. The acrobats shine and soar 'with unearthly access of grace'. Less spectacularly, among pigs and hay and manure mud, in Nicholas Ferrer and his family the fire of God.

Burned down to the blue calm
They called God's look, and through years illumed
Their fingers on the bibles, and gleamed

From the eagle of brass.

The same fire kept Dick Straightup alive as he lay in the freezing gutter, the tramp in 'November' in the sodden ditch.

These are, of course, so exceptional as to be scarcely human. 'Nothing mortal' falters the poise of the racers; the acrobats flash above 'the dullness of flesh'; Nicholas Ferrer 'housekept in fire of the martyrs'; Dick Straightup was more like a tree bole, the tramp more like a hedgehog or a thorn-root, than a man.

A life without doubts or obstructions is either more or less than human. Streamlined efficiency is for angels, animals and machines. Which of these is the saint or the genius? In the ordinary man the energies are there, but not available for efficient unified action, creative or destructive. Rather they sabotage all his efforts by warring with each other and demanding mutually exclusive satisfactions he cannot provide.

One problem for the ordinary man is that he cannot be 'blent in the prayer' ('Thrushes') until he has given his god a face. It is one of the characteristics of single vision to be able to see the Energies only in their destructive forms. The Angel in Blake's Memorable Fancy, for example, can see the Powers of the air only as 'the most terrific shapes of animals sprung from corruption'. One of these is Leviathan, whose mouth and red gills tinge the 'black deep with beams of blood'. The Angel flees in horror, leaving Blake alone:

And then this appearance was no more, but I found myself sitting on a pleasant bank beside a river by moonlight hearing a harper who sung to the harp, and his theme was, The man who never alters his opinion is like standing water, and breeds reptiles of the mind. (*The Marriage of Heaven and Hell*)

Hughes' grandfather and alter ego, Crag Jack, calls continually 'On you, god or not god', to reveal himself other than with a wolf's head and eagle's feet.

Hughes knows that the horror with which we view 'Nature red in tooth and claw' is partly a product of our own preconceptions and tendency to take 'portions of existence' (Blake) and fancy them to be the whole. He knows that not until he has begun to understand nature in its own terms will it show him any other face. Many of the poems in *Lupercal* are strategies and experiments for evoking, confronting and negotiating with the Powers. Until that transformation begins, he will see everything, even the thrushes on the lawn, as terrifying. He forces himself to confront the Energies at their most ugly, savage and, apparently, pointless, to look into 'the shark's mouth / That hungers down the blood-smell even to a leak of its own / Side and devouring of itself' ('Thrushes'). Perhaps, here again, Hughes was remembering *Moby Dick*:

They viciously snapped, not only at each other's disembowelments, but like flexible bows, bent round, and bit their own; till those entrails seemed swallowed over and over again by the same mouth, to be oppositely voided by the gaping wound. Nor was this all. It was unsafe to meddle with the corpses and ghosts of these creatures. A sort of generic or Pantheistic vitality seemed to lurk in their very joints and bones, after what might be called the individual life had departed. Killed and hoisted on deck for the sake of his skin, one of these sharks almost took poor Queequeg's hand off, when he tried to shut down the dead lid of his murderous jaw.
    'Queequeg no care what god made him shark,' said the savage, agonisingly lifting his hand up and down; 'wedder Fejee god or Nantucket god; but de god wat made shark must be one dam Ingin.'[8]

Blake, we remember, thought the god who made the tiger must be 'one dam Injin', especially if he also made the lamb.

One of the strategies Hughes adopts to try to escape from the limitation of single vision is to let nature speak for itself, through the mouth of a hawk:

Actually what I had in mind was that in this hawk Nature is thinking. Simply Nature. It's not so simple maybe because Nature is no longer so simple. I intended some Creator like the Jehovah in Job but more feminine. When Christianity kicked the devil out of Job what they actually kicked out was Nature . . . and Nature became the devil. He doesn't sound like Isis, mother of the gods, which he is. He sounds like Hitler's familiar spirit.[9]

The strategy does not work because Hughes cannot yet get behind the fallen nature of our tradition, and therefore cannot render the hawk's vision other than in terms of deranged human vision – the vision of Canute or Richard III or Hitler.

'What you find in the outside world is what has escaped from your own inner world', Hughes said in a recent broadcast. It follows that to understand nature, it is not going to be enough to study the behaviour of animals. Our own energies and those of the natural world are the same energies. Fourfold vision, which is true poetic vision, reveals that creatures are not portions of existence but the whole of existence in little, and the same applies to man. Creatures were, to Lawrence, 'little living myths'.[10] They are symbols of our own forgotten, unfallen selves. They roam our own inner darkness, where we fear to look, and speak to us in the forgotten language of darkness – symbolism. In *Lupercal* Hughes is also beginning to use poems as controlled dreams, as a technique for fishing in the deep pond of his own unconscious to draw up into consciousness whatever is alive there. Perhaps by opening himself to receive whatever might come up from the world under the world, he can bypass single vision and release his own buried powers, his own demon,

> the dream
> Darkness beneath night's darkness had freed,
> That rose slowly towards me, watching.   ('Pike')

IV

In *Wodwo* the window comes in, the wind of the *nagual* sweeps away order and ordinary, the terrible energies are released, Hughes receives 'the flash of the sun, the bolt of the earth' ('Egg-head) and is almost destroyed. What come up from the world under the world are horrors – ghost crabs:

All night, around us or through us,
They stalk each other, they fasten on to each other,
They mount each other, they tear each other to pieces,
They utterly exhaust each other.
They are the powers of this world.
We are their bacteria,
Dying their lives and living their deaths.

Despite his daring invocation of the energies in *Lupercal*, once they come they are far more inhuman and overwhelming than he had supposed, and he cannot handle them. They completely (and usually instantaneously, with a sudden psychic snap) supplant his normal consciousness, leaving him stripped of his defences against identification with the other, so that he finds himself jammed into or taken over by the consciousness of a hare or a rat in its last agony, or cataleptic, like the man after his battle with the rain horse, or sunstruck, or wandering in a circle utterly without bearings, like the man in 'Snow', or lost in a nightmare world, like Ripley in 'The Wound' with a hole in his head. The 'elemental power-circuit of the universe' flows through him all right, but it blows every fuse in his mind.

Blake's symbol for the energies is the serpent or dragon. This is the face Hughes now sees on his god or not-god; the serpent as swallower of everything ('this is the dark intestine'), the dragon waiting with its mouth open for the woman to deliver her child. Nature is all 'one smouldering annihilation', unmaking and remaking, remaking in order to unmake again. How could such a god be worshipped, or even accepted.

This is the dilemma which pushed Hughes, for a while, towards a Buddhistic rejection of the world as Karma:

And a hundred and fifty million years of hunger
Killing gratefully as breathing
Moulded the heart and the mouth

That cry for milk
From the breast
Of the mother

Of the God
Of the world
Made of Blood.

This was a necessary dead-end, the zero-point of Hughes' journey, from which he, being a poet and therefore committed to this world, could only emerge the stronger. It would seem from 'Logos', where God, himself Creation's nightmare,

. . . gives the blinding pentagram of His power
For the frail mantle of a person
To be moulded onto.
. . .

And within seconds the new-born baby is lamenting
That it ever lived —

that the only answer is to close the womb door and put a stop to these
senseless cycles of suffering. The only other answer, the only answer
for the poet, is the tragic view of life, which attaches a creative value to
suffering, and this is the direction Hughes took: 'The infinite terrible
circumstances that seem to destroy man's importance, appear as the
very terms of his importance. Man is the face, arms, legs, etc. grown
over the infinite, terrible All.'[11] He kept his sympathies intact. Purged
of selfhood and single vision, annihilated, reborn, he embarked on
another, perhaps not doomed, bid to live, another round of negotiations
with 'whatever happened to be out there'.[12]

But before we move on to trace Hughes' emergence into threefold
vision, it might be useful to look in some detail at the one poem
'Wings', in which Hughes consciously casts himself in the role of
latter-day Blake.

In this poem Hughes uses, in addition to the ideas already outlined,
another of Blake's formulations, his division of fallen man into
'spectre' and 'emanation'. John Beer explains these terms as clearly as
they allow:

The unified personality is unified by the vision which is allowed to shine
through it; self-love is equivalent to the setting up of an inward barrier. It
creates a new force, the selfhood, which stands between the vision and its free
expression.

As the selfhood begins to assume a life of its own, appropriating to its own
use the energies of the individual, it becomes, in Blake's terminology, the
'spectre'; the imagination which remains is called the 'emanation'.

The terms may perhaps be associated with Blake's critique of eighteenth
century mathematical thought as a way of thinking which divided the forces of
the universe into two distinct phenomena – the 'spectre' sun, the spherical
body which provides a focus for laws of gravitation, and the 'emanation' of
vivifying light, which is mysteriously produced by this apparently dead body. If
men saw even the sun as a divided image it was not surprising that they should
conform to the same pattern, becoming what they beheld: each man became
centre of his own mechanically organised little universe, disregarding his
imagination as a meaningless accessory except in moments when he wished to
relax from the serious clockwork of life. Blake felt, evidently, that if men saw
the sun as he saw it, a form which is imposed on that infinite energy of the
universe which shouts 'Holy, holy, holy is the Lord God Almighty', – and
necessarily imposed if human life is to survive at all – they would see their
own humanity in the same light. Spectre and emanation would disappear, their
functions being integrated back into a human nature which acted no longer as
moonlit mechanism but as an expressive unity of vision and desire, seeing

every thing that lives as holy.

Until such an awakening, the spectre retains power in the individual, permitting his vision to linger on as impotent emanation. In representing the two split forces pictorially, Blake usually gives them both wings: the spectre has the dark sinister wings of the bat, the emanation the coloured iridescent wings of the butterfly.[13]

Blake pictures unified imagination with the soaring pinions of the eagle, his primary symbol for fourfold vision. Single vision he pictures crouching, crawling on hands and knees, or at the bottom of the sea of materialism, like his Newton.

As Blake took real men, Newton and Locke, to stand for fallen vision in his time, so, in 'Wings', Hughes takes a philosopher, Sartre, a writer, Kafka, and a scientist, Einstein, as his exemplars. All have fallen from that true vision which enables you

To see a World in a Grain of Sand
And a Heaven in a Wild Flower,
Hold Infinity in the palm of your hand
And Eternity in an hour.   ('Auguries of Innocence')

What connects three such different men is that each is under a huge broken wing of shadow; each attempts to fly and produces only a grotesque or pathetic parody of flight.

Sartre 'regrows the world inside his skull, like the spectre of a flower'. His extinct eyeball can see neither heaven nor angels, only facts, and all facts subsumed in the fact of mortality. Hughes' closing image of him clearly parallels Blake's image of Newton trying to encompass the universe on a sheet of paper at the bottom of the sea:

He sits on, in the twice-darkened room,
Pondering on the carrion-eating skate,

And on its wings, lifted, white, like an angel's,
And on those cupid lips in its deathly belly,

And on the sea, this tongue in his ear, licking the last of pages.

Nietzsche also knew this type:

Today I saw a sublime man, a solemn man, a penitent of the spirit: oh, how my soul laughed at his ugliness!
Hung with ugly truths, the booty of his hunt, and rich in torn clothes; many thorns, too, hung on him – but I saw no rose.
There is still contempt in his eye, and disgust lurks around his mouth.
He rests now, to be sure, but he has never yet lain down in the sunlight.
His countenance is still dark; his hand's shadow plays upon it.
The sense of his eyes, too, is overshadowed.
To be sure, I love in him the neck of the ox: but now I want to see the eye of the angel, too.[14]

Kafka, for Hughes, 'is an owl'

'Man' tattooed in his armpit
Under the broken wing.

The tattoo can only be seen when the wing is lifted in flight, but the broken wing cannot be lifted. Similarly the large eyes are for seeing in the dark, but Kafka is condemned by his flightlessness to live in the stunning glare, under the arc-lamp of man's rational consciousness. 'He is a man in hopeless feathers', given the need to fly, commanded by his own nature to fly, without the means to fly. It is the predicament he expressed everywhere in his writings: 'There is a goal, but now way' (*Reflections*). *The Castle* in particular expresses the futility of the attempt to approach grace by reason. There may be a way from God to man (if there is a God); but there is certainly no way from man to God. Yet Kafka felt the obligation to keep up his hopeless 'assault on the last earthly frontier' (*Diaries*).

Man has no other equipment for this assault but logic, language and mathematics. Perhaps Einstein flew highest of all, far into space, but without ever escaping from the prison of his own intellect. He saw no miracles in space such as had sustained his ancestors in the desert:

And no quails tumbling
From the cloud. And no manna
For angels.
Only the pillar of fire contracting its strength into a star-mote.

Einstein is presented as being unable to wonder, or weep, or pray, or love. The nearest he gets to prayer is in his playing of Bach. But music is also mathematics:

He bows in prayer over music, as over a well.
But it is the cauldron of the atom.
And it is the Eye of God in the whirlwind.
It is a furnace, storming with flames.

It is a burned-out bottomless eye-socket
Crawling with flies
In fugues.

His prayer for motherly love is answered not by angels but by a rising cloud of flies, not by the pillar of cloud by day, but by the mushroom cloud of a nuclear explosion.

These human deficiencies Hughes attributes to a shifting of the centre of gravity away from 'man's sense of himself, . . . his body and his essential human subjectivity', and a surrender of his individuality to an 'impersonal abstraction'. For a physicist 'the centre of gravity is . . . within some postulate deep in space, or leaking away down the drill-shaft of mathematics'.[15]

The poet and the physicist are exploring 'the same gulf of unknowable laws and unknowable particles', but the poet, not crippled by single vision, not releasing energies he cannot control, not committed to the total comprehensibility of the universe as if it were the mind's mirror, has the truer way. Hughes' metaphor for the poet's way, written as early as 1961, is 'Wodwo'.

Hughes described his wodwo as 'some sort of satyr or half-man or half-animal, half all kinds of elemental little things, just a little larval being without shape or qualities who suddenly finds himself alive in this world at any time'. That Hughes in this poem is expressing, among other things, the attempt of the poet to enter into threefold vision, is clear if we compare the poem with this prose passage:

... the living suffering spirit, capable of happiness, much deluded, too frail, with doubtful and provisional senses, so undefinable as to be almost silly, but palpably existing, and wanting to go on existing ... homing in tentatively on vital scarcely perceptible signals, making no mistakes, but with no hope of finality, continuing to explore.[15]

This could be a paraphrase of 'Wodwo'. In fact, it describes the efforts of a generation of East European poets to come to terms through poetry with the hostile world in which they are obliged to live and to salvage their humanity and self-respect.

The wodwo is also an image for certain aspects of the world of the child:

Theirs is not just a miniature world of naïve novelties and limited reality — it is also still very much the naked process of apprehension, far less conditioned than ours, far more fluid and alert, far closer to the real laws of its real nature. It is a new beginning, coming to circumstances afresh. It is still lost in the honest amoebic struggle to fit itself to the mysteries. It is still wide open to information, still anxious to get things right, still wanting to know exactly how things are, still under the primeval dread of misunderstanding the situation. Preoccupations are already pressing, but they have not yet closed down, like a space helmet, over the entire head and face, with the proved, established adjustments of security. Losing that sort of exposed nakedness, we gain in confidence and in mechanical efficiency on our chosen front, but we lose in real intelligence. We lose in attractiveness to change, in curiosity, in perception, in the original, wild, no-holds-barred approach to problems. In other words, we start the drift away from any true situation. We begin to lose validity as witnesses and participants in the business of living in this universe.[16]

The best example from this period of the child as witness and participant in the universe is 'Full Moon and Little Frieda'. The child is learning words, and using them, like an artist, to recreate the world. The act of naming the moon with such freshness and openness and wonder unifies the whole scene over which the moon presides, including the child and its father. Such unfallen vision is atoning and redeeming.

V

The events of 1963 and 1969 darkened Hughes' vision again. The Energies manifested themselves to him as more dragonish and wantonly destructive than ever. He found it necessary, as Blake had done, to find a way to stand outside his own intolerable experience, to hold it at arms' length so as to see it whole, to objectify and systematise it as myth. Also he had to recapitulate, to go back to the very beginning and start his quest again, with harsher discipline, not to be seduced by beauty and by words, with fewer preconceptions, not even those which seem to define our humanity. He took Leonard Baskin's Crow-Man, gave him features from Eskimo, Red Indian and Celtic crow-lore, then hatched him, clueless, into our world, with the task of trying to understand it, and his place in it.

Crow tries out or witnesses all the techniques of single vision – words and numbers, scripture and physics – the result is war, murder, suicide, madness. He confronts the Energies always as something to be fought and killed – dragon, serpent, ogress – obstacles on his blind quest. Crow's quest, though he does not himself know it, is ultimately the same as Hughes' quest, to achieve fourfold vision and thereby become fully a man, reborn into a redeemed world of joy.

The poems which were gathered in *Crow* (according to the dust-wrapper 'from about the first two-thirds of what was to have been an epic folk-tale') are mainly about Crow's mistakes, his mutually destructive encounters with the Energies, his ego-death, his first glimmerings of conscience, his first tentative steps towards reconstituting himself and reinterpreting the world, with the help of his Eskimo guide. Hughes had brought Crow to the point he had himself reached. Therefore, he could see no way forward for Crow. He abandoned him and sought to by-pass him:

In the little girl's angel gaze
Crow lost every feather
In the little boy's wondering eyes
Crow's bones splintered

In the little girl's passion
Crow's bowels fell in the dust
In the little boy's rosy cheeks
Crow became an unrecognisable rag

Crow got under the brambles, capitulated
To nothingness eyes closed
Let those infant feet pound through the Universe.

Crow's vision is assumed here to be fundamentally at odds with innocence. It is assumed that he can never achieve threefold vision. But Crow refused to be killed off so easily. He lay dormant for a few years waiting for his future to come clear in Hughes' imagination.

Meanwhile Hughes, possibly without at first knowing it, struggled with parallel versions of the same story – Orghast, Prometheus on his Crag, Gaudete, Cave Birds, Adam and the Sacred Nine. The heroes of all these stories – Pramanath, Prometheus, Lumb, the nameless protagonist of Cave Birds, and Adam – are all, to begin with, split or crucified by their inability to unify or reconcile their mortal and immortal natures. All have violated 'material nature, the Creatress, source of life and light'.

Blake's idea of contraries probably derived from his reading of the Smaragdine Tablet of Hermes Trismegistus: 'That which is above is like that which is beneath, and that which is beneath is like that which is above, to work the miracles of one thing.' This is the tablet Hughes had in mind in 'Fragment of an Ancient Tablet'. But the alchemical wisdom of that tablet is fragmented because Crow cannot yet unify his vision, cannot yet see above and below in any other terms than those of such dualistic clichés, single-vision judgements, as 'good and evil', 'beautiful and ugly' . . . His sexual consciousness is as sick as Lear's in his madness: 'But to the girdle do the Gods inherit, / Beneath is all the fiend's.' The only way in which this conflict can be transcended is 'by creating a being which, like Prometheus, includes the elemental opposites, and in whom the collision and pain become illumination'.[17] This illumination is fourfold vision, the recognition of the vulture not as monstrous obscenity, but as Helper and midwife, mother and bride.

Part II of Orghast, Hughes tells us, 'is the story of the tyrant Holdfast in the Underworld, the decomposition of the fallen ego among the voices of its crimes, oversights and victims'.[17] This could equally well be a summary of Cave Birds. The protagonist's crime has been mutilation and attempted murder. His victim was his own innermost demon, who is also Nature, his mother and intended bride. After his decomposition we witness his reconstitution as a man at the hands of his former victim whom he simultaneously reconstitutes. The image for this healing and atonement is, as in Blake, marriage. In earlier poems of the Crow period Hughes had been unable to get beyond the failed, destructive, cannibalistic marriages of 'Lovesong', 'The Lovepet', 'The Lamentable History of the Human Calf' and 'Actaeon'. Now, in 'His legs ran about' and 'Bride and groom', he enters into fourfold vision.

The reassembling of the bits and pieces of disintegrated man which takes place in these poems is, of course, a version of the Osiris story. The process also redeems nature itself by, as it were, sewing it together, reintegrating it as a harmonious unity. As Blake puts it in *The Four Zoas* ('Night the Eighth'): 'So Man looks out in tree & herb & fish & bird & beast / Collecting up the scattered portions of his immortal body.' *Cave Birds*, like *The Four Zoas*, is about man's 'fall into Division' and 'Resurrection to Unity'. That division is seen by Blake as the separation between the male Spectres and their female Emanations, with consequent torment, sterility and loss of vision. Their eventual reconstitution and marriage initiates Jerusalem, a redeemed world of 'organised innocence', vision, unity, holiness, love and joy.

Thus shall the male & female live the life of Eternity
Because the Lamb of God Creates himself a bride & wife
That we his Children evermore may live in Jerusalem
Which now descendeth out of heaven a City yet a woman.   ('Night the Ninth')

The role of nature in this drama is complex in both Blake and Hughes. Blake's quarrel with Wordsworth centred on Blake's rejection of Wordsworth's nature-worship, his claim that nature was Mother of all, creatress of humanity and therefore of the human imagination, a self-validating whole. Wordsworth, too, used marriage as the dominant image of his 'spousal verse'. Paradise was to be regained, or recreated, by wedding 'the discerning intellect of Man' to 'this goodly universe'. Blake believed that neither the mind of man in its fallen state, nor the material universe, were sources of spirit, and called Wordsworth 'pagan'. Wordsworth, he felt, had allowed himself to be seduced by fallen nature, the glamour of the universe, which in *Jerusalem* Blake calls Vala.

In his marginalia on Wordsworth's *Poems* (1815) Blake wrote: 'Natural Objects always did & now do Weaken deaden & obliterate imagination in Me'. We must remember, however, that with fourfold vision there are no natural objects, since every sparrow, every sandgrain, becomes a world of delight closed to the vision dependent on the five senses which imprison man in a barren world of 'Natural Objects' drained of the spiritual significance only the imagination can bestow upon them.

Seest thou the little winged fly, smaller than a grain of sand?
It has a heart like thee, a brain open to heaven & hell.
Withinside wondrous & expansive, its gates are not clos'd.
I hope thine are not.   (*Milton*)

He renounces the corporeal, vegetable world as having no more to do with him than 'the Dirt upon my feet' (*A Vision of the Last Judgment*, 95), but even that dirt is capable of transfiguration.

In so far as Wordsworth meant by nature not so much the external universe as the condition of innocent at-one-ness with it found in children and animals, this was more attractive to Blake, but nevertheless had to be consigned to the category of a false or inadequate paradise of unorganised innocence which was too protected and comfortable to allow the conflict between contraries out of which alone could come progression towards fourfold vision.

Hughes' position is somewhere between Blake and Wordsworth. Nature, as the external universe, he values much more highly than Blake; but he is well aware that only the human imagination, fourfold, can fuse the horror and the beauty, heal the scarred face of the goddess.

Coleridge would have agreed with Blake: 'The further I ascend from men and cattle, and the common birds of the woods and fields, the greater becomes in me the intensity of the feelings of life. Life seems to me there a universal spirit that neither has nor can have an opposite.' Hughes' experience has been exactly the reverse. It was by descending again from the far limits of pain and consciousness into woods and fields, among men and cattle, that he recovered his sense of the sacredness of animated Nature. In the farming poems miracles issue from the mud and the body's jellies. In 'Barley'[18] the process of germination is rendered sacramentally:

And the angel of earth
Is flying through the field, kissing each one awake.
But it is a hard nursery.
Night and day all through winter huddling naked
They have to listen to the pitiless lessons
Of the freezing constellations
And the rain. If it were not for the sun
Who visits them daily, briefly,
To pray with them, they would lose hope
And give up. With him
They recite the Lord's prayer
And sing a psalm.

Hughes' version of the Lord's prayer is given at the end of 'The Golden Boy': [19]

Thanking the Lord
Thanking the Wheat
Thanking the Bread
For bringing them Life
Today and Tomorrow
Out of the dirt.

But two poems in *Cave Birds*, 'A green mother' and 'As I came, I saw a wood', show that Hughes was as aware as Blake of the inadequacy of the idea that 'the earth is a busy hive of heavens' where a man may climb 'to the heavens of the birds, the heavens of the beasts, and of the fish'. The green mother is Beulah, offering the hero a return to the womb, not for rebirth, but for cradling in endless bliss, the everlasting holiday promised by all the religions, without contraries or suffering or consciousness:

This earth is heaven's sweetness.

It is heaven's mother.
The grave is her breast
And her milk is endless life.
                    You shall see
How tenderly she has wiped her child's face clean

Of the bitumen of blood and smoke of tears.

In a wood the hero sees all the animals move 'In the glow of fur which is their absolution in sanctity.' But they have never fallen, so that sanctity in simple being is not available to man, and, in any case, would be something less than fully human: 'And time was not present they never stopped / Or left anything old or reached any new thing.' The only religion the hero's deepest humanity sanctions for him is communion with a world in which gods are perpetually crucified and eaten and resurrected, and men move not in perpetual sanctity, but in the bitumen of blood and smoke of tears. There and only there is the ground of his striving towards an earned atonement.

There is a parallel situation at the beginning of the second book of Blake's *Milton*, where the questing hero, Milton or Blake, is poised on the threshold of Eternity, which is fourfold vision. The last country or condition through which he must pass, from which Eternity can be seen, is Beulah.

It is a pleasant lovely Shadow
Where no dispute can come, because of those who Sleep. . . .
But Beulah to its Inhabitants appears within each district
As the beloved infant in his mother's bosom round incircled
With arms of love & pity & sweet compassion. But to
The Sons of Eden the moony habitations of Beulah
Are from Great Eternity a mild & pleasant Rest.

Eternity, on the other hand, is a place of great Wars, 'in fury of Poetic Inspiration / To build the Universe stupendous'. The Emanations cannot face its brightness and challenge; they cry for 'a habitation & a place / In which we may be hidden under the shadow of wings'. Their prayer is granted:

Into this pleasant Shadow all the weak & weary,
Like Women & Children, were taken away as on wings
Of dovelike softness, & shadowy habitations prepared for them.

But to rest in Beulah, in the state of threefold vision, would, for the questing poet/hero, be failure; for the state of Beulah can only be maintained by his repeated suffering and sacrifice. His task, like that of the hero of *Cave Birds*, and of *Gaudete* is to 'Redeem the Female Shade' (his own Emanation, his mother and his bride, vision, Nature)

From Death Eternal; such your lot, to be continually Redeem'd
By death & misery of those you love & by Annihilation.

Milton takes the final step into Glory, and his Shadow becomes a Dove.

Blake, like Hughes, makes frequent use of theriomorphic images, not least in his mythology of vision. His image for the darkness of single vision is the Raven, for the energy of twofold vision, the Serpent, for the light of threefold vision, the Dove, and for the majesty of fourfold vision, the Eagle, Lion or Tyger.

From the beginning Hughes had been fascinated by the 'murderous innocence' (in Yeats' phrase) of the hawk, its complete mastery of its world. But not until much later was he able to resolve that oxymoron. From the beginning, also, he had represented the energies as snake or dragon. *Lupercal* contains several poems left over from an abandoned sequence of poems about England, its flora and fauna, its betrayal and pollution by single vision. The controlling image was to have been a river, which would metamorphose freely with a snake, an adder, standing for the rejected energies, the buried life of England, almost extinguished. At first there had been no single theriomorphic image for single vision, since that is by definition exclusively human, but in the recapitulation of single vision in *Crow*, Crow is himself such an image, and is brought face to face with his mother the serpent (whom he sees as an enemy to be annihilated) in several poems. In Hughes, too, the light of innocence, repeatedly victimised, shines from the dove. 'An Alchemy' is the poem which celebrates its advent, in terms of the redeeming innocence of Shakespeare's later heroines, especially Cordelia, with a miraculous transformation of both crow and serpent:

                    Lear redivivus
Phoenix-Posthumous
                    Found breath in Marina
Redeemed all Tempest
                    His kiss of life
Stirred the Turtle
                    Of the waters of amnios
The lunar cauldron

Then black Venus
            double tongued

```
Swine-uddered Sycorax
                    Lilith the night-crow
Slid from the Tree
Released the Rainbow
                    Breasted Dove
With a leaf of light
                    Miranda with a miracle
To Adam Adonis
And sank
          In the crucible
                    Tiamat
                              The Mother
The Scales
          The Coil
                    Of the Matter
                              Deeper
Then ever plummet
                    With Prospero's bones
And the sounding Book
```

In *Gaudete* the death which is also a rebirth and a recovery of innocence is rendered in one of the epilogue poems as the shooting of a dove:

Am I killed?
Or am I searching?

Is this the rainbow silking my body?

Which wings are these?

In *Adam and the Sacred Nine* one of the nine birds which come to Adam is a dove, 'her breast big with rainbows', 'a piling heaven of silver and violet', 'a sun-blinding', the sacrificial Christ-bird, always violated, nesting among thorns, to hatch the egg of resurrection.[20] That rainbow is an important image in Blake, too, a promise of the ultimate recovery of Vision.

VI

One pole of Hughes' achievement is the black vision of *Crow*, twofold vision unredeemed by threefold, a vision of destruction and horror. The opposite pole is the affirmative, celebratory vision of *Season Songs*. Suffering and death are not absent from *Season Songs*, but are not given enough weight to disturb the essentially up-beat surge. Perhaps some of these poems could only have been written by a man who has come through to fourfold vision; but they do not contain within themselves the struggle and the payment, the painful moment of transformation of dirt into God. That is the biggest challenge

Hughes has yet set himself, to hold together and fuse, in a single poem or set of poems, the two poles of his vision, to find verbal equivalents for the magical transformation in consciousness. It is not so impossible as it seems, for the vision of Crow was not a vision of reality. Crow was projecting his own blackness and blindness upon the world, like the angel in the 'Memorable Fancy'. When the angel departs, the scene is transformed to reflect instead Blake's own vision of harmony.

The poems in which this is achieved are, it seems to me, the closing poems of *Prometheus on his Crag*, the closing poems of *Cave Birds*, the last poem in *Adam and the Sacred Nine*, a few of the farming poems and odd poems from elsewhere, but, supremely, the Epilogue poems in *Gaudete*. For example:

The grass-blade is not without
The loyalty that never was beheld.

And the blackbird
Sleeking from common anything and worm-dirt
Balances a precarious banner
Gold on black, terror and exultation.

The grim badger with armorial mask
Biting spade-steel, teeth and jaw-strake shattered,
Draws that final shuddering battle cry
Out of its backbone.

Me too,
Let me be one of your warriors.

Let your home
Be my home. Your people
My people.

The Anglican clergyman Lumb has undergone a terrifying ordeal in the underworld, which has destroyed his old split self and enabled him to be reborn of the goddess, simultaneously bringing her to a new birth. He returns to the world, to the West of Ireland, stripped of everything but his vision – the memories of his ordeal, his intimations of atonement, and his new sacramental vision which enables him to perform small miracles such as whistling an otter out of the loch, and to write these poems. The poems contain as much pain as any poems could, but the pain does not cancel the exultation; on the contrary, is felt to be essential to it. In 'Crow on the Beach' Crow grasps something

Of the sea's ogreish outcry and convulsion.
He knew he was the wrong listener unwanted
To understand or help.

The reborn Lumb is the right listener, able to transform the horror:

The sea grieves all night long.
The wall is past groaning.
The field has given up –
It can't care any more.

Even the tree
Waits like an old man
Who has seen his whole family murdered.

Horrible world.

Where I let in again –
As if for the first time –
The untouched joy.

The atoning, healing, transformations take several forms: the predator becomes an angel or midwife, the monster becomes a bride, pain becomes bliss, terror exultation, the dirt God. Some of these I have already discussed; some have been discussed in earlier chapters. Let us look closer now at the transformation of the predator.

The horror of predation was a common theme in earlier Hughes poems, and reached its definitive statement, perhaps, in 'Crow Tyrannosaurus':

The cat's body writhed
Gagging
A tunnel
Of incoming death-struggles, sorrow on sorrow.

The whole of creation, it seems to Crow, is 'a cortege of mourning and lament'. Yet the horror derives not so much from the reality, as from the split vision of an observer unable to resolve the dualisms of happiness/pain and life/death. Even at the level of field observation it is not accurate. The relationship of prey to predator is not only a matter of struggle and scream. Often the victim will go into a sort of trance of acquiescence. Several lions come upon an old buffalo in the middle of a pool. They will not go out of their depth, so the buffalo could outwait them. Or it could fight for its life with its formidable horns. It does neither. It walks slowly towards them, and bows its head, exposing its spinal cord to the lioness already on its back.

The spider clamps the bluefly – whose death panic
Becomes sudden soulful absorption.

A stoat throbs at the nape of the lumped rabbit
Who watches the skylines fixedly.   (Gaudete. 177)

Fourfold vision does not cast the predator, anthropomorphically, in the role of villain. The tiger is one more embodiment of the goddess. The eagle is a god:

And already the White Hare crouches at the sacrifice,
Already the Fawn stumbles to offer itself up
And the Wolf-Cub weeps to be chosen.   ('Eagle')[21]

'Tiger-psalm'[22] was originally · conceived as a dialogue between
Socrates and Buddha. Gradually Buddha's side of the argument was
resolved into a tiger and Socrates' into the principle of machine guns,
'as if the whole abstraction of Socrates' discourse must inevitably,
given enough time and enough applied intelligence, result in machine
guns'. It is an argument between single vision and fourfold vision. The
tiger, unlike the machine-guns, is carrying out a perfectly rational,
restrained and sacred activity:

The tiger
Kills expertly, with anaesthetic hand.
. . .
The tiger
Kills frugally, after close inspection of the map.
. . .
The tiger
Kills like a fall of a cliff, one-sinewed with the earth,
Himalayas under eyelid, Ganges under fur –

Does not kill.

Does not kill. The tiger blesses with a fang.
The tiger does not kill but opens a path
Neither of Life nor of Death:
The tiger within the tiger:
The Tiger of the Earth.
                    O Tiger!
O Brother of the Viper!
                    O Beast in Blossom!

In his report on visions seen by thirty-five subjects after taking the
hallucinogenic drug harmaline in Chile, Claudio Naranjo tells us that
seven of the subjects saw big cats, usually tigers, though big cats are
not seen in Chile, and tigers, of course, are not seen in the New World.
One woman had a tiger guide throughout her journey:

I walk next to him, my arm over his neck. We climb the high mountain. There
is a zig-zag path between high bushes. We arrive. There is a crater. We wait for
some time and there begins an enormous eruption. The tiger tells me I must
throw myself into the crater. I am sad to leave my companion but I know that
this last journey I must travel. I throw myself into the fire that comes out of
the crater. I ascend with the flames towards the sky and fly onwards.[23]

Another subject actually became a tiger:

I walked, though, feeling the same fredom I had experienced as a bird and a
fish, freedom of movement, flexibility, grace. I moved as a tiger in the jungle,

joyously, feeling the ground under my feet, feeling my power; my chest grew larger. I then approached an animal, any animal. I only saw its neck, and then experienced what a tiger feels when looking at its prey.[23]

Naranjo comments: 'This may be enough to show how the tiger by no means stands for mere hostility, but for a fluid synthesis of aggression and grace and a full acceptance of the life-impulse beyond moral judgement.' It may be that most sophisticated urban whites, whose normal vision is single vision, can only achieve this synthesis with the aid of hallucinogenic drugs, but it occurs very frequently in the oral poetry of so-called 'primitive' peoples. Here, for example, is a Yoruba poem called 'Leopard':

Gentle hunter
His tail plays on the ground
While he crushes the skull.

Beautiful death
Who puts on a spotted robe
When he goes to his victim.

Playful killer
Whose loving embrace
Splits the antelope's heart.[24]

Half Naranjo's subjects had ecstatic feelings of a religious nature: 'The sea was in myself. There was a continuity of the external with the internal. . . . The sand and the plants were myself or something of mine. The idea of God was in everything. . . . Beauty, joy, peace, everything I longed for was there. God in myself.'[25] ('All deities reside in the human breast', said Blake.[26]) But there must always be a descent into destruction before this atonement is reached. The characteristic mythic shape of the experience is described by Naranjo:

The complex of images discussed first as portraying the polarity of being and becoming, freedom and necessity, spirit and matter, only set up the stage for the human drama. This involves the battle of opposites and eventually their reconciliation or fusion, after giving way to death and destruction, be this by fire, tigers, drowning, or devouring snakes. The beauty of fluid fire, the graceful tiger, or the subtle and wise reptile, these seem most expressive for the synthetic experience of accepting life as a whole, or, better, accepting existence as a whole, life and death included; evil included too, though from a given spiritual perspective it is not experienced as evil any more. Needless to say, the process is essentially religious, and it could even be suspected that every myth presents us one particular aspect of the same experience.[27]

This, certainly, is the controlling myth of Hughes' career. And one name for that 'given spiritual perspective' is fourfold vision.

VII

Fourfold vision is everywhere apparent in Hughes' most recent work. At the moment of writing, some twenty poems have been published from a forthcoming collection called *The River*.[28] All are fine, and those about salmon seem to me among Hughes' finest. As in the farming poems, Hughes never takes his eye from the object. Never for a moment does the salmon cease to be a real salmon and become a counter for something else. Yet Hughes' vision reveals, without ever saying so, that the salmon is our prototype, its life-cycle a paradigm of nature's purposes and of the religious life.

In 'Salmon Eggs' the mating salmon are 'Emptying themselves for each other'. This selfless giving, generosity, openness, is a form of dedication or worship, as is the acquiescence of the October salmon in his slow death:

All this, too, is stitched into the torn richness,
The epic poise
That holds him so steady in his wounds, so loyal to his doom, so patient
In the machinery of heaven.

The dying salmon is the defeated, torn and sacrificed hero, about to become a god.
Blake asks

How do you know but ev'ry Bird that cuts the airy way,
Is an immense world of delight, clos'd by your senses five?[29]

The same, of course, may be said of every fish, or every living thing: 'If the doors of perception were cleansed every thing would appear to man as it is, infinite'.[30] What Blake means, surely, is that everything contains within itself the clue to the mystery, the principle of the whole, and being continuous with the whole (which cannot be seen in its immensity) witnesses to the whole and makes it accessible to vision. The mystery is 'the redeemed life of joy'. It is a mystery because there is no mechanistic or rational explanation for the transformation of suffering (and everything which cries out for redemption) into joy. The language of poetry can re-enact it. Joy, as Blake or Hughes understands it, has little to do with happiness – a relatively trivial, uncreative state, a distraction, temptation, backwater from the true way through tragic experience. It is the grace of atonement, the exaltation of being used by the goddess for her sacred purposes, 'her insatiable quest'. In an early version of *Gaudete*, one of the prayers to that goddess composed by Nicholas Lumb was addressed to a salmon (in its capacity as our representative):

While the high-breasted, the halved world
Opens herself for you

While your strength
Can enjoy her, lifting you through her

While your face remains free
Of the mesh of numbness

While your spine shivers and leaps
In the spate of your spirit

Before it trickles thin and low
Inhabited only by small shadows

Court the lady of the hill
Press to her source, spend your plunder

For her – only for her –
O salmon of the ghostly sea.

The language of all these river poems is a rich weave of inter-relationships. A poem may be ostensibly about a single creature, but that creature is defined by its relationships with other creatures, with weather and season and landscape. Since 'All things draw to the river' it is therefore the language of atonement. The life of the salmon is the life of the living waters, sea and river, which is the life of earth and sky, which is our only life. Each poem is a microcosm. The salmon is part of a flow which 'will not let up for a minute'. The river is itself an archetypal image for life in time, process, the one-way helpless journey towards death. But a river is by no means a one-way wastage:

Something else is going on in the river

More vital than death – death here seems a superficiality
Of small scaly limbs, parasitical. More grave than life
Whose reflex jaws and famished crystals
Seem incidental
To this telling – these toilings of plasm –
The melt of mouthing silence, the charge of light
Dumb with immensity.
　　　　　　　The river goes on
Sliding through its place, undergoing itself
In its wheel.　　　　　　　　　　　　　　　　　　　　('Salmon Eggs')

And here the poem approaches the mystery. For the wheel, karma, the 'cycles of recurrence', had formerly been for Hughes, as for most religions, images of horror or absurdity, needing to be transcended. Now it seems that the horror was a product of defective vision, the split psyche, the spiritual blindness caused by dualism, the hubristic desire to improve on the given life, to redeem nature. In the words of Lawrence's risen Christ (in *The Escaped Cock*): 'From what, and to what, could this infinite whirl be saved?'

Since logical analysis is the language of single vision, one would expect the language of fourfold vision to be paradoxical synthesis. The very title of Blake's finest work, *The Marriage of Heaven and Hell*, declares that this is so. 'Salmon Eggs' moves through a series of oxymorons – 'burst crypts', 'time-riven altar', 'harrowing, crowned', 'raptures and rendings' – appropriating on the way all the claims of the Christian mystery of transcendence – 'crypt', 'altar', 'liturgy', 'tidings', 'Sanctus', 'mass', 'font' – claiming them all for the wheel itself, 'the round of unending water', and the salmon egg which is its 'blessed issue', towards the river's simple annunciation: *Only birth matters.*

For this poem to work as a spiritually fertilising experience, it is necessary to believe that these words express a truth uttered by the river, and not a theory uttered by Ted Hughes. And that is unlikely to happen unless we have accompanied him imaginatively through the four stages of his arduous quest, through all the horrors, sufferings and deaths his earlier poems enact.

What saved Hughes in those worst years in the sixties from despair and world-denial and a Beckettian absurdism was a Blake-like tenacity, against all the odds, in holding firm to the conviction that the human spirit, with its desire for existence, is 'the only precious thing, and designed in accord with the whole universe. Designed, indeed, by the whole universe',[31] and that the universe knows what it is about: 'The infinite terrible circumstances that seem to destroy man's importance, appear as the very terms of his importance. Man is the face, arms, legs, etc. grown over the infinite, terrible All.'[32] These words were written in 1966. When Hughes came to rewrite his essay on Popa in 1977, he attributed to the Eastern European poets something of the vision to which he had himself come through in the interim:

At bottom, their vision, like Beckett's, is of the struggle of animal cells and of the torments of spirit in a world reduced to that vision, but theirs contains far more elements than his. It contains all the substance and feeling of ordinary life. And one can argue that it is a step or two beyond his in imaginative truth, in that whatever terrible things happen in their work happen within a containing passion – Job-like – for the elemental final beauty of the created world.[33]

Hughes could not have written that final phrase in the sixties. Then he would have regarded beauty with suspicion, as something likely to blind man to the essential elemental starkness and awesomeness of the world. As his vision matured, beauty forced its way in again, and to the centre, not as something cosy and pretty and picturesque, but as a radiance testifying to miracle.

The poem in which Hughes most fully receives and expresses that radiance is the poem with which he has chosen to end his *Selected Poems*, 'That Morning'. In 1980 Hughes and his son Nicholas spent some weeks salmon-fishing in Alaska. The place and its creatures demanded a sacramental response. The sheer profusion of salmon was like a sign and a blessing:

Solemn to stand there in the pollen light
Waist-deep in wild salmon swaying massed
As from the hand of God.   There the body

Separated, golden and imperishable,
From its doubting thought – the spirit beacon
Lit by the power of the salmon

That came on, came on, and kept on coming

. . .

So we stood, alive in the river of light
Among the creatures of light, creatures of light.

The conclusion of Hughes' *Selected Poems* is the same as the conclusion of *The Marriage of Heaven and Hell:* 'For everything that lives is Holy'.

Uncollected and unpublished poems

A large number of interesting poems by Ted Hughes have remained uncollected, or even unpublished. I have made the following selection on three grounds: intrinsic quality and power, interest in terms of Hughes' development, both in technique and vision, and relevance to the essays in this book.

K S

THE LITTLE BOYS AND THE SEASONS

One came out of the wood. 'What a bit of a girl,'
The small boys cried, 'To make my elder brother daft,
Tossing her petticoats under the bushes. O we know,
We know all about you: there's a story.
Well we don't want your tinny birds with their noise,
And we don't want your soppy flowers with their smells,
And you can just take all that make-up off our garden,
And stop giving the animals ideas with your eyes.'
And she cried a cloud and all the children ran in.

One came out of the garden. A great woman.
And the small boys muttered: 'That's not much either,
She keeps my dad out till too late at night.
You can't get through the bushes for her great bosom,
The pond's untidy with her underclothes,
And her sweaty arms round you wherever you go.
The way she wears the sun is just gypsy.
And look how she leaves grown-ups lying about.'
And they all sat down to stare her out with eyes
Hot as fever with hostility.

One came over the hill, bullying the wind,
Dragging the trees out of each other's arms, swearing
At first so that the children could hardly believe it. No-one
Believed the children when they clapped he had come,
And was lying in the market place and panting.
The weathercock would have crowed, but was in his hand,
The yellow-haired harvest fallen asleep in his arms,
The sun was in his haversack with hares
Pheasants and singing birds all silent. Whereon
Parents pointed warningly to barometers.
But the small boys said: 'Wait till his friend gets here.'

Who came out of the sea, overturning the horses,
The hard captain, uniform over the hedges,
Drilling the air till it was threadbare, stamping
Up and down the fields with the nails in his boots
Till the cobbles of the fields were iron as nails.
Birds stood so stiff to attention it was death.
The sun was broken up for sabres. O he was a rough one.
And the little boys cried: 'Hurrah for the Jolly Roger.'
And ran out, merry as apples, to shoot each other
On landscapes of his icelocked battleships.

(First published *Granta*, 8 June 1954)

QUEST

I know clearly, as at a shout, when the time
Comes I am to ride out into the darkened air
Down the deserted streets. Eyes, terrified and hidden,
Are a weight of watching on me that I must ignore
And a charge in the air, tingling and crackling bluely
From the points and edges of my weapons, and in my hair.
I shall never see the monster that I go to kill.

And how it is ever to be killed, or where it is,
No-one knows, though men have ridden a thousand times
Against it as I now with my terror standing in my hair,
Hardly daring risk into my lungs this air the same
As carried the fire-belch and boistering of the thing's breath
Whose mere eye unlidded anywhere were a flame
To stir the marrow deep under most ignorant sleep.

I ride, with staring senses, but in
Complete blackness, knowing none of these faithful five
Clear to its coming till out of the blind-spot
Of the fitful sixth – crash on me the bellowing heaving
Tangle of a dragon all heads all jaws all fangs,
And though my weapons were lightning I am no longer alive.
My victory to raise this monster's shadow from my people

Shall be its trumpeting and clangorous flight
Over the moon's face to its white-hot icy crevasse
With fragments of my body dangling from its hundred mouths.

(First published *The Grapevine*, Feb. 1958)

LINES TO A NEWBORN BABY

Your cries flash anguish and gutter:
Nothing exists, and you drop through darkness.

What could you recognise here? Though your mother's milk already
Toughens you and prepares you to share

The amazement of the baby mandrill
Crying out as the eyeteeth push through,

The helplessness of the poppy,
The lust of the worm that begins and ends in the earth.

There has been some trouble here, you will find.
A gallery of grisly ancestors

Waits in the schoolroom. Perhaps
You came expecting an Eden

Of perpetual fruit and kindness –
Easily credible after your nothingness.

You will find a world tossed into shape
Like a hatful of twisted lots; locked in shape

As if grown in iron: a stalagmite
Of history under the blood-drip.

Here the hand of the moment, casual
As some cloud touching a pond with reflection,

Grips the head of man as Judith
Gripped that one finished with free will

And the winner's leisure, that one
Finished with begging to differ.

Things being as they are, though only by a hair's breadth,
The brain-stuff is some safety.

Limpets, clamped, suck their salty tongues
Under the sea's explosions;

And the snail that spreads its edge so wonderingly
Presents, to a touch, an instant

Coiled caul shell of comprehension.
Soon, you will smile.

2

Though you have come to be called ours
The breadth of America and England generally
Water the roots that flower your eye.

This is the circulating earth, where all limbs
And features constrain their atoms
As the sea-cloud its droplets.

Meltings of the Himalayas, the Congo's
Load of Africa are among the magi
That crowd to your crib with their gifts.

How much is ours when it comes to being born and begetting?
Your Adam was the sun, your Eve the rock,
And the serpent water.

We search for likenesses in your eyes and mouth —
Your little jackets have more of a person about them.
You have dispossessed us.

Some star glared through. We lean
Over you like masks hung up unlit
After the performance.

3

You roam with my every move
Alert as a survivor
Drifting from the Arctic circle
Who tunes his radio's crackle
(Salt-sodden it is, and troubled
By the whole electrical globe)

Till it coughs and clears its throat
To word of salvation —
Intercom conversation
Of some Grimsby fleet
Bearing down, hurrying
To fill England with stale herring.

(Part 1 first published *Texas Quarterly*, winter 1960; parts 2 & 3 as
'To F.R. at Six Months', *Western Daily Press*, 22 Feb. 1961)

O WHITE ELITE LOTUS

Sheer as a bomb – still you are all veins.
Heart-muscle's moulded you.
Rage of heart-muscle, which is the dead, too, with their revenge.

Steel, glass – ghost
Of a predator's mid-air body conjured
Into a sort of bottle.

Flimsy-light, like a squid's funeral bone.
Or a surgical model
Of the uterus of The Great Mother of The Gods.

Out of this world! One more revelation
From the purply, grumbling cloud
And vulcanism of blood.

The killer whale's avalanching emergence
From the yawn
Of boredom this time.

Out of this world, and cruising at a hundred!
But alive, as even in blueprint you were alive,
Even as the little amoeba, flexing its lens,

Ranging in along a death-ray, is alive
With the eye that stares out through it.

What eye stares out through you?

You visor
Of a nature whose very abandoned bones
Will be an outpost of weapons.

(First published *Critical Quarterly*, winter 1964)

CROW WAKES

I had exploded, a bombcloud, lob-headed, my huge fingers
Came feeling over the fields, like shadows.
I became smaller than water, I stained into the soil-crumble.
I became smaller.
My eyes fell out of my head and into an atom.
My right leg stood in the room raving at me like a dog.
I tried to stifle its bloody mouth with a towel
But it ran on ahead. I stumbled after it
A long way and came to a contraption like a trap
Baited with human intestines.
A stone drummed and an eye watched me out of a cat's anus.
I swam upstream, cleansed, in the snow-water, upstream.
Till I grew tired and turned over. I slept.
When I woke I could hear voices, many voices.
It was my bones all chattering together
At the high-tide mark, bedded in rubble, littered among shells
And gull feathers.
                    And the breastbone was crying:
'I begot a million and murdered a milliion:
I was a leopard.' And 'No, no, no, no,
We were a fine woman,' a rib cried.
'No, we were swine, we had devils, and the axe halved us,'
The pelvis was shouting. And the bones of the feet
And the bones of the hands fought: 'We were alligators,
We dragged some beauties under, we did not let go.'
And, 'We were suffering oxen,' and 'I was a surgeon,'
And 'We were a stinking clot of ectoplasm that suffocated a nun
Then lay for years in a cobbler's cellar.'
The teeth sang and the vertebrae were screeching
Something incomprehensible.
                    I tried to creep away—
I got up and ran. I tried to get up and run
But they saw me. 'It's him, it's him again. Get him.'
They came howling after me and I ran.
A freezing hand caught hold of me by the hair
And lifted me off my feet and set me high
Over the whole earth on a blazing star
Called

(First published as 'X': A Dialogue from *Eat Crow*,
Encounter, July 1965)

SMALL EVENTS

The old man's blood had spoken the word: 'Enough'.
Now nobody had the heart to see him go on.
His photographs were a cold mercy, there on the mantel.
So his mouth became a buttonhole and his limbs became wrapped iron.

Towards dying his eyes looked just above the things he looked at.
They were the poor rearguard on the beach
And turned, watering, with all his hope, from the smoke
To the sea for the Saviour

Who is useful only in life.

So, under a tree a tree-creeper, on dead grass sleeping—
It was blind, its eyes matte as blood-lice
Feeding on a raw face of disease.
I set it on dry grass, and its head fell forward, it died

Into what must have cupped it kindly.

And a grey, aged mouse, humped shivering
On a bare path, under November drizzle—
A frail parcel, delivered in damaging mail and still unclaimed,
Its contents no longer of use to anybody.

I picked it up. It was looking neither outward nor inward.
The tremendous music of its atoms
Trembled it on my fingers. As I watched it, it died.
A grey, mangy mouse, and seamed with ancient scars,

Whose blood had said: 'Sleep'.

So this year a swift's embryo, cracked too early from its fallen egg—
There, among mineral fragments,
The blind blood stirred,
Freed,

And, mystified, sank into hopeful sleep.

(First published *Recklings*, 1966)

THE BROTHER'S DREAM

In a blue, deadly brilliance, a parched madness of rock, of dust
And a pounding ache of blood
I go upward
           In a mountain world of fear
And leathery grass.
Of pine-trees, blasted like gibbets,
Holding out fistfuls of needles, bunched at the branch-end,
Bristling, still as coral.
A mountain is lifting me into terror.
With a clatter of little stones
I climb out onto eternity.
My shadow trails with me.
I have come here of my own will.
My voice is ready for any cries needed.
Like a grave, the cave-hole is watching,
In appalling quiet.
              I stand, part of the stillness—
Not the alert lizard's trigger stillness.
Stillness of some skulls, lying in the open.
And a lilac scent of rottenness
Hanging, like a veil, over the retina.
And a scream going on and on, too fierce for the ear-nerve,
Too deep in the air's stillness.
The masked hills trying to tell me, straining their stillness.
Flies meander in and out of the cave.
They settle on the sunny rocks to clean their wrists and behind their
                                 heads.
They settle on my shirt.
The rocks, that stare through the end,
Stare deep into me
With their final faces.
I am very frail, almost nothing.
Not here, yet here. A moment ago, not here.
Suddenly shouting into the cave: 'Come out!'
And 'Come out! Come out!' the echo
Brightens the hills like a bombflash.
Somewhere under the ground, the bear is at home.
The brain, flickering, quicker than any of these flies;
The bunched talons, contented;
The fangs, in their own kingdom,
And the happy blood—
The black well
Too deep to glitter

Where my shout, that clangs among open mountains,
Is already being digested.

For the pine-trees,
And for the sprawled hills, pasturing their shadows,
It is ordinary morning.

But the bear is filling the cave-mouth.
Its aimed gullet, point-blank, blasting
Into my face, the risen bear
Walks to embrace me,
With a scream like a weapon
Twisting into my midriff,
The rib-roofed gape measuring at my head,
And I see black lips, the widening curtains of saliva,
The small eyes brown and wet and full of evil
Locked in a fever of annihilation,
Lifted talons spread out like dungforks
Reaching to drag the sky down
Over my eyes, the bear crashes its mass
Onto me like a conifer

And at that moment I grip it.
I push away those eyes, the maniacs,
And the ripsaw scream,
The hatred like agony,
The jaws like a ghastly injury, widening, widening—
I grip it with my left hand by the shag
And cordage of its gullet and I hold it
At my locked arms length and with my dagger
In this other hand I rip it up
From the belly – up, up, up
I rip it. I am a steel madman.
The bear's scream is sawing at my brains
But I rip upward till the heart-muscle
Kicks at the dagger haft.
And I have opened a river.
And the bear slides from me like a robe
I have cut the cords of. I wade
Out of the daze.
                    A long while I stand
Like a man awakening.
                    The rocks
Wait for me, landmarks
Back to enormous mountain silence.

Time tries to move.
                    I watch blood
Crawling to touch my boot, slowly, blindly
Tasting the dust.

And the treetops stir.
The bluetits are busy and inquisitive.

But the rocks, and the engraved hills, are altered.
Their incomprehensible faces stare at me
With a new fear.

I come back down through the fir-trees
To my companions and the eyes of the dogs
That were afraid to come with me.
I'm bloody as a Caesarian babe – not my blood.
I send them up to strip the carcass.
I sleep, exhausted.

(Broadcast 22 Nov. 1965; first published
Poetry 1900–1965, ed. Macbeth, 1967)

BIRDSONG

First, love is a little bird
That sings in the orchard blossoms
I think it is a wren
It sings in the brambles and out of the wall
It sings out of the wall.

Then love is a fine falcon
Soaring O soaring, brother of the Archer
Or it rests inside the sun
While the whole earth kneels
      kneels
While the whole earth kneels.

Love becomes a cruel leopard
And its voice rips through the locks
A black bagful of emeralds
It leaps to the woods with the crying body
It leaps with the crying body.

Love becomes a nightly owl
All the night it dooms in your ear
All the day it hides in the wood
Gripping skulls in its talons
      talons
Gripping skulls in its talons.

And then love is a madonna
Deep, deep the river of her peace
And drowned are the floating hands
That did not even wave goodbye
That did not wave goodbye.

But love like a circus returns
The elephants stand on their heads
Small eye and huge anus
And the tigers offer their gullets
      gullets
The tigers offer their gullets.

And love is careful stretcher
For an angel, newly fallen,
With a wound as wide as the world
Where a man dare hardly breathe
      breathe
Where a man dare hardly breathe.

And love is a tourniquet
And the tourniquet a garotte
O love is a song from the lifer's cell
By day it is breaking the stones
      stones
By day it is breaking the stones.

Till love becomes a crow
Upon a desolation
The crow makes a drum
The crow begins to dance
      dance
The crow begins to dance.

There is nothing else
The crow has gone mad
Upon a desolation
It drums and it dances
      dances
Upon a desolation.

While the clouds above
Roll their great bodies together
And maybe it is love moves them
They do not have to live
      live
They do not live have to live.

(First published *London Magazine*, Sept. 1966)

FIGHTING FOR JERUSALEM

The man who seems to be dead

With Buddha in his smile
With Jesus in his stretched out arms
With Mahomet in his humbled forehead

With his feet in hell
With his hands in heaven
With his back to the earth

Is escorted
To his eternal reward
By singing legions

Of what seems to be flies

(First published *Times Literary Supplement*, 9 Oct. 1970)

SONG OF WOE

Once upon a time
There was a person
Wretched in every vein —
His heart pumped woe.
Trying to run it clear
His heart pumped only more muddy woe.
He looked at his hands, and they were woe.
His legs there, long, bony and remote
Like the legs of a stag in wet brambles,
They also were woe.
His shirt over the chair at night
Was like a curtain over the finale
Of all things.

He walked out onto a field
And the trees were grief —
Cemetery non-beings.
The clouds bore their burdens of grief
Into non-being.
The flowers
The birds, the spiders
Staring into space like sacrifices
Clung with madman's grip
To the great wheel of woe.

So he flung them out among the stars —
Trees, toppling clouds, birds and insects,
He was rid of them.
He flung away the field and its grass,
The whole grievous funeral,
His clothes and their house,
And sat naked on the naked earth
And his mouth filled his eyes filled
With the same muddy woe.

So he abandoned himself, his body, his blood —
He left it all lying on the earth
And held himself resolute
As the earth rolled slowly away
Smaller and smaller away
Into non-being.

And there at last he had it
As his woe struggled out of him
With a terrific cry

Staring after the earth
And stood out there in front of him,
His howling transfigured double.

And he was rid of it.
And he wept with relief,
With joy, laughing, he wept —

And at last, tear by tear,
Something came clear.

(First published *Critical Quarterly*, summer 1970)

EXISTENTIAL SONG

Once upon a time
There was a person
Running for his life.
This was his fate.
It was a hard fate.
But Fate is Fate.
He had to keep running.

He began to wonder about Fate
And running for dear life.
Who? Why?
And was he nothing
But some dummy hare on a racetrack?

At last he made up his mind.
He was nobody's fool.
It would take guts
But yes he could do it.
Yes yes he could stop.
Agony! Agony
Was the wrenching
Of himself from his running.
Vast! And sudden
The stillness
In the empty middle of the desert.

There he stood – stopped.
And since he couldn't see anybody
To North or to West or to East or to South
He raised his fists
Laughing in awful joy
And shook them at the Universe

And his fists fell off
And his arms fell off
He staggered and his legs fell off

It was too late for him to realize
That this was the dogs tearing him to pieces
That he was, in fact, nothing
But a dummy hare on a racetrack

And life was being lived only by the dogs.

(First published *London Magazine*, July/Aug. 1970)

ANECDOTE

There was a man
Who got up from a bed that was no bed
Who pulled on his clothes that were no clothes
(A million years whistling in his ear)
And he pulled on shoes that were no shoes
Carefully jerking the laces tight – and tighter
To walk over floors that were no floor
Down stairs that were no stairs
Past pictures that were no pictures
To pause
To remember and forget the night's dreams that were no dreams

And there was the cloud, primeval, the prophet;
There was the rain, its secret writing, the water-kernel
Of the tables of the sun;
And there was the light with its loose rant;
There were the birch trees, insisting and urging.
And the wind, reproach upon reproach.
At the table he cupped his eyes in his hands
As if to say grace

Avoiding his reflection in the mirror
Huddled to read news that was no news
(A million years revolving on his stomach)
He entered the circulation of his life
But stopped reading feeling the weight of his hand
In the hand that was no hand
And he did not know what to do or where to begin
To live the day that was no day

And Brighton was a picture
The British Museum was a picture
The battleship off Flamborough was a picture
And the drum-music the ice in the glass the mouths
Stretched open in laughter
That was no laughter
Where what was left of a picture

In a book
Under a monsoon downpour
In a ruinous mountain hut

From which years ago his body was lifted by a leopard.

(First published *Northwest Review*, fall-winter 1967–8)

CROW FAILS

'Look,' said God, 'I've had an inspiration,'
And he showed Crow his Creation –

Nailed up by its four corners,
With a crown of fatal and firepoint everlastings,
With blood and water coming out,
With its gape-silence, after the birth-cry.

'You can have it,' said God. 'Only don't spoil it.'
'It is beautiful,' said Crow.

                            And he wore it on a chain,
And he ate it and he drank it,
He did his courting in its secret places,
He strung it and strummed it and sang to it

And he rode it through space
But vain and again vain
Were his attempts to defend it

From the black flock of God's second thoughts.   (Unpublished)

CROW COMPROMISES

God flung a glamour—
And the Cosmos became a clockwork.
Crow happily chimed.
Or, when he got tired of chiming, he pointed.
This cosmos stirred him to the depths.

God flung another glamour—
The Cosmos became an optical oscillation
Between Being and Nothing, Nothing and Being—
Crow ducked under his brain, he hid in his body,
Hung his limbs with black and danced to his drum

Adoring the Serpent of Intestine
Coiled in the tree of bone and crowned with teeth

Alias the Serpent of Begetting
Coiled in the crotch and crowned with prickly ecstasies

Propitiating with feasts and foolish songs
With leaves of blood and a woman on a rude altar

The Faceless

God with Two Faces.   (Unpublished)

A LUCKY FOLLY

Crow heard the maiden screaming – and here came the dragon.
He fantasied building a rocket and getting out fast —
Not a hope.
O for a castle – battlements. A pinnacle prison.
Too late. The dragon surrounded him like a seaquake
And the maiden cried lamentably.
Crow cut holes in his nose. He fingered this flute,
Dancing, with an occasional kick at his drum.

The dragon was dumbfounded – he was manic
For music. He began to grin.
He too began to dance. And in horror and awe
The maiden danced with him, incredulous.
'O do not stop,' she whispered, 'O do not stop.'
So the three danced – and Crow dared not stop —

To the creaking beak pipe and the kicked drum.

But, at last, Crow's puff ran out and he stopped.
The maiden paled.
But the dragon wept. The dragon licked Crow's foot
He slobbered Crow's fingers —
'More, more' he cried, and 'Be my god.'

(First published *Workshop* 10, 1970)

A CROW HYMN

Flame works at the sun, the sun at the earth
The moon works at the sea the sea
Works at the moon and works at the earth
And the wind at the sea and the earth
And the seasons work at all life
And the sun works at all life
The earth works at all life

And all life works at death

The queen ant works at eggs
The maneater works at its own life
The mosquito works at its own life
Life works at life using men and women

Atoms work at the flame that works at the sun
That works at the seasons and the winds
And the sea and the earth
And men and women who work at life and at death

The leaves working at life and at death
The viper working at life and at death
And the blowfly and the labour
Of weddings bells and the hungry man
Working at life and at death
Are not busier than the stars

All are parts of a strange engine
Flying through space, with the power of all the suns

A huge insect, towards marriage

(First published *A Crow Hymn*, Sceptre Press, 1970)

BONES

Bones is a crazy pony.
Moon-white – star-mad.
All skull and skeleton.

Her hooves pound. The sleeper awakes with a cry.

Who has broken her in?
Who has mounted her and come back
Or kept her?

She lifts under them, the snaking crest of a bullwhip.

Hero by hero they go —
Grimly get astride
And their hair lifts.

She laughs, smelling the battle – their cry comes back.

Who can live her life?
Every effort to hold her or turn her falls off her
Like rotten harness.

Their smashed faces come back, the wallets and the watches.

And this is the stunted foal of the earth —
She that kicks the cot
To flinders and is off.

(First published *The Listener*, 1 Oct. 1970)

SONGS AGAINST THE WHITE OWL

The white owl got its proof weapons
Bequests of its victims.

And it got those eyes that look beyond life
From fluorescence of old corpses.

It snatched its bones as it could
From the burnings of blizzard.

Death loaned it a belly.
It wears a face it found on the sea.

Twisting sinews of last breaths
It bent these oddments together.

With a ghostly needle of screech
It sewed a coat of the snow

From the knobbed and staring ice
Wringing blood and fat.

O stare Owl stare
Through your glacier wall
At a fatal terrain
Of weeping snow and the leaf of the birch

Where I spoon your soul from a bowl
And my song steams.

(First published *London Magazine*, July/Aug. 1970)

SNOW SONG

In the beginning of beginning
A sea of blood: it heaved under hair.
Stamped hooves, hoisted antlers.
Ran. Firstman caught it. Flayed it.
Bit into its heart. It was a bear
Running roaring. He caught it. Flayed it.
Bit into its heart. It was a salmon
Slipping through walls of water. He caught it
Ate its heart. But spared its eggs.

Night: bones and dung.
He scraped the blood off his muscles.
Faced upwards. Slept.
Floated his ghost clear of bloody fingers
Hung it on the stars.
Mother Of All Things – she washed it.
He awoke with a new life.

The Red Fox was afraid: he feared for his hide.
He bit the Elk: it became a dead tree at the earth's edge.
He bit the salmon: it sank anchor
To sea mud.
He bit the bear it slept a snarl
Of stony roots.

In skin too small for his bones
With a twist of rotten grass in his gut
Firstman wept.
And the Mother Of All Things wept.
And the Fox laughed under the earth.

Then the Mother Of All Things swelled and the bloodsea split
Its plenty for man's hunger.
But the Fox gripped shut her belly.
He seemed to be licking a stone.
His fangs gripped shut her belly.
He seemed to be crunching a tomtit
Or gnawing at a piece of old leather.
So his teeth spittled and the grip grinned
And nothing could be born.

And so, Firstman wept on his rock of hunger
And the Mother Of All Things wept.
Her tears fell. Only her tears fell. Nothing could be born.
Only the tears fell, freezing as they fell

Faltering over the earth
Herding towards Firstman 'We love you, we love you.'

They licked at his mouth. They nuzzled his eyes.
They nestled into his hands.

But the Fox grinned in heaven.

Man's cry sharpened. The snow deepened.

(First published *Crow Wakes*, April 1971)

CROW'S SONG ABOUT GOD

Somebody is sitting
Under the gatepost of heaven
Under the lintel
On which are written the words: 'Forbidden to the living'
A knot of eyes, eyeholes, lifeless, the life-shape
A rooty old stump, aground in the ooze
Of some putrid estuary,
His fingernails broken and bitten,
His hair vestigial and purposeless, his toenails useless and deformed,
His blood filtering between
In the coils of his body, like the leech life
In a slime and ochre pond
Under the smouldering collapse of a town dump,
His brain a hacked ache, a dull flint,
His solar plexus crimped in his gut, hard,
A plastic carnation
In a gutter puddle
Outside the registry office—
Somebody
Sitting under the gatepost of heaven

Head fallen forward
Like the nipped head of somebody strung up to a lamp-pst
With a cheese-wire, or an electric flex,
Or with his own belt,
Trousers round his ankles,
Face gutted with shadows, like a village gutted with bombs,
Weeping plasma,
Weeping whisky,
Weeping egg-white,
He has been choked with raw steak it hangs black over his chin,
Somebody
Propped in the gateway of heaven
Clinging to the tick of his watch
Under a dream muddled as vomit
That he cannot vomit, he cannot wake up to vomit,
He only lifts his head and lolls it back
Against the gatepost of heaven

Like a broken sunflower
Eyesockets empty
Stomach laid open
To the inspection of the stars

The operation unfinished
(The doctors ran off, there was some other emergency)
Sweat cooling on his temples
Hands hanging – what would be the use now
Of lifting them?
They hang
Clumps of bloodclot, varicose and useless
As afterbirths—

But God sees nothing of this person
His eyes occupied with His own terror
As he mutters
My Saviour is coming,
He is coming, who does not fear death,
He shares his skin with it,
He gives it his cigarettes,
He cuts up its food, he feeds it like a baby,
He keeps it warm he cherishes it
In the desolations of space,
He dresses it up in his best, he calls it his life—

He is coming.

(First published *Poems: Fainlight, Hughes, Sillitoe,*
Rainbow Press, April 1971)

CROW'S SONG ABOUT ENGLAND

Once upon a time there was a girl
Who tried to give her mouth
It was snatched from her and her face slapped
She tried to give her eyes
They were knocked to the floor the furniture crushed them
She tried to give her breasts
They were cut from her and canned
She tried to give her cunt
It was produced in open court she was sentenced

She stole everything back

She was mad with pain she humped into a beast
She changed sex he came back

Where he saw her mouth he stabbed with a knife
Where he saw her eyes he stabbed likewise
Where he saw her breasts her cunt he stabbed

He was sentenced

He escaped lobotomised he changed sex
Shrunk to a little girl she came back

She tried to keep her mouth
It was snatched from her and her face slapped
She tried to keep her eyes
They were knocked to the floor and furniture crushed them
She tried to keep her breasts
They were cut from her and canned
She tried to keep her cunt
It was produced in open court she was sentenced

She did life

(First published: *Poems: Fainlight, Hughes, Sillitoe*,
Rainbow Press, April 1971)

THE NEW WORLD

I
It is not too long you'll be straddling the rocket,
My children,
The rocket that will carry you far
To crash you on to an unknown star.

It's a long, long time, little children,
With the moon in your mouth
Riding the bones
Of Eohippus
Over the craters
Into the sunset.

2
When the star was on her face
I held her by the hair
Higher than the moon
She cleared the gate of bone.

We rode into the land of light
Where trees beat their boughs
As at the birthroom midnight window
The dead make hopeless mouths.

All the earth's light was our cloak
We wrapped ourselves. We left
Naked to night the frosty mud
The bare twigs, and the shores.

3
A star stands on her forehead.
In her moving hands
She has cupped the moon.
Her smile says it does not burn.

The earth has been woven
Its animals and flowers
And that is her dress.
It is under her dress
You must seek the sun.

Emptiness of space
Makes her the only Island
Where I can live.

This is the new world.
These are its seven wonders.

4
I said goodbye to earth
I stepped into the wind
Which entered the tunnel of fire
Beneath the mountain of water.

I arrived at light
Where I was shadowless,
I saw the snowflake crucified
On the nails of nothing.

I heard the atoms praying
To enter his kingdom,
To be broken like bread
On a warm sill, and to weep.

5
The street was empty and stone
Like the Himalayas.
The moon was like a low door,
In half sleep I stepped through it.
The stair toppled niagara
I rose floating with the dust.
The room was like a grave
I was the one life left on earth.
The bed was like a star
Like a soul, a singing.
I reached, I groped
Through all of dark space.

I fell asleep
Shaken with laughter of foxes
Who had put something in my hand.

Centuries, centuries later
I woke.

The ice age leaned on the window.

6
Where did we go?
I cannot find us.

Only a tie, draped on the sun.
Only a shoe, dangling on the moon.

We did not land on a star.
Where did we go?

I roam the corridors of space
But the black between the stars

Is like the honeymooner's door,
Locked night and day.   (Set by Gordon Crosse in 1969; first published
                                      Three Choirs Festival Programme, 1972)

AN ALCHEMY

War in the egg
            Lustig the Moor
Aaron began it
            When Salt Tamora
In full blush of Lucretia
            Dawned on Leontes
Icicle Angelo
            Died Adonis' agony
Butchered by Richard
            The lineal Boar
Who darkened darkness
            With ravishing strides
And an Ass's horn
            To gore Titania
Queen of Fays
            For a pound of blood
Stinging Prince Hal
            To Portia's answer
Who defrocked
            Moses' Serpent
On the Hebrew Tree
            Anathalamia
Collapsed as Falstaff
            In the Boar's Head
The Knight of Venus
            After his Feast
Under Herne's acorns,
            Belated as bloated
A mushroom Caesar
            The wounds of Rome
Mouthing prophesy
            From which flittered
A mourning dove

Ancestral her sorcery
            Helena the Healer
Diana her owl side
            Outwitted Angelo
Who walled up Ophelia
            She wept to Othello
Willow Willow
            As he lopped his rivals

A Fortinbras steeled
                    To close with Gertrude
Who Came again

Desdemona rising
                    The Nun of Vienna
From killing her swine
                    The ring-dove's advent
Hamlet's muse
                    Hamlet's madness
Soused by Tempest
                    To Venus's Island
With her weird sisters
                    The blue Hag Hecate
Deflecting the dagger
                    With some rough magic
Into the Sanctum
                    Of Saintly Duncan
Double Macbeth
                    The crown's contagion
Drawn by the blade of Tarquin
                    Cordelia guiding
Blinded Gloucester
                    cutting to the brain
Then Lear saw nine-fold
                    The under-crown lightning
The Boar's Moons mangling
                    His sainted flesh
Lear Furens

He snapped its fang
                    It was Regan's body
He plucked out Goneril
                    Still it gored him
His third effort it vanished
                    And it had been his nothing
It had been his Joy
                    His truth beyond telling
In a warm body
                    Rock-dove of Aphrodite
Leaving a feather only

That Timon damned with gold

That carried Coriolanus
                    Crushed from Caesar
It was Old Nile's Serpent
                    Moon-browed Isis
Bride and Mother
                    Mourning a Rome
Leontes banished
                    Lear redivivus
Phoenix-Posthumous
                    Found breath in Marina
Redeemed all Tempest
                    His kiss of life
Stirred the Turtle
                    Of the waters of amnios
The lunar cauldron

Then black Venus
                    double tongued
Swine-uddered Sycorax
                    Lilith the night-crow

Slid from the Tree

Released the Rainbow
                    Breasted Dove
With a leaf of light
                    Miranda with a miracle
To Adam Adonis

And sank
        In the crucible
                    Tiamat
                        The Mother
The Scales
        The Coil
                Of the Matter
                        Deeper
Than ever plummet
                With Prospero's bones
And the sounding Book.

(First published *Poems for Shakespeare* 2, 1973)

THE LAMENTABLE HISTORY OF THE HUMAN CALF

O there was a maiden, a maiden, a maiden
And she was a knock-out.
Will you be my bride, I sighed, I cried, I was ready to die.
And she replied, what did she reply?

'Give me your nose, for a kiss' she sighed. 'It's a fair pawn!'
So I sliced off my nose
And she fed it to her puppy.

Lady, are you satisfied?

'O give me your ears, to share my fears, in the night, in my bed,
    where nobody hears, my darling!'
So I sliced off my ears
And she fed them to her puppy.

'Now let me have your legs, lest they carry you far, O my darling,
    far from my side,' she cried.
So I chopped off my legs and she gave them to her puppy.

Lady, are you happy?

'O I want your heart, your heart, your heart, will it never be mine?
    Let me hold it,' she cried.
So I sliced me wide, and I ripped out the part
And she fed it to her puppy.

Lady, are you satisfied?

'O give me your liver, or I'll leave you for ever.
Give me your tongue, your tongue, your tongue
Lest it whisper to another.
Give me your lungs that hurt you with their sighs,
She cried.
With tears of love, with tears of love, I hacked out those dainties
And she fed them to her puppy.

Lady, are you satisfied?

'O give me your eyes, your rolling eyes,
That splash me with their tears, that go roving after others.
And give me your brains, that give you such pains
With doubting of my love, with doubting of my love.
And give me your arms, that all night long when you're far from
    my side they'll clasp me, clasp me'
And she cried, 'I'll be your bride!'
So I tore out my eyes and I gouged out my brains and I sawed off
    my arms and I gave them to my darling

And she fed them to her puppy.

Lady, are you satisfied?

'No, give me your skin, that holds you in,
O pour out your blood in a bowl and let me drink it, be mine.
O slice off your flesh and I'll nibble your bones, my darling!'
So I dragged off my skin and I brimmed it with my blood and I rolled up
    my flesh and I basketted my bones and I laid them at her door and
    she cried and she cried

Puppy, puppy, puppy.

Lady, I said, though I'm nothing but a soul, I have paid down the price,
    now come to be my bride.
But the puppy had grown, the puppy was a dog, was a big fat bitch, and
    my darling wept

'Take my dog' she wept, 'O take it.
You are only a soul, how can we be married?
So take my dog for this dog it is my soul,
I give you my soul!' And she gave me her dog.

Lady, are you satisfied?

Now I live with a bitch an old sour bitch now I live with a bitch a bitch
    a bitch so I live with a bitch an old sour bitch and there was a maiden
    a maiden a maiden . . .

(First published *New Departures*, 7/8, 9/10, 1975)

THE ADVOCATE

Not the birth-cry
But the wound in the air – its blooed-edged breathing.

Not the stony engines and trembling wings of the Mass
But the self, staring, sightless, dropping through darkness.

Not your days – their alternating flash
Of certainty and doubt, equally polished,

Your millionaire honesty in paper money

But the speechless upside-down corpse
Hanging at your back
Who has paid in kind.

I am his advocate. I am the balance.

I am hypodermic. My first word
Will start the truth shining from your pores.

Here I sit on your brow, a mosquito,
Totting the count.

(Unpublished)

TWO DREAMS IN THE CELL

I

I sat

With the armour of light on my eyes.
And my brain tight
In the status quo, buckled with fixed stars.

My legs at ease, ready for sniper questions.
The trusty wall for my lamp.
My fingers

Gauntletted with studded words.
What had been forged by the rising and the setting sun
Bright across my knees, a vigil blade.

And my spine
Deep into the sub-soil, immovable
Like a stake I was tied to,

Waiting for the demon.

2

Feathers on end, scorched, blood-spiky,
Shrapnel-jagged, Nebuchadnezzar
Lifted his eagle claw from the burning.

Bone-splinters stuck out of charred bandages.
He looked like a Guy Fawkes at dawn
Rising from the rained-out bonfire.

His grin cracked and blood shone.
'St John Chrysostom,' he said
'Stole a saintly kiss from God's mother

But I paid for it.'

He dug up earth and began to eat it

As if he were alone in the forest.

(Unpublished)

YOUR MOTHER'S BONES WANTED TO SPEAK, THEY COULD NOT

You thought they were clods of dirt

Which cannot argue, being dumb as bones,
The dirty bones that are broken to crusts of dirt.

They are faceless, like the smell of smoke.
And beyond appeal
Like electrons. Unarguable
Like the signature on a warrant —

Which is wholly human
Yet wholly unarguable.

Like the whole body – wholly human
Wholly unarguable.

Under the doomsday light of your mother's bones
Your paltriest words, your fleetest imaginations

Move like chains
Like bullets

Like iron pens
Carving your signature in the papery flesh.

(Unpublished)

SHE IS THE ROCK

The air is that sort of rock
As well as the mountain
Which sprouts grass.

Your thirst flies
But the sun's
Elixir
Only roasts your mouth black finally.

You fall
Again into her to be healed
In the end by her inner stoniness, as
Before you were delivered
From her globe of egg.

What happens on earth
Is the struggle of as-if-hewn stone
To prove
You freed yourself, yourself yourself's
World-mark lonely maker.

She sends faces to trap you
And drugs between legs
To quicken
The first and last addiction
And lay you in the bonds of dark bliss.

Resting, as even eagles
Rest
In the grave of eagles.

(Unpublished)

LIGHT

Eased eyes open, showed leaves.

Eyes, laughing and childish
Ran among flowers of leaves
And looked at light's bridge
Which led from leaf, upward, and back down to leaf.

Eyes, uncertain
Tested each semblance.
Light seemed to smile.

Eyes ran to the limit
To the last leaf
To the least vein of the least flower-leaf.

Light smiled
And smiled and smiled.

Eyes
Darkened

Afraid suddenly
That this was all there was to it.

(First published *Granta*, April 1976)

SKIN

Made out the company of grass.

Grass pricked it
In its language
Smelling fellow earth, but nervous.

Skin tightened
Suppressing its reflex
Shudder of dawn

Thinking, it is beginning – first fingerings
At my knots
Then will come rendings, and drenchings of world-light

And my naked joy
Will be lifted out, with shouts of joy —

And if that is the end of me
Let it be the end of me.

(First published *Granta*, April 1976)

ABBREVIATIONS
USED IN THE NOTES

Page references are to the English edition unless otherwise stated.

WORKS BY TED HUGHES

Hawk *The Hawk in the Rain*, Faber & Faber 1957; US edition Harper, 1957.
Lupercal *Lupercal*, Faber & Faber 1960; US edition Harper, 1960.
Wodwo *Wodwo*, Faber & Faber 1967; US edition Harper & Row, 1967.
Poetry *Poetry in the Making*, Faber & Faber, 1967; US edition as *Poetry Is*, Doubleday, 1970.
Odedipus *Seneca's Oedipus*, adapted by Ted Hughes, Faber & Faber, 1969; US edition Doubleday, 1972.
Coming *The Coming of the Kings*, Faber & Faber, 1970; US edition as *The Tiger's Bones*, Viking, 1974.
Crow *Crow*, Faber & Faber, 1970; US edition Harper & Row, 1971.
Season Songs *Season Songs*, Viking, 1975; UK edition Faber & Faber, 1976.
Gaudete *Gaudete*, Faber & Faber, 1977; US edition Harper & Row, 1977.
Cave Birds *Cave Birds*, Faber & Faber, 1978; US edition Viking, 1978.
Remains *Remains of Elmet*, Faber & Faber, 1979; US edition Harper & Row, 1979.
Moortown *Moortown*, Faber & Faber, 1979; US edition Harper & Row, 1980.
Choice *A Choice of Shakespeare's Verse*, Faber & Faber, 1971; US edition as *With Fairest Flowers While Summer Lasts*, Doubleday, 1971.
Myth 1 'Myth and Education', *Children's Literature in Education*, no. 1, 1970.
Myth 2 'Myth and Education', *Writers, Critics and Children*, ed. G. Fox *et al.*, Heinemann, 1976; US edition Agathon Press, 1976.

OTHERS

Pilinszky *Janos Pilinszky: Selected Poems*, translated by Ted Hughes and Janos Csokits, Carcanet, 1976.
Popa *Vasko Popa: Collected Poems, 1943–1976*, translated by Anne Pennington with an introduction by Ted Hughes, Carcanet, 1978.
Sagar *The Art of Ted Hughes*, by Keith Sagar, Cambridge University Press, second edition, 1978.
Faas *Ted Hughes: the Unaccomodated Universe*, by Ekbert Faas, with selected critical writings by Ted Hughes and two interviews, Black Sparrow Press, Santa Barbara, 1980.

CHAPTER 3

1 The Apocrypha, I Maccabees, 1:38−9.
2 Daniel, x: 7−10.
3 Daniel, x: 3.
4 Daniel, VIII: 17.
5 'The Movement' is a kind of critical shorthand for what was never a recognised school of poetry − rather a coherence of attitude. By the mid-1950s, these poets had taken over many of the avenues of poetry publishing. *Delta 8*, spring 1956, devotes most of its pages to a discussion of the situation. Christopher Levenson's introductory article gives the reason for this as being a deep sense of unease at the swiftness with which the *coup d'etat* had been effected and apprehension as to the attitudes to life and art of these poets, which he, and others, regarded as 'negative and dangerous'. In the following issue, *Delta 9*, Donald Davie replies, and supports the assumption of a *coup d'etat* having taken place. Davie deplores the fact that at a time when they are most in need of exacting criticism, these poets have been place in the position of 'having splendidly and ultimately arrived'.
6 A view he still holds. This phrase comes from 'The Right Lines', an essay in *The Abomination of Moab* (London, 1979), p. 270.
7 Robert Conquest, 'Humanities', *New Lines*, p. 79.
8 *Ibid.*
9 John Holloway, 'Warning to a Guest', *ibid*, p. 16.
10 Kenneth Allot, *Penguin Book of Contemporary Verse* (Harmondsworth, 1962), p. 35.
11 *New Lines*, p. XIV.
12 Kingsley Amis, 'Against Romanticism', *New Lines*, p. 45.
13 *Ibid.*
14 Donald Davie, *Purity of Diction in English Verse* (London, 1952), Davie argues for 'Urbanity' in poetry: Mathew Arnold's 'tone and spirit of the centre' (p. 87) as opposed to the 'provincial' − not of any actual metropolis or province but a 'spiritual quality' (p. 88). The achievement of urbanity becomes a moral achievement: 'a product of integrity and equilibrium in the poet' (p. 88).
15 Faas, p. 201.
16 'Creon's Mouse', *Brides of Reason* (Fantasy 1955), *Collected Poems 1950−1970*, London 1972), p. 9.
17 *New Lines*, p. 67.
18 *Ibid.*, p. XV.
19 The description of the nuclear bomb by J. Robert Oppenheimer, one of its creators.
20 *Wilfred Owen: Collected Letters* (Oxford, 1967), Letter 664.
21 *Collected Poems* (London 1967), p. 38.

22 George Steiner, 'Humane Literacy', (1963), in *Language and Silence* (London, 1967), p. 22.
23 *Death in Life*, p. 541.
24 Edwin Muir, 'The Day Before the Last Day', *Selected Poems* (London, p. 22).
25 See *Poetry of the 1950's* for Larkin's statement that he does not want recourse to 'tradition' or a 'common myth-kitty' and, 'Four Conversations', *London Magazine*, vol. 4 no. 8, 1964, for a confirmation of his attitude: ' . . . to me the whole of the ancient world, the whole of classical and bibilical mythology means very little, and I think that using them today not only fills poems full of dead spots but dodges the writer's duty to be original'.
26 *Death in Life*, p. 541.
27 'A Woman Unconscious', *Lupercal*.
28 Hughes, in a review of *Men Who March Away: Poems of the First World War*, in *The Listener*, 5 August, 1965. Hughes calls this war 'our number one national ghost'. It is more than a national ghost. The imagery of the First World War pervades the literature of the Second World War. Norman Mailer's *The Naked and the Dead* starts 'Every hundred yards Cummings steps up onto the parapet and peers cautiously into No Man's Land.' Kurt Vonnegut's experience of the fire bombing of Dresden is encapsulated in his Billy Pilgrim's catching the stench of 'roses and mustard gas'. Eliot in 'East Coker' (1940) uses the image of trench warfare to describe the writing of poetry:
>   And so each new venture
>   Is a new beginning, a raid on the inarticulate
>   With shabby equipment always deteriorating
>   In the general mess of imprecision of feeling,
>   Undisciplined squads of emotion . . .
>   . . .
>   There is only the fight to recover what has been lost
>   And found and lost again and again . . .
29 *Ibid.*
30 *Choice*, p. 198.
31 Faas, p. 202.
32 The phrase recurs in the New Testament in Matthew xxiv:15 and in Mark xiii:14, but in both cases is a reference back. See Matthew: 'When therefore ye shall see the abomination of desolation, spoken of by Daniel the prophet, stand in the holy place . . .'.
33 Blake, *Jerusalem I*, 10: lines 7ff.
34 Blake, *Milton II*, 48: lines 1ff.
35 Blake, the closing sentence of *A Vision of the Last Judgement*, Nonesuch *Blake*, p. 652: 'I question not my Corporeal or Vegetative Eye any more than I would Question a Window concerning a Sight. I loook thro' it & not with it.'
36 Myth 1, p. 56.
37 *Ibid*, p. 60.
38 *Ibid*.
39 'Egg-Head', *Hawk*.
40 Myth 2.
41 C. G. Jung, 'Archaic Man', *Modern Man in Search of a Soul* (London, 1961), p. 144 (first published 1933).
42 'Desk poet', an interview with John Horder, *The Guardian*, 23 March 1965.
43 'The Jaguar', *Chequer*, Nov. 1954. The fourth and fifth stanzas of this

version are:

> As if in a sudden frenzy: slavering jaw hanging,
> The crazed eye satisfied to be blind in fire,
> By the bang of blood in the brain deaf the ear.
> But what holds them, from corner to corner swinging,

> Swivelling the ball of his heel on the polished spot,
> Jerking his head up in surprise at the bars,
> Has not hesitated in the millions of years,
> And like life-prisoners they through bars stare out.

44 Faas, p. 199.

45 'Myth' 2, p. 90.

46 *Ibid*, p. 85.

47 'Ghost Crabs', *Wodwo*.

48 *Gaudete*, Epilogue, poem 2.

49 Hughes has said that he is in broad agreement with many of the findings of Jungian depth psychology. The 'Myth and Education' essays bear this out. Eric Neumann's *Depth Psychology and the New Ethic* contains many of the theses that Hughes proposes in his work. Relevant to the argument at hand is the Appendix to this book: Neumann holds that it is the projection of the shadow side of the psyche, and scapegoat psychology engendered by the 'old ethic', which 'leads to wars and the extermination of groups holding minority opinions'. See also Jung, *The Undiscovered Self*, p. 101: 'If a world-wide consciousness could arise that all division and all antagonisms are due to the splitting of opposites in the psyche, then one would really know where to attack. But if even the smallest and most personal stirrings in the human soul – so insignificant in themselves – remain as unconscious and unrecognised as they have hitherto, they will go on accumulating and produce mass groupings and mass movements which cannot be subjected to reasonable control or manipulated to a good end.'

50 Myth 2, p. 58.

51 Myth 2, p. 91.

52 Faas, p. 190.

53 Hughes, *The Head of Gold*, written for the 'Living Language' series of the B.B.C. Home Service (Schools). Broadcast on the 21, 28 September and 5 October 1967. The work is based, loosely, on the canonical Daniel, and reference is made to the Apocryphal Bel and the Dragon.

54 Undoubtedly, the strangest aspect of the Book of Daniel is Nebuchadnezzar's seemingly unreasonable demand that his dream be interpreted when even he cannot remember it. Daniel redreams the king's dream. The inescapable conclusion one draws is that the poet of Daniel anticipates Jung's *collective unconscious* by some two thousand years.

Donald Davie's attitude to this concept is one of suspicion: '. . . from Jung the poet learns about the hypothetical "collective unconscious"; and an uncritical reading of some of the older anthropologists or of Robert Graves' *The White Goddess* suggests that if the poet, looking for symbols, can dredge deep enough in his own mind, he comes across the archetypes, eternally recurrent myths and symbols which underlie all Christian and other mythologies just as they underlie the dreams of the sleeping individual. We have to be careful here . . .' 'Professor Heller and the Boots' (March 1954), in *The Poet in the Imaginary Museum* (Manchester, 1977), p. 22.

55 Blake, Notes on 'Observations on the Deranged Manifestations of the Mind, or Insanity', Spurzheim (Nonesuch *Blake*, p. 817). 'Cowper came to me and said: "O that I were insane always. I will never rest. Can you not make me truly insane? I will never rest till I am so. O that in the bosom of God I was hid. You retain health and yet are as mad as any of us all – over us all – mad as a refuge from unbelief – from Bacon, Newton and Locke'.

56 Hughes, 'Desk poet'.

57 Faas, p. 204.

58 Myth 2, pp. 91–2 (Faas, p. 191–192).

59 Blake, *Jerusalem I*, 1: lines 18–21.

CHAPTER 4

1 T. S. Eliot, 'Verse pleasant and unpleasant', *The Egoist*, 1918, quoted in John Press, *A Map of Modern English Verse* (Oxford, 1969), p. 118.

2 Ted Hughes, sleeve notes to *Poetry International 1969*, Argo MPR 262–3.

3 Ezra Pound, *Literary Essays* (Norfolk, Conn. and London, 1954), pp. 3–14. In his Cheltenham Lecture of October 1977, Hughes referred to poetry as 'a very suspect way of speaking', prone to 'too many flourishes' and 'over flamboyant'.

4 Zbigniew Herbert, quoted in Introduction to *Selected Poems*, translated by John Carpenter and Bogdana Carpenter (Oxford, 1977), p. XII.

5 Ted Hughes, Introduction to *Selected Poems: Keith Douglas* (London, 1964), pp. 12–13.

6 Zbigniew Herbert, quoted in *World Authors 1950–1970*, ed. John Wakeman (New York, 1975), pp. 634–6.

7 Pilinszky, p. 9.

8 Zbigniew Herbert, 'Biology Teacher', *Selected Poems, ed. cit.* p. 26.

9 Miroslav Holub, 'The Lesson', *Selected Poems*, translated by Ian Milner and George Theiner (Harmondsworth, 1967), p. 69.

10 Zbigniew Herbert, *ed. cit.*, p. 40.

11 Popa, p. 2. It is worth recalling that Poland, Hungary, Yugoslavia and Czechoslovakia have existed as modern nations only since 1918. Prior to that date they experienced centuries of occupation by Prussians, Russians, Austrians and Turks, during which time language 'survived as the sole badge of national identity, and the poets have become, through language, the acknowledged custodians of national aspirations' (Clive Wilmer, *London Magazine*, Feb.–March 1981, p. 135).

12 Ted Hughes, Cheltenham Lecture, 1977.

13 *Modern Poetry in Translation*, 5, Czech Poets, editorial, 1969.

14 *Ibid.*

15 Popa, p. 2.

16 Kingsley Amis, *Selected Poems*, Penguin Modern Poets, 2 (Harmondsworth, 1962). Certainly not until the late 1950s and early 1960s were there poets of quality in England who could cope with the enormity of Auschwitz and Hiroshima. In *For the Unfallen* by Geoffrey Hill (London, 1959) in the poem 'Of Commerce and Society' we have the lines

> Many have died. Auschwitz
> Its furnace chambers and lime-pits
> Half-erased, is half-dead: a fable
> Unbelievable in fatted marble.

In *A Group Anthology*, ed. Edward Lucie-Smith and Philip Hobsbaum (Oxford, 1963) we find 'Annotations of Auschwitz' by Peter Porter. Above all, we have Sylvia Plath's *Ariel* poems, bringing the subject to our attention. Hughes' first volumes, *The Hawk in the Rain* and *Lupercal* refer to the First World War predominantly, although 'A Woman Unconscious' does deal with the threat of nuclear war. In the *Selected Poems: Ted Hughes and Thom Gunn*, published by Faber & Faber in 1962, 'wounds', 'war' and 'beach-heads' are for Gunn mere metaphors in love-lyrics.

17 Popa, p. 1.
18 Zbigniew Herbert, quoted in *World Authors, op. cit.*, pp. 634–6.
19 Zbigniew Herbert, quoted in *Selected Poems, ed. cit.*, p. XII.
20 *Ibid.*, p. 22–4.
21 Zbigniew Herbert, *Selected Poems*, translated by Peter Dale Scott and Czeslaw Milosz (Harmondsworth, 1968), p. 21.
22 Miroslav Holub, *Selected Poems*, pp. 27–9.
23 Popa, p. 4.
24 Miroslav Holub, *Selected Poems*, p. 72.
25 *Ibid.*, p. 40.
26 Pilinsky, p. 19.
27 *Ibid.*, p. 26.
28 *Ibid.*, p. 36.
29 *Ibid.*, p. 52.
30 George Steiner, *Language and Silence* (Harmondsworth, 1979), p. 189.
32 Popa, p. 3.
33 Robert J. Lifton, *Death in Life: the survivors of Hiroshima* (London and New York, 1968), quoted by Anne Cluysenaar, in *British Poetry since 1960* ed. M. Schmidt and G. Lindop (Manchester, 1972) p. 219.
34 Pilinsky, pp. 12–13.
35 *Ibid.*, p. 13.
36 Popa, 'One bone to another', *ed. cit.*, p. 53.
37 Keith Douglas, *Collected Poems*, ed. Waller, Fraser and Hall (London, 1966), p. 86.
   That volatile huge intestine holds
   material and abstract in its folds:
   thought and ambition melt and even the world
   will alter, in that catholic belly curled.
38 'A wind flashes the grass', *Wodwo*, p. 29.
39 Ted Hughes, Interview with Peter Orr, *The Poet Speaks*, XVI, British Council, 1963.
40 Popa, p. 61. In 'Return to Belgrade' from *Earth Erect*, he refers to his poems as 'ripened stones', p. 119
41 Zbigniew Herbert, *Selected Poems*, translated Peter Dale Scott and Czeslaw Milosz, *ed. cit.*, p. 108.
42 Ted Hughes, Cheltenham Lecture, 1977.
43 Popa, p. 37.
44 Popa, p. 25.
45 *Ibid.*, p. 26.
46 Zbigniew Herbert, *Selected Poems*, translated John Carpenter and Bogdana Carpenter, *ed. cit.*, p. 47.
47 Pilinsky, p. 48.
48 Popa, p. 28.
49 Miroslav Holub, *Selected Poems*, p. 42.
50 Sylvia Plath, 'Mushrooms', *The Colossus*, (London, 1960), p. 34.

51 W. B. Yeats, *Collected Poems* (London, 1933), p. 211.
52 Miroslav Holub, *Selected Poems*, p. 50.
53 Pilinsky, 'Trapeze and Parallel Bars', p. 18.
54 Popa, p. 48.
55 A. Alvarez, Introduction to *Selected Poems: Zbigniew Herbert*, translated Peter Dale Scott and Czeslaw Milosz, *ed. cit.*, p. 13.
56 Myth 2.
57 Sylvia Plath, *The Colossus*, p. 87.
58 Cf. Hughes' comments in Faas, p. 207. 'Popa, and several other writers one can think of, have in a way cut their losses and cut the whole hopelessness of that civilization off, have somehow managed to invest their hopes in something deeper than what you lose if civilization disappears completely and in a way it's obviously a pervasive and deep feeling that civilization has now disappeared completely. If it's still here it's still here by grace of pure inertia and chance and if the whole thing has essentially vanished one had better have one's spirit invested in something that will not vanish.'
59 Quoted from B. Fletcher, J. Fletcher, W. Bachem, B. Smith, *A Student's Guide to the Plays of Samuel Beckett* (London, 1978), p. 33.
60 Ted Hughes in Faas, p. 204: 'one poem never gets the account right. There is always something missed. At the end of the ritual up comes a goblin. Anyway within a week the whole thing has changed, one needs a fresh bulletin.'
61 Geoffrey Thurley, *The Ironic Harvest* (London, 1974), p. 186.
62 Faas, pp. 203–4.
63 Popa, p. 8.
64 *Ibid.*, p. 9.
65 A. Alvarez, Introduction to *Selected Poems: Zbigniew Herbert*, translated Peter Dale Scott and Czeslaw Milosz, *ed. cit.*, p. 10.
66 Popa, p. 4.
67 Faas, p. 204.
68 'The owl flower', *Cave Birds*, p. 58.

CHAPTER 5

1 Faas, p. 197. The remarks were made during Hughes' first interview with Faas (1970).
2 Thomas Wilson, *The Arte of Rhetorique* (London, 1560, fol. 26r); Erasmus' epistle is taken from *De conscribendis*. Erasmus argued (in Wilson's translation, fol. 24r): 'It were a foule thinge, that brute beastes should obeye the Lawe of Nature, and menne like Giauntes, should fighte againste Nature.' A succinct expression of a contrary view was recently provided by 'Nameless' in Alexander Zinoviev's novel *The Radiant Future* (London, 1981), p. 111: 'there is one thing I am certain of: everything that is bestial comes from nature: everything that is human comes from God, that is, it has been invented'.
3 F. R. Leavis, *The Common Pursuit* (Harmondsworth, 1962), p. 132; reprinted from *Scrutiny*, vol. XII no. 4 (autumn 1944).
4 Both Leavis's attitude towards Othello and Dr Johnson's protest that 'the *garner* and the *fountain* are improperly conjoined' are discussed at greater length in my essay, "Leavis, *Othello*, and self-knowledge", *Dutch Quarterly Review*, vol. 9 (1979), No. 3, pp. 218–231.
5 See Part 3 for full text.

6 'Preface to Shakespeare'; quoted from *Johnson*, ed. Mona Wilson (London, 1963), p. 499.

7 F. R. Leavis, 'Johnson as Critic', *Scrutiny*, vol. xii No. 3 (summer 1944), p. 193.

8 See, for example, G. R. Hibbard, 'The early seventeenth century and the tragic view of life', *Renaissance and Modern Studies*, vol. 5 (1961), pp. 5–28; also John M. Wallace, *Destiny his Choice* (Cambridge, 1968), p. 65.

9 Quoted from *The Basic Writings of Sigmund Freud*, tr. and ed. A. A. Brill, (New York, 1938), p. 563. Brill's translation seems preferable in this case to that given in the Hogarth Press 'Standard Edition', vol. vii, p. 149.

10 Czeslaw Milosz, 'The Nobel Lecture 1980', *New York Review of Books*, vol. xxviii No. 3 (5 March 1981), p. 12. Milosz writes that to 'contemplate Being' is the poet's 'true vocation'.

11 *Correspondence of Alexander Pope*, ed. George Sherburn (Oxford, 1956), vol. ii, p. 351.

12 Robert Graves, *The White Goddess* (London 1961, revised and enlarged ed.), p. 426.

13 Hughes, 'Introduction to the poetry of Vasko Popa', *Popa: Selected Poems*, Penguin Modern European Poets (Harmondsworth, 1969), p. 10. The introduction was written by or in 1967, when the first *Crow* poems were beginning to appear in print. Whether its tenor is easily reconciled with that of *Crow* or the complementary essay on Shakespeare may be debated, and Hughes' remarks on Popa perhaps apply more clearly to Miroslav Holub and Zbigniew Herbert. I assume that both Holub and Herbert would be fundamentally opposed to Hughes' later remarks on the need for 'ritual and dogma' in the 1970 interview with Dr Faas. Half of the Popa selection is taken from *Secondary Heaven (Sporedno Nebo)*, which was published in Yugoslavia in 1968, after Hughes had written his essay. Hughes' relation with these East European poets is of exceptional interest, while the discussion of *Wodwo* in Dr Faas' study shows how damaging careless mistakes about the chronology of Hughes' writings can be.

14 Faas, pp. 200–1. In the interview, Hughes speaks movingly of the need to 'have one's spirit invested in something that will not vanish . . . a new divinity, one that won't be under the rubble when the churches collapse' (p. 207). The question is, whether the reliance on Jungian notions and the supposedly shamanist relation to the Goddess are likely to be above the rubble, or should rather be seen as another example of the imaginative retreat Orwell discussed in *Inside the Whale*.

15 In the essay on Shakespeare, the 'Complete Works' are the 'tribal dream'; Hughes applies this phrase specifically to *The Tempest* (comparing it with *Parzifal* and Andrae's *Chymische Hochzeit*) in his second interview with Fass (1977): Faas, p. 212. I would think that *The Tempest* is too radical, personal and sceptical to be seen in this way, and that the seventeenth-century work with the strongest claims to be considered as a 'tribal dream' is *The Pilgrim's Progress*.

16 Hughes made this point about Hopkins in Granada Television's South Bank Show (15 February 1981).

17 'Crow's Song About England' is in Part 3; 'Crow's Song about Prospero and Sycorax' appeared in the handsome limited edition of *Crow* published by Faber in December 1973. It is collected in *Moortown* as 'Prospero and Sycorax'.

18 Faas, pp. 56, 57, 57, 59. Dr Faas' conclusion that Cambridge was 'a prison term' that 'stifled all creative impulse' seems misleading, particularly

when we remember that Hughes followed Part I in English with Part II of the Archaeology and Anthropology Tripos.

CHAPTER 6

1 *Approaching the Unconscious*, essay, 1964.
2 *The Spectator*, 21 March 1970.
3 Faas, p. 206.
4 *The Listener*, 29 October 1964. Review of *Shamanism* by Mircea Eliade and *The Sufis*, by Idries Shah (London, 1964). Reprinted in part in Faas, pp. 174–5.
5 R. M. Underhill, *Singing for Power*, (Berkeley, Calif., 1976,) p.7.
6 The shaman's ability to 'see' closely resembles Wordsworth's experience in *The Prelude*, II 348, when 'Oft in these moments such a holy calm would overspread my soul, That bodily eyes were utterly forgotten'. The result of this experience is the same for the shaman as for the Romantic poet. 'Through the strangely sharpened senses of the shaman, the sacred manifests itself' (Mircea Eliade, *Myths, Dreams and Mysteries*). Wordsworth also instinctively sought solitude, the isolation in which the barrier between the sacred and the profane is dissolved. This 'natural supernatural-ism' can be seen in the philosophy of the Eskimo shaman, Igjuquarjuk – 'True wisdom is only to be found far away from people, out in the great solitude, and it is not to be found in play [cf. Wordsworth's rebuke by Nature when boating on Ullswater], but only through suffering. Solitude and suffering open the human mind, and therefore a shaman must seek his wisdom there' (quoted in Joan Halifax, *Shamanic Voices*, p. 169. (see note 12). Hughes' own Romantic affiliations are closest to Blake who saw God sitting in a tree – who emphasized energy and animal vitality – who wrote songs of both Innocence and Experience.
7 Faas, pp. 200–1.
8 *Ibid.*, p. 199.
9 *Ibid.*, p. 200.
10 *Ibid.*, p. 163.
11 'The Poet Speaks', xvi, British Council, 1963.
12 Joan Halifax, *Shamanic Voices*, (New York 1979; Pelican ed. 1980), p. 32.
13 Faas, p. 207.
14 *Shamanic Voices*, p. 33.
15 Harrold ed. Thomas Carlyle, *Sartor Resartus*, (New York, 1937), p. 194.
16 *Choice*, p. 199.
17 Jung, *The Meaning of Psychology for Modern Man*, essay, 1933/4. In *Collected Works*, vol. 10.
18 Myth 1, p. 61.
19 Myth 2, p. 92; Faas, p. 192.
20 Faas, p. 175.
21 *Structural Anthropology* (Penguin, ed., pp. 186–205) in an essay entitled The Effectiveness of Symbols.
22 *Ibid.*, p. 181, essay, *The Sorcerer and his Magic*.
23 Interview with John Horder, *The Guardian*. Hughes has been talking about *Lupercal*.
24 A similar progress can be seen in Hughes' development from the use of a dialectic of myth (the reconciling of opposites such as life and death, wild and tame, nature and culture), through an emphasis on legend, the myth

recounted, to the ritual which is the myth enacted.

25 Faas, p. 206.
26 Above, p. 8.
27 *Primitive Mythology*, p. 253.
28 *Poetry*, p. 19.
29 For instance the poems 'The Perfect Forms', 'Two Wise Generals', 'Phaetons', 'Egghead','Urn Burial', 'Fire-eater'.
30 'For the archaic and traditional cultures, the symbolic return to chaos is indispensible to any new Creation', Eliade, *Myths, Dreams and Mysteries* (Fontana ed., London, 1968, p. 79).
31 *Ibid.*, p. 80.
32 Faas, p. 205.
33 Recent examples of this are 'Life is trying to be life' and 'A Citrine Glimpse' 1 and 2, both in *Moortown*.
34 Joan Halifax, *Shamanic Voices*, p. 109.
35 *Eat Crow* (London, 1971). p. 18.
36 The broadcast is described in *The Listener*, July 1970. This is the source of the quotations here.
37 pp. 81–7. Note also 'Crow's Battle Fury'. This poem recreates the heroic initiation described by Eliade in *Rites and Symbols of Initiation*.
38 J. Evans-Wentz edition, p. 149.
39 Faas, p. 206.
40 Halifax, *Shamanic Voices*, p. 31. ' . . . At the moment when he or she is transported to a place that is beyond mortality, the poetry breaks forth to overwhelm, a potent and aesthetic resolution.'
41 p. 181. It is interesting that Thurley puts Hughes in the 'English Existentialist tradition', because of this emphasis on the experience of suffering. Hughes is in fact in an immeasurably older tradition.
42 See also 'And the Phoenix has come' in *Moortown*.
43 'After the first fright', third poem in the 1978 Faber edition of *Cave Birds*.
44 This is the basis of *The Teachings of Don Juan*, by Carlos Castenada, which is a modern enquiry into the shamanic experience.
45 Eliade, *Myths, Dreams and Mysteries* (Fontana, ed. London, 1968. p. 186).
46 'Crow and Mama'
47 'Peredur Son of Evrang', *The Mabinogion* (Penguin 1976) pp. 248–49.
48 'What will you make of half a man', *Gaudete*, p. 173.
49 Cf. 'Having first given away pleasure', *Gaudete*, p. 192.
50 Sagar, p. 189.
51 Walter F. Otto, *Dionysus, Myth and Cult*, (Indiana, 1965), p. 78.
52 *Ibid.*, p. 193.
53 *Ibid.*, p. 143.
54 Mircea Eliade, *Rites and Symbols of Initiation* (New York, 1958), p. 61.
55 Mircea Eliade, *Myths, Dreams and Mysteries*, p. 73

CHAPTER 7

1 Letter to Neil Roberts, 2 October 1979.
2 *Guardian*, 23 March 1965. does not corroborate Hughes' view of the destructiveness of Cambridge. In an interesting autobiographical article in *New Universities Quarterly* (1980) he says that while he found there a 'machine geared to conformity and show' he also found 'a new force abroad that meant personal salvation for me'. This force for Redgrove, who was a scientist, was Downing English.

3 Blurb to *The Wise Wound* (New York, 1978).
4 Interview with John Haffenden, *London Magazine*, June 1979.
5 *Poetry*, p. 61.
6 Quoted in 'A gift for being in touch', an interview with Anthony Bailey, *Quest*, Jan/Feb. 1978.
7 Interview with Mike Erwin and Jed Rasula, *Hudson Review*, vol. VIII No. 3, autumn 1975.
8 Review of *Shamanism* by Mircea Eliade, *The Listener*, October 1965.
9 Interview with Blake Morrison, *New Statesman*, February 1980.
10 Letter to Neil Roberts, 26 October 1979.
11 Interview with Caroline Walsh, *The Irish Times*, 6 December 1975.
12 P. V. Glob, *The Bog People* (1965, English translation London, 1969, edition used Paladin paperback, 1971), pp. 77–8.
13 Bernard Harrison: 'Poetry and the language of feeling', *Tract* 27, Feb. 1979.
14 Letter to Terry Gifford and Neil Roberts, 1 October 1979.
15 Geoffrey Thurley, *The Ironic Harvest* (London, 1974), p. 188.
16 Letter to Neil Roberts, 19 December 1977. For the essay that provoked this letter see *Delta* 57, 1977. The essay compares *Gaudete* with Redgrove's excellent radio play *The God of Glass*. The latter has been turned, not entirely successfully, into a novel with the same title (London, 1979).
17 *Poetry Society Bulletin*, summer 1979.
18 Ted Hughes and R. S. Thomas read and discuss selections from their own poems, The Critical Forum, Norwich Tapes Ltd., 1978.
19 Interview with Mike Erwin and Jed Rasula, *Hudson Review*, vol. VIII, No. 3, autumn 1975.
20 Myth 2; Faas, p. 191.

CHAPTER 8

1 This and the following quotations are from *Letters Home* by Sylvia Platt, ed. by Aurelia Schober Plath (New York, 1977), pp. 316, 273, 249, 253, 316, 266.
2 *Lyonnesse* (London, 1971), p. 7.
3 *Ibid.* See also Margaret Dickie Uroff, *Sylvia Plath and Ted Hughes* (Urbana, Ill., 1979), pp. 72–3.
4 'Notes on the chronological order of Sylvia Plath's poems', *The Art of Sylvia Plath*, ed. Charles Newman (Bloomington, Ind., 1971), pp. 187–95 (p. 187).
5 Judith Kroll, *Chapters in a Mythology: the Poetry of Sylvia Plath* (New York, 1976), pp. 166ff.
6 *Ariel* (London, 1965), p. 19.
7 *Cave Birds*, p. 56. For more detailed information concerning some of the issues touched upon in the following argument, see Faas. I should like to take this opportunity to correct a printing error in that study. The fifth sentence on p. 86 beginning 'By contrast, the poems . . . ' should read: 'By contrast, about half of the poems were written after the death of Sylvia Plath, and under its impact seem to record the poet's descent into a Bardo of self-destruction.' As a comparison of the present essay and the 'Postscript' to Faas will make clear, I also admit to a slight change in my understanding of 'Bride and groom' and its place in the poet's development.
8 *The Colossus* (London, 1960), pp. 86–8.
9 *African Folktales*, selected and edited by Paul Radin, Bollingen Series XXXII (Princeton, N.J., 1964), pp. 250–3 (P. 252). See also Jon Rosenblatt, *Sylvia*

Plath: the Poetry of Initiation (Chapel Hill, N.C., 1979), pp. 34–7.

10 This and the following quotations are from *Letters Home*, pp. 352, 303, 394.

11 Review of John Greenway, *Literature Among the Primitives* etc., *New York Review of Books*, vol. 5, No. 9 (9 December 1965), p. 35.

12 This and the following quotations are from *The Art of Sylvia Plath*, ed. C. Newman, pp. 192–3.

13 This and the following quotations are from *Letters Home*, pp. 141, 143.

14 *Johnny Panic and the Bible of Dreams and Other Prose Writings* (London, 1977), p. 166.

15 Nancy Hunter Steiner, *A Closer Look at Ariel: a Memory of Sylvia Plath*, introduction by George Stade (New York, 1973), p. 64.

16 This and the following quotations are from *The Bell Jar* (London, 1966), pp. 226, 257.

17 This and the following quotations are from *Ariel*, pp. 55–6, 18, 20, 21.

18 *Winter Trees* (London, 1971), p. 19.

19 *Letters Home*, pp. 559–60.

20 This and the following quotations are from *Ariel*, pp. 14, 15.

21 *Audience*, vol. 8, No. 2 (spring 1961), pp. 77–105 (p. 99).

22 Faas, p. 203.

23 *Wodwo*, p. 121.

24 Faas, p. 210.

25 This and the following quotations are from *Wodwo*, pp. 122–3, 131–2, 144, 143, 133, 145.

26 *Eat Crow* (London, 1971), pp. 19–21.

27 Faas, p. 213.

28 *Ibid.*, 77–78, 85.

29 *Ibid.*, 213.

30 'Crow's Song About God', see Part 3.

31 'Crow's Song About England', see Part 3.

32 'Crow's Courtship', *Poems – Ruth Fainlight, Ted Hughes, Alan Sillitoe* (London, 1971), p. 15.

33 Review of Max Nicholson, *The Environmental Revolution, Your Environment*, vol. 1, No. 3 (summer 1970), pp. 81–82, 83.

34 This and the following quotations are from *Choice*, pp. 181, 187, 196–97, 198.

35 Faas, pp. 117–18.

36 *Ibid.*, p. 215.

37 *Gaudete*, pp. 14–15.

38 For a more detailed interpretation of this sequence, see Faas, pp. 126f.

39 This and the following quotations are from *Gaudete*, pp. 102, 103, 104, 105–6.

40 See Faas, p. 125.

41 This and the following quotations are from *Gaudete*, pp. 186, 178, 181.

42 Faas, p. 207.

43 This and the following quotations are from *Gaudete*, pp. 190, 177, 192, 198.

44 I find little evidence to support Keith Sagar's more literal reading of the Epilogue poems where Lumb is described as 'even, almost inadvertently, carr[ying] out his healing task . . . As for Lumb himself, we assume his life henceforth will be to make his small contribution, here and there, to the great task of restoring to others a sense of the sacred, and a spiritual orientation towards life which makes it possible to experience nature as, in spite of everything, healing, revivifying, and worthy of service' (Sagar, pp.

210, 212). The Lawrentian didacticism which such words seem to attribute to *Gaudete* is precisely the tone, I think, which Hughes, on account of his ironic techniques, avoids so successfully.

45 This and the following quotations are from *Gaudete*, pp. 176, 182—3.
46 This and the following quotations are from *Choice*, pp. 182, 181, 195.
47 This and the following quotations are from *Cave Birds*, pp. 30, 44, 52, 7, 56.
48 'Lovesong' and 'The Lovepet' both appear in the American edition of *Crow*. 'The Lovepet' and 'Actaeon' are both in *Moortown*.
49 Faas, p. 213.

CHAPTER 9

1 Subtitles for the three sections of 'Wings' ('M. Satre considers current affairs', 'Kafka writes' and 'Einstein plays Bach') appear only in the Faber & Faber British edition, published 18 May 1967. The British edition also contains 'Logos' and sections II and III of 'Gog', not found in the American Harper & Row edition of 22 November 1967. Omitted in the British edition are 'Scapegoats and Rabies' and 'Root, Stem, Leaf'. The British and American editions of *Wodwo* are otherwise the same, following the same sequence of poems and with no line variations.
2 'The poetry of Keith Douglas', *The Listener*, vol. 67 (21 June 1962), pp. 1068—70; 'The crime of fools exposed', *New York Times Book Review* (12 April 1964), pp. 4, 18; *The Listener*, vol. 74 (5 August 1965), p. 208.
3 See Sylvia Plath, *Letters Home*, ed. Aurelia Schober Plath (New York, 1975), pp. 378, 434. Ted and Sylvia were present at the terminus of the seven mile long column of people who marched from the atomic bomb plant at Aldermaston to Trafalgar Square in April 1960, and were affected by the cold war scares of atomic fallout and the 1961 fallout shelter boom in America.
4 See Hughes' own comments on this change in style in Faas, pp. 208—11.
5 Alan Moorehead, *Gallipoli* (London, 1956), pp. 360—1.
6 For well-documented summary discussions of Freud's thoughts on aggression, 'archaic heritage' and the Thanatos death instinct, see Liliane Frey-Rohn, *From Freud to Jung*, trans. F. E. Engreen & E. K. Engreen (New York, 1974), pp. 126—132; Richard Wollheim, *Sigmund Freud* (New York, 1971), pp. 206—13. The principal source for Freud's comments on the repetition—compulsion organic drive is the *New Introductory Lectures on Psycho-Analysis*, trans. W. J. H. Sprott (1933; rpt. London, 1962), pp. 132—9.
7 Faas, pp. 197—201; Myth 1, pp, 56—7, 66, 68—70; Myth 2, pp. 87—90. On the repression of the instincts in Christianity see also the poem 'Logos' in the British edition of *Wodwo*.
8 Faas, pp. 182—4.
9 Faas, p. 186
10 D. T. Suzuki, *Mysticism: Christian and Buddhist* (New York, 1957), p. 28.
11 See Robert Hume, 'An outline of the philosophy of the Upanishads', in *The Thirteen Principal Upanishads*, trans. & ed. Hume, 2nd ed. (1931; rpt. New York, 1977), pp. 42ff.
12 P. Y. Deshpande, *The Authentic Yoga* (London, 1978), pp. 41ff.; Ernest Wood, *Yoga*, rev. ed. (1962; rpt. Harmondsworth, 1972), pp. 43—4, 72.
13 D. T. Suzuki, *Living by Zen* (London, 1950), pp. 46—88; Suzuki, 'The oriental way of thinking', *Japan Quarterly*, vol. 11 (1955), pp. 51—8.

14 Heinrich Zimmer, *Myths and Symbols in Indian Art and Civilisation*, ed. Joseph Campbell (New York, 1946), pp. 175–84.

15 Faas, p. 204.

16 Faas, p. 207.

17 Reprinted in Hume, ed., p. 142. See also *Chāndogya Upanishad* (2.21.4), in Hume, ed., p. 199.

18 Wood, pp. 60–1, 68ff.

19 D. T. Suzuki, *Essays in Zen Buddhism, Second Series*, ed. Christmas Humphreys (1950; rpt. London, 1958), pp. 30–6; Suzuki, Erich Fromm & Richard De Martino, *Zen Buddhism and Psychoanalysis* (New York, 1960), pp. 17–18, 49–56.

20 Sir James Frazer, *The Golden Bough*, abridged ed. (1922; rpt. New York, 1940), pp. 628–9, 664.

21 Robert Graves, *The White Goddess*, 2nd ed. (London, 1966), pp. 169, 176.

22 Joseph Campbell, in *The Masks of God: Creative Mythology* (New York, 1970), p. 288, discusses the left side as the feminine side of feeling, mothering, seduction, enchantment and nourishment, as well as wrath and revenge, sorcery and delusion. In mythological systems the right side is usually the masculine side, the source of analytic reason, action, strength, hero-deeds, justice, brute force, egotism, aggression and malice. This corresponds to the popular bicameral 'split brain' theory, wherein the right lobe (which controls the left side of the body), views reality holistically, intuitively, spatially, and the left lobe (which controls the right side of the body), analyses reality through reason and linear, sequential thought. (In left-handed people, the lobes may be reversed, or functions shared.)

23 Gareth Knight, *A Practical Guide to Qabalistic Symbolism* (1965; rpt. New York, 1978), I, pp. 90–4; Dion Fortune, *The Mystical Qabalah* (1935; rpt. London, 1941), pp. 139, 156–7.

24 D. T. Suzuki, *The Essentials of Zen Buddhism*, ed. Bernard Phillips (New York, 1962), pp. 327, 396, 400.

25 Mircea Eliade, *Shamanism*, trans. Willard R. Trask (Princeton, N.J., 1964), pp. 58–64, 434–36; Joseph Campbell, *The Masks of God: Primitive Mythology* (New York, 1964), pp. 334ff.

26 Mircea Eliade, *The Myth of the Eternal Return*, trans. Willard R. Trask (New York, 1954), pp. 6, 9, 12–17.

27 Campbell, *The Masks of God: Primitive Mythology*, pp. 334–49.

28 Graves, pp. 411–2. The response portion of the first stanza of the chant, which is not reprinted in the epigraph to 'The Harvesting', specifically mentions the greyhound as pursuer. To Graves this is evidence of the White Goddess as hag-destroyer of the masculine principle – nature in its predatory aspect. In 'The Harvesting' a white greyhound is mentioned early in the story; it is doubtless the same dog in the last paragraph that opens its enormous white head to attack Grooby.

29 Deshpande, pp. 19–24; Wood, p. 15.

30 See Faas, pp. 205–6; Plath, *Letters Home*, 354, 371, 399. Hughes' libretto has unfortunately never been published.

31 Lama Anagarika Govinda, 'Introductory foreword' to W. Y. Evans-Wentz, ed., *The Tibetan Book of the Dead*, trans. Lama Kazi Dawa-Samdup, 3rd ed. (1957; rpt. New York, 1960), pp. LX–LXI. In the *Bardo* text itself see also p. 151. Subsequent references to this 3rd edition will be abbreviated *Bardo*.

32 *Bardo*, pp. XXXIX, XL, XLVI.

33 *Bardo*, p. 123.

34 D. T. Suzuki, *Essays in Zen Buddhism, First Series*, ed. Christmas

Humphreys (1949; rpt. New York, 1961), pp. 214–66; Suzuki, *The Essentials of Zen Buddhism*, p. 359.

35 D. T. Suzuki, *Zen and Japanese Culture* (1938; rpt. New York, 1959), p. 350.

36 Thomas Merton, *Mystics and Zen Masters* (New York, 1967), p. 14.

37 Suzuki, *The Essentials of Zen Buddhism*, pp. 362–3.

38 Suzuki, *Mysticism: Christian and Buddhist*, pp. 100–2; *Zen Buddhism and Psychoanalysis*, p. 12; *The Essentials of Zen Buddhism*, pp. 360–1.

39 Faas, p. 172.

40 D. T. Suzuki, 'Zen in the modern world', *Japan Quarterly*, vol. 5 (October-December 1958), p. 458.

41 Suzuki, *The Essentials of Zen Buddhism*, p. 358. Similar poems using negations, written by other Zen masters, are reprinted in Lucien Stryk, ed., *World of the Buddha: a Reader* (Garden City, N.Y., 1968), pp. 311, 353.

42 Suzuki, *The Essentials of Zen Buddhism*, p. 357.

43 Suzuki, *Living by Zen*, p. 76.

44 *Poetry*, pp. 62–3.

45 Mircea Eliade, *Myth and Reality*, trans. Willard R. Trask (New York, 1963), pp. 85–6.

46 *Bardo*, pp. 171, 177, 186; see also Eliade, *The Myth of the Eternal Return*, pp. 98–9.

47 Suzuki, *The Essentials of Zen Buddhism*, p. 236. This image of wiping clean the *karmic* mirror is one of the most common in all of Oriental literature. See, for instance, Śvetāśvatara Upanishad, 2:14, in Hume, ed., p. 399; Yoka Daishi's 'Song of enlightenment' in Suzuki, *Manual of Zen Buddhism* (Kyoto, 1935), p. 107.

48 *Bardo*, p. 188.

49 Suzuki, *Essays in Zen Buddhism, First Series*, pp. 225–6,191, 263.

50 See *Kena Upanishad*, 4:29, in Hume, ed., p. 339; Suzuki, *Essays in Zen Buddhism, First Series*, pp. 261, 245.

51 Zimmer, pp. 70, 183, and plate No. 53.

52 Carl Jung, 'On the psychology of the trickster figure', in Paul Radin, *The Trickster* (New York, 1956). pp. 202–9.

53 Reprinted in Robert Sohl and Audrey Carr, eds., *The Gospel According to Zen* (New York, 1970), p. 28.

54 D. T. Suzuki, *The Essence of Zen Buddhism* (London, 1947), pp. 13–14.

55 'O White Elite Lotus', see Part 3.

56 Reprinted in E. A. Burtt, ed., *The Teachings of the Compassionate Buddha* (New York, 1955), pp. 211–12.

57 Zimmer, pp. 37–8, 89.

CHAPTER 10

1 Telephone interview with Ted Hughes, 3 August 1980.

2 Letter, 5 April 1961, in Sylvia Plath, *Letters Home*, ed. Aurelia Schober Plath (New York, 1975), p. 416.

3 Letter, 9 July 1960 in Plath, p. 389.

4 James Hogg, 'Ted Hughes and the drama', *Salzburg Studies in English Literature: Poetic Drama and Poetic Theory*, vol. 22 (1974), No. 1.

5 Plath, pp. 392, 407, 409, 431, 446 *and passim*.

6 Faas, pp. 189–90.

7 *Choice*, p. 9.

8 *Ibid*.

9 *Audience*, vol. 8 (1961), pp. 77−105.

10 No. 6 (1961), pp. 12−13.

11 No. 4 (1961), pp. 146−8.

12 'Bridegroom and His Ideals', London Times, 22 January 1963, p. 14.

13 A. C. H. Smith, *Orghast at Persepolis* (London, 1972), pp. 154−5.

15 *Encounter*, vol. 25 (1965), pp. 20−1.

16 Telephone interview with Hughes. Other poems derived from *Difficulties of a Bridegroom* are 'The Lamentable History of the Human Calf', 'Waking' and 'Gog', Part III.

17 London, 1967.

18 London, 1969.

19 Telephone interview with Hughes.

20 *Performance*, No. 1 (1971), pp. 65−5.

21 Smith, pp. 91−7.

22 Faas, p. 206.

23 *Choice*, pp. 181−200.

24 Faas, p. 209.

25 Part 2 of *The Head of Gold*. First broadcast 28 September 1967.

26 First broadcast 16 November 1980.

27 Ted Hughes, *The Tiger's Bones and Other Plays for Children* (New York, 1974), pp. 93−108. First broadcast 29 January 1971.

28 *Coming*, p. 61. First broadcast 2 December 1965.

29 *Coming*, p. 81. First broadcast 2 May 1968.

30 First broadcast 22 September 1966.

31 *Crow*, p. 86.

32 First broadcast 1 February 1962. First produced 12 July 1972.

33 London, 1971.

34 First broadcast 21 January 1963.

35 Faas, p. 209

36 First broadcast 12 February 1964.

37 Faas, p. 192.

38 *Seneca's Oedipus*, adapted by Ted Hughes. First performance 19 March 1968.

39 First produced Easter 1970.

40 T. S. Eliot, *Selected Essays: 1917-1932* (New York, 1932), pp. 123−5

41 *Choice*, p. 195.

42 Actually, ICTR, The International Centre of Theatrical Research, but 'known to the in-set as CIRT'. John Heilpern, *Conference of the Birds* (London, 1977), p. 26.

43 First performed 1 September 1971.

44 Geoffrey Reeves, 'The Persepolis follies of 1971', *Performance*, No. 1 (1971), pp. 54, 56.

45 Faas, p. 191.

46 Smith, pp. 96−7.

47 Peter Wilson, 'Interview with Ted Hughes: author of Orghast', *5th Festival of the Arts: Shiraz Persepolis*, 1 August, September [sic] 1971, pp. 1−2.

48 Smith, pp. 217−18.

49 Faas, p. 212.

50 Farid Ud-din Attar, *The Conference of the Birds*. Trans. C. S. Nott (London, 1954).

51 Letter from Keith Sagar, 26 October, 1980.

52 Margaret Crogden, *Lunatics, Lovers and Poets: the Contemporary Experimental Theatre* (New York, 1974), p. 279.

53 Kenneth Tynan, 'Director as misanthropist: on the moral neutrality of Peter Brook', *Theatre Quarterly*, 25 (1977), pp. 26–7.
54 London, 1978.
55 London, 1975; London, 1978.
56 *Choice*, p. 183.

CHAPTER 11

1 Told by Lewy Costima to Melville Jacobs, *Northwest Sahaptin Texts*, vol. II, *Columbia University Contributions to Anthropology*, vol. xix(1934), pp. 238–9.
2 Calvin Bedient, *Eight Contemporary Poets* (Oxford, 1974), p. 116.
3 Faas, p. 205.
4 'Leaves' in *Season Songs*, p. 43.
5 Paul Radin, ed., *The Trickster* (New York, 1956), pp. 202–3.
6 Claude Lévi-Straus, *Structural Anthropology* (New York, 1967), pp. 220ff.
7 *The Listener*, 30 July 1970, p. 149.
8 'Crow and the cartoons', *Critical Quarterly*, spring 1971.
9 Elizabeth and Melville Jacobs, *Nehalem Tillamook Tales*, (Eugene, Oreg., 1959), pp. 198–9.
10 E. Lucie-Smith, ed., *British Poetry Since 1945* (Harmondsworth, 1970), p. 390.
11 *The Listener*, 30 July 1970, p. 149.
12 *Myth and Reality* (New York, 1963), pp. 21ff.
13 Adolphe Franck, *The Kabbalah* (New York, 1967), p. 130.
14 *Ibid.*, 129.

CHAPTER 12

1 Ian Hamilton, 'Ted Hughes' Crow', *A Poetry Chronicle* (London, 1963), p. 166.
2 C. G. Jung, *Modern Man in Search of a Soul* (London, 1973).
3 *Ibid.*, p. 180.
4 *Ibid.*, p. 183.
5 *Ibid.*, p. 189.
6 Charles Newman, ed., *The Art of Sylvia Plath* (London, 1970), p. 187 (Faas, p. 180).
7 C. G. Jung, *Archetypes of the Collective Unconscious*, vol. 19, para. 172.
8 See 'The Rock', an autobiographical essay in *Worlds: Seven Modern Poets*, ed. Geoffrey Summerfield (Harmondsworth, 1974), pp. 122–7.
9 C. G. Jung, *Mysterium Coniunctionis*, vol. 14, pp. 90–1.
10 *Oedipus*, pp. 16–18.
11 James Joyce, *Ulysses* (Penguin, ed., p. 43).
12 'The Christian's ordinary conception of God is of an omnipotent, omniscient, and all-merciful Father and Creator of the world. If this God wishes to become man, an incredible *kenosis* (emptying) is required of Him, in order to reduce His totality to the infinitesimal human scale. Even then it is hard to see why the human frame is not shattered by the incarnation' Jung, *Memories, Dreams, Reflections* (Fontana ed., London, 1967, pp. 370–1).
13 Hughes, 'Secret Ecstasies': a review of Mircea Eliade's *Shamanism*, *The Listener*, 29 Oct. 1964, p. 678.

14 Hughes, 'Patrick White's "Voss"', a review of *Voss*, *The Listener*, 5 Feb. 1964, p. 230.

15 Joseph Campbell, *The Hero With a Thousand Faces* (New York, 1949).

16 John Keats, 'Epistle to J. H. Reynolds'.

17 Herman Melville, *Moby Dick* (Collins Classics ed., 1968, p. 331. See p. 264, in the chapter 'The Shark Massacre', for what is probably a witnessed account of the phenomenon to which Hughes is referring.

18 *Choice*.

19 'Prospero and Sycorax', *Moortown*, p. 148.

20 Eric Neumann, *Origins and History of Consciousness* (New York, 1954), p. 163

21 Hughes, *Prometheus on His Crag* (London, 1973), now in *Moortown*.

22 C. G. Jung, *Psychology and Alchemy, Collected Works*, vol. 12, p. 50.

23 *Cave Birds* was first presented at the Ilkley Festival on 30 May 1975. It was broadcast on B.B.C. Radio 3 with very minor alterations, on 23 June 1975. These versions have major differences from the book version. In addition to a linking narrative, read by Hughes, there are two poems which are omitted from the book: 'The Advocate' and 'Your Mother's Bones Wanted to Speak'. These are printed in Part 3.
'The Plaintiff' has been shortened in the book, leaving out the section quoted in this essay, regarding the 'criminality' of the accused – 'What Herod', etc. 'The Gatekeeper' has been altered. The lines 'Then an answer, so this is what I am, finally, / Finally horror', have been omitted. The poem which in the book version is entitled 'A Riddle', in the Ilkley and Radio 3 versions is 'An Incomparable Marriage'. Since some of the assertions made in this essay rest on material which has been omitted from the book version, it follows that, to me, the earlier version of *Cave Birds* was more satisfactory.

24 Jean-Paul Sartre, *Nausea* (Penguin ed., pp. 183–4).

25 Faas, p. 186.

26 Popa, p. 3.

27 C. G. Jung, *Psychology and Religion: West and East, Collected Works*, vol. 11: 'It is only through the psyche that we can establish that God acts upon us, but we are unable to distinguish whether these actions emanate from God or from the unconscious. We cannot tell whether God and the unconscious are two different entities. Both are borderline concepts for transcendental contents. But empirically it can be established, with a sufficient degree of probability, that there is in the unconscious an archetype of wholeness which manifests itself spontaneously in dreams etc., and a tendency, independent of the conscious will, to relate other archetypes to this centre. Consequently, it does not seem improbable that the archetype of wholeness occupies as such a central position which approximates it to the God-image. The similarity is further borne out by the peculiar fact that the archetype produces a symbolism which has always characterised and expressed the Deity ... Strictly speaking, the God-image does not coincide with the unconscious as such, but with a special content of it, namely the archetype of the self ... ' (para. 757, pp. 468–9).

28 Hughes, 'The genius of Isaac Bashevis Singer', *New York Review of Books*, 22 April 1965, pp. 8–10. This essay is a review of the 'poetic' achievement of Singer. In a summary of his work, Hughes states that Singer has 'raised Jewishness to a symbolic quality', and is writing 'specifically about man in relationship to God', 'The Jew becomes the representative modern man of

suffering, and understanding, and exile from his Divine inheritance' – 'He is a typical modern hero'.

29 Faas, p. 204.
30 *Ibid.*
31 'But poetic imagination is determined finally by the state of negotiation – in a person or a people – between man and his idea of the Creator. This is natural enough, and everything else is naturally enough subordinate to it. How things are between a man and his idea of the Divinity determines everything in his life, the quality and connectedness of every feeling and thought, and the meaning of every action' *Choice*, pp. 184–5.

CHAPTER 13

This essay is an extended version of a talk given to the University of Aberdeen's Literary Society in February 1980.

1 See, in particular, Hughes' review of Mircea Eliade's *Shamanism* (from which his remark about the 'romantic' temperament is taken), *The Listener* vol. 72 (29 October 1964), and remarks on shamanism in the *London Magazine* interview of 1970, now conveniently reprinted in Faas.
2 I discuss the relationship between Hughes and Campbell in 'Ted Hughes' 'Crow' as Trickster-hero', *The Fool and the Trickster*, ed. P. V. A. Williams, (Ipswich and Totowa, N.J., 1979), pp. 83–108, 134–7.
3 The summary appears in A. C. H. Smith, *Orghast at Persepolis* (London, 1972), pp. 132–3.
4 Myth 1, pp. 55–70.
5 Hughes, *How the Whale Became and Other Stories* (Penguin ed. London, 1971), p. 66.
6 See Alan Brodrick, *Lascaux: a Commentary* (London 1949), pp. 81–4, and A. Sieveking, *The Cave Artists* (London, 1979), p. 121.
7 For the quotation from Hughes see Faas, p. 205. Given Hughes' further comment – 'He impressed me all right' – it's surprising that little attention has been given to this. See Calvin Bedient's chapter on Hughes in *Eight Contemporary Poets* (Oxford, 1974), and my essay on *Crow*, *op. cit.*, pp. 101–3.
8 See the 1877 entries on *Anna Karenina* in Dostoyevsky's *Diary of a Writer* and the account of Turkish atrocities in Book V, chapter 4 of *The Brothers Karamazov*.
9 Joseph Campbell, *The Masks of God*, 4 vols. (London, 1960-8), vol. 2 ('Oriental Mythology'), p. 6.
10 Sagar, pp. 243–4. Subsequent references to this indispensable book are incorporated into the text.
11 Carl Jung, *Mysterium Coniunctionis*, tr. R. F. C. Hull (London, 1963), p. 496. Subsequent references in the main text are to this edition.
12 Faas, p. 212.
13 Jung, *Psychology and Alchemy*, tr. R. F. C. Hull (London, 1953), p. 333.
14 It may be worth remarking that Graves discusses poetry as 'a form of psychotherapy' in *On English Poetry* (London, 1922), p. 85: 'Being the transformation into dream symbolism of some disturbing emotional crisis in the poet's mind ... poetry has the power of homeopathically healing other men's minds similarly troubled, by presenting them under the spell of hypnosis with an allegorical solution of the trouble'.

15 *The Renaissance Philosophy of Man*, ed. E. Cassirer, P. O. Kristeller and J. H. Randall, Jr. (Chicago, Ill., 1956), p. 335.

16 Cyprian Rice, *The Persian Sufis* (London, 1964), p. 37. Rice's fourth chapter discusses the seven stages, and the seventh chapter is devoted to 'fana', cf. p. 77: '. . . as the refining process proceeds, the rhythm is speeded up. Bewilderment (*tahayyur*) and the sense of estrangement from the world of limits and multiplicity increase. In the perfection of *fana*, *fana* itself is no longer adverted to . . . The soul, going all out to God, no longer has any return upon itself.'

17 Foxcroft's translation of *Chymische Hochzeit* is reprinted, with a very full commentary, in the second volume of John W. Montgomery's *Cross and Crucible* (The Hague, 1973).

18 Although it is not concerned with Ted Hughes, the title essay in Philip Rahv's *Literature and the Sixth Sense* (London, 1970), offers a thoughtful discussion of literary mythologising.

CHAPTER 14

My thanks to Terry Gifford, Ashby Wilson, and the Children's Department of the Greensboro Public Library for their help.

1 Myth 1, p. 56.

2 Myth 1, pp. 56, 57.

3 Myth 2, p. 91.

4 Space does not permit consideration of Hughes' other children's books, all of which are notable. *How the Whale Became* is a charming collection of animal fables, a droll updating of the *Just So Stories*. *The Iron Man* (entitled *The Iron Giant* in America) is the imaginative story of a benign monster who redeems the world through his heroic ordeals. The children's plays of *The Coming of the Kings and Other Plays* (called *The Tiger's Bones and Other Plays* in the expanded American edition) are marvellous Hughesian reworkings of traditional stories. All students of Hughes should know *Poetry in the Making*, for, among other things, it is one of the best guides to his own poetic practice.

5 The English first edition of 1961 and English paperback of 1977 are illustrated by George Adamson, the American edition of 1973 by Mila Lazarevitch.

6 *Poetry*, p. 104.

7 Keith Sagar, *Ted Hughes* (Harlow, 1972), p. 15.

8 Gerald Rose is the English illustrator, Jan Pyk the American.

9 *Poetry*, p. 110.

10 Sagar, pp. 237–8.

11 Faas, p. 184.

12 Thomas Lask, review of *Season Songs*, *New York Times Book Review*, 21 December 1975, p. 8.

13 Geoffrey Wolff, review of *Season Songs*, *New Times*, 28 November 1975, p. 56.

14 Ted Hughes, introduction to a reading from *Season Songs*, 6 September 1977, BBC Radio 3 and 4.

15 J. M. Newton, 'For Children?': review of *Season Songs*, *Cambridge Quarterly* vol. VII (1976), p. 84.

16 Sagar, p. 159.

17 *Poetry*, p. 18.
18 Sagar, p. 161.
19 Sagar, p. 167.
20 Faas, p. 187.

CHAPTER 15

1 'Ted Hughes and R. S. Thomas read and discuss selections from their own poems', Norwich Tapes Ltd., 1978.
2 Radio 3, 10 May 1980.
3 *Poetry*, p. 17.
4 *Poetry*. p. 38.
5 *Remains*.
6 'Justifying one's valuation of Blake', *The Human World*, vol. 7 (May 1972), p. 61.
7 *Song at the Year's Turning* (London, 1963), p. 54.
8 *New Republic*, 31 January 1976.
9 The first paragraph quoted here is from the Norwich Tape (see note 1). The rest was broadcast on Radio 3, 10 May 1980.
10 Norwich Tape.
11 *Orts*, (London, 1978), poem 21.
12 Norwich Tape.
13 Quoted in Sagar, p. 243.
14 Radio 4, 18 December 1979.
15 Henry Williamson, *Tarka the Otter* (Puffin edition, revised 1963, p. 163.

CHAPTER 16

1 *The Marriage of Heaven and Hell* Plate 19.
2 Carlos Castaneda, *Tales of Power*(London, 1974), p. 176.
3 *Ibid.*, pp. 172–3.
4 Herman Melville, *Moby Dick* (Signet ed., New York, 1962, pp. 396–7).
5 Faas, p. 206.
6 Faas, p. 200.
7 Faas, pp. 200–1.
8 Melville, *op cit.*, p. 295.
9 Faas, p. 199.
10 D. H. Lawrence, *Twilight in Italy* (Penguin ed., 1976, p. 88).
11 Popa, p. 8.
12 Faas, p. 201.
13 John Beer, *Blake's Visionary Universe* (Manchester, 1969), p. 39–40.
14 Nietzsche, *Thus Spake Zarathustra* (Penguin ed., 1975, pp. 139–40).
15 Popa, p. 3.
16 *Children as Writers 2*, (London, 1975), p. v.
17 A. C. H. Smith, *Orghast at Persepolis*, (London, 1972), pp. 132–3.
18 Michael Morpurgo, *All Around the Year* (London, 1979), pp. 12–13.
19 *Season Songs*, p. 40.
20 *Moortown*, p. 167.
21 Ted Hughes, *Under the North Star*, (London 1981), p. 46.
22 *Moortown*, pp. 150–1.
23 Michael J. Harner, ed., *Hallucinogens and Shamanism* (Oxford, 1973), pp. 184–5.

24 Ruth Finnegan, ed., *The Penguin Book of Oral Poetry* (Harmondsworth, 1978), p. 163.

25 Harner, *op. cit.*, p. 188.

26 *The Marriage of Heaven and Hell*, Plate 11.

27 Harner, *op. cit.*, pp. 189–90.

28 The twenty poems from *The River* so far published are:

'Whiteness', *Hand and Eye*, ed. Geoffrey Elborn, Tragara Press 1977; *Saturday Night Reader*, ed. Emma Tennant, W.H. Allen 1979.

'Salmon Taking Times', *Poetry Supplement*, Poetry Book Society 1979.

'The Word River', *New Departures* 12, 26 September 1980.

'Low Water', *London Review of Books*, 2 October 1980.

'Last Act', 'The Merry Mink', 'The Moorhen' and 'September Salmon', *Quarto* 11, October 1980.

'Nymet', *London Review of Books*, 4 December 1980.

'Catadrome', *Three River Poems*, Morrigu Press, 1 February 1981.

'An October Salmon', *London Review of Books*, 6 April 1981; *Selected Poems 1957–1981*, Faber 1982.

'Caddis', *Three River Poems*, Morrigu Press, 27 April 1981.

'Visitation', *Three River Poems*, Morrigu Press, 29 April 1981.

'The Dead Vixen', *Times Educational Supplement*, 5 June 1981.

'Go Fishing', *New Statesman*, 26 June 1981.

'Fairy Flood', *Poetry Review*, September 1981.

'In the Dark Violin of the Valley' and 'Salmon Eggs', *Grand Street*, Autumn 1981; 'Salmon Eggs' also in *Selected Poems 1957–1981*.

'That Morning', *A Garland for the Laureate*, Celandine Press 1981; *London Review of Books*, 3 December 1981: *Selected Poems 1957–1981*.

'River of Dialectics', *Poetry Supplement*, Poetry Book Society 1981.

29 *The Marriage of Heaven and Hell*.

30 *Ibid.*

31 Popa, pp. 2–3.

32 Popa, p. 8.

33 Popa, p. 2.

INDEX OF WORKS BY TED HUGHES

Part 3 is not indexed